Internal Security in India

MODERN SOUTH ASIA

Internal Security in India

Violence, Order, and the State

EDITED BY AMIT AHUJA

and

DEVESH KAPUR

OXFORD
UNIVERSITY PRESS

OXFORD
UNIVERSITY PRESS

Oxford University Press is a department of the University of Oxford. It furthers
the University's objective of excellence in research, scholarship, and education
by publishing worldwide. Oxford is a registered trade mark of Oxford University
Press in the UK and certain other countries.

Published in the United States of America by Oxford University Press
198 Madison Avenue, New York, NY 10016, United States of America.

Library of Congress Cataloging-in-Publication Data
Names: Ahuja, Amit and Kapur, Devesh, editor.
Title: Internal security in India : violence, order, and the state /
edited by Amit Ahuja and Devesh Kapur.
Description: New York, NY : Oxford University Press, [2023] | Series: Modern South Asia series |
Includes bibliographical references and index.
Identifiers: LCCN 2022029942 (print) | LCCN 2022029943 (ebook) |
ISBN 9780197660348 (paperback) | ISBN 9780197660331 (hardback) |
ISBN 9780197660362 (epub) | ISBN 9780197660355 | ISBN 9780197660379
Subjects: LCSH: Internal security—India.
Classification: LCC HV6295.I4 I55 2023 (print) | LCC HV6295.I4 (ebook) |
DDC 363.320954—dc23/eng/20220909
LC record available at https://lccn.loc.gov/2022029942
LC ebook record available at https://lccn.loc.gov/2022029943

DOI: 10.1093/oso/9780197660331.001.0001

1 3 5 7 9 8 6 4 2

Paperback printed by Marquis, Canada
Hardback printed by Bridgeport National Bindery, Inc., United States of America

CONTENTS

LIST OF FIGURES

LIST OF TABLES

ACKNOWLEDGMENTS

This volume began its journey with a conversation we had in 2018 about the Indian state's performance in producing internal security. As it progressed, we realized that there is limited work that takes an integrated look across different aspects of internal security, their inter-linkages with each other and with external security. We wanted to produce a volume that took on this challenge. We are thankful to all those who supported us in this endeavor.

Partial funding for this volume came from a grant from the Smith Richardson Foundation, and we are grateful to Allan Song for making part of the grant available to put together this book. The grant was originally given when one of us (Devesh Kapur) was Director of the Center for the Advanced Study of India (CASI) at the University of Pennsylvania, and we are thankful to Juliana Di Giustini and Georgette Rochlin at CASI for their full support and careful management of the grant.

We also received funding from the Jaideep and Rachel Khanna Foundation, and we are grateful to Jaideep Khanna for his unstinted support and encouragement and Vivian Walker and Ada Ho at the Paul Nitze School of Advanced International Studies (SAIS) at Johns Hopkins University for their help in managing this grant.

The chapters in this volume were originally scheduled to be presented at a workshop in New Delhi in March 2020. However, the outbreak of COVID put paid to those plans. We eventually held a virtual workshop in September 2020. For the multiple arrangements (and cancellations) in hosting the workshop and related issues we are thankful to Ruchika Ahuja and Eswaran Sridharan at the University of Pennsylvania Institute for the Advanced Study of India (UPIASI), New Delhi, for all their help.

We are also indebted to the commentators at the workshop, who provided invaluable feedback on individual chapters—Aparna Chandra, M. R. Madhavan, Shivshankar Menon, Anit Mukherjee, Ujjwal Kumar Singh, and Anjana Sinha. We owe a special thanks to the external reviewers, who diligently went through the entire volume and provided perceptive and constructive feedback and suggestions that were very valuable to all the chapter authors in revising their drafts.

We were shocked and saddened by the sudden passing away of Shakti Sinha in October 2021. We remember him fondly and remain grateful for his chapter and engagement with our volume. Many of our contributors suffered personally during the pandemic, and still they persevered. Our volume bears testimony to their resilience.

Emma Andersson, Jashan Bajwa, Ishani Srivastava, Rajkamal Singh, Daniel Stone, and Zehra Siddiqui were immensely helpful in putting together some of the data used in the volume. Michael Rodgers, Alaine Johnson, Neesha Patel, and Elizabeth Floyd helped edit and put the volume together. We owe a special debt to the team at Oxford University Press, New York, and especially David McBride, Ashutosh Varshney, Pradeep Chhibber, and Emily Benitez for their strong support and forbearance.

ABBREVIATIONS AND ACRONYMS

AASU	All Assam Students Union
ACLED	Armed Conflict Location & Event Data Project
AFSPA	Armed Forces Special Powers Act
AKPM	Akhila Karnataka Police Mahasangha
AR	Assam Rifles
ARC	Aviation Research Centre
ASGP	All Assam Gana Sangram Parishad
ASP	Assistant Superintendent Police
ATS	Anti-Terrorism Squad
BADP	Border Area Development Programme
BDOs	Block Development Officers
BGFs	Border Guarding Forces
BJP	Bharatiya Janata Party
BPRD	Bureau of Police Research and Development
BSF	Border Security Force
CAA	Citizenship Amendment Act
CAG	Comptroller and Auditor General
CAPFs	Central Armed Police Forces
CBI	Central Bureau of Investigation
CBS	Corps Battle Schools
CCTNS	Crime and Criminal Tracking Network and Systems
CDS	Chief of Defense Staff
CERT.In	Computer Emergency Response Team, India

CI	Counter Insurgency
CIAT	Counter Insurgency and Anti-terrorism Schools
CIJWS	Counterinsurgency and Jungle Warfare School
CISF	Central Industrial Security Force
CMS	Communications Monitoring System
COAS	Chief of Army Staff
CoBRA	Commando Battalions for Resolute Action
COFOG	Classification of Functions of Government
CORAS	Commandos for Railway Security
CPI	Communist Party of India
CrPC	Criminal Procedure Code
CRPF	Central Reserve Police Force
CyCord	Cyber Cooperation Centre
DAA	Disturbed Areas Act
DAR	District Armed Reserve
DGP	Director General of Police
DM	District Magistrate
DSPEA	Delhi Special Police Establishment Act
DRDO	Defense Research and Development Organization
DRSCs	Departmentally Related Standing Committees
DSCO	Doctrine for Sub-Conventional Operations
DSSC	Defence Services Staff College
ECI	Election Commission of India
ED	Enforcement Directorate
EEVFAM	Extrajudicial Execution Victims Family Members
FCRA	Foreign Contribution Regulation Act
FRS	Facial Recognition System
FRT	Facial Recognition Technology
GOI	Government of India
GoM	Group of Ministers
GOs	Gazetted Officers
IAF	Indian Air Force
IAS	Indian Administrative Service
IB	Intelligence Bureau

ICJS	Inter-operable Criminal Justice System
IDPs	Internally Displaced Persons
IG	Inspector General
IGP	Inspector General of Police
IM	Indian Mujahideen
IPC	Indian Penal Code
IPS	Indian Police Service
IRBs	India Reserve Battalions
IS	Internal Security
ITBP	Indo Tibetan Border Police
J&K	Jammu & Kashmir
JIC	Joint Intelligence Committee
KRC	Kargil Review Committee
LIC	Low Intensity Conflict
LOC	Line of Control
LWE	Left-Wing Extremism
MAC	Multi Agency Centre
MCOCA	Maharashtra Control of Organised Crime Act
MGNREGA	Mahatma Gandhi National Rural Employment Guarantee Act
MHA	Ministry of Home Affairs
MOS	Minister of State
NAFRS	National Automated Facial Recognition System
NATGRID	National Intelligence Grid
NCB	Narcotics Control Bureau
NCO	National Classification of Occupation
NCRB	National Crime Research Bureau
NCT	National Capital Territory
NCTC	National Counter-Terrorism Centre
NDA	National Democratic Alliance
NDFB	National Democratic Front of Bodoland
NDPS	Narcotic Drugs and Psychotropic Substances
NE	Northeast
NEFA	Northeastern Frontier Agency
NETRA	Network Traffic Analysis

NFFU	Non-functional Financial Upgrade
NFHS	National Family Health Survey
NHRC	National Human Rights Commission
NIA	National Investigation Agency
NIC	National Integration Council
NRC	National Register of Citizens
NSA	National Security Advisor
NSA	National Security Act of 1980
NSC	National Security Council
NSCN-IM	Nationalist Socialist Council of Nagaland–Isaac Muivah
NSDP	Net State Domestic Product
NSG	National Security Guard
NTRO	National Technical Research Organisation
OBC	Other Backward Classes
PAC	Provincial Armed Constabulary
PDP	People's Democratic Party
PIL	Public Interest Litigation
PLFS	Periodic Labor Force Survey
PMO	Prime Minister's Office
POTA	Prevention of Terrorism Act
PPKS	Police Parivar Kalyan Samiti
QRTs	Quick Response Teams
RAF	Rapid Action Force
RAW	Research and Analysis Wing
RBI	Reserve Bank of India
RJMP	Rakshak Jan Morcha Party
RPKP	Rajya Police Karmchari Parishad
RR	Rashtriya Rifles
RTI	Right to Information
SAG	Special Action Group
SAP	State Armed Police
SAPs	State Armed Battalions
SC	Scheduled Castes
SFs	Security Forces

SHO	Station House Officer
SI	Sub-Inspector
SIB	Subsidiary Intelligence Bureau
SIMI	Students' Islamic Movement of India
SOP	Standard Operating Procedure
SP	Superintendent of Police
SPIR	Status of Police in India Report
SPS	State Police Service
SRE	Security Reimbursement Expenditures
SSB	Service Selection Board
SoO	Suspension of Operation
TADA	Terrorist and Disruptive Activities (Prevention) Act
UAPA	Unlawful Activities Prevention Act
UAPA 2019	Unlawful Activities Prevention Amendment Act, 2019
UAV	Unmanned Aerial Vehicles
ULFA	United Liberation Front of Asom
UP	Uttar Pradesh
UPA	United Progressive Alliance
UPP	Uttar Pradesh Police
UPSC	Union Public Service Commission
VHP	Vishva Hindu Parishad

CONTRIBUTORS

Amit Ahuja is an Associate Professor in the Department of Political Science at the University of California, Santa Barbara.

Yashovardhan Azad (IPS) was former Secretary, Security, Cabinet Secretariat, Special Director Intelligence Bureau, Government of India.

Anubha Bhonsle is a journalist and founder of a new media storytelling platform, Newsworthy and was formerly the Executive Editor at CNN-IBN.

Saikat Datta is a journalist, author, and public policy specialist.

Sahana Ghosh is an Assistant Professor of Anthropology in the Department of Sociology and Anthropology at the National University of Singapore.

Nirvikar Jassal is an Assistant Professor of Political Science in the Department of Government at the London School of Economics and Political Science.

Beatrice Jauregui is an Associate Professor, Centre for Criminology & Sociolegal Studies, University of Toronto.

Arjun Jayadev is Professor of Economics at Azim Premji University.

Devesh Kapur is Starr Foundation Professor of South Asian Studies at the School of Advanced International Studies at Johns Hopkins University.

Akshay Mangla is an Associate Professor, Saïd Business School, University of Oxford.

Paaritosh Nath is an Assistant Professor at the School of Policy and Governance, Azim Premji University.

Dr. Hanif Qureshi (IPS) is the Commissioner of Police in Panchkula, Haryana.

Srinath Raghavan is Professor of International Relations and History, Ashoka University.

Nirvikar Singh is Distinguished Professor of Economics and Co-Director of the Center for Analytical Finance, University of California–Santa Cruz.

Sushant Singh is a Senior Fellow at Centre for Policy Research, New Delhi. He is a former Army officer and was the Deputy Editor of *The Indian Express*.

Shakti Sinha (IAS) was former director of the Nehru Memorial Museum and Library.

Paul Staniland is Professor of Political Science and faculty chair of the Committee on International Relations, University of Chicago.

Raeesa Vakil is a postdoctoral fellow at the Centre for Asian Legal Studies, National University of Singapore.

1

The State and Internal Security in India

AMIT AHUJA AND DEVESH KAPUR

Even as the intensifying military competition between the world's two preeminent powers, the United States and China, regularly grabs headlines, their equally massive efforts involving the immense number of personnel and financial resources devoted to their internal security gets much less attention. In recent years, there has been much concern about China's military modernization and increasingly aggressive military posture, buttressed by rapidly increasing defense spending. However, what is less well known is that China has been spending even more on domestic security. According to estimates, China's annual spending on domestic security was around $200 billion in 2020, having tripled since 2007. As the world's superpower, the United States' defense expenditures dwarf those of any other country, including China. However, even the United States spends more than nearly half as much on internal security as on conventional defense expenditures.

An estimated 11.2 million personnel are involved in China's internal security, including 3.6 million law enforcement personnel, 2.8 million auxiliary personnel, and 4.8 million security guards. The corresponding number for the United States is about 2.7 million, encompassing 970,000 state law enforcement personnel, 132,000 in federal law enforcement, 444,000 National Guard personnel, and 1.1 million private security "protective services."

The reality that even the world's superpowers have to pay so much attention to internal security reveals just how much it matters within the wider "security sector." This now encompasses a broad range from simple policing and law enforcement to conventional armies and strategic forces. In between lies a wide spectrum from intelligence to incarceration, from private security to paramilitary forces, and more recently, from counterterrorism to cyber-security.

Worldwide internal security expenditures amount to about half of conventional military expenditures. Internal crime and violence is estimated to cost about a tenth of global GDP.[1] The human costs of weak internal security are even higher. Homicide is far more lethal than conflicts and terrorism. In 2017, there were 464,000 victims of homicide, four times more than the 89,000 killed in armed conflicts and the 26,000

Amit Ahuja and Devesh Kapur, *The State and Internal Security in India* In: *Internal Security in India*. Edited by: Amit Ahuja and Devesh Kapur, Oxford University Press. © Oxford University Press 2023. DOI: 10.1093/oso/9780197660331.003.0001 fatal victims of terrorist violence that year.[2] This century, fatalities from organized crime—an average of about 65,000 killings annually—have roughly matched those from all armed conflicts across the world combined. Almost a fifth of all homicides in 2017 were related to gangs and organized crime.

Analysts and scholars of conflict have noted that the incidences of armed conflict in the world decreased substantially in the past few decades before increasing in 2014–2015 due to the conflict in Syria and in neighboring Iraq and in Ukraine subsequently. While territorial and other disputes between countries persist, inter-state war (that is, war between states) has become a rarer event. Intra-state armed conflict—civil wars, terrorism, and related political violence—peaked in the early 1990s following the dissolution of the Soviet Union and Yugoslavia and declined thereafter, before the wars in Syria, Ethiopia, and Ukraine partially reversed those trends beginning in 2014. Nonetheless, deaths in armed conflict are lower now than in the early 1990s or in previous decades.[3]

In Latin America, for example, from the 1960s to the 1980s, a major source of internal conflict was right-wing governments battling leftist opponents, leading to the deaths of hundreds of thousands of people. Military-backed governments kidnapped and secretly killed their leftist opponents. This century, the nature of conflict has changed. More than 79,000 people have disappeared in Mexico, most of them since 2006, caught in the drug war that has engulfed the country.[4]

In Brazil, approximately 94,000 citizens were murdered in the state of Rio between 2003 and 2020. It is estimated that almost 60 percent of the city's territory and more than 20 percent of the greater metropolitan area is now controlled by mafia syndicates. Brazil and Mexico, however, are not alone. "Of the fifty most violent cities in the world, forty-three are in Latin America. Of the twenty-five countries that boast the highest murder rates, nearly half are south of the Rio Grande. Latin America as a whole, a region that accounts for a mere 8 percent of the world's population, is responsible for 38 percent of the world's criminal killings."[5]

Africa is besieged with threats of jihadism, organized crime, and insurgencies, which together make parts of the continent ungovernable. Nigeria, the continent's most populous country and home to its largest economy, is struggling to cope with a variety of internal security threats. The country's northeast is overrun by some of the continent's deadliest Islamist insurgencies led by Boko Haram and Islamic State. Gangs of kidnappers are terrorizing the northwest, while Biafran secessionism seems to be reviving in the oil-rich southeast. In the first nine months of 2021, 2,200 people were kidnapped for ransom and 8,000 were directly killed in different conflicts. Hunger and disease triggered by fighting have claimed hundreds of thousands of lives, and conflict has displaced more than 2 million Nigerians.[6]

These shifts in the nature and locus of violence necessitate an analytical shift as well.[7] During the years of the Cold War, much of the analytical work on the "security sector" focused on external security. Subsequently, there was a shift to internal security-related issues, initially insurgencies and civil war, and later, terrorism and cyber-security. More recently, there is growing attention on the societal and political effects resulting from the actions of the providers of the security forces themselves, whether police brutality or surveillance activities of the "deep state." But while these literatures have greatly improved our understanding of specific aspects of internal security, there is a paucity of work that takes an integrated look across different aspects of internal security and their interlinkages with each other and with external security. This book seeks to address this lacuna, focusing on internal security in India.

What Is Internal Security?

As an analytical category, "internal security" can be capacious, encompassing activities ranging from natural disasters to strikes and protests. In the wake of the COVID global pandemic, countries are grappling with the need to broaden the definition of national security within the broader state security apparatus. They have awakened to so-called soft national-security threats, such as infectious diseases and climate change, that may well pose existentialist threats to a much greater degree than insurgencies or antagonistic neighbors.

However, this book has a narrower focus: how has the Indian state managed the core concern of internal security—violence and order. Internal security is deeply embedded in wider political and societal contexts. Political competition, the structure and social base of parties, and the actions and decisions of political leaders affect internal security in multiple ways. This is exemplified by the Punjab crisis and the scourge of endemic communal violence. Internal security can also be generated through the involvement of civil society actors. Additionally, internal security reflects the legitimacy and exercise of authority—and its fallibility.[8]

The role of political and social actors in security production has been discussed elsewhere.[9] In this volume, we focus on the statist view of security production. We do so for three reasons: (1) Ultimately the provision of security is the state's responsibility and it is through the state that a polity generates the capacity to produce security. (2) The trends related to violence and order as well as state capacity that are discussed in this volume span many decades. They capture the long-term pathologies of the Indian state overseen by multiple governments and parties. (3) When it comes to the production of internal security, even as political actors shape state behavior, politics itself is shaped by the state's long-standing approaches, not to mention its capacity. Opening the black box of the state and its constituent institutions is therefore fundamental to understanding the dynamics of internal security and its management.

The run-up to India's independence and its immediate aftermath—the bloodbath and ethnic cleansing surrounding Partition and the contested integration of some of the princely states—shaped the Indian state's ideas about internal security at its foundational moment as an independent sovereign state. The violent conjunctures that marked the emergence of a national, territorial, republican polity in India were soon overcome—but the scars ran deep.

Almost immediately, the state had to meet three challenges that contested its sovereignty—in its north, in the contested accession of the princely state of Jammu and Kashmir; in its northeast, Nagaland and Manipur; and in central India, where a communist-led revolutionary movement in Telangana was gathering momentum. Seven decades later, these issues have continued to fester. The tens of thousands of lives lost in these conflicts attest to the harsh reality that a close relationship between state making and violence is—perhaps—an "integral part of the process of accumulation of power by the national State. . . . [and] necessary for the imposition or maintenance of order."[10] The history of state making in the United Kingdom or the United States, two countries closely associated with the making of Western democracy, attest to this reality.

Public violence (as distinct from private violence) involves some kind of claim-making and is one set of options located within larger processes of political and social negotiation, bargaining, and political understandings. Public violence "emerges from the ebb and flow of collective grievances and struggles for power. It interweaves incessantly with non-violent politics, varies systematically with political regimes, and changes as a consequence of essentially the same causes that operate in the non-violent zones of collective political life."[11]

At one level, violence seems to be ubiquitous in India. In an interview with *Indian Express*, Historian Upinder Singh states that "There are border conflicts, insurgencies of various types, the threat of terrorism, the fear of communal flare-ups, violent crimes, and various forms of social violence. While the modern Indian state has several instruments to control violence, these can be subverted to serve the interests of those in power."[12]

Order, or its absence, is another major challenge and is central to the function of any state. Singh has argued that ancient texts in the subcontinent were unanimous in the view that the state exists to maintain order, to prevent the strong from preying on the weak, and to protect and give justice to the people (*praja*). The debates (as in the Mahabharat) were about the use of "necessary force in politics" and the line separating legitimate force from violence.[13]

In the modern era, Max Weber's canonical definition of the state as the "human community that (successfully) claims the monopoly of the legitimate use of violence within a given territory" lays the foundation of violence and its control within modern societies. To this, we can add Huntington's observation on the importance of order: "The primary problem is not liberty but the creation of a legitimate public order. Men may, of course, have order without liberty, but they cannot have liberty without order. Authority has to exist before it can be limited."[14] Hence security—external (army) and internal (police)—has been viewed as a classic public good, and the most essential function of any state.

However, the state as Leviathan is Janus-faced. As Acemoglu and Robinson have argued, "One face resembles what Hobbes imagined: it prevents War (state of anarchy), it protects its subjects, it resolves conflicts fairly, it provides public services, amenities and economic opportunities: it lays the foundations for economic prosperity. The other is despotic and fearsome: it silences citizens, it is impervious to their wishes. It dominates them, it imprisons them, maims them. . . . It steals the fruits of their labor or helps others do so."[15]

This Janus face of the state is reflected at three levels. At the micro-level is the policeman's dilemma: how does one ensure that when policemen stop a car or come upon illicit goods (money, jewelry, drugs) through their investigations, they do the right thing when no one is looking over their shoulders?

At the organization level, how do police systems behave ethically? Not just in the confines of a jail while interrogating a suspect in an empty room, but also in the public glare as crowds demand an arrest, an "encounter," or the reverse— a declaration of innocence. All this, as pressures from politicians mount and moral mountains become molehills (exemplified in India by the abject failures of bringing the perpetrators of communal violence to justice) and vice versa, makes all transgressions appear equal when they are not.

At the national level is the well-known Madisonian dilemma: "In framing a government which is to be administered by men over men, the great difficulty lies in this: you must first enable the government to control the governed; and in the next place oblige it to control itself."

While this volume does not explicitly address these dilemmas, which shape the contours of internal security, the contributions help to understand them better. An Indian government report defined internal security as "security against threats faced by a country within its national borders, either caused by inner political turmoil, or provoked, prompted or proxied by an enemy country, perpetrated even by such groups that use a failed, failing or weak State, causing insurgency, terrorism or any other subversive acts that target innocent citizens, cause animosity between and amongst groups of citizens and communities intended to cause or causing violence, destroy or attempt to destroy public and private establishment."[16]

To this we can add the security threats faced by the citizens of the country from the state itself—as both the solution and the source of the problem. Citizen consent is a necessity for the production of internal security. Democracies rely on persuasion, and when consent is not readily given, some turn to coercion (to varying degrees) to obtain it. India's long counterinsurgency campaigns, a record of extrajudicial killings by security forces, struggles with crowd management, and extraordinary legal protections given to security forces (in the form of the Armed Forces Special Powers Act) have tested, and not infrequently, sullied its democratic reputation.

Three broad and interrelated questions organize the discussions in this volume. First, what has been the record of the Indian state on the objectives of controlling violence and preserving order? Second, how have the approaches and capacity of the Indian state evolved to attain these twin objectives? And third, what have been the implications of the Indian state's approach toward internal security for civil liberties and the quality of democracy?

The Indian state has grappled with a variety of internal security challenges since independence from colonial rule and the bloodbath of Partition. Insurgencies, terrorist attacks, communal violence including large-scale massacres, mob violence, and electoral violence have claimed more lives than all of India's external wars put together. After showing a sharp upswing in the 1980s and 1990s, a number of violence-related indicators have declined over the past two decades. This drop in violence, its cause and implications, have largely gone unnoticed.

At the same time, in response to its internal security challenges and with more resources at its disposal, the Indian state has expanded its capacity across multiple sectors. The increase has been lopsided and has mostly occurred at the federal level, however. The army has substantially enhanced its counterinsurgency capacity. The size of the Central Armed Police Forces (CAPFs) has doubled over the last three decades. Simultaneously, the institutional infrastructure overseeing internal security at the federal level has also expanded. New agencies and new laws have appeared. By contrast, the state police forces, preventive agents, and first responders to acts of violence and disorder remained understaffed, underequipped, badly trained, and poorly led. Separate from the state, a fast-expanding private security sector has emerged. It currently employs around nine million personnel, which is about three times all the central and state police forces put together.

India's internal security approach has come at a deeply troubling price for the quality of the country's democracy. The Indian Constitution privileges national security over individual civil liberties in ways that is uncommon for long-standing democracies. Numerous national security laws, weak oversight mechanisms within and outside the security forces, and judicial forbearance for human rights violations in the name of national security reflect and enhance the bias against civil liberties. Extrajudicial killings by security forces, a high number of custodial deaths, the use of torture to extract information and confessions, wrongful detentions of suspects for long durations, and the use of national security laws to suppress political dissent and harass citizens are some of the quotidian practices that have come to be accepted in the name of internal security.

Internal Security and State Building

Internal security provision is one of the fundamental responsibilities of the modern state. But how does it shape the state, especially in the Global South, where internal security threats typically are more varied and larger in magnitude? While external wars are moments of unity and consensus, which facilitate investments in state capacity, internal conflict is by definition divisive and destructive. Consequently, wars and external threats are said to assist with state making.[17] Internal conflict is supposed to have the opposite effect on state capacity.[18] The Indian state's spending on internal security as a share of GDP has remained steady over the past four decades. While high economic growth since the 1980s has provided the state with more money to spend on internal security in absolute terms, this increase has been modest in real per capita terms. Still, our volume suggests that its internal conflicts, and more broadly, its approach toward confronting internal security threats, have shaped the Indian state in profound ways.

The enhancement of internal security-related state capacity has been mostly concentrated at the Center and has further tilted a federal structure with unitary tendencies toward centralization. The seventh schedule of the Indian Constitution holds states responsible for the subject of law and order. Still, whether it is controlling communal riots and mob violence, or preventing terrorist attacks, state governments have gradually become more dependent on the Center to meet their security needs. While modest expenditures by state governments on their police forces has enfeebled capacity, it has been severely amplified by the active political undermining of professional norms. Across the country, especially in the cities, understaffed and poorly trained police forces have contributed to the conversion of policing from a public to a private good, leading to the growth in the private security industry.

While most insurgency-hit states in India are not major contributors to the country's tax revenue, they do make a claim on state resources. The financial and personnel resources for these internal wars are not raised locally for the most part and are instead provided by Delhi. When the state has either defeated the insurgency or has brought violence under control, the Center continues to underwrite the peace; the federal forces often stay, and financial support endures. Gradually, state building occurs. Transport and communication links improve. Local special forces are raised. While these changes have the potential to deepen the ties of these regions with the rest of the country, as long as the bureaucratic capacity of the state outside the security sector remains stunted, and the alienation of the local population continues, the underlying issues will fester and integration into the national fabric will not materialize.[19]

How Effective Has the Indian State Been in Providing Internal Security?

Measures of Violence and Order

After the communal carnage surrounding Partition, the first major internal security challenge was a communist-led peasant insurrection in Telangana in the erstwhile princely state of Hyderabad. Almost as soon as it ended in 1951, an insurgency erupted in Nagaland in India's North East in 1952. At the end of the decade, a famine in Mizoram and a pitifully indifferent response by the Indian state would spark the Mizo insurgency. In 1966, in an embarrassing episode, the Indian Air Force was forced to bomb Aizawl as the insurgents threatened to overrun the Assam Rifle battalion headquarters. The insurgency would continue for a quarter century until the peace accord of 1986, one of the more successful peace settlements in the troubled region.

In many ways, the onset of wider internal security challenges began after the 1967 elections, which marked the end of the hegemony—but not predominance—of the Congress. As electoral competition heated up and the economy struggled, the core internal security challenges from the late 1960s to the early 1980s were around labor strife, student protests, agrarian unrest, and localized caste and communal conflicts. A violent left-wing insurgency in West Bengal—the Naxalite movement—led to assassinations and murders of numerous policemen, government officials, businessmen, landlords, professionals, and political leaders. After "Presidents Rule" was declared, the state struck back, crushing the movement with extralegal means from fake encounters to police atrocities to jailing movement members. The anarchy left not only a deep impact on West Bengal's economy as capital fled, but a political culture marked by violence that has been exceptional by Indian standards. The Naxal leadership scattered and quietly rebuilt the movement in the forests of central India over the next two decades.

The 1980s marked a sharp deterioration in India's internal security. The Punjab crisis brought a full-fledged insurgency at the doorstep of India's capital. In the beginning of the decade, dozens of people were being killed annually. By the middle of the decade, this jumped to hundreds and by the end of the decade to thousands.

But the decade also marked some of the most reprehensible massacres of innocent people killed by marauding mobs with official complicity. In 1979, the massacre of Namasudra refugees (a Dalit sub-caste) by the West Bengal police, who allegedly killed thousands of people, in Marichjhapi island in the Sundarbans went largely unreported.[20] The Nellie massacre of Bengali Muslims in rural Assam in 1983 was probably the most gruesome communal slaughter since Independence. The report of the state government appointed Commission of Inquiry (Tewary Commission on Assam Disturbances) was never formally released. However, press reports based on leaked parts of the report claim that between January to April 1983, 2,072 people were killed in group clashes, and 235 were killed in police firings.[21] More large-scale massacres followed in the next two decades, including the killing of around three thousand Sikhs in Delhi in 1984 in the aftermath of Mrs. Gandhi's assassination,[22] about a thousand (mostly Muslims) killed in the Bhagalpur riots in 1989,[23] nearly 900 in Mumbai in 1992–1993,[24] and more than a thousand (again largely Muslims) across many districts of Gujarat in 2002.

India's internal security took a marked turn for the worse as it entered the 1990s. As with Punjab, a series of terribly short-sighted political partisan moves in Kashmir led to an uprising whose echoes continue to reverberate. Now for the first time, a new security threat emerged—violence perpetrated by Jihadi and other fundamentalist groups. The Ministry of Home Affairs' (MHA) Annual Report of 1991–1992 made grim reading:

> The assassination of Rajiv Gandhi in a bomb blast in Tamil Nadu in May, 1991 evoked widespread reaction and led to country wide protests and large-scale violence in Andhra Pradesh. West Bengal and Tripura. . . . The gazetting of the Interim Award of the Cauvery Water Dispute Tribunal on December 11, 1991 led to widespread violence mainly in Karnataka which resulted in the exodus of a large number of Tamilians from Karnataka into Tamil Nadu [and also] exodus of some Kannadigas from Tamil Nadu to Karnataka. . . . The situation in Punjab and Jammu & Kashmir continued to be grave. The overall law and order situation in the country during the year continued to cause serious concern due to terrorist and secessionist activities, communal conflicts, and violence by left wing extremists. The Sikh terrorist activities in some States registered increase and posed problems for the law enforcing agencies during the year. The year was also marked by caste related tension and agitations on reservation for backward classes in some States. The communal front which had aggravated in an unprecedented manner in 1990, remained disturbed and vulnerable and further vitiated the law and order situation in the country.

That year, electoral violence claimed 350 lives in about 3,300 poll-related violent incidents; leftist extremist violence claimed 473 lives in 1,870 violent incidents; in Punjab, 2,030 militants and 474 members of the security forces were killed along with more than two thousand civilians; in the North East, violence in Manipur and Nagaland claimed 42 lives in 27 violent incidents; and in Assam, 278 violent incidents led to 130 killings. The whole state was declared a disturbed area and the army had to be inducted in aid of civil authorities.[25]

Since around 2000, insurgency-related violence in Jammu and Kashmir and in the northeastern states became more episodic and its footprint contracted. Peace and political settlements still elude these conflicts, and the specter of violence has ebbed but hardly ended in these troubled regions. The 2000s also saw the geographic spread of Naxal presence and accompanying violence across the tribal belt in central India. Overall, more lives have been lost in this insurgency than in the North East and more civilians have lost their lives than in even the Kashmir conflict. The fact that this could happen in the geographic heart of the country is a striking indictment of governance and development failures in this region since independence, especially the lamentable treatment of its tribal population. Gradually, however, the state has been able to bring this deadly conflict under control and violence has declined and geographically concentrated. Importantly, while some old insurgency-related fires continue to burn, albeit with less intensity, new insurgencies have not appeared. Since 2002, India has not experienced ethno-religious massacres on the scale of Gujarat 2002, Delhi 1984, or Nellie 1983. But, as incidents of communal violence like in Muzaffar Nagar in 2013 and in Delhi in 2020 testify, this form of violence and their facilitators remain active, on tap, as it were. In these cases, the state is not the deterrent; it is the facilitator.

Below the threshold of communal riots and large-scale massacres, there lurks another form of violence motivated by everyday communalism.[26] Acts of intimidation and lynching carried out by vigilantes on various pretexts, be it discouraging interfaith marriages or cattle smuggling, have been occurring with some regularity. Often when these circulate on social media and the state looks the other way, their impact is both chilling and felt broadly.

In contrast to the 1980s and 1990s, however, current levels of electoral violence and high-profiled political assassinations have plummeted. The landscape of violence, then, has undergone a substantial shift in recent decades. Many of the key indicators of violence have declined sharply, which we discuss next.[27]

Homicide

An important indicator of violent crime, homicide deaths, has declined steadily over the past three decades. While homicide rates have declined worldwide—from 6.8 per 100,000 in 1990 to 5.8 in 2018—India's decline has been steeper—from 5.1 to 3.1 in the same period (Figure 1.1). Interestingly, male homicide rates account for most of this decline. Between 1999 and 2018, male homicide rates declined from 6.1 to 3.4 (per 100,000), while for women the decline was negligible—from 2.9 to 2.7—a reflection of the fact that family members rather than strangers are the main source of violence directed at women.[28]

India's strict arms control laws, together with controls on access to ammunition, appear to have contributed to lower homicide rates than in Latin America or Africa. In 2018, the total stock of arms licenses issued by states was about 3.6 million (60 percent were in just three states—Uttar Pradesh, Punjab, and Jammu and Kashmir). These are state-specific licenses for small-bore arms issued primarily for crop protection and sporting purposes.[29] Between 2018 and 2020, the number of new arms licenses issued with "all India permission" was about 8,000 annually, while another 33,000 such licenses were renewed annually during this period (there are of course many illegal manufacturers as well as smuggled weapons).[30]

However, while this might explain a lower level of violence, it does not explain the declining trend. Remarkably, these declines have occurred even as a strong predictor of homicides, the proportion of the population aged between fifteen and twenty-nine years, remained largely unchanged during this period. Two other likely predictors, an increase in the police-to-population ratio and the percent of population in jail, also changed little. However, for much of this period India's economy

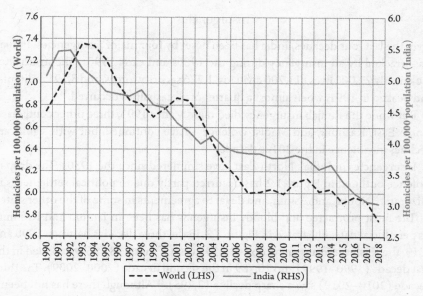

Figure 1.1 Trends in homicide rates: India vs. World
Source: World Bank

grew at unprecedented rates. Did greater prosperity contribute to less violence, and might this reverse as India's economy slows?

Terrorism

According to data from the Global Terrorism Index 2020, 8,749 people were killed in India in terrorist attacks since 2001, but there has been a declining trend since 2010. The number of terrorist incidents (excluding Jammu and Kashmir) declined by 70 percent from 71 to 21 between the years 2000–2010 and the following decade.[31]

The pattern on hijackings has also shifted over the past two decades. Beginning with the hijacking of an Indian Airlines plane on its way from Srinagar to Jammu (which was hijacked and flown to Lahore in 1971), hijackings emerged as high-profile terrorist actions. They often achieved their purpose of seriously embarrassing the Indian state in addition to the loss of life and property.[32] There were three hijackings in the 1970s, seven in the 1980s, and five in the 1990s.[33] Two hijackings occurred outside India (an Air India flight in Seychelles by a group of mercenaries in 1981 and another Air India flight hijacked by Palestinians linked to the Abu Nidal group in Karachi in 1986). However, there have been none since the hijacking of an Indian Airlines flight in December 1999 (flying from Kathmandu and taken to Kandahar), both because of stronger efforts in the country and because of the tightening of global airport security measures after 9/11.

Insurgencies

Over the last four decades, India has been beset by four major insurgencies. Punjab was wracked by an insurgency during the 1980s and early 1990s. The insurgency took nearly 22,000 lives (11,700 civilians, 1,776 security forces, and 8,191 militants) and peaked in 1991, when almost a quarter of all casualties occurred.[34]

But while the Punjab insurgency died rapidly after 1993, three other conflicts—North East, Kashmir, and Maoist violence—have continued, but with significant declines in violence in the 2010s decade.

Insurgencies in India's North East have simmered since the 1950s. The drop in violence outlined in Figure 1.2 has occurred partly due to political settlements in Mizoram, Tripura, and Assam, and de facto agreements in some of the other states.

The most protracted and bloody insurgency has been in Jammu and Kashmir. As per official data, illustrated in Figure 1.3, in the three decades between 1990 and 2019, the Kashmir insurgency took 41,859 lives. Of these, 18,775 were killed in the first decade (1990–1999) and 20,789 in the second decade (2000–2009). The third decade (2010–2019) saw a sharp decline (2,295).[35] Although there has not been a significant upsurge of violence after the revocation of Article 370 in 2019 (which had enshrined the state's special status), that is largely due to the iron fist of a repressive internal security dragnet.

Incidents of violence due to Left Wing Extremism (LWE) (also referred to as Naxalites/Maoists) declined by almost two thirds from 6,061 in the period 2008–2010 to 2,168 a decade later (2018–2020). The number of civilian and security

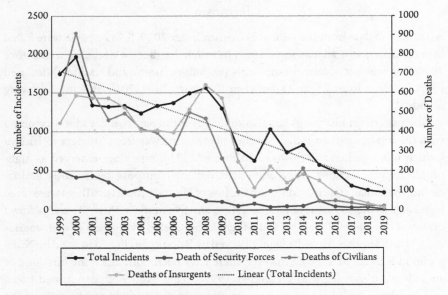

Figure 1.2 Insurgencies: North East, 1999–2019
Source: MHA Annual Reports

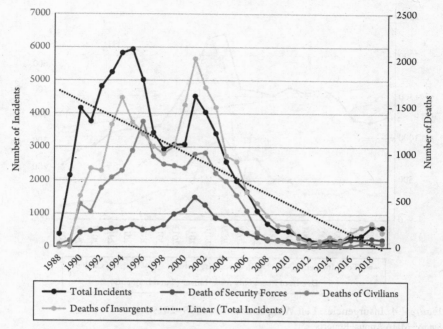

Figure 1.3 Insurgencies: Jammu and Kashmir, 1988–2019
Source: MHA Annual Reports

force deaths declined even more sharply, from 2,632 in the earlier period to 625 in the most recent period—a decline of more than three fourths (see Figure 1.4). The geographical spread of LWE violence contracted from 76 districts in 2013 to 53 in 2020.

An important reason is the much larger presence of the Indian state, through the deployment of CAPFs, provision of helicopters and UAVs, funding the State's India Reserve Battalions (IRBs)/Special India Reserve Battalions, and fortified police stations. The presence of the state has also been manifest in the construction of more than 5,000 km of new roads, installation of mobile towers, and increasing bank branches, post offices, health, and education facilities.[36] Various central schemes such as the Security Related Expenditure Scheme, Special Infrastructure Scheme, and Special Central Assistance have also provided additional funds (about Rs. 1,100 crores annually).[37]

The total death toll in the three ongoing insurgencies over two decades has been 53,199 (Table 1.1). The toll has been highest in Kashmir, but civilian casualties have been highest in the LWE insurgencies. The decline of violence is more due to enhanced state capacity and less the sorts of political settlements that would provide consent of the governed and ensure that new cycles of violence do not occur.

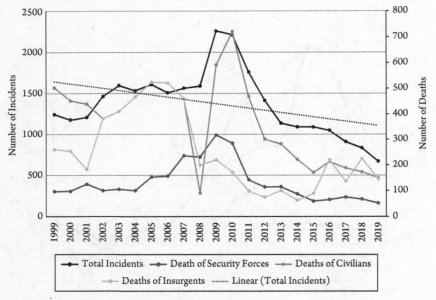

Figure 1.4 Insurgencies: Left Wing Extremism, 1999–2019
Source: MHA Annual Reports

Table 1.1 **Deaths in insurgencies (1999–2019)**

	Security Forces	*Civilians*	*Insurgents*	*Total*
LWE	2,779	7,725	5,202	15,706
North East	1,394	6,150	6,865	14,409
Kashmir	3,552	6,772	12,760	23,084
Total	7,725	20,647	24,827	53,199

Source: MHA data

Communal Violence

Communal violence has been the scourge of independent India. After the horrific carnage around Partition that resulted in over a million deaths and displaced an estimated 10 million people, communal violence fell markedly in the 1950s. It increased in the 1960s before again falling in the 1970s. Hindu-Muslim violence was particularly virulent for about a quarter century from the late 1970s to 2002, when the bloodbath in Gujarat ensued. Since then, it has been relatively stable according to official data (see Figures 1.5 and 1.6).[38] The 1980s also saw for the first

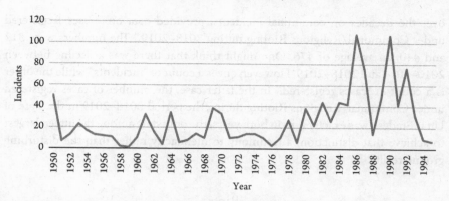

Figure 1.5 Hindu-Muslim communal violence, 1950–1995
Source: Varshney, Ashutosh, and Wilkinson, Steven. Varshney-Wilkinson Dataset on Hindu-Muslim Violence in India, 1950–1995, Version 2.

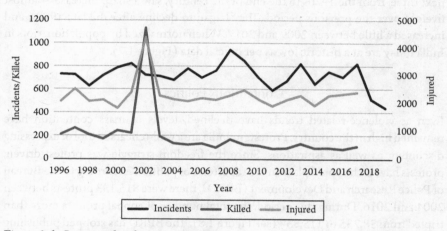

Figure 1.6 Communal violence, 1996–2019
Note: These data include all communal violence.
Source: MHA

time Hindu-Sikh violence, marked most horribly by the 1984 Delhi riots, but after the early 1990s, this virus died out.

After 2017, the MHA has stopped providing data on communal violence. In response to a question in Parliament in 2018, the government had put forward data that the number of communal incidents during the years 2014, 2015, 2016, and 2017 was 644, 751, 703, and 822 respectively, with an annual average of 730. By far, the highest share was Uttar Pradesh, with 22.1 percent. Uttar Pradesh accounted for a fifth of all "communal incidents" between 2010 and 2014.[39] In March 2021, in response to another question in Parliament, the government provided data for two years on communal incidents. But this statement, in contrast to reporting by MHA over the decades on communal incidents, provided data on "Cases Registered under Communal/Religious Rioting during 2018–2019." The numbers were 512 and 440, an average of 476. One might think that there was a decline between 2010–2014 and 2018–2019. However, one is a count of "incidents," while the other is a count of "cases registered." In the latter case, the number of cases registered under Communal/Religious Rioting during the period 2018–2019 in the state of Uttar Pradesh was exactly zero in both years, the only state among the fifteen largest to achieve that distinction, a testimony to mendacity rather than the disturbing ground reality.

Riots

In many ways, changes in the occurrence of riots over time is a good reflection of shifts in order in independent India. The first decades were relatively stable. The next three, from the 1970s to the end of the century, saw a sharp increase—almost fivefold over the previous period. They began to decline after the late 1990s, and increased a little between 2009 and 2017. When normalized by population, riots in India today are at a historic low as per official data (Figure 1.7).

Contentious Politics

Even as violence-related trends have declined, levels of mass contention have remained high in the country. Protests in India are a well-rehearsed tool of expressing discontent as well as aspirations. Since the freedom struggle was protest-driven, protests have an honored place in the repertoire of politics. According to the Bureau of Police Research and Development (BPRD), there were 815,133 protests between 2004 and 2016. During this period, the total number of annual protests more than tripled from 38,235 to 115,837 (see Figure 1.8). The BPRD has stopped publishing protest data after 2016. Another data repository that relies on newspaper reports of

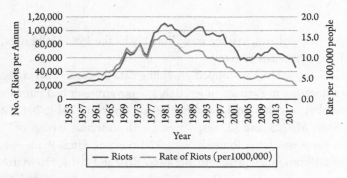

Figure 1.7 Riots, 1953–2019
Source: Bureau of Police Research and Development (BPRD)

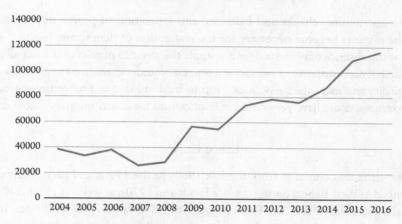

Figure 1.8 Protests in India, 2004–2016
Source: Bureau of Police Research and Development (BPRD)

protests—the Armed Conflict Location & Event Data Project (ACLED)—points to a similar trend between 2016 and 2019. The number of protests it tracked jumped from 9,689 in 2016 to 15,837 in 2019.

But the massive difference in the number of protests as reported by BPRD and ACLED in one common year, 2016—an almost twelvefold difference—serves as a strong caveat on such data compiled by global sources. Many protests that take place in rural India go unreported by the press and hence do not register in data that rely on media reports.

Most protests are small in size and remain nonviolent. Large-scale protests, while much fewer, can paralyze cities and transport, and be much more damaging when they occasionally turn violent. The Ram Janambhoomi protests and processions in 1990, caste-based agitations to demand greater share in reservations in state jobs, including the Gujjar protests in Rajasthan in 2008, the Patidar agitation in Gujarat in 2015, and the Jat protests in Haryana in 2016 are illustrative of such types of protests. The yearlong farmer protests ranging from mid-2020 to mid-2021 were remarkable in their duration while remaining relatively peaceful. One reason protest activity has clocked a sharp rise in recent years is due to falling costs of collective action. The increase in access to social media has made coordination for collective action much easier across the world. The same pattern is visible in India. Higher protest activity puts additional pressure on a severely understaffed police force.

In his final speech to the Constituent Assembly on November 25, 1949, B. R. Ambedkar warned against the use of protest politics in a constitutional democracy, viewing them as a "Grammar of Anarchy." He felt that a constitutional democracy provided institutional avenues to articulate, aggregate, and represent collective grievances and demands. One interpretation of rising protest activity is that it is a symptom of the failure of institutional politics. As Acemoglu and Robinson argue, when institutions, checks and balances, and separation of power stop working, public protests become necessary for the restoration of democratic health.[40] But, just as the absence of protests does not imply the absence of grievances, not all protest activity is restorative of democracy, especially under conditions of graded social inequality and majoritarian politics. Protests by dominant and subordinate groups, for example, could have very different implications for constitutional democracy.

Labor Unrest

Labor strife was common from the late 1960s to the 1990s and particularly pronounced in West Bengal during the late 1960s and 1970s, as well as in Maharashtra, Kerala, and Tamil Nadu. The Railway Strike of 1974 was the peak of the pan-India labor movement, although other major labor strikes such as the textile mills in Mumbai in the early 1980s and periodic strikes in the public sector–dominated banking industry have continued. While in 1970, 1.5 million workers went on strike and strikes outnumbered lockouts nine to one, by 1990 striking workers dropped to 804,000, about half the number in 1970. The person-days lost in disputes came down from 20 million in 1970 to 12 million in 1990.

Post economic liberalization, as the balance shifted toward capital, formal sector employment grew much more slowly relative to the massive numbers entering the work force. This undermined the power of unions, and one consequence has been a sharp decline in labor disputes and the number of person-days lost (Figures 1.9 and 1.10).

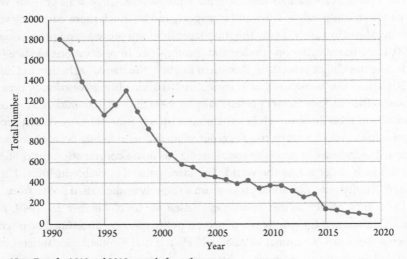

Note: Data for 2018 and 2019 are only for strikes.

Figure 1.9 Labor disputes (strikes + lockouts)
Source: Labour Bureau and Annual Reports, Ministry of Labour and Employment

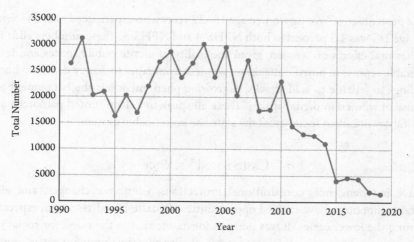

Figure 1.10 Person-days lost in labor disputes (thousands)
Source: Labour Bureau and Annual Reports, Ministry of Labour and Employment

Electoral Violence

As Indian elections became more competitive at the state and national levels in the mid-1960s and the number of political parties increased sharply, election-related violence began to rise. Then from the 1990s onward, the trend reversed, and electoral violence fell sharply. According to an internal Home Ministry note, between 1989 and 2019, electoral violence declined across multiple indicators. The number of incidents at the polling station fell by 25 percent, electoral violence–related deaths dropped by 70 percent, and injuries were reduced by 60 percent. This occurred despite the size of the electorate increasing by over 80 percent and the number of polling stations nearly doubling. This reduction in violence has been made possible by a closer supervision of the polls by the Election Commission of India and the extensive use of central and state police forces to secure the elections.[41]

Gender-Based Violence

One area where reported violence has increased is gender-based violence. However, the data here are extremely unreliable since so much of this violence occurs in private spaces and goes unreported. About one in three women in India are subject to intimate partner violence, but only one in ten of these women formally reports the offense.[42] Perhaps the best All-India survey data come from the National Family Health Survey (NFHS). In response to the question, "Ever-married women age 18–49 years who have ever experienced spousal violence," the percentage of women who answered affirmatively dropped from 37.2 percent in NFHS-3 (2005–2006) to 31.2 percent in NFHS-4 (2015–2016) and 29.3 percent in NFHS-5 (2019–2021).

The percentage of "Young women age 18–29 years who experienced sexual violence by age 18" was 1.5 percent in both NFHS-4 and NFHS-5. These numbers elide the behavioral effects on women, given the reality of unsafe public spaces and innumerable reports of horrific attacks on women, from rapes to dowry deaths to honor killings to feticide to acid attacks. A growing phenomenon is the harassment and abuse of women in digital spaces. These all speak to a deep-rooted patriarchy and misogyny in Indian society that the state has been unable to stem.

Caste-Based Violence

Since independence, constitutional protections, economic changes, and electoral competition have created opportunities for caste-based assertion, especially among the lower castes. It was perhaps inevitable that in the quest for social justice and equality among the lower castes, challenging the dominant castes' imperative to maintain their power and privileges would result in tumult and violence. As dominant castes resorted to threats, humiliation, and violence to preserve their control, subordinate groups turned to the state for their protection and occasionally hit back with violence. The struggle has not infrequently resulted in mass violence. In 1968, the powerful landlords of the Kilvenmani village in Tamil Nadu burned 44 Dalits to death when they protested to demand higher wages. In 1981, armed gangs of higher castes gunned down 24 Dalits in Dehuli and a few days later 12 more Dalits in Sarhupur in Uttar Pradesh. In 1997, six Dalits were hacked to death by the local dominant castes when a Dalit was elected to the position of Panchayat president in the district of Madurai in Tamil Nadu. In the 1990s, Bihar experienced caste wars. Maoist groups led by OBCs and made up of Dalit foot soldiers killed members of the landed Bhumihar castes. In retaliation, Ranvir Sena militiamen drawn from among Bhumihars slaughtered Dalits; 21 Dalits were gunned down in Bathani Tola in 1996 and 58 were killed in Laxmanpur Bathe in 1997. The frequency of such large-scale attacks has diminished in the last couple of decades even though instances of caste-based conflicts across different parts of the country remain high.

Two aspects of mass violence–related trends should be noted here. First, the type of mass violence that is at the center of discussions in this volume are those that not only threaten individual liberty but also threaten the state, the guarantor of order and liberty. There are other forms of everyday violence that rob individuals of liberty without directly threatening state institutions.[43] Our volume does not focus on these forms of violence. Second, although mass violence has taken multiple forms in India, these acts have seldom triggered attempts at reconciliation that would force state and society to face up to the consequences of violence. As a result, violence is remembered differently across groups, its memory fuels resentment, and groups remain polarized.

Security Force Fatalities

The trend of falling public violence is mirrored in the fatality figures of security forces. As Figures 1.11 and 1.12 illustrate, police, CAPF, and army fatalities have declined in the last decade.

Internal Security Institutional Framework

While every situation in which the security of the state is threatened is a public order problem, not all public order problems threaten the security of the state. Similarly, public disorder inevitably entails law and order problems, but the converse is not true—not all law and order problems are public order problems. This is schematically illustrated in Figure 1.13. Often, challenges to public order, especially protests and strikes, are ways in which citizens draw attention to their grievances that have gone unheeded. Sometimes the state views challenges to public order as threats to the security of the state, and in so doing, precipitates the very crisis it seeks to check.

Under the Constitution, "Public Order" and "Police" are in the State List (List II) of the Seventh Schedule. The states are responsible for prevention, detection, and investigation of such crime through their law enforcement machinery. The Union Government's role is to help state governments by sharing intelligence, providing armed and paramilitary forces to the states if required, and providing financial assistance for strengthening their policing infrastructure. The legal framework comes from Article 256, which empowers the Union to issue directions to a state to ensure such compliance. Under Article 355, the Union has the duty "to protect every State against external aggression and internal disturbance and to ensure that the government of every State is carried on in accordance with the provisions of this Constitution." In addition to these powers, Article 356 confers extraordinary powers on the Union to deal with a constitutional breakdown in a state and take over all functions of the State Government.

The internal security architecture of the Union Government has four elements:

A. *Political*: Cabinet and the Cabinet Committee on Security.
B. *Administrative*: Ministry of Home Affairs; Prime Minister's office; Cabinet Secretariat.
C. *Intelligence*: The Intelligence Bureau (which reports to the Home Minister); Research and Analysis Wing (which falls under the Cabinet Secretariat, and hence, reports to the Prime Minister); the Joint Intelligence Committee (JIC), National Technical Research Organisation (NTRO), and Aviation Research Centre (ARC) all report to the National Security Advisor (NSA); and the National Security Council Secretariat under the NSA, which serves the National Security Council.[44] A different set of agencies monitors

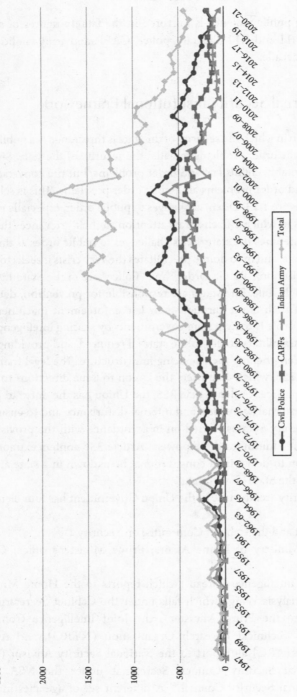

Figure 1.11 Security force fatalities over time

Sources: National War Memorial website, https://nationalwarmemorial.gov.in/ and government figures provided in response to questions asked in the parliament. Civil Police and CAPF data until 2018 are from Indian Police Journal, November- December 2018. For 2018-19, https://www.indiatoday.in/india/story/292-cops-martyred-in-india-from-sep-2018-to-aug-2019-police-1611235-2019-10-20; for 2019-20, https://www.deccanherald.com/national/35398-police-personnel-killed-on-duty-since-independence-264-in-past-one-year-905158.html; for 2020-21 https://indianexpress.com/article/cities/chandigarh/police-commemoration-day-hary ana-dgp- pays-tributes-to-police-martyrs-377-bravehearts-in-khaki-remembered-7583990/

financial intelligence: Directorates in the Income Tax, Customs and Central Excise departments; the Financial Intelligence Unit; and the Enforcement Directorate. These are all under Ministry of Finance.

D. *Enforcement*: The Central Armed Police Forces (CAPFS), including the Central Reserved Police Force (CRPF), Border Security Force (BSF), Central Industrial Security Force (CISF), Indo-Tibetan Border Police (ITBP), Assam Rifles, Shashastra Seema Baal (SSB), and the National Security Guard (NSG).

The MHA is the nodal agency for enforcement. As Shakti Sinha explains in his chapter, its size and often the stature of its political leadership reflect its power. In addition to the CAPFs, MHA also manages several other central police organizations.[45] The MHA's role is to manage both vertical (between Center and states) and horizontal (among states) coordination. The latter is a necessity to deal with organized crime.[46] At present, there is no legislation or institutional mechanism that mandates coordination across state police forces. The failure of coordination was manifestly visible in the botched response to the 26/11 attacks and the lengthy amount of time it took to bring LWE under control as insurgents moved and operated across state borders. These coordination challenges are even greater in fast-emerging security threats such as cyber-crime and cyber-attacks.

But the Home Ministry's ambit is so broad—from disaster management to checking counterfeit currency to managing the census or the official language policy—that its attention to internal security gets diluted. There is also a larger political dynamic that affects the trust between the central and state governments that is so critical for better internal security. The trust deficit becomes much greater when there is a perception that security agencies of the central government are being used for partisan purposes which severely risks undermining internal security.

This perception has always plagued the Intelligence Bureau (IB), which is tasked with intelligence collection and dissemination and also acts as a security advisor to the federal and state governments. It is widely perceived to be used as an instrument of governments to spy on opposition figures or even members of the ruling party. A number of government agencies, including the IB, have broad wiretap powers in the name of national security. The lack of oversight makes this process highly vulnerable to abuse. Just such a misuse seems to have occurred when intelligence services allegedly used the Pegasus software (developed by an Israeli company NSO and acquired by the Indian government in 2017) to surveil political opponents, journalists, human rights activists, and even an election commissioner.[47]

The chapter by Saikat Datta suggests that it is hard to gauge the effectiveness of the IB. Given the manner in which it recruits its personnel and deploys them, its analytical capabilities are questionable. It has expanded rapidly in recent years to an organization with a Rs. 2,500 crore budget. While intelligence services are by nature nontransparent, the lack of regulatory frameworks or parliamentary oversight

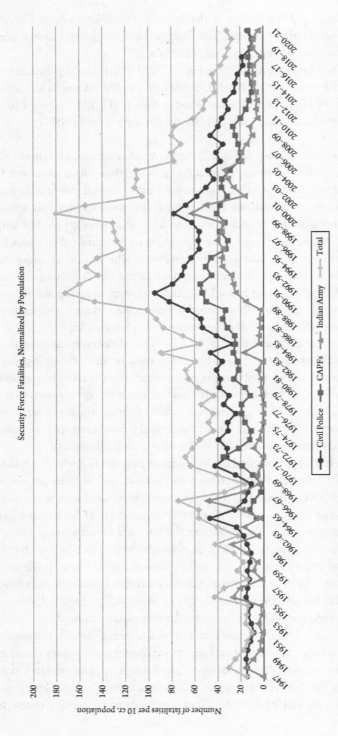

Figure 1.12 Security force fatalities, normalized by population

Source: Civil Police and CAPF data until 2018 are from Indian Police Journal, November– December 2018. For 2018-19, https://www.indiatodayin/india/story/292-cops-martyred-in-india- from-sep-2018-to-aug-2019-police-1611235-2019-10-20; for 2019-20, https://www.deccanherald.com/national/35398-police-personnel-killed-on-duty-since- independence-264-in-past-one-year-905158.html; for 2020-21 https://indianexpress.com/article/cities/chandigarh/police-commemoration-day-haryana-dgp- pays-tributes-to-police-martyrs-377-bravehearts-in-khaki-remembered-7583990/

Law & Order

Public Order

Security of the State

Figure 1.13 Law and order, public order, and security of the state
Source: Second Administrative Reforms Commission, Fifth Report, "Public Order," June 2007.

in India makes it worse. The reality that no government has sought to put in such frameworks speaks volumes of the partisan uses of the IB.

Similarly, the effectiveness of the CBI, which is under the Ministry of Personnel and is the key investigative agency on corruption cases, eroded as it began to be used for partisan purposes, leading the Supreme Court in 2013 to denounce it as a "caged parrot" and "its master's voice."[48] Nonetheless, it is undoubtedly often the case that in politically sensitive cases in states, the mistrust of the local police runs even deeper, leading to a clamor to get it investigated "outside," that is, to call in the CBI. But the reverse is also true, with jurisdictional arbitrage being leveraged for political purposes.

Since the BJP-led government came to power in 2014, there was a significant increase in investigations launched by central agencies, such as the CBI and ED, against the government's rivals and critics. Between 2014 and 2021, central agencies launched investigations against 570 of the government's political rivals and critics (and their family members as well), compared to just 39 individuals linked to the BJP or its allies. While this asymmetry has been true of past governments as well—the UPA-2 government launched investigations against three of its rivals for every one of its own—the ratio rose to 15:1 under the NDA government, a fivefold increase.[49] Election financing is riddled with corruption across the board, making politicians and political parties easy targets for the ED. Between 2012 and 2022, the ED filed a total of 24,893 cases under the provision of the Foreign Exchange Management Act, 1999 (FEMA) and 3985 under the Prevention of Money Laundering Act (PMLA).[50] Among these, a third of FEMA cases and more than half of all PMLA cases were filed in 2020–21 and 2021–22.

But actions have consequences. Under the Delhi Special Police Establishment (DPSE) Act, which gives power to the CBI, a state government can withdraw general consent to the CBI to investigate crimes within the state. Starting in 2015 when Mizoram withdrew "general consent" given to the CBI, seven other states—Maharashtra, Punjab, Rajasthan, West Bengal, Jharkhand, Chhattisgarh, and Kerala followed suit thereby requiring the agency to get consent from the concerned state governments for every individual case it registers in their states. Except Mizoram, all were ruled by opposition parties, and their decision was driven by mounting concerns that the CBI was serving the partisan political interests of the ruling party. In an affidavit to the Supreme Court in November 2021, the CBI submitted that about 150 requests for sanction to investigate were pending with these eight state governments since 2018, a testament to partisanship and distrust.[51] This is not new. A similar pattern was visible in earlier periods of political polarization between the ruling and opposition parties. During 1974–1979, Andhra Pradesh, Tamil Nadu, and Karnataka each withdrew consent wholly or partially, and subsequently periodically revoked or restricted consent. Haryana, Nagaland, Mizoram, and Sikkim did not give their consent to the Prevention of Corruption Act 1988, while others (Andhra Pradesh, Assam, Himachal Pradesh, Madhya Pradesh, Mizoram, Punjab, Uttar Pradesh, and West Bengal) gave only conditional consent.

In contrast to the CBI, the legislation creating the National Investigation Agency (NIA) gives it jurisdiction across the country without prior permission from state governments. The National Investigation Agency (NIA) Act 2008 provides for constitution of Special Courts, registered by NIA, where such cases are heard on a day-to-day basis and get precedence over other cases, thereby "fast-tracking" such cases.[52] This is also the case with the Enforcement Directorate (ED), whose authorization comes under the PMLA and FERA Acts.

But all these agencies are under the control of the Union Government and vulnerable to political pressure. That has undermined their credibility and with it, their effectiveness. To retaliate against this behavior, opposition-controlled states have also begun to use their police forces to file cases against elected members of the ruling BJP and their allies. These actions will only further politicize both federal and state police agencies and inevitably reduce their effectiveness.

Doctrine

The Indian state does not have a formal or set strategy and doctrine that it has followed in confronting the variety of insurgencies since independence. The chapters by Paul Staniland and Sushant Singh in this volume remind us that its approach has varied, demonstrating some flexibility. It is much more uncompromising in dealing with ethnoreligious insurgent groups in bordering states and with those that have connections with Pakistan. It has been brutal, but it has also been open to negotiations when insurgent demands stop short of secession. The state has used a range of tactics across the insurgencies, including buying of insurgents, strategic hamleting, and even outsourcing extralegal actions to state-supported militia. It has raised theater-specific forces. Rashtriya Rifles has been at the forefront of counter-insurgency in Jammu and Kashmir, Assam Rifles in the North East, and the CAPFs in the LWE insurgency belt. Unlike American counterinsurgency operations in Iraq and Afghanistan, or domestic counterinsurgency warfare in Pakistan and Sri Lanka, the Indian state has refrained from using weapons like air power and heavy artillery against the rebels outside of exceptional circumstances. Its actions have caused far less population displacement as compared to similar operations in the country's neighborhood. Still, recently the counterinsurgency strategy has shifted to focus on exercising control, and away from the process of building public consent in support of the state. The measures used to judge performance of security forces are revealing. Amit Ahuja and Srinath Raghavan note that army units are evaluated more on the number of insurgent kills and the kinetic operations undertaken than on their record on preserving peace and winning over the population.

While the counterinsurgency strategy and tactics have asserted the state's territorial control and achieved significant reduction in violence, it is striking to observe that many of these insurgencies have persisted for decades, and the state has failed to convert reduced violence into political settlements. As a result, conflicts have not ended. They have merely gone off the boil and continued to simmer.

The absence of a national internal security doctrine is understandable, for ambiguity affords state policy more flexibility. However, Sushant Singh in his chapter observes a lack of ongoing deliberation on this issue, giving credence to the belief that the Indian state's response to old and emergent challenges remains reactive and crisis-driven. The horrific 2008 Mumbai terrorist attacks, which took 164 lives, is illustrative.

It took a shock of this magnitude, exposing the country to shame and ridicule, to shake the system to undertake a flurry of actions in very reactive ways. A Multi Agency Centre (MAC) was created as a coordinating mechanism across all relevant agencies, with counterpart subsidiary-MACs in each state capital where all agencies operating at the state level (especially the Special Branch of the state police) were represented.[53]

The Unlawful Activities (Prevention) Act 1967 was amended to reincorporate provisions similar to earlier counterterrorism legislation, especially the Terrorist and Disruptive Activities (Prevention) Act 1985 (TADA) and the Prevention of Terrorism Act 2002 (POTA). The former was allowed to lapse under a sunset clause in 1995 and the latter was repealed in 2004, in part because of serious human rights violations. A National Investigation Agency (NIA) was created for undertaking investigation and prosecution of offenses affecting India's national and internal security. These legislations were passed by both houses of Parliament, cutting across party lines.

A more ambitious effort was to network all multiple stand-alone databases, which led to the creation of NATGRID. Originally envisaged to be up and running within two years, it was hobbled by turf wars and took more than a decade to become operational. Another ambitious attempt—a National Counter Terrorism Centre (NCTC)—failed to take off at all.

Beyond the fight against insurgencies and terrorists, a troubling aspect of the Indian state's approach toward violence and order is the tolerance of political party–linked vigilantes that Paul Staniland flags in his chapter. Their significant capacity for violence and their ready availability means that they can be called upon to unleash serious chaos at short notice. The persistence and in certain cases the growth of party-connected vigilante groups, and their ability to act with impunity, suggests that the recent downward trend of mob violence, riots, and large-scale massacres is fragile and can be reversed easily. For now, the Indian state confronts the challenge of controlling violence and preserving order through a burgeoning security apparatus at its disposal.

Boots on the Ground: Organizations and Personnel

On the ground, four sets of personnel provide internal security in India: the 1.3 million strong Indian Army (until recently, one third of its infantry troops have been used for an internal security role); the one million strong federal CAPFs, that serves as paramilitary forces; the two million strong state police forces; and another nine million private security guards. In addition, the Indian Railway Protection Force Service has another 75,000-odd personnel, including a new commando unit (CORAS—Commandos for Railway Security). There are also smaller localized forces for specialized purposes, such as the approximately 60,000 rangers deployed for wildlife protection.[54]

Under the British Raj, one third of the colonial army was devoted to internal security. While the army's familiarity with internal security management was an important reason why it was inducted into this role soon after independence, it was nonetheless a surprising development. Conventional wisdom on coup-proofing suggests that young democracies should refrain from using their military for internal security. However, as Ahuja and Raghavan argue in their chapter, contravening this wisdom, the Indian government used the Indian military widely for state consolidation purposes and fighting counterinsurgency following independence. The 1980s and the 1990s saw a significant expansion in the army's internal security role as it was tasked with controlling insurgencies in Punjab, Jammu and Kashmir, and Assam, in addition to its ongoing counterinsurgency role in other North East states. To meet these demands, the army created the Rashtriya Rifles, a counterinsurgency force mustered from within the organization, with a current strength of 75,000 personnel. The North East–focused and army-led counterinsurgency force, Assam Rifles, saw substantial expansion.

In the three decades between 1990–2020, the size of India's CAPFs almost doubled (with commensurate increases in expenditures) even as the personnel strength of virtually all other major ministries of the federal government has declined. In 1991, CAPFs were 45.6 percent of the size of the army. By 2020, this

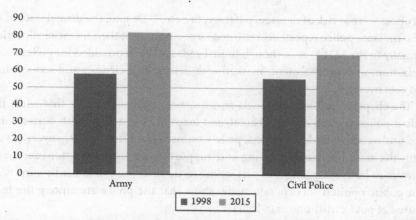

Figure 1.14 Personnel strength of CAPF as a percentage of army and civil police, 1998 and 2015
Source: Data on army from the International Institute for Strategic Studies, and on civil police from BPRD

had increased to 84.1 percent. However, the size of CAPFs relative to the civil police—about half—has been roughly similar at the beginning and end of this period (see Figure 1.14).

Police Forces: The Weak Link

The bedrock of internal security in any country is the civil police, and this foundation is the Achilles heel of India's internal security. The harsh reality of the functioning of the Uttar Pradesh police (in India's most populous state) is illustrative. A CAG report found that despite sharp increases in crime, the problem of understaffing persists in police forces as less than half of police personnel were in place relative to their authorized strength. Staff shortages in the forensic labs were at 67 percent and shortages of traffic police were between 70 to 90 percent.[55] The number of police stations was considerably less than the already low Indian norms, while mobility was hampered by shortages of police vehicles. At the same time, the police department "purchased ten bulletproof Tata Safari and eight General Safari vehicles for Chief Minister's security . . . purchasing more expensive and luxurious vehicles (Mercedes Model M-Guard) for Chief Minister's security instead of Land Cruiser sanctioned earlier," using funds earmarked to replace junked police vehicles, "thus depriving the district police of their sanctioned fleet of vehicles."[56] The state police lacked modern weapons with about half the police force using point-303 bore rifles that had been declared obsolete by the MHA more than two decades ago. This issue is further compounded by chronic ammunition shortages. The sole storage facility for arms and ammunitions in the state "lacked proper storage buildings, fire security system and surveillance system and, therefore, arms & ammunitions worth crores of rupees were at risk of damage, pilferage, fire etc."[57] Despite the dismal state of affairs, the state police repeatedly returned large amounts of their financial allocation annually to the MHA, even though these funds had been provided for police modernization, with procurement "marked with delays, inefficiencies and serious time and cost overruns."

The chapters by Akshay Mangla and Beatrice Jauregui reiterate that while the Indian police is often corrupt, brutal, and inept in how it deals with citizens, it is also understaffed, underequipped, poorly trained, and often severely overworked. With the state just barely training and supporting its police functionaries—and policemen both struggling and pretending to do their job—it is hardly surprising that public opinion surveys repeatedly show that the police are among the least trusted of public institutions in India.[58]

In 2007, the Second Administrative Reforms Commission highlighted a litany of problems facing the police in India: poor civil police-to-population ratio; long delays in filling up of vacancies; a legal framework, embedded in the Police Act 1861, that was out of sync with the needs to combat emerging crimes such as terrorism, cyber-crimes, sophisticated economic crimes, crimes pertaining to violation of human rights, etc.; and the need to separate investigation and prosecution assistance wings from the other normal police duties.

It also highlighted glaring organizational lacunae: poor working conditions (several studies have pointed out that an average policeman has to work up to 12 to 14 hours a day, often seven days a week); lack of housing; limited number of police stations with weak infrastructure, both physical and human, for existing stations; outmoded recruitment and training systems and obsolete equipment; and, of course, the perennial problem of insulating the police from political and other extraneous influences.

Efficient policing and successful investigation and prosecution of crimes are not just a *sine qua non* for rule of law, but they also lead to stronger internal security. Mounting arrears of undetected crimes, delayed and denied justice, and acts of violence that go unchecked all generate a sense of impunity among those engaging in such actions on the one hand, and frustration and anger in those at the receiving end. The widening gap between the two is an obvious threat to internal security.

One visible implication of the state of affairs is that the state police force is yet to emerge as the centerpiece of a counterinsurgency response. Despite their many deficiencies, they are the first responders to insurgencies and terror attacks, where they have achieved some notable successes. On December 13, 2001, when the Indian Parliament was assaulted by five well-armed attackers on a suicide mission, they were stopped by the Delhi police personnel stationed in the complex. But, more often than not, when tested, state police forces have been overwhelmed by insurgencies and embarrassed by terrorists. At the same time, when well-supported and well-led state police forces have had frontline roles in confronting insurgencies, the results have been promising, as seen in Punjab, Jammu and Kashmir, Andhra Pradesh, and Tripura. Moreover, according to the Status of Policing in India Report 2021, although 39 percent of respondents in conflict zones find the police force to be corrupt, about half as many (20 percent) judge the army and paramilitary similarly. Nonetheless, 60 percent of respondents in these areas trust the police more than the army or the CAPFs. The experience of counterinsurgency has been that while national armed forces can help suppress insurgents, the task of restoring public order invariably involves careful and sustained police work.[59]

The problems rooted in their training, capacity, and organizational culture also surface when police forces confront violent protests. The Haryana police defected along ethnic lines when facing rioting mobs of co-ethnics in 2016. A panicked state government turned to the CAPFs and the army for help, as highlighted by Nirvikar Jassal and Hanif Qureshi in their chapter. In Kashmir, CAPFs and state police have used pellet guns as a nonlethal means of crowd control, blinding hundreds of protesters. In Tamil Nadu, the police opened fire against protesting workers at a copper plant, killing 11 protesters in 2018. Arvind Varma identifies police leadership as a key factor in explaining police performance.[60] He contends that even a poorly trained force learns enough in the field and is capable of delivering good policing if led by skilled and determined officers. Such officers lead from the front and are willing to defend their force from political pressure and outside criticism.

The leadership of the central and state police forces is drawn from the elite IPS, whose authorized size was 4,982 in early 2020, with a vacancy rate of nearly one fifth. In recent decades, the political clout of the IPS officers has risen sharply as compared to other civil services. This change is driven by two factors. Greater political interference in police forces has increased the likelihood of IPS officers becoming subservient to politicians.[61] At the same time, since the police is aware of the illegal and criminal activities of politicians and either actively assist in it or look the other way, many politicians in power at the state and district levels get indebted to the police at an early stage. The perception of the Indian state prioritizing internal security and law and order has further empowered the IPS officers since they are at the head of the CAPFs and the police forces; across these forces, IPS officers command close to three million personnel. Two out of five NSAs, and the most powerful ones, have been IPS officers.[62] Chapters by Akshay Mangla and by Beatrice Jauregui point to the damagingly weak downward accountability of leadership in the police. The same concern extends to the CAPFs.

Are IPS officers adequately rooted in the culture of the units they are commanding within the police and CAPFs? In his chapter on the CAPFs, Yashovardhan Azad rightly notes the strengths IPS officers bring to their positions by being part of a national cadre. But this then places on them the onus of rooting themselves in the culture of their units. The record of these officers is uneven at best. By contrast, because of regimentation, quality of leadership as well as downward and upward accountability is stronger within the army. The same, however, cannot be said about the CAPFs, which are led mostly by IPS officers who are parachuted into the CAPF units.

In the army, careers rarely survive serious operational failures. Officers feel accountable to the men they lead because of a strong *esprit de corps*. For example, abandoning a unit's casualties, as well as the weapons (without destroying them) in the battlefield, is considered sacrilegious in the army. As demonstrated in the 2010 ambush of CRPF units, which cost the lives of 76 troops and another ambush in 2021 in which 22 troops were lost, CAPFs are yet to meet similar standards of accountability or a shared spirit of comradeship. In both instances, units cracked under hostile fire, leaving the dead and injured soldiers behind and abandoning weapons. There appear to have been few adverse career consequences for the leadership of these forces, highlighting the disjuncture between the leadership monopoly of the IPS and weak accountability.

However, these shortcomings notwithstanding, the induction of the army into internal security operations is not the answer. In their chapter, Amit Ahuja and Srinath Raghavan argue that for the sake of the health of civil-military relations and military's preparedness for its primary role—protection from external threats—the Indian military's internal security posture needs to be reduced, not expanded. This has already begun to occur in the North East.[63] Instead, the state must redouble its effort to bolster the training and capacity of the CAPFs and state police forces. Despite being raised for specialized tasks, CAPFs are often inducted into roles that fall outside their mandate, a tendency that should be checked. As Nirvikar Jassal and Hanif Qureshi show in their chapter, the Rapid Action Force that was created to quell riots is often engaged in providing VIP security or police *bandobast* (arrangements). The repurposing of the Assam Rifle from an effective counterinsurgency force to an all-purpose CAPF is illustrative of the same point.

Representativeness of the Security Forces

Given their widespread deployment to confront a variety of identity conflicts across a diverse country, the representativeness of the security forces matters. The CAPFs and the police forces have gradually improved caste and gender diversity, although at very low levels for the latter. However, the religious representativeness of security forces remains a serious concern. Moreover, inclusion has not always meant integration. How personnel are integrated and find a sense of belonging within an organization is important.

Of the 2.1 million-odd police personnel in states/UTs at the beginning of 2020, 10.3 percent (215,000) were women. There are large interstate variations. Contrary to expectations, the share of women in Bihar's police force (25.3 percent) is three and a half times that in Kerala (7.2 percent), while their share in Tamil Nadu's police force is more than three times compared to neighboring Andhra Pradesh (18.5 versus 5.85 percent). The central government has sought to increase the representation of women in the CAPFs by reserving 33 percent posts at constable level for women in CRPF and CISF and 14–15 percent posts at constable level in border guarding forces (i.e., BSF, SSB, and ITBP). These efforts have a long way to go—women were barely 3.7 percent of CAPFs by end 2021.[64,65]

Sahana Ghosh's chapter examines a case of efforts to integrate women in the BSF and illuminates the challenges given wider societal attitudes. In the civil police, women are now about 10 percent, a marginal increase from the 7 percent in 2017. Interestingly, the state that leads in female police representation is Bihar, where one out of four police personnel is a woman.[66] These low levels reflect the overall low levels of female labor force participation in India, as well as the lack of basic infrastructure amenities for women in the police, such as toilets.

The CAPFs have broad based regional and caste representation. Sixty percent of vacancies are allotted among states/UTs on the basis of population ratio, while 20 percent in the Border Guarding Forces (BGFs—BSF, ITBP, SSB, and Assam Rifles) are allotted to border districts that lie within the responsibility of the force. Another 20 percent of vacancies in the BGFs are allotted to areas affected by militancy, that is, Jammu and Kashmir, North East states, and LWE-affected areas (the districts affected by militancy are notified by the government periodically). This ratio increases to 40 percent in non-BGFs (CRPF and CISF).

Data from 1991 show SC representation between 14.4–19 percent and ST between 5.7–8.5 percent in the different CAPFs. At that time, combined SC/ST representation in the IPS was 22.2 percent. By 2020, overall representation of SCs and STs in CAPFs was 17 percent and 11 percent respectively. However, in other more "elite" security agencies, the representation falls. The percentage of representation in SPG, NSG, and RAW of SCs/STs was 10.0, 7.8, and 7.7 (in 1996).

The one yawning lacuna in representation is Muslims, reflecting the wider marginalization of the community and their low presence in all public-sector jobs, which is even more pronounced in the security forces. The Muslim component of the military falls between 2 to 3 percent, making them the most underrepresented religious group in the Indian military. The Sachar Committee found that the Muslim share among police constables was 6 percent. During the 1990s, Muslims accounted for between 1.8 percent (in ITBP) to 5.5 percent (in CRPF) in the CAPFs.[67] In 2014, minorities representation was just under 10 percent, while that of Muslims was 4.8 percent.[68] While the ratio is slightly higher for the Rapid Action Force, which was specifically created for controlling riots and communal violence, it is still under 7 percent. However, in agencies like NSG, SPG, and RAW, there are almost no Muslims or Sikhs.

The long-standing deliberate exclusion of minorities is consequential. Take the example of the intelligence establishment, a substantial part of which is either directly or indirectly Pakistan-facing. The lack of religious diversity within these organizations, especially the absence of Muslims, makes these outfits more vulnerable to communalization than would have been the case had these been more diverse.

Although historically such an outcome was largely avoided—a credit to their professionalism—this appears to have changed since 2014. One manifestation of this change has been that investigations into terror groups targeting Indian Muslims by Hindu extremist outfits have been either buried or closed.[69] By turning a blind eye to the activities of these groups, these agencies are jeopardizing the very goals they are charged with, namely strengthening India's internal security.

Welfare of Security Forces

Welfare of security forces, especially the CAPF and police personnel, remains an ongoing concern. Beatrice Jauregui argues in her chapter that festering of grievances among the ranks undermines the capacity of security forces. The decades of the 1970s and 1980s witnessed multiple instances of breakdown of discipline among the security forces. Many were triggered by strike action within police forces, and often these incidents boiled over into mutinies in the ranks; eight mutinies occurred among state police forces and CAPFs between 1978 and 1982. The government turned to the army to crush five of these mutinies, whereas the other three were subdued by CAPFs. Since then, discontent has not triggered a similar wave of mutinies across the security forces.[70]

According to official data until mid-2020, 35,398 police personnel (including CAPFs) have lost their lives in action in the country since independence, about 500 a year. In 2019–2020, central police forces (the CAPFs and RPF) accounted for 42 percent of the 264 deaths. Between 2010 and 2017, 1,968 CAPFs died during their service period/on-duty. However, those killed on active duty was considerably less—400, about a fifth of those who died. Another 301 committed suicide and 798 died of heart attacks.[71] Between 2012 and 2021, on average 120 CAPF personnel per year committed suicide. For 2020 and 2021, this average had ticked up and stood at 150, placing the suicide rate for the CAPFs at 16 per 100,000. The comparable rate for the entire country was 11.3 per 100,000 in 2020.[72]

The high number of deaths is in large part due to poor working conditions. A Parliamentary Committee was "anguished to find that 16% of BSF, 82% of ITBP, 78% of SSB and 43% Assam Rifles BOPs/COB are yet to be provided clean and safe drinking water," that there was an "acute shortage of dwelling units for CAPFs" (which was less than 40 percent), and inadequate medical personnel (more than 40 percent vacancies), despite the "critical" need "for providing medical care to various battalions."[73] The one notable change that has occurred is greater benefits to the next of kin of those killed in the course of duty.[74]

Private Security

Even as (or perhaps, because) the state police forces have remained understaffed and under-resourced, a fast-expanding private security sector has ballooned in India.

Private security services are the 11th largest sector by employment, employing 8.9 million people in 2017 and a projected 12 million by 2022.[75] As Arjun Jayadev and Paaritosh Nath document in their chapter, India is an outlier in the high ratio of private security providers to public security providers—almost 5:1. While the majority of private security providers work in the informal sector—the quintessential *durwan, chowkidar,* etc.—the formal sector's share is around 40 percent and has been growing at 20 percent annually.[76] While there are a few large players (e.g., G4S employs around 1.25 lakh), there are many small vendors (often run by ex-servicemen) who provide guards to the big companies. While the majority are employed in manned guarding, cash delivery guarding services has emerged as an important segment of this market.

The growing presence of private security providers led to calls for regulating the sector, and the Private Security Agencies (Regulation) Act was passed in 2005. A Private Security Agencies Central Model Rules was formulated in 2006 and updated in 2020 (by then 12,299 PSAs were registered). A National Skill Qualification Framework for training personnel working in this industry was formulated in 2018, prescribing detailed norms for entry-level training for private security guards. New regulations on private security agencies required owners to go through a six-day training on subjects like internal security and disaster management and to verify antecedents of their employees.[77]

The rapidly expanding private security market highlights some uncomfortable realities. At one level, these numbers underscore the inability of the Indian state to provide a sense of security to its citizens. Citizens have low trust in the state's ability to fulfill its primary responsibility. At another level, private security is increasingly being viewed as a status marker in a society in which the haves are constantly trying to wall themselves from the have-nots, weakening the public consensus of security as a public good.

The Costs of Internal Security: Financial Resources

Security and order are classic public goods, but like all public goods, their supply requires financial resources. Public expenditures on internal security raise important questions. First, there is the issue of the *level* of expenditures. All financial resources have opportunity costs, and increasing security-related expenditures may well crowd out expenditures on other basic public goods like education, health, or infrastructure that could increase public welfare and social cohesion, and thereby reduce the need for security expenditures. However, lower expenditures could also result in greater disorder and violence, and thereby weaken social cohesion.

A second question is the distribution of expenditures *within* the security apparatus, that is, between salaries, pensions, capital equipment, and training. For instance, the training period to be a police officer in the United States ranges from 10 to 36 weeks, whereas in countries like Finland and Norway, officers must attend their nations' three-year police universities, and leave with degrees that are equivalent to a bachelor's. In India, the vast bulk of police are constables with poor prior education, and even then, the total police budget spent in training in 2019–2020 was just 1.13 percent.[78] Since most policemen don't get leave, they rarely get in-service, as well as other specialized training, to update their skills. There is an additional hurdle—a paucity of training institutions. On average, each of the 11 police training institutes in Uttar Pradesh has to train over 37,700 personnel annually.

Nirvikar Singh's chapter examines these issues and finds that after years of neglecting the police force, some of the larger Indian states have begun to spend relatively more on their police, with the growth rate of spending matching that on both social services and on economic services. Using RBI data, he shows that in 2019–2020, combined state budgets on police touched Rs. 1.475 trillion, covering expenditures on salaries, weapons, housing, and transport. Nonetheless, even after an increase in recruitment in state police forces, crucial vacancies at the officer level are still almost a third.

Due to inadequate spending on the part of states, the Center had to spend more on its own six police forces, whose budget growth consistently outpaced that of any of the big-ticket spending items of the government. Between 2010–2011 and 2019–2020, total expenditure on the police by states increased from 47,040 crores in 2010–2011 to 147,544 crores in 2019–2020.[79] One of the fastest-growing elements of central government spending was on CAPFs, increasing from Rs. 25,075 crores in 2010–2011 to Rs. 60,980 crores in 2019–2020.[80]

The deterioration in internal security by the late 1960s led the GOI to initiate various schemes for financial assistance to states for modernizing their police forces. As with central schemes, they incentivize states to put in resources that the Center more than matches (either 75:25 or 60:40). Under these schemes, the central government sanctioned and provided funds for India Reserve Battalions (IRBs), armed units of state police forces. This began in 1971 with the initial raising costs borne by the central government. By 2020, 191 IRBs had been sanctioned, while 144 had been raised by the states. Additional schemes provided central assistance for the acquisition of advanced weaponry and intelligence equipment.

The criteria determined for interstate distribution of funds by the central government include population, sanctioned strength of police force, number of police stations, and crime intensity. However, a substantial fraction of these resources has gone unused. Similarly, other specialized funds, such as the Nirbhaya Fund, set up in 2013 to provide states with funds to improve women's safety, have seen barely half of the funds utilized, a reflection of the states' priorities.

Emerging Issues: New Technologies, New Threats, and the Emergence of Hybrid Warfare

According to an IBM report, India was the second most attacked country by cyber criminals in Asia Pacific in 2020 after Japan. The previous year (2019), "the largest (data breach) was in India, where the government ID database, Aadhaar, reportedly suffered multiple breaches that potentially compromised the records of all 1.1 billion registered citizens."[81] The country's nodal cyber-security agency Indian Computer Emergency Response Team (CERT-In), which is mandated to track and monitor cyber security incidents in India, reported 1,402,809 security incidents in 2021.[82] A report from Recorded Future (the world's largest provider of intelligence for enterprise security) revealed a cyber campaign conducted by a China-linked group, targeting ten Indian organizations in the power generation and transmission sector and two organizations in the maritime sector with potential pre-positioning of network access to support Chinese strategic objectives.[83] There is every reason to believe that targeting the computer network operations of strategically important organizations in India will only grow.

At the same time, the rise of social media and the speed and scale in which fake news can spread and simultaneously trigger and amplify conflict is a new challenge to internal security. With the technology to produce deep fake images and videos easily available, divisive news items and fake videos targeting communities as well as security force personnel can threaten social order. Political parties and extremist groups have used these technologies to push divisive messages. Moreover, if India's insurgencies in border states have manifestly demonstrated the links between internal and external security, the manner in which hostile powers can leverage social media to exploit internal polarization and fan conflict shows how the lines between internal and external security are blurring.

To add to it, India itself "has emerged as a hot spot for online fraud in which perpetrators are rarely punished. Cases have become so common in recent years that the Indian authorities have dedicated special units to dealing with the problem."[84] The number of cases registered for cyber-crimes almost doubled in just two years from 2018 to 2020 (from 27,248 to 50,035).

Cyber-security is an example of how new technologies reshape internal security challenges and priorities, while also providing the state with new tools. Officially, India has formulated a Cyber Crisis Management Plan and set up specialized groups including CERT In, the National Critical Information Infrastructure, and the National Cyber Coordinator Centre. The MHA is adding more: a CyCord (Cyber Cooperation Centre) under the IB focusing on tracking hacking and online investigations, the National Cybercrime Threat Analytics Unit, the Platform for Joint Cybercrime Investigation Team, the National Cybercrime Forensic Laboratory, and the Cybercrime Ecosystem Management Unit. While impressive on paper, there is very little substantive information about these organizations and their effectiveness.

While leveraging technology has become an important part of the Indian state's attempts to improve internal security,[85] this has been most evident in digital technologies. In 2009, in the aftermath of the Mumbai attacks, the GOI approved the Crime and Criminal Tracking Network and Systems (CCTNS) project—a Rs. 2,000 crores initiative to provide a common nationwide digital networking tracking system on "Investigation of crime and detection of criminals." The scope later expanded to include the key pillars of the country's criminal justice supply chain—police, forensics, prosecution, courts, and prisons—into a common plat-form, the "Inter-operable Criminal Justice System" (ICJS). The system is supposed to improve crime-fighting capabilities by facilitating the collection, storage, re-trieval, analysis, transfer, and sharing of data by the police across the country. It should also serve to help citizens better access services from the police such as registering petitions, requests for certificates, verifications, and permissions and grievance registration.[86]

By late 2020, the overall progress of the CCTNS project was deemed at 81.6 per-cent, with Bihar, West Bengal, and the North East states lagging, and 308 million digitized criminal records available in the CCTNS.[87] But as with e-governance in general, the reach substantially exceeds the grasp. A CAG report on the Delhi police—the best manned and equipped in the country—found that while CCTNS was operational in all locations, the quality of data entered into the system was often "still populated by junk data or left blank." Vulnerabilities in the security architec-ture of CCTNS—largely due to an obsolete technology stack on which CCTNS is based—were unaddressed. An enterprise-wide data integration and intelligence gathering project, Safe and Secure Delhi, had to be "shelved after repeated attempts to finalize vendors failed."[88]

The explosion of digital surveillance can have positive impacts for national and individual security but has serious implications for individual privacy and freedoms. The line between digital governance and Chinese-style, techno-authoritarianism is a thin one, and there is significant risk of digital governance tipping over into digital control.[89] The Supreme Court in the K. S. Puttaswamy case, involving the right to privacy, held that interception (of communications) has to meet the rigor of "necessity, proportionality and due process." It is unclear how this will be monitored as the country rapidly builds its surveillance capability and a nationwide facial recognition database, collecting images from CCTV feeds and newspapers, for example. The use of facial recognition technology as a law-enforcement tool by the police—in 2019 amid protests against a citizenship law, as well as the farmer protests in 2021—occurred despite the absence of a national law to define limits on its use.

According to tech research group Comparitech, with about 10 CCTV cameras per 1,000 people, Delhi has become the 20th most heavily monitored city in the world. The Delhi Police Commissioner claimed that "technology was used extensively to investigate over 750 cases related to the Delhi riots in February 2020 that left 53 people dead and led to the arrest of over 200 people."[90] The police claimed that a majority were identified through FRS (Facial Recognition System) when matched with criminal records and the rest were identified through driving license photographs. As per the official account, video analytics and FRS were used to analyze CCTV footage, deleted data from an electronic device was retrieved, geolocations were ascertained to place the presence of the accused, and drone mapping was used for crime scene reconstruction. DNA fingerprinting, e-Vahan database, facial recognition, fund flow analysis, and forensic teams comprising physical, chemical, biological, and ballistic analysis of videos and photographs through open sources were apparently also used to investigate the cases.[91]

Yet all this technology notwithstanding, it seemed manifest that many perpetrators of the violence, and even more key, the instigators were untouched—reaffirming a half century of hoary tradition of impunity in communal violence. Technology may propose but politics will dispose.

Nonetheless, the reality is that Facial Recognition Technology (FRT) systems are here to stay, and with 79 FRTs across different states and cities with an investment of nearly 1,000 crores, their use is likely to become ubiquitous.[92] The National Automated Facial Recognition System (NAFRS) was launched in 2021 despite the absence of standards in place to regulate the technology or certify the quality of different FRTs. There was no legal architecture that authorized the use of NAFRS, identified the agencies authorized to use it, or provided safeguards and redressal mechanisms for wrongly implicated victims.[93]

At the time of writing, a draft personal data protection bill had been introduced in Parliament, India's answer to the EU's General Data Protection Regulation. While it provided new protections for India's internet users, it also had broad exemptions for public authorities to access personal data. It also permits the central government to exempt any agency from privacy obligations on broad grounds, such as maintaining public order. The potential for massive surveillance with nontransparent oversight risks shifting power to the state—and this includes both central and state governments—at the expense of civil and political liberties, at a time of broader concerns about growing authoritarianism in the country.

The Costs of Internal Security: Liberties and Human Rights

If coercion is the inevitable corollary of state building, coercion as the glue of nation building rarely succeeds for long. For Tolstoy, nonviolence meant "the rejection of coercion as the glue of the commonwealth." But the state's monopoly of violence has been the very definition of the state. Indeed, this was precisely why Gandhi was skeptical of the state since "the state can never be weaned away from violence to which it owes its existence."

Security is a means to an end. The question is what is the end here? The trade-off between order and liberty is especially important in a democracy, and even more so if marginalized communities have to bear the brunt of the costs of the curtailment of liberties. It might well be, as Benjamin Franklin put it, "those who would give up essential liberty to purchase temporary safety deserve neither liberty nor safety."

The birth of independent India occurred in a seething cauldron of carnage, insecurity, and fear. As the Constituent Assembly debated what would emerge as one of the most progressive constitutions of its time, it also inserted Article 22 in Part III, allowing the government to detain anyone without trial for at least three months and giving Parliament permission to decide what should be the maximum time for which a person can be thus detained. Defending this provision, B. R. Ambedkar, the architect of the Indian Constitution, argued, "I do not think that the exigency of the liberty of the individual should be placed above the interests of the State," perhaps reflecting the exigencies of the time.[94] In March 2021, a special NIA court rejected the bail application filed by Stan Swamy, an 83-year-old Jharkhand-based tribal rights activist arrested in the Bhima Koregaon case, observing that "the collective interest of the community would outweigh the right of personal liberty of the applicant."[95]

Article 22 was challenged in the first fundamental rights case heard by the Indian Supreme Court involving A. K. Gopalan, a freedom fighter and communist leader, who was detained under its provisions.[96] The Court ruled on behalf of the State. As Raeesa Vakil points out in her chapter, citing Chandrachud, the Court was "heavily influenced by the desire to avoid striking down a statutory provision that was conceived as an essential part of the national security apparatus and which the government asserted as being crucial in dealing with the challenges of the time."

Vakil places the Indian Supreme Court's historical reluctance in striking down internal security laws unconstitutional within the wider deference shown by the Court to the legislature, stemming from its unwillingness to interfere with laws that were enacted when Parliament was competent to do so by the provisions of the Constitution. The lacuna is especially glaring in the case of anti-terror legislation, where the Court has notably failed in enforcing constitutional principles or even granting effective relief or enforcement, even as it doubled down on the rhetoric of rights.

The combination of growing internal security challenges and the Court's deference led to an accretion of laws meant to improve internal security but with clear negative implications for civil liberties. These included the Unlawful Activities Prevention Act 1967 (UAPA), Prevention of Insults to National Honour Act 1971, National Security Act 1980, Prevention of Damage to Public Property Act 1984, the Information Technology Act 2000, and the Unlawful Activities (Prevention) Amendment Act 2019 (UAPA). Under UAPA alone, 5,111 cases were filed and

6,009 arrested between 2015 and 2019. Interestingly, the largest number of cases in 2019 were registered in Manipur (about one fourth), while the largest number of arrests (also about a fourth of the total) were in Uttar Pradesh. Another act that is being widely misused is the National Security Act. An investigation of the Allahabad high court's judgments on 120 cases (of which 70 were brought against Muslims) related to the NSA between 2018 and 2020 showed that close to 80 percent of cases filed by the Uttar Pradesh government were quashed by the court.

Yet another act prone to severe misuse is the Narcotic Drugs and Psychotropic Substances (NDPS) Act, which came into effect in 1985. The act "is so unique, draconian, impractical, ineffective, exploitative and prone to misuse that to use the familiar description for laws would be an insult to the ass." While "it's gone through several iterations and dilutions over nearly four decades, and yet remains a disaster for the citizen, a blessing for headline-hunting and corrupt policemen, a jackpot for the lawyers and a pain for the judges."[97]

The suppression of civil liberties has been even more apparent in the deluge of sedition cases. Sedition was defined in the Indian Penal Code in 1872 and widely used by the British to imprison those fighting for India's freedom. The British charged Gandhi under the sedition law. During his trial in 1922, he described the law as "the prince among the political sections of the Indian Penal Code designed to suppress the liberty of a citizen." It was abolished in the United Kingdom itself in 2009, but it continues to thrive in India even though the Supreme Court had ruled in 1962 and 1995 that the sedition law could only be used when there was incitement to violence, or if there was intention to create disorder.[98] An investigative report found that 11,000 individuals had been charged in 816 sedition cases since 2010.[99] There was a 28 percent increase in the number of sedition cases filed between 2014 and 2020 compared to the annual average between 2010 and 2014, during the second term of the United Progressive Alliance (UPA). Much of this increase is due to a surge in sedition cases against activists involved in protest movements, such as those against the Citizenship Amendment Act (CAA) in 2019, or against celebrities who spoke out against lynching and intolerance and those who allegedly raised "pro-Pakistan" slogans. The misapplication and misuse of this law is not confined to the federal government or one particular party; it also extends to the state governments controlled by different parties. Its widespread misuse ensures that the conviction rate under the law remains minuscule. At the time of writing, the Supreme Court had suspended the enforcement of the sedition law until it ruled on its constitutionality. Chief Justice Ramana has observed that sedition or Section 124A of the Indian Penal Code was prone to misuse by the government. "The use of sedition is like giving a saw to the carpenter to cut a piece of wood and he uses it to cut the entire forest itself," he said.[100]

If the illiberal use of laws to widen the dragnet for preventive arrests has undermined civil liberties, two other widespread practices have been a pernicious blot on India's human rights record. The first is the deeply disturbing issue of "encounter killings." It is widely presumed to have been used against hundreds of terrorists in Punjab in the 1980s,[101] the Mumbai underworld in the 1990s, Gujarat in the 2000s, and people associated with Students' Islamic Movement of India (SIMI) in 2016. In the North East, this has been manifest in Manipur where allegedly there have been allegations of more than 1,500 extrajudicial killings by the Manipur Police and security forces. Few security personnel were held accountable in all these cases.

According to the NHRC, 2,560 deaths during encounters with police were reported between 1993 and 2008. The NHRC pointedly termed nearly half (1,224) as "fake encounters."[102] In 2012 in a case involving alleged encounter killings, the Supreme Court emphasized that when police personnel liquidate criminals and cover it as an encounter, such killings "amount to State sponsored terrorism."[103] At the same time, it also observed that "one cannot be oblivious of the fact that there are cases where the police, who are performing their duty, are attacked and killed. There is a rise in such incidents and judicial notice must be taken of this fact. In such circumstances, while the police have to do their legal duty of arresting the criminals, they have also to protect themselves."

The issue once again came to the fore in 2019 when the police in Hyderabad, Telangana, gunned down four suspects after arresting them for the gang rape and murder of a young woman. The officers involved were feted and garlanded. In 2020, in another case, the Uttar Pradesh police shot a criminal, Vikas Dube, when he was being shifted from the adjoining state after surrendering publicly, following the killing of eight policemen during an earlier attempt to arrest him. Five of his aides were also shot in similar actions, considered part of Uttar Pradesh Chief Minister Yogi Adityanath's policy to shoot down (thok-do) criminals.[104] The system's infirmities have justified "creating order by trampling on law," which is publicly popular and hence politically successful.[105]

A second troubling issue is the use of torture by sundry security forces. Torture can persist as a generalized practice even in democratic societies. Weak procedural protections, few consequences for perpetrators, and the militarization of policing, which introduces a mentality that treats criminal suspects as though they were enemies in wartime, make this possible.[106] In 2020, the Supreme Court passed directions for installation of CCTV cameras and recording equipment in the premises of all central investigating agencies that carry out interrogations and have the power of arrest. Its effects are unclear as of yet.

Deaths in police custody in the country have averaged between 100–150 annually over the past decade. Custodial deaths are often the result of torture going too far. While India signed the United Nations Convention against Torture in 1997, it has not ratified it despite voicing repeated commitments. Guidelines laid down by the NHRC require each death in police or judicial custody to be reported within twenty-four hours of its occurrence to the NHRC as well as a post mortem report, magisterial inquiry report, viscera report, etc. for ascertaining whether the death in custody resulted from foul play or negligence by public servants. The NHRC's findings suggest that it often does not buy into the official stories of encounter killings and custodial deaths, but at most insists on financial compensation, with the state offering "blood money," as it were.

There is little systematic evidence of action taken against the security officials responsible for such cases. Between 2009 and 2019, 867 cases were registered against policemen in connection with custodial deaths. Of 394 policemen charged, just 29 were convicted (Figure 1.15). According to the "Status of Policing in India Report 2019," one out of five surveyed police personnel felt that killing a dangerous criminal was better than a legal trial, 75 percent felt that there is nothing wrong in being violent toward criminals, and 83 percent approved of beating criminals.

The Roman orator Cicero is credited with the phrase *Silent enim leges inter arma*: when swords are drawn the laws fall silent. In internal security, this is particularly true of COIN operations. It has been argued that in the absence of a strong commitment to the rule of law in COIN operations, the long-term costs are likely to be much higher, whether in terms of military resources, civilian life, or international legitimacy.[107] However, as shown in Anubha Bhosle's poignant examination of the persistence of AFSPA—often for decades in some parts of the country—such thinking does not appear to have convinced the stewards of India's internal security. Yashovardhan Azad points out that the problem of impunity is not confined to the army. The CAPFs, who are not similarly protected by the AFSPA, nevertheless remain unaccountable for their actions against civilians in counterinsurgency theaters. The normalization of state violence in the name of internal security has

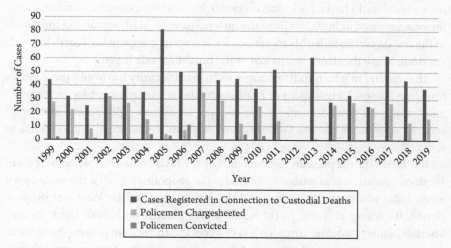

Figure 1.15 Cases in connection with custodial deaths, 1999–2019
Source: NCRB

far-reaching and dangerous implications for civil liberties and more broadly for Indian democracy.[108] In the name of internal stability and security, the state can command immense power and curtail citizen freedoms without facing many institutional obstacles.[109]

Internal Security and External Relations

External relations clearly matter for internal security. But the converse is also true. India's internal security affects its external relations. This is especially true of India's relations with its neighbors. The better India's relations with countries with which it shares borders, the more manageable its internal security. While this is most evident in India's relations with Pakistan—the Punjab and Kashmir insurgencies, the Mumbai blasts of 1992, the 2008 terrorist attacks, or Pulwama—it is also the case with other neighbors. India's ability to temper violence in the North East has, in part, been facilitated by its neighbors in the region—Bangladesh, Bhutan, and Myanmar—becoming less willing to provide sanctuary to the leadership of many insurgent groups operating in the region.

Insurgent groups, and especially their leadership, find safe havens in the neighboring countries, who harbored them either passively or actively, and use them as bargaining chips with India. Between 2009 and 2014, Bangladesh arrested and handed over at least 17 top leaders of various groups, leading others to surrender to India.[110] In 2017, the director general of the BSF stated camps and hideouts of Indian insurgent groups in Bangladeshi soil were "almost zero."[111]

Similarly, in 2020, Myanmar handed over nearly two dozen insurgents to India and its actions, as with Bangladesh, served as a deterrent. The United Arab Emirates, once considered a haven for Indian criminals, has also been deporting criminals and terrorists wanted in India.[112] Given the internal turmoil in Myanmar and the nature of the terrain on the India-Myanmar border, insurgent groups in the North East will continue to use the dense forests across the border for safe haven.

The manner in which India manages its internal security has implications for its foreign relations. Its treatment of Muslims creates an environment for recruitment and training by powers hostile to the country. Its human rights record in internal security operations has led Germany and Belgium to ban small arms exports to India.[113]

But international pressure on human rights, which comes almost entirely from Western countries, is inextricably enmeshed in geopolitics. Unlike the early 1990s when India was relatively weaker and the preeminence of the West was unquestioned, it's a very different world today. India's records on human rights or civil liberties, while troubling, are much less of a concern to Western powers than how to deal with an assertive and belligerent China. Consequently, pressure from Western countries is likely to be muted.

The Perennial Issue: *Quis custodiet ipsos custodies?*

In all societies, there is a perennial tension between better managing internal security challenges while restraining their coercive institutions. The fundamentals of internal security begin with street-level safety, which entails the civil police. As Akshay Mangla's chapter reveals, a robust police system is to a country's internal security what public health is to national health. It is not only the first line for defense but also is the part of the internal security apparatus in a democracy that matters most for the daily lives of most citizens. The rich can buy private security from gated communities to private transport, the *durwans*, and private security guards. The implications of Thucydides perceptive observation that "the strong do what they can and the weak suffer what they must" is that a well-functioning police system is important to protect the marginalized and the poor. But that has certainly not been the case in India.

In order to improve the functioning of the police, the Union Government set up various commissions and committees including the National Police Commission (1977), the Ribeiro Committee (1998), the Padmanabhaiah Committee (2000), and the Malimath Committee on Criminal Justice (2002). Subsequently, the government constituted a review committee headed by R. S. Mooshahary to review the recommendations of the previous Commissions and Committees on Police Reforms in 2004.[114] The Committee short-listed 49 recommendations and formulated a Model Police Act in 2006. Since law and order is constitutionally a state subject, these were sent to state governments for them to take appropriate action.

The same year (in 2006), in response to a PIL filed by a retired DIG of police (Prakash Singh) a decade earlier, the Supreme Court gave specific directions to the central and state governments to carry out structural changes in the police with a view of insulating it from extraneous pressures and making it accountable to the people. However, a decade after the Supreme Court's directive, a review found meager progress by most states. Not even one state was fully compliant with the directives, and the majority of states were noncompliant with most of the directives, especially the most critical ones.

The failure to comply with the directives reveals the extent to which governments of all political stripes have little interest in putting into place systems of checks and balances to make policing more professional and accountable.[115] This is hardly surprising given the well-documented nexus between politicians, criminals, and the police.[116] Forty-three percent of the winners in the 2019 general election had criminal cases—an increase of 44 percent in the number of MPs with declared criminal cases since 2009. The chances of winning for a candidate with declared criminal cases was 15.5 percent, compared to just 4.7 percent for a candidate without any cases. In 2021, of the 78 ministers in the Union Cabinet, 42 percent had criminal cases against them and 31 percent of ministers had serious criminal cases including cases related to murder, attempt to murder, robbery, etc. All three Ministers of State for Home—the very ministry charged with curbing these activities—had serious criminal charges against them.[117] Crime pays and comes with political protections that elected office in India brings. The sight of elected officials with heinous cases against them being provided with protection by a police force meant to put them behind bars is a telling testimony that echoes the madly rational king in Shakespeare's *King Lear*, who cries out, "Change places, and, handy-dandy, which is the justice, which is the thief?"

The state as Leviathan gives it power to use legitimate force to protect its citizens—but who protects citizens from the state if this power serves partisan political and personal interests rather than national interests?

At one level, there are state actions that create internal security challenges. The actions of the central government in Punjab that left the country reaping the whirlwind, the 1984 Delhi riots, the manipulations of elections in Kashmir, the periodic lighting of communal fires, the Gujarat riots, and most recently the violence that followed the imposition of a Citizenship Amendment Act are but some examples of when the firefighter becomes the arsonist.[118]

Another disturbing facet is when the state decides to hound its own citizens, on either fabricated or flimsy grounds, to make a political point. This could be students or a minor actor, not because they pose any internal security threats but to set an example to others contemplating dissent, akin to the Chinese proverb "Kill the chicken to scare the monkey."[119] It's almost impossible to know since the "deep state" is opaque. As Yashovardhan Azad reminds us, Section 24 of the RTI Act exempts the main organs of internal security of the central government—all six CAPFs, NIA, NSG, IB, SPG, DRI, and Directorate of Enforcement—from disclosing information.[120] So if they act on political instructions, how would anyone know? Then who will guard the guardians?

In principle, a democratic society puts checks on the executive branch. These can come from the legislature, the courts, independent agencies, civil society (activists and the media), and international pressure.

In a parliamentary system, legislative pressures come primarily from opposition parties and from rival camps in the ruling party. A weak opposition is unlikely to hold the government to account in any substantive way. The Home Ministry's parliamentary standing committee generally stays away from any controversial topics. Importantly, most opposition parties have little interest in fundamental reforms that would limit their future discretion or hold security forces accountable.

Another plausible check is the professionalism and institutional pride of public officials. But despite the substantial constitutional protections enjoyed by the civil services, somewhere the foundations of power in state bureaucracy have shifted from being rooted in the prestige and professional ethos of the administrative or police services to political patronage and personal gains. To be sure, for many public officials discretion is the better part of valor. But whatever the cause, the erosion of professionalism within the security-related institutions has undermined their capacity to protect the integrity of their own organizations and the rights of citizens from arbitrary state power.

The courts too have lost their former zeal to hold the executive to account. Their quiet acquiescence to the executive is evident in its pusillanimous defense of the writ of habeas corpus, guaranteed under Article 32 of the Indian Constitution. The writ of habeas corpus has been a critical tool of judicial power, its main enemy often the elected branches that fear that power, particularly during a security crisis.[121] Habeas corpus has not been suspended—rather, it has been whittled away by expanding detention powers.

Statutes to restrict habeas corpus are less surprising than the judiciary's deference to Parliament's authority. The suspension statutes do not prevent supervision of detentions by judges—and it is here that their inactions have perhaps been most troubling. The Court's abdication of a key function led an observer to excoriate the Court's "slipping into judicial barbarism. . . . This usually means weak protection for civil liberties and dissenters and an unusual degree of deference to State power, especially in constitutional matters . . . a politics that sees protest, dissent, and freedom of expression all through the prism of potential enemies of the State."[122]

In the early 1990s, as India was battling bloody insurgencies in Kashmir and Punjab, its human rights record came under mounting international criticism. To forestall it, the National Human Rights Commission was set up under the provisions of the Protection of Human Rights Act, 1993.

In 2018, on the occasion of its 25th anniversary, NHRC highlighted its achievements—from disposal of more than 1.7 million cases, orders for payment of more than Rs. 1 billion to victims of human rights violations, efforts to spread awareness of human rights across the country, interventions in the 2007 Nandigram violence in West Bengal, and strictures again state-created militia (Salwa Judum).[123]

The reality is more somber. Both the Supreme Court and its own chairperson (a former chief justice of India) have called the NHRC a "toothless tiger." Its design is flawed—it lacks powers to investigate human rights violations involving the armed forces and it can't do much if state governments do not cooperate with it. Despite a substantial increase in complaints, it is perennially short-staffed and inadequately funded (about 300 staff and Rs. 44 crore budget in 2018), perhaps deliberately.[124] The NHRC's autonomy is severely compromised by a serious conflict of interest. The administrative ministry for the NHRC—the MHA—is the overseer of the country's internal security apparatus and the source of some of the very human rights violations that the NHRC investigates. The government can make the NHRC ineffectual by simply not filling key positions, as it has been doing in recent years.

The lawyer and activist K. G. Kannabiran had opposed the NHRC, arguing that bypassing the courts was not the solution. Instead, the criminal courts needed to be strengthened and violations of human rights needed to be prosecuted through the courts and through private complaints, following up cases to ensure that policemen who violate the law were punished under criminal law and made to pay compensation from their own pockets. Any other form of dealing with human rights would be a palliative, and that seems to be the Indian reality.[125]

The Centrality of Violence?

In his book *The Law of Force: The Violent Heart of Indian Politics*, the anthropologist Thomas Blom Hansen argues that "violence has moved to the centre stage of Indian public life. [This] development signals a deep problem, a deformation and a pathology that may present a danger to the future of democracy."

There is no question that democracy will struggle in any polity where violence is at the center of public life. But the claim that violence has become central to Indian public life seems to contradict some of the empirical findings of this book. Violence in public life can take many forms: from riots to electoral violence, from caste to religious and ethnic violence, from insurgencies to terrorism, from political assassinations to hijackings. As we have seen earlier, in many of these indicators, violence is less—in some cases substantially less—than the peak quarter century from the late 1970s to early 2000s. This decline parallels a substantial decline in private violence (as measured by homicide rates).

It is certainly the case that public violence, such as riots and insurgencies, has persisted (albeit less virulently) even as new forms of public violence such as vigilantism and lynch mobs seem to be sprouting like an ugly cancer across the country. Yet, notwithstanding this trend, aggregate levels of violence in India—public and private—have declined in the first two decades of this century compared to the previous two decades.

Nonetheless, the absence of evidence does not necessarily imply evidence of absence. This is evident in contemporary India in at least four distinct ways. The philosopher Amia Srinivasan has argued that, "The privation of safety doesn't just mean the exposure to forms of physical harm or even psychological harm; it also means the erosion of our sense of selves as agents in the world."[126] More than "exposure to bodily threat and assaults on dignity" is the "creation of an insidious uncertainty, one that closes down the sense of individual possibility and control. Without some guarantee of safety, we cannot plan, and we cannot dream." Violence and humiliation have for long curtailed the life opportunities of Dalits and women. Even as some of these substantial constraints have moderated, India's religious minorities, especially Muslims, are also endangered by a growing threat of violence, humiliation, and diminishing safety. Take the use of lynching as an instrument of terror. The actual numbers of deaths in lynching are relatively small compared to many other acts of violence. But its effects are much larger, akin to terrorism. The violence of lynching is targeted not just at the individual but to send a message to certain communities about their subordinate position. Speaking about the lynching of African Americans in the United States, the historian Amy Louise Wood argued that although, "Compared to other forms of terror and intimidation that African Americans were subject to under Jim Crow, lynching was an infrequent and extraordinary occurrence," yet, "despite, or even because of, its relative rarity, lynching had a singular psychological force, generating a level of fear and horror that overwhelmed all other forms of violence."[127]

Second, in certain regions, epitomized by Kashmir, the curbing of violence is the result of an iron fist emanating from a massive security presence. The Indian state's actions hardly seem to vindicate a government seeking to reach out to its citizens.

But it is two other features that are more worrying. The first is the changing nature of the Indian state. Of particular concern is the erosion of the necessary institutional checks and balances which, from Parliament to courts to the media, can scrutinize and curb the excesses of the multiple security agencies that comprise the "deep" state. Some of these attributes have been a feature of state and national level politics for decades. But, they have reappeared in such a pronounced manner for the first time since the political emergency that lasted from 1975 to 1977. At the time of writing, the misuse of the coercive apparatus of the state for stifling dissent, muzzling civil liberties and pursuing political vendettas has become routine. Still, state abuse can be stopped and corrected. Weaponization of social prejudice, however, is more difficult to reverse, and therefore, poses a more long-lasting threat.

The second feature, rooted in Indian society, as Hansen points out, is "why so many ordinary people in India today seem to either tacitly endorse, or actively participate in public violence?", be it encounter killings by the police, or violence by *gauraksha* vigilantes and lynch mobs. It is the tacit, if not explicit, support or threat of violence among large sections of the public that weakens a powerful check on the state. With street and online mobs being allowed to act with impunity, and incendiary commentary going unchallenged in the public sphere, gradually society is being weaponized against itself. These actions are undermining the authority of the state.[128] Experience from across the world, including India's own neighborhood, suggests that this process could easily spin out of control and significantly undermine state capacity to control violence. The decline of violence, then, is no assurance of social harmony. If both the state and society find ways to rationalize exclusionary politics, violence will become de facto legitimized. The resultant weakening of the critical guard rails does not necessarily portend much greater levels of violence, but it certainly increases its likelihood.

In the book that follows, Part I of the volume discusses in four chapters the legal, institutional, and financial frameworks that are foundational to the Indian state's response to the internal security-related challenges. Laws on internal security empower the state in extraordinary ways to assert its authority at the expense of constitutional freedoms of citizens. Anchoring her chapter in the Constituent Assembly debates, Raeesa Vakil traces the gradual empowerment of the state in general and the central government more specifically in the name of internal security. She delves into the oversight role the judiciary has performed with respect to the security forces and its willingness to address state excesses, including extrajudicial killings. Anubha Bhonsle explores the origins and survival of extraordinary legal protections given to security forces in the form of the Armed Forces Special Powers Act (AFSPA), a law that at its birth was already being compared to martial law by lawmakers. Shakti Sinha's chapter examines the powerful Ministry of Home Affairs, which carries the day-to-day burden of securing India internally, but whose coercive powers are also undermining the very democracy it seeks to protect. Nirvikar Singh examines the public finances of internal security and how public spending has varied over time and across states and issue areas.

Part II delves into the internal security doctrine and strategy across two chapters. Paul Staniland situates India's approach to internal security in a comparative perspective while highlighting the substantial variation we observe in the state's approach over time and across regions. Sushant Singh discusses and critically evaluates aspects of the internal security doctrine as practice rather than doctrine as policy.

The six chapters in Part III engage the range of the state's coercive capacity available through their internal security providers. Amit Ahuja and Srinath Raghavan examine the continuity and change in the military's long-standing role in providing internal security. Yashovardhan Azad discusses the expansion and varied roles of the Central Armed Police Forces (CAPFs) and the challenges these forces confront. Akshay Mangla vividly illustrates the types of law and order tasks performed by police forces and how poor training, equipment, and the heavy hand of politics undermine their effectiveness. Nirvikar Jassal and Hanif Qureshi provide a first-ever systematic study of the Rapid Action Force, a specialized outfit created to quell communal violence. Arjun Jayadev and Paritosh Nath generate a comprehensive empirical picture of the rapidly expanding private security industry. Finally, Saikat Datta decodes the role of the Intelligence Bureau in the provision of internal security.

Intra-organizational changes and struggles of the principal internal security providers—the CAPFs and the police forces—and their impact on internal security are the focus of the two chapters in Part IV. Sahana Ghosh provides an account of gender inclusion in the Border Security Force and illustrates the roadblocks in the path of integrating female recruits into a predominantly male organization. Beatrice Jauregui highlights the efforts made by the rank-and-file personnel of the police force to unionize themselves to demand better treatment by their own organization.

Notes

1. Bernard Harborne, William Dorotinsky, and Paul M. Bisca, *Securing Development: Public Finance and the Security Sector* (Washington, DC: The World Bank, 2017).
2. United Nations Office on Drugs and Crimes (UNODC), *Global Study on Homicide 2019* (Vienna: UNODC, 2019).
3. Thomas S. Szayna, Stephan Watts, Angela O'Mahony, Bryan Frederick, and Jennifer Kavanagh, "What Are the Trends in Armed Conflicts, and What Do They Mean for U.S. Defense Policy?,"

(Santa Monica, CA: RAND Corporation, 2017), https://www.rand.org/pubs/research_repo rts/RR1904.html.

4. Mary Beth Sheridan, "The Search for the Disappeared Points to Mexico's Darkest Secrets," *Washington Post*, December 3, 2020, https://www.washingtonpost.com/graphics/2020/ world/mexico-losing-control/mexico-disappeared-drug-war/.

5. Marie Arana, *Silver, Sword and Stone: The Story of Latin America in Three Extraordinary Lives* (London: Weidenfeld & Nicolson, 2019).

6. United Nations Development Programme (UNDP), *Assessing the Impact of Conflict on Development in North-east Nigeria* (Abuja, Nigeria: UNDP, 2021), https://www.ng.undp.org/ content/nigeria/en/home/library/human_development/assessing-the-impact-of-conflict-on-development-in-north-east-ni.html.

7. For an excellent articulation of this line of thinking, see Rachel Kleinfeld, *A Savage Order* (New York, NY: Knopf Doubleday Publishing Group, 2018).

8. Atul Kohli, *Democracy and Discontent: India's Growing Crisis of Governability* (Cambridge: Cambridge University Press, 1990).

9. Examples include Sumit Ganguly, Nicolas Blarel, and Manjeet S. Pardesi, *The Oxford Handbook of India's National Security* (Oxford: Oxford University Press, 2018), which encompasses a very broad understanding of security; for a focus on one specific internal security concern such as ethnic violence see: Ashutosh Varshney, *Ethnic Conflict and Civic Life: Hindus and Muslims in India* (New Haven, CT: Yale University Press, 2002); Steven Wilkinson, *Votes and Violence: Electoral Competition and Ethnic Riots in India* (Cambridge: Cambridge University Press, 2004); Sudha Pai and Sajjan Kumar, *Everyday Communalism: Riots in Contemporary Uttar Pradesh* (Oxford: Oxford University Press, 2018); or counterinsurgency, for example, Paul Staniland, *Ordering Violence: Explaining Armed Group-State Relations from Conflict to Cooperation* (Ithaca, NY: Cornell University Press, 2021); Mona Bhan, *Counterinsurgency, Democracy, and the Politics of Identity in India: From Warfare to Welfare?* (London: Routledge, 2013); Sumit Ganguly and David P. Fidler, *India and Counterinsurgency: Lessons Learned* (London: Routledge, 2009); or Left Wing Extremist violence, for example see Shivaji Mukherjee, *Colonial Institutions and Civil War: Indirect Rule and Maoist Insurgency in India* (New York, NY: Cambridge University Press, 2021).

10. Youssef Cohen, Brian R. Brown, and A. F. K. Organski, "The Paradoxical Nature of State Making: The Violent Creation of Order," *American Political Science Review* 75, no. 4 (1981): 901–910.

11. Charles Tilly, "Violence, Terror, and Politics as Usual," *Boston Review* 27, no. 3–4 (Summer 2002): 21–24.

12. Seema Chishti, "We must not glorify ancient India. . . but learn from it: Historian Upinder Singh," *Indian Express*, October 29, 2017, https://indianexpress.com/article/lifestyle/ books/historian-upinder-singh-glorify-ancient-india-learn-from-it-4911049/.

13. Upinder Singh, *Political Violence in Ancient India* (Cambridge, MA: Harvard University Press, 2017).

14. Samuel P. Huntington, *Political Order in Changing Societies* (New Haven, CT: Yale University Press, 1968), 8–9.

15. Daron Acemoglu and James Robinson, *The Narrow Corridor: States, Societies and the Fate of Liberty* (New York: Penguin, 2019).

16. Commission on Center-State Relations, Report of the Task Force—5, "Criminal Justice, National Security and Centre-State Cooperation" (2010).

17. See Charles Tilly, "Reflections on the History of European State-making," in *The Formation of National States in Western Europe* (Princeton, NJ: Princeton University Press, 1975). Richard Stubbs, "War and Economic Development: Expert-Oriented Industrialization in East and South East Asia," *Comparative Politics* 31, no. 3 (1999): 337–355; Michael Desch, "War and Strong States, Peace and Weak States?" *International Organization* 50, no. 2 (1996): 237–268.

18. See Timothy Besley and Torsten Persson, "Wars and State Capacity," *Journal of the European Economic Association* 6, no. 2–3 (2008): 522–530; Miguel Centeno, *Blood and Debt: War*

and the Nation-State in Latin America (University Park: Pennsylvania State University Press, 2002); Fernando Lopez-Alves, *State Formation and Democracy in Latin America 1810–1900* (Durham, NC: Duke University Press, 2000).

19. States in the global south, including those in the Indian subcontinent, possess uneven state capacity within their territories as a lingering effect of colonial governance. For one rendition of this argument see Adnan Naseemullah, *Patchwork States: The Historical Roots of Subnational Conflict and Competition in South Asia* (Cambridge: Cambridge University Press, 2022).

20. Deep Halder, *Blood Island: An Oral History of the Marichjhapi Massacre* (New Delhi: HarperCollins Publishers India, 2019).

21. Makiko Kimura, *The Nellie Massacre of 1983: Agency of Rioters* (Thousand Oaks, CA: Sage, 2013).

22. Officially, 2,733 Sikhs were reported to have been killed in Delhi alone during the anti-Sikh massacre according to the R. K. Ahuja Committee. Unofficial estimates place this figure close to 4,000 persons.

23. R. C. P. Sinha and Shamsul Hasan, "Report of the Commission of Inquiry to Inquire into the Communal Disturbances at Bhagalpur, 1989" (Bihar, Patna: Superintendent Secretariat Press, 1995).

24. Report of the Justice B. N. Srikrishna Commission on the Mumbai riots of 1992–1993.

25. MHA, *Annual Report 1991–92*, Government of India, New Delhi.

26. See Pai and Kumar, *Everyday Communalism*. Thomas Hansen, *The Law of Force: The Violent Heart of Indian Politics* (New Delhi: Aleph Book Company, 2021), argues that the weaponization of crowds against outgroups is a long-standing practice in Indian politics not confined to Hindu Nationalists alone. He suggests that for those who participate and support it, violence holds the promise of empowerment.

27. Since our aim is to capture long-term trends for indicators of violence and order, we draw substantially on data gathered by the state. It is the only source for time series data for these outcomes. Some of these indicators may not be the most accurate measure of a particular outcome. Still, we are confident of the trends that these data represent. In some instances, these trends corroborate each other, and in other instances, they are backed by scholarly accounts and press reporting.

28. United Nations Office on Drugs and Crimes (UNODC), India Country Profile, https://dataunodc.un.org/content/Country-profile?country=India.

29. Lok Sabha, *Unstarred Question No. 1254*, December 18, 2018.

30. Lok Sabha, *Unstarred Question No. 1459*, September 20, 2020.

31. Lok Sabha, *Unstarred Question No. 4937*, July 23, 2019.

32. According to one account, one of the hijackers, Hashim Quereshi, was a double agent in the BSF. See T. V. Rajeswar, *India. The Crucial Years* (New Delhi: HarperCollins, 2015), 104.

33. In 1978, Indian Airlines Flight 410 was hijacked by Bholanath Pandey and Devendra Pandey (both rumored to be members of Youth Congress). The Congress Party rewarded them with party tickets to contest not just the state assembly election in Uttar Pradesh, but the Lok Sabha polls as well, four times in a row.

34. Pramod Kumar, "Violence in Retrospect," In *Punjab in Prosperity and Violence*, ed. J. S. Grewal and Indu Banga (New Delhi: Manohar Publishers, 1998), 136.

35. A linear regression and Mann-Kendell test on the annual number of incidents both suggest a significant decline at a 95 percent confidence interval.

36. Ashutosh Bhardwaj, "Chhattisgarh Maoists Suffering from Betrayal, Fewer Leaders and Weapons, and Too Many Roads," *ThePrint*, February 12, 2021, https://bit.ly/2PvDdQw.

37. Rajya Sabha, *Unstarred Question No. 390*, September 26, 2020.

38. Between 1961 and 2003, there were more than two dozen reports by commissions of inquiry of the Communal Riots. *Report of Working Group of National Integration Council to Study Reports of the Commissions of Inquiry on Communal Riots* (2007), https://bit.ly/32UKa0E.

39. Abheet S. Sethi, "Uttar Pradesh, India's Communal Tinderbox," *The Wire*, October 7, 2015, https://bit.ly/3sYFH7u.

40. Acemoglu and Robinson, *The Narrow Corridor*.

41. See R. Tripathi, "More Security Forces for Lok Sabha Polls than Operation Brasstacks," *The Economic Times*, May 21, 2019, https://bit.ly/3sYFH7u.

42. Yuvaraj Krishnamoorthy, Karthika Ganesh, and Karthiga Vijayakumar, "Physical, Emotional, and Sexual Violence Faced by Spouses in India: Evidence on Determinants and Help-Seeking Behaviour from a Nationally Representative Survey," *Journal of Epidemiology & Community Health* 74 (2020): 732–740.

43. For example, see Harsh Malhotra, "How Does Caste Shape Vulnerability to Violent Crime in India?" Working paper no. 322, Centre for Development Economics, Delhi School of Economics, November 2021, http://www.cdedse.org/pdf/work322.pdf.

44. The armed forces have their own intelligence agencies, one each under the army, navy, and air force, and an umbrella body, the Defence Intelligence Agency.

45. These include the National Crime Records Bureau (NCRB); Bureau of Immigration (BOI); Narcotics Control Bureau (NCB); National Investigation Agency (NIA); Directorate of Coordination—Inter State Police Wireless; National Intelligence Grid (NATGRID); Intelligence Bureau (IB); Police Training Institutes; and Central Forensic Science Lab (CFSL).

46. See Lucia Michelutti, "The Inter-State Criminal Life of Sand and Oil in North India," in *The Wild East: Criminal Political Economies in South Asia*, ed. Lucia Michelutti and Barbara Harris-White (London: UCL Press, 2019), 168–193.

47. The software completely takes over phones and can track every activity with access to the device's camera and microphone.

48. Originally set up as the Delhi Special Police Establishment in 1946 to investigate bribery and corruption, it was renamed the Central Bureau of Investigation (CBI) in 1963. The CBI's powers of investigation cover three distinct issue areas: the Anti-Corruption Division, which investigates cases against central government employees as well as all cases against state government employees entrusted to the CBI by the state; the Special Crimes Division, which handles prominent cases of conventional nature such as offenses relating to narcotics and psychotropic substances, murders, etc.; and the Economic Offences Division, which investigates financial crimes, bank frauds, money laundering, illegal money market operations, etc.

49. Mariyam Alavi with Jain Sreenivasan, "Under BJP Government, Cases against Political Rivals Explode," *NDTV*, December 22, 2021, https://www.ndtv.com/india-news/under-bjp-government-cases-against-bjp-rivals-explode-ndtv-analysis-2665911.

50. See Lok Sabha, *Unstarred Question No. 1338*, July 25, 2022.

51. Deeptiman Tiwary, "General Consent for the CBI: The Law, and Political Reasons for Its Denial," *Indian Express*, November 12, 2021, https://indianexpress.com/article/explained/sc-state-government-consent-cbi-investigation-7617317/.

52. At the time of writing, forty-nine such courts had been designated as Special NIA courts across the country.

53. Shishir Gupta, *The Indian Mujahideen: The Enemy Within* (New York, NY: Hachette, 2011).

54. Between 2012 and 2017, India accounted for nearly 31 percent (162 of 526) of ranger deaths, about as many as the next five countries on the list—Congo, Thailand, Kenya, United States, and South Africa—combined.

55. Comptroller and Auditor General of India, *Performance Audit of Modernisation and Strengthening of Police Forces, Government of Uttar Pradesh*, Report No. 03 of the year 2017 (2017), https://cag.gov.in/uploads/download_audit_report/2017/Report_No.3_of_2017_Performance_Audit_of_Modernisation_of_Police_Forces_Government_of_Uttar_Pradesh.pdf.

56. Ibid., xii.

57. Ibid., xi.

58. See "Politics and Society between Elections," CSDS and Azim Premji University (2019), https://azimpremjiuniversity.edu.in/SitePages/pdf/politics-and-society-between-elections-2019-report.pdf.

59. C. Christine Fair and Sumit Ganguly, *Policing Insurgencies: Cops as Counterinsurgents* (New Delhi: Oxford University Press, 2014).

60. Arvind Verma, "Role of Police in Containing Mob Violence," *Economic and Political Weekly*, no. 36 (2012): 65–73.

61. Observers trace the decline in the professionalism of the police officers to Indira Gandhi's rule. Prakash Singh sees three phases. In the first, while political masters appreciated the honest officer, they transferred him when he became inconvenient, but sent him to places which were as prestigious. In the second, the politicians maltreated the officers who would not toe their line and saw to it that they were dumped in insignificant assignments. In the third and the current phase, officers who take a stand against the politicians are hounded; they may be suspended, framed in cases and their pension may be stopped. See Prakash Singh, *The Struggle for Police Reforms in India: From Ruler's Police to People's Police* (New Delhi: Rupa Publications, 2022).

62. Sanjaya Baru, *India's Power Elite Class, Caste and a Cultural Revolution* (New York: Penguin Random House, 2021).

63. IANS, "Army Pulls Out in Some Areas of Western Assam Where Normalcy Has Returned," *Business Standard. Business-Standard*, April 18, 2021, https://www.business-standard.com/article/current-affairs/army-pulls-out-in-some-areas-of-western-assam-where-normalcy-has-returned-121041800398_1.html.

64. Lok Sabha, *Unstarred Question No. 4224*, March 29, 2022.

65. Lok Sabha, *Unstarred Question No. 4167*, March 29, 2022.

66. *India Justice Report*, 2020.

67. Omar Khalidi, *Khaki and Ethnic Violence in India* (Gurgaon: Three Essays Collective, 2003), Table 1.

68. PTI, "Muslims Account for Less than 5% of Paramilitary Personnel," *Economic Times*, August 6, 2014, https://bit.ly/2QHtqat.

69. Adrian Levy and Cathy Scott-Clark, *Spy Stories: Inside the Secret World of the RAW and the ISI* (New Delhi: Juggernaut, 2021), make this point about RAW and IB.

70. Douglas Makeig, "'Aid-to-Civil': *Indian Army and Paramilitary Involvement in Domestic Peacekeeping*," Federal Research Division and Library of Congress, 1984.

71. Rajya Sabha, Department-related Parliamentary Standing Committee on Home Affairs, *Two Hundred Fifteenth Report, Working Conditions in Non-Border Guarding Central Armed Police Forces (Central Industrial Security Force, Central Reserve Police Force and National Security Guard)*. (Presented to Rajya Sabha on 12th December 2018; Laid on the Table of Lok Sabha on 12th December 2018), https://rajyasabha.nic.in/rsnew/Committee_site/Committee_File/ReportFile/15/107/215_2019_11_14.pdf.

72. Lok Sabha, *Unstarred Question No. 4187*, March 29, 2022.

73. Rajya Sabha, *Two Hundred Fourteenth Report, Working Conditions in Border Guarding Forces (Assam Rifles, Sashastra Seema Bal, Indo-Tibetan Border Police and Border Security Force)*. (Presented to the Rajya Sabha on 12th December 2018; Laid on the Table of Lok Sabha on 12th December 2018), https://rajyasabha.nic.in/rsnew/Committee_site/Committee_File/ReportFile/15/107/214_2019_11_11.pdf.

74. This included increasing central ex-gratia lump-sum compensation from 2016 from Rs. 15 lakh to Rs. 35 lakh for death on active duty and from Rs. 10 lakh to Rs. 25 lakh for death on duty; extra ordinary pension based on last pay drawn; ensuring access to all service benefits including death-cum-retirement gratuity, leave encashment, Central Government employees group insurance scheme, Provident Fund; (iv) Force level welfare schemes.

75. Ministry of Skill Development and Entrepreneurship, *Annual Report 2019–20*, Table 3.

76. FICCI, *Private Security Industry: Job Creation and Skill Development*, 2018, http://ficci.in/spdocument/23012/Private%20Security%20Industry%20Report.pdf.

77. They can do this by accessing electronic databases through the police like the Crime and Criminal Tracking Networks and Systems (CCTNS) and the Interoperable Criminal Justice System (ICJS).

78. Bureau of Police Research & Development, *Data on Police Organizations, January 2020*, 41.

79. Data are from RBI's *State Finances: A Study of Budgets.*

80. *MHA Annual Report, 2019–20*, 147–148.

81. World Economic Forum, *The Global Risks Report 2019*, 16.

82. See Lok Sabha, *Unstarred Question No. 541*, July 20, 2022.

83. "China-Linked Group RedEcho Targets the Indian Power Sector," https://go.recordedfuture.com/redecho-insikt-group-report.

84. Sameer Yasir and Hari Kumar, "Indian Call-Center Plot Fooled Americans into Paying Over $14 Million," *New York Times*, December 17, 2020, https://www.nytimes.com/2020/12/17/world/asia/india-call-center-scam.html.

85. The Central Government has provided assistance to state for acquiring advanced weaponry and intelligence equipment (such as UAVs, Night Vision Devices, CCTV systems, and body-worn camera systems), modern communication equipment, and better equipment and training for forensics, cybercrime, and traffic policing.

86. "Crime and Criminal Tracking Network & Systems (CCTNS)," *National Crime Records Bureau*, https://ncrb.gov.in/en/crime-and-criminal-tracking-network-systems-cctns.

87. Rajya Sabha, *Unstarred Question no. 1793, to be answered on 10th March 2021.*

88. CAG, *Report no.15 of 2020—Performance Audit of Manpower and Logistics Management in Delhi Police*, 2020.

89. The Chinese government's use of surveillance technology suggests that the same technologies used to terrorize and remold those who are thought to resist the party's authority can be deployed to coddle and reassure those who accept its rule. Josh Chin and Liza Lin, "The Two Faces of China's Surveillance State," *Wall Street Journal*, September 2, 2022, https://www.wsj.com/articles/the-two-faces-of-chinas-surveillance-state-11662130940?st=089qm2dp17htacq&reflink=desktopwebshare_permalink.

90. PTI, "Technology Used Extensively to Investigate Northeast Delhi Riots Cases: Delhi Police Chief," *Indian Express*, February 19, 2021, https://indianexpress.com/article/cities/delhi/technology-used-extensively-to-investigate-northeast-delhi-riots-cases-delhi-police-chief-7195703/.

91. Ibid.

92. The data are from the Pantopic Tracker of the Internet Freedom Foundation.

93. The technology is not foolproof and can give high false positives

94. Shuti Kapila argues that in laying the foundations for India's legal infrastructure, for very different reasons, both Ambedkar and Patel gave state's sovereignty primacy because they were wary of the potential for violence entrenched in a diverse society. By contrast, Tilak, Savarkar, and Gandhi placed the idea of sovereignty with the people. Shuti Kapila, *Violent Fraternity: Indian Political Thought in the Global Age* (Princeton, NJ: Princeton University Press, 2021). The Indian state's selective exercise of its sovereignty in confronting violence would suggest that both principles are still in use.

95. Apoorva Mandhani, "'Community Interest Outweighs Right of Personal Liberty': Why Court Denied Bail to Stan Swamy," *ThePrint*, March 23, 2021, theprint.in/judiciary/community-interest-outweighs-right-of-personal-liberty-why-court-denied-bail-to-stan-swamy/626906/.

96. *A. K. Gopalan v. State of Madras* (AIR 1950 SC 27).

97. Shekhar Gupta, "Aryan Khan Isn't a Show to Enjoy. NDPS Is a Weapon Vengeful State Could Use on You or Your Kids," *ThePrint*, October 23, 2021, https://theprint.in/national-interest/aryan-khan-isnt-a-show-to-enjoy-ndps-is-a-weapon-vengeful-state-could-use-on-you-or-your-kids/755219/.

98. *Kedar Nath Singh v. State of Bihar; Balwant Singh & Bhupinder Singh v. State of Punjab.*

99. Kunal Purohit, "Our New Database Reveals Rise in Sedition Cases in the Modi Era," *Article 14*, February 2, 2021, https://www.article-14.com/post/our-new-database-reveals-rise-in-sedition-cases-in-the-modi-era. Sedition cases are registered under the Indian Penal Code (IPC)'s

Section 124A, which deals with sedition, a nineteenth-century law used against Indians by the colonial government.

100. Krishnadas Rajagopal, "Supreme Court to Hear 2 Petitions against Sedition Law on April 27," *The Hindu*, April 26, 2022, https://www.thehindu.com/news/national/supreme-court-to-hear-2-petitions-against-sedition-law-on-april-27/article65358177.ece.

101. A. Laws and V. Iacopino, "Police Torture in Punjab, India: An Extended Survey," *Health and Human Rights* 6, no. 1 (2002): 195–210.

102. United Nations Human Rights Council, *Report of the Special Rapporteur on Extrajudicial, Summary or Arbitrary Executions*, Christof Heyns, April 26, 2013, https://www.ohchr.org/Documents/HRBodies/HRCouncil/RegularSession/Session23/A.HRC.23.47.Add.1_EN.pdf.

103. *Om Prakash & Ors v. State of Jharkhand & Anr* (September 26, 2012).

104. Vipul Mudgal, "India's Police Forces Turning Into Private Armies Of Elected Rulers," *Article14*, April 22, 2021, https://www.article-14.com/post/india-s-police-forces-turning-into-private-armies-of-elected-rulers.

105. Pratap Bhanu Mehta, "Thoki Raj: Creating Order by Trampling on Law Is One of the Elements of Adityanath's Ideological Success," *Indian Express*, July 11, 2020, https://indianexpress.com/article/opinion/columns/vikas-dubey-encounter-case-up-police-6499823/.

106. Beatriz Magaloni and Luis Rodriguez, "Institutionalized Police Brutality: Torture, the Militarization of Security, and the Reform of Inquisitorial Criminal Justice in Mexico," *American Political Science Review* 114, no. 4 (2002): 1013–1034.

107. Humza Kazmi, "Counterinsurgency and the Rule of Law," *University of Pennsylvania Journal of International Law* 33, no. 3 (2012): 871–905.

108. For a strong warning see Joseph Josy, *The Silent Coup: A History of India's Deep State* (Chennai: Generic, 2021).

109. In this context, it is worth remembering that suspension of democracy between 1975 and 1977 under the national emergency provisions was proclaimed in the name of internal security. "Any situation which weakens the capacity of the national government to act decisively inside the country is bound to encourage dangers from outside. It is our paramount duty to safeguard unity and stability. The nation's integrity demands firm action," Indira Gandhi had said in her speech justifying the emergency on June 26, 1975.

110. Devesh Pandey, "17 Indian Insurgent Leaders Arrested in Bangladesh in Five Years," *The Hindu*, March 7, 2015, https://www.thehindu.com/news/international/17-indian-insurgent-leaders-arrested-in-bangladesh-in-five-years/article6967230.ece.

111. PTI, "First Time: Insurgent Camps on Bangladesh Soil Reduced to Zero, Says BSF," *The Economic Times*, July 14, 2018, https://economictimes.indiatimes.com/news/defence/first-time-insurgent-camps-on-bangladesh-soil-reduced-to-zero-says-bsf/articleshow/62105460.cms.

112. Shishir Gupta, "HT Exclusive: Nudged by Ajit Doval, Myanmar Army Hands Over 22 Northeast Insurgents," *Hindustan Times*, May 16, 2020, www.hindustantimes.com/india-news/ht-exclusive-myanmar-flushes-out-northeast-insurgents-hands-over-22-to-india/story-x3CcZ88zxPj54l6XtqTj6L.html.

113. Imran Ahmed Siddiqui, "Kashmir: Army Human Rights Record Raises Barrier before German Arms Exports," *Telegraph India*, February 20, 2021, www.telegraphindia.com/india/security-forces-human-rights-record-raises-barrier-before-germanys-arms-exports-to-india/cid/1807272.

114. "Police Reforms Debates in India," *Commonwealth Human Rights Initiative*, 2011.

115. "Government Compliance with Supreme Court Directives on Police Reforms an Assessment," *Commonwealth Human Rights Initiative*, September 2020.

116. Milan Vaishnav, *When Crime Pays: Money and Muscle in Indian Politics* (New Delhi: HarperCollins, 2016).

117. "PM Modi's New Council of Ministers: 42% Have Criminal Cases, 90% Are Millionaires," *Indian Express,* July 15, 2021, https://indianexpress.com/article/india/pm-modi-council-of-ministers-criminal-cases-millionaires-7398120/.

118. Sixty-nine people died in the protests and riots that followed. Vijaita Singh, "69 Killed in 79 Days since Parliament Passed Citizenship Amendment Act," *The Hindu,* February 29, 2020, www.thehindu.com/news/national/citizenship-amendment-act-69-killed-in-79-days-since-parliament-passed-law/article30945131.ece.

119. Sruthisagar Yamunan, "How the Might of India's Federal Investigative Agencies Came to Be Trained on One Young Woman," *Scroll,* August 30, 2020, https://bit.ly/3tZV1Cp.

120. Ankur Mishra, "Section 24 of the Right to Information Act, 2005," *Institute of Law, Nirma University,* 2019, https://cic.gov.in/sites/default/files/Section%2024%20of%20the%20RTI%20Act%20-%20Ankur%20Mishra.pdf.

121. Paul D. Halliday, *Habeas Corpus: From England to Empire* (Cambridge, MA: Harvard University Press, 2010).

122. Pratap Bhanu Mehta, "SC Was Never Perfect, but the Signs Are That It Is Slipping into Judicial Barbarism," *Indian Express,* November 18, 2020, https://indianexpress.com/article/opinion/columns/supreme-court-arnab-goswami-bail-article-32-pratap-bhanu-mehta-7055067/.

123. Apurva Vishwanath, "NHRC Turns 25—and That's Pretty Much All It Has Achieved," *ThePrint,* October 16, 2018, https://theprint.in/india/governance/nhrc-turns-25-and-thats-pretty-much-all-it-has-achieved/132716/.

124. *NHRC Annual Report 2017–18.* By March 2021, its annual reports for 2018–19 and 2019–20 had not been published.

125. Henri Tiphagne, "Defending Human Rights, Challenging State Impunity: Henri Tiphagne's Talk at Kannabiran Lecture," *Live Law,* February 13, 2021, www.livelaw.in/columns/defending-human-rights-challenging-state-impunity-henri-tiphagnes-talk-at-kannabiran-lecture-169816.

126. Amia Srinivasan, "The Politics of Safety," *Financial Times,* August 13, 2021.

127. Amy Louise Wood, *Lynching and Spectacle: Witnessing Racial Violence in America, 1890–1940* (Chapel Hill: University of North Carolina Press, 2011).

128. Praveen Swami, "India's Turned a Blind Right Eye to Hindutva Violence, but It Can Be a Threat to State Itself," *ThePrint,* April 17, 2022, https://theprint.in/opinion/security-code/indias-turned-a-blind-right-eye-to-hindutva-violence-but-it-can-be-a-threat-to-state-itself/918092/.

PART I

INTERNAL SECURITY

The Legal, Institutional, and Financial Framework

2

Internal Security and India's Constitution

RAEESA VAKIL

"A nation is not governed which is perpetually to be conquered."[1]
—Edmund Burke

In 1949, the Constituent Assembly of India witnessed one of its most impassioned debates as members discussed constitutional provisions that would allow the federal government to declare a state of "emergency" in any part of the Union. The proposal under discussion would allow the enforcement of fundamental rights to be suspended during such emergencies,[2] leading one outraged Assembly member, Mr. H. V. Kamath, to describe these clauses as a "grand negation" of the draft Constitution itself.[3] Mr. Kamath was opposing an argument that was heard in the debates and is still common today: that threats to the security of India, both internal and external, can only be countered by a strong central executive that is unencumbered by legal constraints. Mr. Kamath did not disagree with this in principle, but offered a nuanced compromise. A strong Center, he said, included not only the executive, but an empowered legislature and judiciary as well. "Make all the three strong," he urged, "but not one at the expense of the other two, not the Executive at the expense of the Judiciary or the Legislature."[4]

Mr. Kamath's pleas, based on the experiences of the Indian population under British security laws, were not entirely successful. A strong Center was established, with a powerful executive government that had authority to act against potential threats. To moderate concerns, the drafters of the Constitution provided three forms of recourse. The first was to defer complex decision-making on controversial questions to future legislators, resting firmly on the hope that these constitutional interstices would be filled by laws that conformed with constitutional principles they had espoused. The flexibility that this afforded rested on faith in a performing legislature that would prioritize the rule of law over the needs of the moment, a faith that is, today, demonstrably misplaced.[5] Although a national emergency has not been declared since one notable instance in the 1970s, a number of anti-terror and preventive detention laws created in its wake have clearly established that

Raeesa Vakil, *Internal Security and India's Constitution* In: *Internal Security in India*. Edited by: Amit Ahuja and Devesh Kapur,
Oxford University Press. © Oxford University Press 2023. DOI: 10.1093/oso/9780197660331.003.0002

the situations that the Constituent Assembly envisioned as exceptional—even improbable—have become increasingly part of the daily architecture of the state. Moreover, notable lacunae remain unfilled by the legislature; even as the surveillance apparatus of the state expands, India still does not have a law protecting personal data, and laws that were designed in a colonial state to secure compliance from a subject population remain unrepealed long after independence.[6]

The second recourse that the Constituent Assembly had in mind was to trust that the nascent Supreme Court would act as Mr. Kamath had suggested—as a counterweight to consistently protect against the "arbitrary fiat of the executive."[7] This was not borne out; the Supreme Court of India, despite some notable resistance to executive power during the Emergency in the 1970s, has otherwise interpreted the Constitution in a manner that prioritizes public order over the liberty of the individual.[8] Finally, the inclusion of provisions that affirmed a "strong Center" in the Constitution were premised on the hope that they would never be used unless absolutely required. Instead, each instance of a threat to national security has been utilized as the basis to expand executive authority further, especially by the creation of security institutions that operate without significant oversight, such as the Central Bureau of Investigation, the National Investigation Agency, and India's biometric identity program, Aadhar. Accountability within these security institutions remains minimal, and reforms in the police and paramilitary forces have been few and far between.[9]

Today, the Indian Supreme Court, the Union Government, and Parliament grapple with a range of internal security challenges that include separatist movements, violent political actions, communal and caste-led suppression by majoritarian movements, and internal acts of terror. Legal fragmentation occurs especially in conflict zones, such as Kashmir or the North East, where martial law allows military and paramilitary forces to act with impunity and little accountability. Although the exact scope and range of these problems may not have been anticipated by the drafters of the Indian Constitution at the time of drafting, their intention was to design a constitution that would remain robust against new challenges over time. In this chapter, I examine the evolution of internal security and Indian constitutional law in three parts beginning with the legislature, then the executive, and finally, the judiciary, to consider whether they succeeded. The width of the legal issues involved in internal security necessarily limit the ambit of this chapter, and discussions on certain subjects (such as the institution of the police) may be abbreviated, particularly when they are the subject of interventions in other chapters of this volume. Nevertheless, I hope to reveal the underlying structural concerns in the legal architecture of internal security and how they have served the Indian state. In doing so, I demonstrate that the intention of creating exceptional legal frameworks for security have instead, through institutional and structural weakness, evolved into the norm.

The Legislature
The Union and the States

June 13, 1949, witnessed a contentious session in the Constituent Assembly of India, as members debated the allocation of legislative powers between the Union and the still-fragmented states in the draft Constitution of India. It was accepted that this allocation would be tilted toward the Center, and a proposal to enumerate limited state powers and leave the residue to the Union was considered and rejected. Instead, the Assembly remained in favor of three lists consisting of Union, state, and concurrent legislative powers.[10] In the Constitution that was adopted, the balance still tilts in favor of the Union; repugnancy, or conflicts between the Union and states on how these legislative powers are to be exercised, is to be resolved in favor of the Union if it has already legislated on the field, and matters not included on the list fall automatically under Union powers of legislation.[11] Additionally, four specific fields are reserved for the Union: one concerns the power to legislate to give effect to international treaties,[12] and the remaining three are concerned, more or less, with national security. The Union legislature may ignore the allocation of powers in Schedule VII in order to *firstly*, establish special courts; *secondly*, to enact on matters in the state list during an Emergency, and finally, to legislate on state matters even outside Emergencies, if a majority of the Parliament votes that it is "necessary or expediency in national interest."[13]

The inclusion of a provision allowing the Union to legislate "in national interest" outside of Emergencies was met with skepticism by the Assembly, chiefly on the grounds that having such legislation periodically ratified would be cumbersome and unnecessary. The Assembly was divided on this, with some, such as H. V. Pataskar, noting, "if it is really a matter of national interest I do not understand why the State itself will not either pass the legislation itself or be willing to consent to legislation by Parliament. Why should we presume that the State will assume such an anti-national attitude?"[14] Opposing him, others like Mahavir Tyagi warned about the dangers to the Union posed by states in language not unlike some modern-day Indian rhetoric: "There are certain provinces in which a certain class of people are in a majority: they desire to be independent of the Centre."[15]

An amended provision was finally adopted, allowing states to vote to allow such laws to be passed for a period of one year, following which an annual ratification would be required to keep such laws in force. The "national interest" that the members of the Constituent Assembly envisioned for this provision was not necessarily security-related; Shibban Lal Saxena and O. V. Alagesan spoke of a "an emergency about food,"[16] T. T. Krishnamachari discussed a precedent concerning the enactment of a law regarding an inter-state river project,[17] and Brajeshwar Prasad spoke of issues of national importance in the context of the economy, which was in an "incipient stage of development."[18] The only context in which security issues were discussed were when Alagesan hypothesized a law-and-order situation in which the Union Government stepped in and took over from the state government, stating, "Sir, I am sure that it will be a mockery of provincial autonomy if such a thing happens."[19] Such "mockery" was to occur repeatedly, thereafter.

A great deal of Mr. Alagesan's criticism may have rested on the painstaking allocation of powers across the lists contained in Schedule VII. Although general powers were spread across these three lists, those concerning the security of the state were cleanly delineated: armed forces lay squarely within the Center's control, while law and order, and the police, remained state subjects.[20] With conflicts and residuary powers being allocated to the Center, it may have appeared that this was a coherent and complete allocation, allowing the Center to address external, or internal inter-state threats, while allowing the states to concern themselves with their own law and order. In practice, periodic conflicts between state and federal governments revealed the limitations of this arrangement, demonstrating that they were not easily addressed within the constitutional framework.

A singular point of conflict arose from Article 355 of the Constitution, which places a duty on the Union Government to protect states not only against external aggression, but also "internal threats."[21] The roots of this conflict go back to the allocations of power in Schedule VII: when asked about how the state's power to legislate on police would affect paramilitary union forces such as the then-Home Guards, Dr. Ambedkar said, "If it is not Police, then it will go under the Union Government. "*Police*" is used in contradiction to "*Army.*" Anything that is not "*Army*" is police."[22] At that time, the chief concern was to secure the union against a potential threat or recession by the unintegrated states; consequently, the converse issue of protecting the states from federal intervention was not raised at all, with the discussion concluding with Ambedkar stating, "I am sure if a province is going to play a fraud on the Constitution, the Centre will be strong enough to see that that fraud is not perpetrated."[23]

The faith of the members of the Assembly in their successors' intentions left this latter question open, and led almost immediately to complex constitutional conflicts. In 1955, the Central Reserve Police Force was constituted; despite the name, members of the force were recruited not under the Police Act 1861, but under the Central Reserve Force Act 1955, and consequently were neither army, nor police.[24] They were given limited, non-investigative powers generally accorded to the police under the Code of Criminal Procedure, but were organized according to the model of the Indian Army.[25] The CRPF was to function under the state governments and act to aid them, but had significant operational independence over how to carry out those functions.[26] The Border Security Force (BSF) established by the Union Government in 1968 allowed BSF members to perform law-and-order functions of state magistrates under their direction, but allowed them to function independently of state authorities if they found that communication was inconvenient.[27] This is in addition to the centrally controlled army's own role in counterinsurgency efforts within India; as Ahuja and Raghavan point out in their chapter in this volume, counterinsurgency work constitutes "the largest claim on the Army's resources."

A related, and second question that the Constitution did not address was whether the Union could deploy these forces into states without their prior consent. Although the Sarkaria Commission (appointed in 1988 to review the Constitution) described this arrangement as frictionless, noting that "there is no state government which has not at some time or the other made use of the Union forces,"[28] they nevertheless polled states to consider their views on the uses of such forces by the Union. While some states suggested that the use of federal security forces was a valuable aid to state police, others noted that the constitutional text did not specifically authorize the Union to deploy federal forces in a state without the state's consent. The language of Entry 2A of List I in Schedule VII was specifically invoked to note that federal forces could be used "in *aid* of the civil power" of state governments, although this language does not clearly articulate whether the consent of state governments was required.[29]

Legal disputes between federal units are nominally to be resolved by the Supreme Court, which has the jurisdiction to determine suits between states, or between the Center and states.[30] In practice, this provision has been used in an extremely limited fashion, and rarely on issues concerning national security, and the courtroom is a limited space for negotiating issues without public scrutiny. Accordingly, the Sarkaria Commission entertained the suggestion that the Inter-State Council envisioned in Article 263 of the Constitution should be utilized more effectively as a space for the resolution of federal issues, and to obtain such consent wherever necessary.[31] This view was opposed by the then-Union Government, which affirmed that the use of the word "duty" in Article 355 indicated that the Union Government could, at its discretion, deploy federal forces into states to address emergency threats that did not constitute ordinary law-and-order concerns.[32] The Sarkaria Commission ultimately conceded the point, interpreting Article 355 in favor of the Center to suggest that states could request assistance, but the Center was also free to act on its own and deploy Union forces such as the Central Reserve Police or the Border Security Force in states.[33]

At the time of the Sarkaria Commission Report, Union forces had been deployed in states to quell internal disturbances three times: in Kerala to secure Union offices and employees during a general strike; in West Bengal, for a different strike; and to protect the Farakka Barrage.[34] In current times, questions on the extent of Union powers under Article 355 with reference to national security have expanded from the deployment of paramilitary forces to examining the role of union investigative agencies, such as the Central Bureau of Investigation,[35] affirming the constitutionality of the Armed Forces (Special Powers) Act 1958, which allows the Union to declare a "disturbed area" within a state and deploy Union forces to resolve the disturbance,[36] and validating a Union law that allowed it to enforce measures to address illegal migration into Indian territory.[37] Arguments that these were not the intended use of Article 355 have been unsuccessfully raised by both critics of the Supreme Court as well as by the Court itself.[38] In 1994, the Court unsuccessfully attempted to link the use of Article 355 to emergencies alone, but was unable, among a bench of nine judges, to arrive at a consensus on this specific point.[39] It had become evident, over time, that the faith that the Assembly had placed on Parliament and the executive's ability to resolve complex constitutional questions was perhaps misplaced, and that federalism was vulnerable to the strong Center's expansionist tendencies.

The Functioning of Parliament

The ambiguities that Parliament was intending to resolve in the framing of Article 355 rested on a specific understanding of the legislative function that undercut many of the deliberations of the Constituent Assembly. The legislative framework in India was designed so that Parliament in India would operate in close conjunction with the executive, which plays a predominant role in drafting, presenting, and securing the passage of legislation.[40] The inherent dangers in allowing too much executive control were to be countermanded by faith in future parliamentarians, who would, it was assumed, act as a deliberative body, to take measured decisions in the national interest. On this assumption, Dr. B. R. Ambedkar was able to quell opposition on ambiguous wording and deferrals in the Constitution regarding complex issues. On legislative qualifications, for instance, he argued, "Parliament will certainly have more time at its disposal than the Drafting Committee had and Parliament would have more information to weigh this proposal,"[41] a position predicated on faith that Parliament would exercise its time in order to weigh evidence and "arrive at some via media which might be put into law."[42]

In practice, the Indian Parliament abdicates its deliberative function to large extent in favor of allowing the executive great rein.[43] This is particularly apparent in the case of national security legislation, which undergoes limited scrutiny and is characterized by reactionary lawmaking. Immediate, and occasionally ill-considered, responses to emerging issues have resulted in laws that are drafted with extensive borrowing, either from historical precedents designed to quell colonized populations, or from previous laws already passed and struck down by Indian courts, without addressing the inherent defects in either source. When discussing constitutional guarantees of personal liberty in the Constituent Assembly Debates, the specter of colonial laws that were used to quell political demands for freedom lingered. Pandit Thakur Dass Bhargava cited the Rowlatt Act 1918, which introduced the power to allow detention without trial, and sparked nationwide protests, asking, "where is the guarantee that this House or the provincial legislatures will not enact a law like that Act?"[44] His demand was that the Constitution should provide sufficient and specific safeguards that prevented the replication of Rowlatt-style restrictions by legislatures; the idea that one could have a law in independent India that allowed for conviction despite *"no vakeel, no daleel, no appeal"* (no lawyer, no evidence, no appeal) was abhorrent.[45] Despite this, the power to enact preventive detention laws were explicitly granted to legislatures by the text of the Constitution, and against Bhargava's urge to protect the people of India from their future legislators. It was argued that this Article 22,[46] which sought to limit such powers, was too explicit. Naziruddin Ahmad said, "As, to what should be done for a man who is under preventive detention should be left to the Legislature," pointing out that no amount of detail could cover every potential instance that might arise.[47] The Home Ministry, led by Sardar Patel, accordingly advocated for preventive detention and ultimately won, with the inclusion of Article 22 in the Constitution.

Preventive detention has been listed on the union, and on concurrent lists, allowing both state legislatures and Parliament to frame laws on the subject.[48] In attempting to balance personal liberty with public order, the Assembly left it open to Parliament to "by law, prescribe" the classes of cases in which preventive detention laws might be allowed, the procedure to be followed by monitoring boards, and the period for which preventive detention might be allowed.[49] These powers were utilized almost immediately; in order to prevent pre-constitutional legislation that authorized preventive detention laws from lapsing with the Constitution coming into force, the Government of India, on January 26, 1950, passed an executive order extending these laws to the independent state.[50] As courts began to test these laws against the newly enacted Constitution, a central Preventive Detention Act 1950 was substituted, and was invalidated in part by the Supreme Court for not complying with Article 22.[51] Subsequent acts carefully complied with the letter of this ruling and were upheld by the Supreme Court until the Emergency in 1960,[52] which led one scholar to note that in the first ten years of independence, "India has never been without a law of preventive detention."[53]

Preventive detention laws have since been enacted by both Parliament and state legislatures, and following criticism and allegations of misuse, have been periodically repealed. The preventive detention act that was introduced soon after the Constitution came into force was soon replaced with a series of ordinances that replicated its broad intent. In 1987, reacting to the assassination of Prime Minister Indira Gandhi and to threats posed by militants in disturbed areas of India, Parliament passed the Terrorist and Disruptive Activities (Prevention) Act 1985 (TADA), directly attacking constitutionally protected safeguards concerning trials, criminal procedure, and the established judicial framework. TADA had a time limit: in two years, the law would expire, but it was challenged before that by the Supreme Court on the grounds that it had exceeded the Union's legislative powers. This contention was not accepted, with the Court now drawing an established link between national security and law and order.[54] TADA was sustained long past its inbuilt "sunset" of two years by means of periodic legislative renewals, despite a letter from the chairman of the National Human Rights Commission to Parliament, urging them to repeal it since "provisions of the statute have yielded to abuse."[55]

It was only repealed in 1995 after it was found that despite its aggressive limitations on personal liberties and sweeping investigative powers, the conviction rate for offences under TADA remained "abysmally low."[56]

TADA was replaced by the Prevention of Terrorism Act 2002 (POTA), enacted following attacks on the Indian Parliament. Although POTA replicated provisions of TADA, it was explicitly modelled on a state law—the 1999 Maharashtra Control of Organised Crime Act (MCOCA). In Parliament, MCOCA's higher conviction rate was invoked to authorize this by L. K. Advani (the deputy prime minister) as a viable precedent, and MCOCA has since been replicated in other states, with Gujarat attempting to have a slightly more powerful law enacted thrice, against repeated rejections by the president for its apparently unconstitutional restraints on personal liberty.[57] MCOCA, and subsequently POTA, allowed vaster powers of surveillance along with preventive detention, and like TADA, permitted self-incrimination by admitting as evidence, in confessions made to police officers. Criticisms of these laws followed the enactment of POTA, resulting in its eventual repeal, but the contentious provisions from POTA were merely reinserted into the current Unlawful Activities (Prevention) Act 1967 (UAPA).[58] The UAPA itself has been repeatedly amended by governments ranging across the political spectrum, each time expanding executive powers further in 2004, 2008, and 2014. Constitutional challenges to each of these amendments on the grounds of the expansion of legislative power at the cost of individual liberty have consistently failed, with the Supreme Court at best reading down a provision that automatically criminalized membership in banned organizations.[59] Additionally, attempts to apply the UAPA to political actors have been on the rise, with increasing recognition that it is being applied specifically to stifle freedom of expression and dissent.[60]

In their acts of repetition and replication, legislators have frequently ignored both internal opposition as well as external sources of criticism of national security laws. Repeals of such laws have only been possible through periods of sustained political opposition, and internal safeguards to the parliamentary process have often failed to check these errors. M. R. Madhavan has pointed out that the reference of bills for review before passage to Departmentally Related Standing Committees (DRSCs) is not mandatory, and in practice has been particularly lax on security and law and order issues, allowing such bills to be passed with limited to no scrutiny.[61] He points out that neither the Criminal Law Amendment Bill 2013, which substantially altered multiple criminal codes, nor the National Investigation Agency (NIA) Act, which establishes a federal authority for investigating crimes related to national security, were referred to DRSCs.[62] Indeed, the UAPA was amended in 2019 without allowing the bill to be referred to a DRSC, although the amendment allows the government to take the extreme step of designating any person as a "terrorist" for the purpose of the act without disclosing rationale or providing a judicial appeal against this order.[63]

Being unable to determine how security and liberty might be balanced in specific cases, the Assembly had left these questions for the legislatures and courts to determine by interpretation and enactment of laws.[64] The inherent conflict at the heart of these constitutional provisions, allowing legislatures to frame these laws in times of peace as well as war while simultaneously constricting the operation of these laws, reflected the divided mind of the Constituent Assembly on this. As Sagar points out, "Parliaments are not immune from panic; they may be misled; they may lack access to classified information; and they may lack courage."[65] Parliamentary scrutiny has failed to address the flaws inherent in the constitutional design, and has, on occasion, allowed temporary measures to linger indefinitely, turning a reaction into the status quo long after the instigating event has passed. In articulating such laws, the challenge faced by Parliament is to ensure that public safety and the liberty of the individual are both provided for. In reality, wide drafting allows the executive great latitude, while constraining the individual's ability to seek remedies against unfair action.

The Executive

The prime minister remains the head of the Indian government, exercising control over the Government of India following his or her appointment by the president.[66] Constitutionally, prime ministers and their cabinets are accountable to the lower house of Parliament (i.e., the Lok Sabha), an arrangement that is mirrored with governors and chief ministers at the state level. Executive power, as interpreted by the Supreme Court of India, constitutes the residue of all state functions once judicial and legislative powers are removed.[67] The executive has powers that co-extend with legislative powers, and the government does not always require prior legislation in order to act on these powers.[68]

The Indian model of separation of powers, which describes the relationship between the executive, legislature, and judiciary, does not mirror the explicitly articulated American model, nor the more loosely defined Westminster model. While the unenforceable directive principles of state policy in the Constitution task the Indian state with striving to separate the judiciary from the executive,[69] this is not mandated within the constitutional framework. The consequent balance among the state, court, and legislature for control has led some commentators to suggest that rather than any of these three branches, "In India, the Constitution is supreme."[70] This is an argument that is fraught with difficulties, particularly when security agencies and legislation function within the interstices of the constitutional framework. In practical terms, the constrained use of parliamentary oversight and the outsize role played by the executive in enacting legislation ensures that it is the executive holding authority over the remaining two organs.[71]

In addition to the executive powers that co-extend with the legislature, the Union Government is constitutionally granted immense powers to address situations of emergency, including both internal and external threats to the nation. Legislative interventions have expanded the scope of investigation, surveillance, and detention by delegating their powers back to the government, and the government frequently exercises these, not only to engage in actions to protect internal security, but also to establish institutional frameworks that allow it to organize and channel these responses. In this section, I discuss three aspects of executive power relating to emergencies, ordinances, and institutions, to demonstrate that the unchecked latitude given to the executive has lent itself to abuses in the name of protecting internal security.

Executive Powers and Emergencies

The Indian Constitution notably contains "emergency" powers that allow it to assume control of state governments when there is "failure of constitutional machinery."[72] As Sagar and Subramaniam have both argued, the roots of current emergency powers rest not only in imminent threats to the security of the state, which are provided for in Article 352 ("war," "external aggression," or "armed rebellion").[73] Instead, the powers under Article 356 and 355 that impose a duty on the Union to protect states against "internal disturbances" were framed to also allow a response to internal political opposition that threatened the Indian state.[74] In contrast to Article 352, Articles 355 and 356 have been widely used, enabled by the Supreme Court's facilitative interpretations of the legal constraints embedded in these provisions.[75] As the preceding discussion on Article 355 and legislation demonstrates, the Union's ability to deploy central forces to states challenges not only the state's legislative power, but also its executive authority.

The Sarkaria Commission's ultimate recommendation was that "it is desirable that the State Government should be consulted, wherever feasible. . . . However, prior consultation with the State Government is not obligatory."[76] As a result, broad emergency powers not only empower the executive, but tilt such powers toward the Union Government, preventing states from acting within the federal framework to check Union power. A key instance of this is found in legislation such as the Armed Forces (Special Powers) Act 1956 (AFSPA), which has remained in force since a pre-Constitution period. The AFSPA allowed a state to notify an area as "disturbed," which triggers special provisions that allowed armed forces to use force, arrest and conduct searches and seizures without warrant, detain in custody any person, and be granted immunity from legal prosecution.[77] An amendment extended the power of notification to the central government as well, with Article 355 as the validating authority for this exercise.[78] AFSPA was a concentration of executive power at the Center; the Code of Criminal Procedure already made provisions for armed forces to assist state police in quelling disturbances, but implicit in this was the need for a state official to ask for their assistance.[79] By contrast, AFSPA allowed the Center to overrule state consent either directly or through their delegate: the unelected governor of the state. As Bhonsle points out in her chapter in this volume on AFSPA, this has allowed the Center to effectively designate an area as "disturbed" for extended periods, some ranging from the 1950s into the present, regardless of states' objections.[80]

AFSPA and Article 355 envisioned states of exception: emergencies or extraordinary situations in which the executive might intervene in state affairs to secure law and order.[81] Coupled with these, the Constitution authorized legislatures to enact preventive detention legislation, including this in the union and the concurrent lists in Schedule VII, with limited checks on how this detention might be carried out contained in Article 22 of the Constitution. The latitude that Article 22 grants to legislatures and the executive on preventive detention has been described as a "vast power virtually free from judicial restraint and the protection of the other fundamental rights," chiefly by virtue of the fact that this provision was included within the section containing these fundamental rights in the Constitution.[82] Modern security laws have therefore expanded upon these to grant the Union power to indefinitely detain, question, and hold citizens on suspicion.[83] The Constitution accordingly grants significant and largely uncontrolled powers to the executive in times of both peace and conflict to address issues of public order and security, leaving little room for states to resolve conflicts within the federal framework.

Executive Legislation

The act of legislation is not constrained to Parliament and state legislatures alone in India. The president is granted the power to enact ordinances, which have the effect of law, when Parliament is not in session.[84] This power is replicated in the states, with the governor also having the power to promulgate ordinances.[85] In both cases, the requirement is only that the legislatures not be in session; the threshold applied is the personal satisfaction of the president and the governor that such ordinances are necessary in the immediate circumstances.[86] In practice, this power is exercised by the government, that is, the prime minister or chief minister, acting on the advice of their cabinets.[87] Ordinances require subsequent legislative ratification, can be renewed infinitely, and are subject to only limited judicial review.[88] Despite the language of exceptionalism, ordinances are routine, and as Dam has indicated, are often preferred over the process of legislation.[89]

The use of executive ordinances is particularly evident in the field of national security, where the executive can, and does, use periods of parliamentary recess to enact laws without having to encounter their opposition. A systematic review by Dam of ordinances enacted between 1950 and 2009 reveals that apart from TADA, all security-related laws in India have been preceded by an ordinance.[90] POTA, for instance, was based on the previously issued Prevention of Terrorism Ordinance

2002, and the Unlawful Activities (Prevention) Ordinance of 2004 preceded the act of the same name.[91] The link to emergent and immediate needs has been challenged as tenuous at best. POTO was enacted days before Parliament began its winter session in 2002, leading to accusations that it was an attempt to deliberately subvert the democratic process and deepen government powers.[92] In addition, the Armed Forces (Special Powers) Act 1956, which continues in force in parts of North East India as well as in Jammu and Kashmir today, began its life as an ordinance directed at Assam and Manipur, and was extended in application to Punjab and Jammu and Kashmir over time before being enacted into a law by Parliament.[93]

Contemporary governments now rely heavily on ordinances to introduce security-related legislation when opposition is anticipated, using majorities to push legislative ratification through after the fact. When passing bills is impossible for political reasons, lapsed bills are increasingly renotified as ordinances instead, allowing the government to legislate without question.[94] A key instance of this is the ordinance establishing the national biometric identity system—Aadhar—which began as an ordinance and was eventually passed as a law by utilizing money bills, which are intended for authorizing budgetary allocations and consequently have lower legislative thresholds for passage.[95] The law as it was enacted contained an exception on the grounds of "national security," allowing confidential biometric and personal data to be disclosed to anyone by the Union Government.[96] This provision was ultimately struck down by the Supreme Court because it contained inadequate safeguards and oversight to prevent the misuse of disclosed information.[97]

The language of exceptionalism, evident in ordinances, can also be see in the drafting of security laws such as anti-terror legislations. Like the Aadhar Act, these laws grant sweeping investigative, custodial, and surveillance powers to investigative agencies and governments in India. Loosely defined offenses of "terrorism" and "disruptive" activities allowed police officers to invoke TADA in virtually any case, resulting in the Punjab government's having to direct officers not to apply TADA when an offense was criminalized already.[98] This legislative drafting allows the executive to expand on its powers, using national security as the basis for political action as well. A recent survey revealed that the National Security Act 1980, a preventive detention law, was being widely used in cases concerning political protests, even if they were nonviolent, as well as to detain persons accused of offenses criminalized under acts unrelated to national security (such as cow slaughter).[99] In their increasing use of executive ordinances, the executive, in considerations of national security, has excluded legislative oversight as well as legislative control.

Institutions and the Law

The police in India today are still governed by the colonial-era Police Act 1861, and draw their power to enforce concerns of internal security as well as law and order under several colonial-era legislation, including the 1860 Indian Penal Code, which defines offenses such as sedition; the 1872 Evidence Act; and the 1885 Indian Telegraph Act, which authorizes surveillance powers. The transition from colonial police to independent police with minimal reforms and restructuring is evident from the fact that after the two colonial police commissions that established the police (in 1860 and 1902), the next set of reforms were only initiated post-Emergency, in 1978's National Police Commission.[100] Structural divisions in the police force place senior IPS officers under the Union's control, with state officers subordinate to magistrates.[101] Several scholars have argued, including Mangla in this volume, that limitations in the state police forces' training and structure constrain their ability to effectively act on law and order, and that continuing political interference instills doubts in their capacity and autonomy.

In addition to the challenges posed within states to ensure that policing is in line with constitutional mandates on fair procedures, fundamental rights, and constitutional writs, a second challenge arises from the rise of federal agencies that control aspects of investigation and police work in India.[102] Their work frequently brings them into conflict with existing state forces and gradually erodes state power, demonstrating the weakness of the Constitution's federal framework in this regard. This has been marked by gradual expansionism: the creation of a National Investigative Agency in 2008 was not fraught with conflict over the usurpation of state power, primarily because the list of offenses that the Agency was empowered to investigate was limited to laws that enforced defense concerns, such as the Atomic Energy Act 1962, the Anti-Hijacking Act 1982, and so on.[103] The inclusion of the Unlawful Activities (Prevention) Act 1967 did not attract much public comment, despite the criticisms directed against that legislation itself. However, in 2019, the amended act had expanded its scope to cover investigation of a wider range of offenses that directly infringed on state power, including Chapter VI of the Indian Penal Code itself.[104]

The conflict is most apparent in the functioning of the Central Bureau of Investigation, which is an institution established by an executive order in 1983, under the Ministry of Home Affairs, even though the Constitution explicitly allows the Union to establish such a body by legislation.[105] In addition to its weak legal basis, it functions to date under a legislation aimed at providing for the investigation of corruption in the military during World War II.[106] The CBI, as one former Union minister put it, "has no independent standing in law. It is a piece of legal fiction whose underpinnings in law are tenuous to say the least."[107] Section 6 of this Act requires the consent of states before the CBI can investigate an offense in their jurisdiction. In 2020, following political conflicts with the Union Government, the Rajasthan government was one of nine states that withdrew "general consent" allowing the CBI to investigate cases within its territory, requiring the CBI to take individual consent for each case.[108] This represents a remarkable shift, as interventions by the CBI have historically been sought by the state governments themselves, and is linked, perhaps, to increasing conflicts over the extent of central control in the CBI's internal functioning, particularly in the appointment of its leadership.[109] In response to this retreat from centralization, the Supreme Court in 2020 attacked the federal allocation once again, ruling that the requirement for consent need not apply in certain cases, including those wherein the CBI was investigating state officials themselves.[110]

The CBI is not the only institution whose legal underpinnings originate in executive fiat. The National Human Rights Commission (NHRC), which performs an important, albeit limited function in checking excesses by security forces, was established by ordinance in 2006, although unlike the CBI it was subsequently ratified by specific legislation.[111] The NHRC has been directed in an ongoing litigation concerning police reform to study the question of whether the investigation of crimes concerning internal and external security in India should be entrusted to the CBI instead of state police using the powers in Article 355.[112] A pending challenge to the constitutionality of the CBI still hangs before the Supreme Court while the CBI, nevertheless, continues to function and investigate cases that go far beyond its original scope of tackling corruption.[113] Finally, as Datta demonstrates in his chapter on Intelligence Bureau (IB) in this volume, the IB, a well-funded executive body, was established by the British colonial government on the basis of a telegram sent by Her Majesty, and continues to function under independent India's governments with little to no oversight or legal constraints. In his chapter, Datta argues that the limited constraints that do exist (such as the IB's inability to arrest or prosecute) have operated to expand its power to perform other functions unchecked by a need to be held accountable to a court.

Security institutions in India have also focused on expanding powers of surveillance as a means of securing internal security. A recent report indicates that ten central agencies now have wide-ranging surveillance and investigative powers.[114] These include the Intelligence Bureau, the Research and Analysis Wing, several tax and revenue authorities, and the Delhi Commissioner of Police.[115] Information is sourced through three bodies: a Communications Monitoring System (CMS), a Network Traffic Analysis body (NETRA), and the National Intelligence Grid (NATGRID). As Bhandari and Lahiri have pointed out, the executive's discretion to engage in surveillance is not subject to any independent oversight, and any evidence obtained by such surveillance, even if it controverts the law on evidence, is usually admissible in courts.[116] The absence of any law protecting personal data, even though the Supreme Court recognizes privacy as a right, allows these bodies to exercise their powers in the absence of legal frameworks for control and accountability.[117] Consequently, an incentive for the executive to comply with Indian evidence laws is lacking, with little to no control over their compliance. In December 2020, the Delhi High Court has begun hearing a challenge to their constitutionality of these surveillance bodies,[118] but for the present, the only bulwark against them is the judiciary, and judicial review over security institutions is neither systemic nor consistent.

The Judiciary

The Supreme Court of India performs three functions in its exercise of judicial review: it interprets the Constitution, it tests legislation for validity against the Constitution, and it tests executive action for validity against legislation and the Constitution. Often the latter two functions are combined in a challenge, allowing the Court to determine whether a law and the action taken under that law are valid.[119] In the field of national security, the Court has demonstrated that in each of these functions, it prioritizes public order over personal liberty, reading down constitutional and legislative safeguards to allow the legislature to enact permissive laws extending state power, and to allow the executive to exercise these powers with great latitude.[120]

Interpreting the Constitution

The Indian Supreme Court's much-lauded procedural and substantive innovations in public interest litigation rest chiefly on the foundation of Article 21, which protects the right to life and personal liberty, subject to "procedure enacted by law."[121] The phrase "procedure established by law" was intentionally adopted, with the Constituent Assembly explicitly rejecting an American-style "due process" clause out of concern that Indian courts would, like their American counterparts, use it to invalidate social and economic legislation.[122] While this fear did not come true, the Supreme Court has established that it will not read "procedure enacted by law" as authorizing Parliament to take away life or personal liberty at will. A wider reading of this provision allows the Court to interrogate legislative provisions on whether the procedure they establish is fair, just, and proper.[123] This substantive procedural justice, in theory, ought to allow the Court to act as a guardian to the citizen against the excesses of the state. Together with Articles 20 and 22, these constitutional provisions form a code that establish the fairness of the criminal process: persons are protected from the retrospective application of laws and from self-incrimination and double jeopardy.[124]

Regrettably, despite these apparently robust protections, lacunae in the constitutional text have been filled by judicial interpretation, which tends toward the protection of public order over the guarantee of personal liberty. As early as 1960, P. K. Tripathi had written that the protections in these provisions had "undergone a process of contraction,"[125] largely because of judicial interpretation of preventive detention laws. The Court's failure to uphold personal liberties against state justifications of preventive detention, according to him, "verge[d] on total abandonment of the unfortunate individuals who happen to fall under their shadow."[126] The Supreme Court in *Maneka Gandhi v. Union of India* had famously articulated the need for a fair trial while confirming that it was impossible to clearly define the standards that would establish fairness.[127] Although the Supreme Court has acted to protect some

aspects of fair trials, including the need for legal representation, the right to be provided with evidence and to cross-examine, and the right to appeal, the rights of the
individual have been balanced by the Court against the need for public order.[128] In
jurisprudence on bail and the conduct of trial, the Court, according to Chandra
and Sen, is "more concerned with State security and truth-seeking than individual
liberty . . . it creates a systemic presumption of criminality against accused persons
as a class."[129]

This is particularly evident in provisions on the law concerning illegally obtained
evidence. The only protection that the Constitution provides is against compelling self-incrimination,[130] and despite this bar, the Supreme Court has interpreted
these provisions to allow various forms of evidence that do not constitute active
disclosures.[131] This reading allows the executive to engage in surveillance without
checks or safeguards to obtain admissible evidence; for example, methods such as
phone tapping or using illegally obtained evidence to secure convictions have received judicial ratification.[132] Until a recent Supreme Court decision in 2020, legislation governing narcotic drugs and related offenses allowed the admission of
confessions made to police officers as well—an otherwise prohibited act that had
been permitted through the use of a legal fiction that allowed police officers to be
treated as government officials for that law's purposes.[133] The ratification of surveillance to obtain evidence, and the guarantee that such evidence will be admissible,
however obtained, have been exacerbated by the simultaneous expansion of surveillance, coupled with the absence of privacy legislation in India. The Constitution
does not guarantee the right to privacy, and although the Court has read Article
21's protection of life and liberty to recognize that such a right exists,[134] the failure
of the Court to enforce it against the state renders this recognition largely symbolic.
Indeed, the Court's ruling has been that privacy must be weighed against the public
interest.[135]

In addition to procedural rights, all fundamental rights in Part III of the
Constitution are subject to textual exceptions. These generally refer to the per-
missibility of reasonable restrictions to secure "public order," "the security of the
state," and "the interests of the general public."[136] The Supreme Court interprets
"reasonableness" in this context to restrain the state from overreaching its powers,
particularly when the legislature has lapsed and left legal provisions open to misuse
without adequate provisions to safeguard the exercises of power.[137] The Supreme
Court's rulings on internal security do lend some credence to the view that their
engagement with judicial review is not so much an exercise in interpretation as it is
an exercise in political negotiation.[138]

Unconstitutionality

The Court has been historically reluctant to declare laws unconstitutional, prefer-
ring, wherever possible, to "read them down" by interpreting them in line with the

Constitution. In the case of anti-terror legislation, the Court has notably failed in enforcing constitutional principles and declined to grant effective relief or enforcement, which simultaneously reiterates the rhetoric of rights. The Court tends to defer to the legislature, ruling in *AK Gopalan v. State of Madras*[139] that Parliament did not have to indicate the specific need the preventive detention legislation was addressing, and that an invocation of the constitutional text authorizing preventive detention laws was sufficient.[140]

In *Kartar Singh v. Union of India*, the Supreme Court first established a warning on the dangers of disturbing substantive due process by allowing confessions to police officers, but then went on to allow it, upholding provisions of the Terrorist and Disruptive Activities (Prevention) Act 1986.[141] As Chandrachud has pointed out, the Court's decision was "heavily influenced by the desire to avoid striking down a statutory provision that was conceived as an essential part of the national security apparatus and which the government asserted as being crucial in dealing with the challenges of the time."[142] Even as the Court in *Kartar Singh* noted that the Act lent itself in practice to "sheer misuse and abuse" by the police, it was reluctant to strike it down entirely.[143] The limitations of judicial logic on the unconstitutionality of national security laws were also evident when the Armed Forces (Special Powers) Act 1956 was challenged in the Supreme Court. A bench of five judges upheld the constitutionality of the law, despite finding that they needed to endorse the need for compensating abuses, as well as adopting a list of "dos and don'ts" that was submitted by the attorney general for the armed forces to follow in exercising extraordinary powers of arrest, detention, and force.[144]

The deference granted to the invocation of Article 352 is particularly notable in the case of *Makhan Singh Tarsikka*, when Justice Gajendragadkar refused to intervene in examining the constitutionality of the Defence of India Act during the proclamation of an emergency. The Court, in Gajendragadkar's opinion, was not a true anti-majoritarian institution; that was a political function, best discharged by "the existence of an enlightened, vigilant, and vocal public opinion."[145] In *ADM Jabalpur v. Shivakant Shukla*[146] the Court infamously ruled that writ petitions for habeas corpus could not be moved during the declaration of an emergency. Even though the ruling in *ADM Jabalpur* has been declared by the Supreme Court to no longer be good law, the issue of the justiciability of Emergency Proclamations continues to be undecided.[147]

Article 352 has since remained unexercised; however, the Court's failure to express in clear terms the impact of judicial review over detention orders in an emergency implies that future threats to national security are to be addressed through unclear law.[148] The Court has refused to articulate standards on which such declarations of emergency may be reviewed, while continuing to affirm their power to review such declarations. The minority in *S.R. Bommai* described these standards as impossible to articulate, with Justice Verma stating that "judicial scrutiny of the same is not permissible for want of judicially manageable standards."[149]

Even though the majority disagreed, they failed to articulate "judicially manageable standards," noting that they could examine the material basis on which a proclamation of emergency had been declared, but that "it would be more appropriate to deal with concrete cases as and when they arise."[150] The point of consensus in *Bommai* was that proclamations could be issued to prevent state governments from violating the Constitution's "basic structure"—a term articulated but, once again, not defined by the Court.[151]

The effect of *Bommai* and the Court's subsequent interpretations places political conflicts, such as hung assemblies, on the same footing as internal security threats, and allows intervention on both grounds. In sum, judicial decisions on unconstitutionality, whether they refer to amendments to the Constitution, national security laws, or executive action, combine the rhetoric of rights protection while actively working to safeguard state power.

Remedies and Reforms

The citizen's chief remedy against state action in India is in the form of writ petitions filed under Articles 226 and 32, to the High Courts or the Supreme Court, respectively. These petitions allow the citizen to ask these courts to enforce fundamental rights and seek, in remedy, directions that constrain state action. Dr. B. R. Ambedkar described Article 32 as the "very soul of the Constitution."[152] Removing this provision in the Constitution, Ambedkar argued, could only be done by a constitutional amendment, and accordingly, "we need not therefore have much apprehension that the freedoms which this Constitution has provided will be taken away by any legislature merely because it happens to have a majority."[153] A short, ill-fated attempt to amend the right to remedies occurred during the Emergency, but was thereafter undone by the Supreme Court's articulation of the basic structure in *Kesavananda Bharati*, rendering the writ remedy to be unamendable going forward.[154]

Internal security laws that allow relaxation in criminal procedure and enhance the state's powers to detain and interrogate persons indicate more urgently the need for these writ remedies. The common law writ of habeas corpus, requiring the state to produce a person before a court so that their well-being and safety (and indeed, life) may be established, acts as an immediately available check on the potential abuses of these relaxations, such as indefinite detentions or custodial violence and torture. The overruling of an emergency-era judgment in which the Supreme Court failed to enforce this light was lauded in 2017 as having undone a historical wrong;[155] the majority described the enforcement of the writ of habeas corpus as essential to the survival of democracy. Despite this, in 2020, the Supreme Court was lax in hearing and deciding habeas corpus petitions, leaving citizens, and particularly, political dissidents, without remedy for the breach of their fundamental rights. Writ petitions filed in 2019 are still being heard without any immediate remedies, with the Court, on at least two occasions, dispensing with such petitions by directing the petitioner to go visit the detained person instead of having them produced before the Court, as the law requires.[156] In cases such as these, the failure of the Court to treat an immediate remedy as urgent can effectively result in defeating the purpose of the remedy itself, allowing the state to exercise wider powers of detention and custodial interrogation than the Constitution would allow.

In prioritizing public order claims over individual liberties, the Court has adopted strategies of innovating remedies instead of enforcing fundamental rights. Lapses in procedural protections by police forces have not resulted in rulings on enforcing these existing laws. In 2008, a question about whether the police are required to mandatorily file a First Information Report on complaints (thus triggering the criminal process under law) was raised in the Supreme Court, and remained pending until a ruling in 2013. The 2013 ruling by five judges in *Lalita Kumari v. Govt. of U.P.*[157] found that the registration of the report was mandatory in such cases, and issued a set of guidelines for the police, demanding that they complete a preliminary inquiry in seven days and file a FIR if needed. Although this is laudable in intention, the guidelines were issued without reference or consideration for research on police procedure, and had to be promptly modified on request from the police, who argued that seven days might not be sufficient.[158] The Supreme Court, however, has also recognized in a number of cases that there have been instances of lapses and abuses by police officers,[159] and has on occasion ordered compensation to be granted to those affected.[160] This remedy derives from the public exchequer, as the Supreme Court is willing to grant remedies but not enforce punitive measures. Consequently, they neither prevent the original offense nor penalize the offender.

In addition to remedies, the Court has also engaged in projects of reform. While still refusing to strike down the AFSPA for unconstitutionality, the Court was willing to adopt a set of guidelines proposed by the Government of India, constituting "dos and don'ts" for the armed forces to follow in disturbed areas. These guidelines were subsequently cited by the Government of India as adequate protection against abuses in a case where a court-monitored investigation found that security forces had been responsible for custodial deaths of at least seven persons in Manipur, where AFSPA was in force.[161] Once again, the order in this case was for compensation, as military officers are exempted from standing trial in civil courts, and instead must face court-martials at the military's discretion instead.[162] Despite years of documented abuse by armed forces under AFSPA, there has only been one disclosed instance of a court-martial, in a case involving a faked "encounter" in Machil, Kashmir, where six Army personnel were sentenced to life imprisonment for the deaths of three civilians.[163] The sentence was awarded in 2015, and then suspended by an Armed Forces Tribunal in 2017.[164]

The Court's biggest project of legislation in the field of national security has been in the case of *Prakash Singh v. Union of India*, in which a retired police officer approached the Supreme Court seeking structural reform in Indian police forces to decrease corruption and increase accountability. The Court, in ongoing litigation, has directed states to constitute local Police Complaints Authorities, limit politically controlled transfers of personnel, and increase checks on abuse of police powers. Like the executive foundations of the CBI, these judicially created bodies often misdirect attention to concerns that do not strike at the heart of issues emerging in the functioning of the police.[165] A limited survey suggests that local complaint authorities, when constituted, can be productive;[166] however, the majority of states have not complied with these directions altogether.[167] These acts of judicial legislation, and the consequent injustices that they have allowed to flourish, demonstrate accurately the limits of the Court's approach to national security and civil liberties. With their focus on public interest litigation and legislative reform, and their simultaneous neglect of precedent and procedure, the Court increasingly treats cases as though they occur in vacuums, and not as part of a continuing pattern of executive expansion, enabled by their own jurisprudence.

Conclusion

During the drafting of the Indian Constitution, amid an animated debate on provisions concerning the qualifications of members to legislature, the incensed Lakshmi Kant Maitra, representing Nabadwip in West Bengal, turned his ire on the Drafting Committee. "Your practice has been that whenever there has been any difficulty," he said, "you pass it on to the future Parliament; you offer no solution."[168] He was accused of allowing his "temper to outrun his discretion,"[169] but his words proved prescient, not specifically to the subject of legislative qualifications, but to the Drafting Committee's faith in future legislators to resolve the conflicts that they could not.

The relegation of thorny constitutional questions to future Parliaments to resolve was not an unreasonable decision. Scholars like Hanna Lerner have argued that the deferral of such questions to the future is valuable; "constitutional flexibility" expands the range of options available to political leaders and therefore allows time for the creation of consensus, instead of imposing a majoritarian view on a burgeoning republic.[170] The Indian model of constitutionalism rests heavily on mechanisms that are predicated on the founders' faith in the republic to negotiate and arrive at a solution that remains true to the principles they established. In practice, this requires a parliament that engages with the law it is framing, an executive that carefully exercises the powers that it is given, and a court that limits arbitrariness and abuse.

The Indian Constitution is, despite all deferrals to the legislature, one of the longest in the world, containing granular detail on the ordinary functioning of the state. This curious dichotomy is apparent from Ambedkar's vision of constitutional morality, which was rooted in a detail-rich constitution, resting on the premise that "it is perfectly possible to pervert the Constitution, without changing its form by merely changing the form of the administration.... In these circumstances it is wiser not to trust the Legislature to prescribe forms of administration. This is the justification for incorporating them in the Constitution."[171] The continued tension between these complex politics of deferral and detail were intended to be resolved by parliamentary legislation and judicial interpretation, and as this chapter demonstrates, was especially so in the case of questions of national security.

In current practice, the Indian Parliament's abdication of its responsibilities, coupled with the executive's expansionist tendencies, has placed immense pressure on the Court to carry forward its precolonial legacy of aggressively protecting liberties and acting as a counter-majoritarian institution. The Court has, of late, increasingly stumbled on this responsibility, leading commentators to describe it as "executive-minded,"[172] in its tendency to resolve constitutional questions in favor of expanding government power. With the notable exception of the articulation of basic structure, the Court has tended toward permissive deference on issues of national security, failing to enforce fundamental rights, and often deciding these questions on limited and secret evidence handed over the bar in a sealed envelope to the judges by government lawyers.[173] In December 2020, the Supreme Court came under criticism for expediting and granting bail to a controversial and famous news anchor, while denying and not hearing bail petitions filed by other citizens accused of crimes. "Every case is different," said the chief justice in response to an argument that the rule of bail ought to be applied consistently across cases.[174] This approach allows the Court to treat both, precedent and procedure, as flexible references instead of binding norms, and gives them room to provide the executive with the latitude it needs to operate without judicial oversight. This deferral to executive concerns is not by any means a new conundrum, but an exacerbation of existing tendencies in independent India.

Internal security in India operates in fields of legal exceptionality; its location in the interstices of the constitutional framework result in security institutions that function outside the framework of the law, resting on colonial inheritances and hastily enacted laws, easily lending itself to political manipulation. Scholarship in India increasingly advocates the indigenous roots of Indian democracy, arguing against an existing school of thought that suggests the lingering presence of colonial institutions and practices lays down an authoritarian foundation for the Indian Constitution.[175] While this may be true in understanding the underlying principles represent constitutional consensus, most concede that the process of constitutional dialogue that established this consensus left several conflicts unresolved, particularly on security.[176] Dr. Sachchidananda Sinha, acting as the chairman of the Constituent Assembly, addressed the drafters as their deliberations began, speaking of the temporality of their work. "The Constitution that you are going to plan," he said, must be "reared for immortality . . . a structure of adamantine strength, which will outlast and overcome all present and future destructive forces."[177] Within the rhetoric was also a sense of the practical: he went on to say, "reasonable agreements and judicious compromises are nowhere more called for than in framing a Constitution for a country like India."[178] These reasonable agreements and judicious compromises have until now ceded the liberties of the individual to the concerns of public order and national security; going forward, a better balance requires not just constitutional commitments from the Supreme Court, but an active legislature, and a sturdy federal framework to check the excesses of the executive.

Notes

1. Edmund Burke, *On Conciliation with America* (1775), quoted by B. R. Ambedkar in Lok Sabha, Parliament of India, *Constituent Assembly of India Debates*, vol. I (17 December 1946), 1.7.29, http://164.100.47.194/Loksabhahindi/cadebatefiles/cadebates.html.

2. The term "fundamental rights" refers specifically to a list of rights enumerated in Part III of the Indian Constitution. These rights are enforceable through judicial writs, against the state. Constitution of India 1950, Part III, Articles 12–32.

3. *Constituent Assembly Debates*, vol. IX (August 20, 1949), 9.120.114.

4. *Constituent Assembly Debates*, vol. IX (August 20, 1949), 9.120.121.

5. See M. R. Madhavan, "Parliament," in *Rethinking Public Institutions in India*, ed. Devesh Kapur, Pratap Bhanu Mehta, and Milan Vaishnav (New Delhi: Oxford University Press, 2017).

6. See Vrinda Bhandari and Karan Lahiri, "The Surveillance State, Privacy and Criminal Investigation in India: Possible Futures in a Post-Puttaswamy World," *University of Oxford Human Rights Hub Journal* 3, no. 2 (2020): 15–46, https://ohrh.law.ox.ac.uk/wp-content/uploads/2021/04/U-of-OxHRH-J-The-Surveillance-State-Privacy-and-Criminal-Investigation-1-1.pdf; Rohit De, "Constitutional Antecedents," in *The Oxford Handbook of the Indian Constitution*, ed. Sujit Choudhury, Madhav Khosla, and Pratap Bhanu Mehta (Oxford: Oxford University Press, 2016), 17, 23; Mithi Mukherjee, *India in the Shadows of Empire: A Legal and Political History, 1774–1950* (New Delhi: Oxford University Press, 2010).

7. *Constituent Assembly Debates*, vol. IX (August 20, 1949), 9.120.122.

8. See Aparna Chandra and Mrinal Satish, "Criminal Law and the Constitution," in *Oxford Handbook of the Indian Constitution*, ed. Sujit Choudhury, Madhav Khosla and Pratap Bhanu Mehta (Oxford: Oxford University Press, 2016), 794, 795.

9. See Ujjwal Kumar Singh, *The State, Democracy and Anti-Terror Laws in India* (Los Angeles: Sage Publications, 2007).

10. *Constituent Assembly Debates*, vol. VIII (June 13, 1949), 8.103.2 *et seq*. This later became Schedule VII in the Constitution of India 1950.

11. Constitution of India, 1950, Article 254, 248.

12. Constitution of India, 1950, Article 253.

13. Constitution of India, 1950, Article 249.

14. *Constituent Assembly Debates*, vol. VIII (June 13, 1949), 8.103.67.

15. *Constituent Assembly Debates*, vol. VIII (June 13, 1949), 8.103.78.

16. *Constituent Assembly Debates*, vol. VIII (June 13, 1949), 8.103.62, 8.103.68.

17. *Constituent Assembly Debates*, vol. VIII (June 13, 1949), 8.103.69.

18. *Constituent Assembly Debates*, vol. VIII (June 13, 1949), 8.103.70.

19. *Constituent Assembly Debates*, vol. VIII (June 13, 1949), 8.103.68.

20. Constitution of India 1950, schedule VII, list 1, entry 2, 2A and list II, entry 1–2.

21. Constitution of India 1950, Article 355.

22. *Constituent Assembly Debates*, vol. IX (September 1, 1949), 9.129.371.

23. *Constituent Assembly Debates*, vol. IX (September 1, 1949), para 9.129.371.

24. Government of India, Inter-State Council, "Report of the Sarkaria Commission" (1988) 7.7.10, http://interstatecouncil.nic.in/wp-content/uploads/2015/06/CHAPTERVII.pdf.

25. Inter-State Council, "Report of the Sarkaria Commission," 7.7.11–14.

26. Inter-State Council, "Report of the Sarkaria Commission," 7.7.11–14.

27. Inter-State Council, "Report of the Sarkaria Commission," 7.7.18.

28. Inter-State Council, "Report of the Sarkaria Commission," 7.7.20.

29. Inter-State Council, "Report of the Sarkaria Commission," 7.2.01–05.

30. Constitution of India 1950, Article 131.

31. Inter-State Council, "Report of the Sarkaria Commission," 7.2.01–05.

32. Inter-State Council, "Report of the Sarkaria Commission," 7.2.07–08.

33. Inter-State Council, "Report of the Sarkaria Commission," 7.2.09.

34. Inter-State Council, "Report of the Sarkaria Commission," 7.3.12.

35. *Union of India v. V. Sriharan* (2016), 7 SCC 1, para. 173.13 (Supreme Court of India). The Supreme Court held that the use of the Central Bureau of Investigation to examine certain offences was warranted, under Article 355, and therefore did not constitute an interference with state powers in the federal scheme.

36. *Naga People's Movement of Human Rights v. Union of India* (1998), 2 SCC 109 (Supreme Court of India).

37. *Sarbananda Sonowal v. Union of India* (2005), 5 SCC 655 (Supreme Court of India).

38. See Jaideep Reddy, "Duty of the Union under Article 355 of the Constitution: Remembering the Constitutional Ideal of Co-operative Federalism," *National University of Juridical Sciences Law Review* 4 (2011): 371.

39. *S. R. Bommai v. Union of India* (1994), 3 SCC 1, para. 57 (Supreme Court of India, per Justice Sawant for himself and Justice Kuldip Singh); para 272 (Justice Jeevan Reddy for himself and Justice Agrawal).

40. Ruma Pal, "Separation of Powers," in *The Oxford Handbook of the Indian Constitution*, ed. Sujit Choudhury, Madhav Khosla, and Pratap Bhanu Mehta, (Oxford: Oxford University Press, 2016), 253, 258.

41. *Constituent Assembly Debates*, vol. IX (July 30, 1949), 9.107.172.

42. *Constituent Assembly Debates*, vol. IX (July 30, 1949), 9.107.172.

43. M. R. Madhavan, "Parliament," 68.

44. *Constituent Assembly Debates*, vol. IX (September 15, 1949), 9.141.70.

45. *Constituent Assembly Debates*, vol. IX (September 15, 1949), 9.141.65 (per Pandit Thakur Dass Bhargava).

46. Constitution of India 1950, Article 22 provides protections to person arrested, but states in clause (3) that these protections will not apply to "enemy aliens" or "to any person who is arrested or detained under any law providing for preventive detention."

47. *Constituent Assembly Debates*, vol. IX (September 15, 1949), 9.141.91.

48. Constitution of India 1950, schedule VII, list I, entry 9; list III, entry 3.

49. Constitution of India 1950, Article 22(7).

50. Granville Austin, *The Indian Experience: Working a Democratic Constitution* (New Delhi: Oxford University Press, 1999), 56.

51. *A.K. Gopalan v. State of Madras* (1950), 1 S.C.R 88 (Supreme Court of India).

52. Austin, *The Indian Experience*, 62–68.

53. P. K. Tripathi, "Preventive Detention: The Indian Experience," *The American Journal of Comparative Law* 9, no. 2 (1960): 219, 222.

54. *Kartar Singh v. State of Punjab* (1994), 3 S.C.C 569 (Supreme Court of India).

55. Poulomi Banerjee, "Setting the Nation to Rights: From Prison Reforms to Refugee Rights, 25 Years of the NHRC," *Hindustan Times*, March 25, 2018, https://www.hindustantimes.com/india-news/setting-the-nation-to-rights-from-prison-reforms-to-refugee-rights-25-years-of-the-national-human-rights-commission/story-5HVKRPHa4OIMOvopkaMJLJ.html.

56. Singh, *The State, Democracy and Anti-Terror Laws in India*, 296.

57. Singh, *The State, Democracy and Anti-Terror Laws in India*, 294–295, 297.
58. Anil Kalhan, Gerald P. Conroy, Mamta Kaushal, Sam Scott Miller, and Jed S. Rakoff, "Colonial Continuities: Human Rights, Terrorism, and Security Laws in India," *Columbia Journal of Asian Law* 20 (2006): 93, 153.
59. *Indra Das v. State of Assam* (2011), 4 S.C.R. 289 (Supreme Court of India); Arun Ferreira and Vernon Gonsalves, "Fifty Years of Unreasonable Restrictions under the Unlawful Activities Act," *The Wire*, March 9, 2017, https://thewire.in/rights/uapa-anti-terrorism-laws.
60. See Mayur Suresh, "The Slow Erosion of Fundamental Rights: How *Romila Thapar v. Union of India* Highlights What Is Wrong with the UAPA," *Indian Law Review* 3, no. 2 (2019): 212–223.
61. M. R. Madhavan, "Parliament," 83.
62. M. R. Madhavan, "Parliament," 83.
63. See Nitika Khaitan, "New UAPA: Absolute Power to State," *Frontline*, October 25, 2019, https://frontline.thehindu.com/cover-story/article29618049.ece.
64. See Abhinav Sekhri, "Article 22—Calling Time on Preventive Detention," *Indian Journal of Constitutional Law* 9 (2020): 173 (arguing that Article 22 as well as Schedule VII authorizations for preventive detention legislation should be repealed).
65. Rahul Sagar, "Emergency Powers," in *The Oxford Handbook of the Indian Constitution*, ed. Sujit Choudhury, Madhav Khosla, and Pratap Bhanu Mehta (Oxford: Oxford University Press, 2016), 213, 224.
66. Constitution of India, 1950, Article 75.
67. *Ram Jawaya Kapur v. Union of India*, A.I.R 1955 S.C. 549 (Supreme Court of India).
68. Constitution of India, 1950, Article 73. See also Shubhankar Dam, "The Executive," in *The Oxford Handbook of the Indian Constitution*, ed. Sujit Choudhury, Madhav Khosla, and Pratap Bhanu Mehta (Oxford: Oxford University Press, 2016), 307, 321–322.
69. Constitution of India, 1950, Article 50.
70. Ruma Pal, "Separation of Powers," 255.
71. Ruma Pal, "Separation of Powers," 255. Pal argues that the Constituent Assembly saw the legislature and executive as irretrievably intertwined and accordingly focused their concerns on separating the judiciary from the executive, alone.
72. Constitution of India, 1950, Article 356.
73. Rahul Sagar, "Emergency Powers," 216; Gopal Subramaniam, "Emergency Provisions under the Indian Constitution," in *Supreme but Not Infallible: Essays in Honour of the Supreme Court of India*, ed. B. N. Kirpal et al. (New Delhi: Oxford University Press, 2000), 134.
74. Rahul Sagar, "Emergency Powers," 216.
75. Rahul Sagar, "Emergency Powers," 225.
76. "Inter-State Council, "Report of the Sarkaria Commission," 7.5.03
77. Armed Forces (Special Powers) Act, 1956, sections 4, 5, and 6; Constitution of India, 1950, Article 355.
78. Government of India, "Report of the Committee, Headed by Justice (Retd) B.P. Jeevan Reddy, to Review the Armed Forces (Special Powers) Act 1958" (2005), 6–7, 20–22.
79. Code of Criminal Procedure, 1973, sections 130, 131.
80. Anubha Bhonsle, "The Persistence of the AFSPA," in this volume.
81. Armed Forces (Special Powers) Act, 1958, section 3.
82. Austin, *The Indian Experience*, 55.
83. See Shylashri Shankar, *Scaling Justice: India's Supreme Court, Anti-Terror Laws and Social Rights* (New Delhi: Oxford University Press, 2009); Ujjwal Kumar Singh, *The State, Democracy and Anti-Terror Laws in India*.
84. Constitution of India, 1950, Article 123.
85. Constitution of India, 1950, Article 213.
86. Shubhankar Dam, *Presidential Legislation in India* (Cambridge: Cambridge University Press, 2014), 4.
87. Ibid.

88. Constitution of India 1950, Article 123, 213; Sujoy Chatterjee, "*Krishna Kumar II*: Laying Re-promulgations to Rest?" *Indian Law Review* 1, no. 3 (2017): 327.
89. Dam, *Presidential Legislation in India*, 5.
90. Dam, *Presidential Legislation in India*, 9.
91. See Kalhan et al., "Colonial Continuities"; Singh, *The State, Democracy and Anti-Terror Laws in India*.
92. Dam, *Presidential Legislation in India*, 7.
93. "Report of the Committee, Headed by Justice (Retd) B. P. Jeevan Reddy, to Review the Armed Forces (Special Powers) Act 1958."
94. Manu Sebastian, "When Lapsed Bills Resurrect as Ordinances," *LiveLaw*, March 5, 2019, https://www.livelaw.in/columns/when-lapsed-bills-resurrect-as-ordinances-143329.
95. K. N. Chaturvedi, "Dangerous Trends in Law Making in India," *Statute Law Review* 39, no. 1 (2018): 63.
96. Aadhar (Targeted Delivery of Financial and Other Subsidies, Benefits and Services) Act 2016, section 33(2).
97. *Justice K. Puttaswamy v. Union of India* (2019) 1 S.C.C. 1
98. See Kalhan et al., "Colonial Continuities," 147.
99. Manish Sahu, "In Uttar Pradesh, More than Half of NSA Arrests This Year Were for Cow Slaughter," *Indian Express*, September 11, 2020, https://indianexpress.com/article/india/in-uttar-pradesh-more-than-half-of-nsa-arrests-this-year-were-for-cow-slaughter-6591315/.
100. David H. Bayley, "The Police and Political Order in India," *Asian Survey* 23, no. 4 (1983): 484, 488.
101. Arvind Verma, "The Police in India: Design, Performance, and Adaptability," in *Rethinking Public Institutions in India*, ed. Devesh Kapur and Pratap Bhanu Mehta (New Delhi: Oxford University Press, 2005), 194, 204–205.
102. Arvind Verma, "The Police in India," 211–213.
103. National Investigation Agency Act 2008, Schedule.
104. National Investigation Agency Act 2019, Schedule.
105. K. S. Subramanian, "Central Bureau of Investigation: Crisis of Legitimacy, Credibility, and Accountability," *Economic and Political Weekly* 49, no. 51 (2014): 13; Constitution of India, 1950, schedule VII, list I, entry 8.
106. Delhi Special Police Establishment Act, 1946.
107. Manish Tewari, "Is CBI a Legal Entity," *Deccan Chronicle*, October 28, 2018, https://www.deccanchronicle.com/opinion/columnists/281018/is-cbi-a-legal-entity.html.
108. PTI, "Rajasthan Withdraws General Consent for CBI amid Political Crisis," *The Times of India*, July 20, 2020, https://timesofindia.indiatimes.com/india/rajasthan-govt-withdraws-general-consent-for-cbi-investigation-amid-political-crisis/articleshow/77072258.cms.
109. A Supreme Court order concerning the summary suspension of the CBI director in 2018 failed to clarify the institutional process for appointments, and investigation of claims of corruption against CBI officers, leading the Opposition and several commentators to publicly question the independence of the CBI as well as the Supreme Court's exercise of jurisdiction. See Pratap Bhanu Mehta, "The Biggest Casualty in the Alok Verma Affair Has Been the SC's Authority," *Indian Express*, January 12, 2019, https://indianexpress.com/article/opinion/columns/tragedy-after-farce-alok-verma-cbi-director-removed-fired-supreme-court-modi-panel-5534312/; Sandeep Phukan and Devesh K. Pandey, "Prime-Minister Led Panel Removes Alok Verma as CBI Director, Rao Back in Charge," *The Hindu*, January 10, 2019, https://www.thehindu.com/news/national/narendra-modi-led-panel-removes-alok-verma-as-cbi-director/article25960822.ece.
110. *Kanwal Tanuj v. State of Bihar* (2020), S.C.C. Online S.C. 395 (Supreme Court of India).
111. The Protection of Human Rights Ordinance 1993 was substituted by the Protection of Human Rights Act 1993. See, on this, Dam, *Presidential Legislation in India*, 84.
112. *Prakash Singh v. Union of India* (2006), 8 S.C.C. 1, paras 32–33.

113. K. S. Subramanian, "Central Bureau of Investigation."

114. "10 Agencies Can Now Snoop on 'Any' Computer They Want," *Economic Times*, December 21, 2018, https://economictimes.indiatimes.com/news/politics-and-nation/10-central-agenc ies-can-now-snoop-on-any-computer-they-want/articleshow/67188875.cms?from=mdr.

115. Ibid.

116. Bhandari and Lahiri, "The Surveillance State, Privacy and Criminal Investigation in India," 46.

117. Ibid.

118. Karan Manral, "Right to Privacy: Delhi High Court Seeks Centre's Stand on PIL against Surveillance Systems," *Hindustan Times*, December 2, 2020, https://www.hindustantimes. com/india-news/right-to-privacy-delhi-high-court-seeks-centre-s-stand-on-pil-against-surveillance-systems/story-6Pcitq50ppYBgfrRgEUAmO.html.

119. See, e.g., *Maneka Gandhi v. Union of India* (1978), in which the Court heard a challenge to the Passports Act as well as an order passed under that Act.

120. See Chandra and Satish, "Criminal Law and the Constitution," 795.

121. Constitution of India, 1950, Article 21.

122. Manoj Mate, "The Origins of Due Process in India: The Role of Borrowing in Personal Liberty and Preventive Detention Cases," *Berkeley Journal of International Law* 28, no. 1 (2010): 216–260.

123. See, generally, Abhinav Chandrachud, "Due Process," in *The Oxford Handbook of the Indian Constitution*, ed. Sujit Choudhury, Madhav Khosla, and Pratap Bhanu Mehta (Oxford: Oxford University Press, 2016), 777; Anup Surendranath, "Life and Personal Liberty," in *The Oxford Handbook of the Indian Constitution*, ed. Sujit Choudhury, Madhav Khosla, and Pratap Bhanu Mehta (Oxford: Oxford University Press, 2016), 756.

124. Constitution of India, 1950, Articles 20–22.

125. P. K. Tripathi, "Preventive Detention: The Indian Experience," 220.

126. P. K. Tripathi, "Preventive Detention: The Indian Experience," 221.

127. *Maneka Gandhi v. Union of India* (1978) See also Raeesa Vakil, "Constitutionalizing Administrative Law in the Indian Supreme Court: Natural Justice and Fundamental Rights," *International Journal of Constitutional Law* 16, no. 2 (2018): 475, on *Maneka Gandhi*'s holding regarding procedural justice.

128. Aparna Chandra and Mrinal Satish, "Criminal Law and the Constitution," 806.

129. Aparna Chandra and Mrinal Satish, "Criminal Law and the Constitution," 813.

130. Constitution of India, 1950, Article 20(3).

131. The definitive case in this regard is *State of Bombay v. Kathi Kalu Oghad*, A.I.R 1961 S.C. 1808 (Supreme Court of India), but see also *Yusufalli Nagree v. State of Maharashtra*, A.I.R 1968 S.C. 147 (Supreme Court of India, holding that secretly recorded phone conversations are admissible against an accused); *Ritesh Kumar v. State of Uttar Pradesh*, A.I.R 2013 S.C. 1132 (Supreme Court of India, allowing the police to direct an accused person to provide a sample voice recording). See, on *Kathi Kalu Oghad*, Abhinav Sekhri, "The Right against Self-Incrimination in India: The Compelling Case of Kathi Kalu Oghad," *Indian Law Review* 3, no. 2 (2019): 180–211.

132. *State of Madhya Pradesh v. Mallah* (2005), 3 S.C.C. 169 (Supreme Court of India, holding that evidence obtained during an unlawful search can be admitted against an accused).

133. *Tofan Singh v. State of Tamil Nadu*, Criminal Appeal 153/2013, Supreme Court of India (October 29, 2020); Samanwaya Rautray, "Supreme Court Says Right to Privacy Will Apply to Accused Charged under NDPS," *Economic Times*, October 29, 2020, https://economicti mes.indiatimes.com/news/politics-and-nation/supreme-court-says-right-to-privacy-will-apply-to-accused-charged-under-ndps/articleshow/78935664.cms.

134. *Justice K. Puttaswamy v. Union of India* (2017), 10 S.C.C. 1 (Supreme Court of India).

135. *Govind v. State of Madhya Pradesh* (1975), 2 S.C.C 148 (Supreme Court of India).

136. Constitution of India, 1950, Articles 19(2) to 19(6).

137. See Lawrence Liang, "Freedom of Speech and Express," in *The Oxford Handbook of the Indian Constitution*, ed. Sujit Choudhury, Madhav Khosla, and Pratap Bhanu Mehta (Oxford: Oxford University Press, 2016), 814.

138. Pratap Bhanu Mehta, "The Inner Conflict of Constitutionalism," in *India's Living Constitution*, ed. Zoya Hasan, E. Sridharan, and R. Sudarshan (New Delhi: Permanent Black, 2002), 179, 188. See also Shylashri Shankar, *Scaling Justice: India's Supreme Court, Anti-Terror Laws and Social Rights* (New Delhi: Oxford University Press, 2009) (arguing that judges in such cases act as "embedded negotiators").

139. A.I.R 1950 SC 27 (Supreme Court of India).

140. Abhinav Sekhri, "Preventive Justice Part 3: An Overview of the Statutes," *Indian Constitutional Law and Philosophy* (December 31, 2016), https://indconlawphil.wordpress.com/2016/12/31/preventive-justice-part-3-an-overview-of-the-statutes/.

141. (1994) 3 S.C.C. 569 (Supreme Court of India).

142. Chintan Chandrachud, *Balanced Constitutionalism* (New Delhi: Oxford University Press, 2017), 168.

143. *Kartar Singh v. Union of India* (1994), 3 S.C.C. 569 (Supreme Court of India).

144. *Naga People's Movement v. Union of India* (1998), 2 S.C.C. 109 (Supreme Court of India).

145. *Makhan Singh Tarsikka v. State of Punjab*, AIR (1964), SC 381 (Supreme Court of India).

146. (1976) 2 S.C.C. 521 (Supreme Court of India).

147. Rahul Sagar, "Emergency Powers," 222.

148. Rahul Sagar, "Emergency Powers," 224.

149. *SR Bommai v. Union of India* (1994), 3 SCC 1, 4 (Supreme Court of India).

150. *SR Bommai v. Union of India* (1994), 219 (per Justice Jeevan Reddy and Justice Agrawal).

151. Rahul Sagar, "Emergency Powers," 230.

152. *Constituent Assembly Debates*, vol. VII (December 9, 1948), 7.70.172.

153. *Constituent Assembly Debates*, vol. VII (December 9, 1948), 7.70.173.

154. (1973) 4 S.C.C. 225 (Supreme Court of India).

155. *Justice K. Puttaswamy v. Union of India* (2017).

156. Arunabh Choudhury, "The Habeas Corpus Conundrum: The Supreme Court Must Resurrect Itself," *LiveLaw*, May 4, 2020, https://www.livelaw.in/columns/the-habeas-corpus-conundrum-the-supreme-court-must-resurrect-itself-156178.

157. A.I.R (2012) S.C. 1515 (Supreme Court of India).

158. *Lalita Kumari v. State of Uttar Pradesh*, Criminal Miscellaneous Petition 5029/2014 in Writ Petition (Criminal) 68/2008, Supreme Court of India (March 5, 2014); "Time Limit for Registering FIR Extended from 7 days to 15 Days; Supreme Court Modifies Lalita Kumari Norms," *LiveLaw*, March 8, 2014, https://www.livelaw.in/breaking-news-time-limit-registering-fir-extended-7-days-15-days-supreme-court-modifies-lalita-kumari-norms/.

159. See, e.g., *Adambhai Sulemanbhai Ajmeri & Ors v. State of Gujarat*, Criminal Appeal Nos. 2295–2296 of 2010, May 16, 2014 (the Supreme Court rebuked the Gujarat police for falsely implicating the petitioners in a terror case).

160. See, e.g., *E.E.V.F.A v. Union of India* (2016), 4 S.C.C. (Cri) 508. (I must disclose that I was legally assisting the court's counsel, the amicus curiae, in this case.)

161. *E.E.V.F.A v. Union of India* (2016).

162. There are valid critiques of the court-martial process as a viable alternative to judicial trials in India, resting particularly on the fact that there is no requirement for any of the adjudicating officers in a summary court-martial to have legal training or qualifications, even though the penalty in these proceedings may amount to a death sentence. See Nikita Doval, "Time to Court Martial the Court Martial," *Livemint*, September 9, 2015, https://www.livemint.com/Opinion/x38SVJm93ISFe41NnAgBzI/Time-to-court-martial-the-court-martial.html.

163. Mir Ehsan, "Machil Fake Encounter: For Families, Justice Brings Some Cold Comfort," *Indian Express*, September 8, 2015, https://indianexpress.com/article/india/india-others/machil-fake-encounter-for-families-justice-brings-some-cold-comfort/.

164. Parvez Imroz, "Machil and the Opaque World of the 'Court Martial,' *Indian Express*, August 1, 2017, https://indianexpress.com/article/opinion/machil-and-the-opaque-world-of-the-court-martial-4776343/.

165. Mihir Desai, "Red Herring in Police Reforms," *Economic and Political Weekly* 44, no. 10 (2009): 8.

166. Shengkuo Hu and Courtenay R Conrad, "Monitoring via the Courts: Judicial Oversight and Police Violence in India," *International Studies Quarterly* 64, no. 3 (2020): 699.

167. V. Venkatesan and Shivangi Mathew, "Police Reforms Still Only Largely on Paper," *Frontline*, August 9, 2019, https://frontline.thehindu.com/dispatches/article28960801.ece.

168. *Constitution Assembly Debates*, vol. IX (July 30, 1949), 9.107.153.

169. *Constitution Assembly Debates*, vol. IX (July 30, 1949), 9.107.150. Mr. Maitra accepted the rebuke and changed his mind, supporting an amendment that deferred the decision on qualifications to the Parliament to decide in the future.

170. Hanna Lerner, "The Indian Founding," in *The Oxford Handbook of the Indian Constitution*, ed. Sujit Choudhury, Madhav Khosla, and Pratap Bhanu Mehta (Oxford: Oxford University Press, 2016), 55, 61.

171. *Constituent Assembly Debates*, vol. VII (November 4, 1948), 7.48.229.

172. Accusations that the present Court is "executive-minded" borrow from a phrase Lord Atkins used, when he said that the Court is "more executive-minded than the executive" in *Liversidge v. Anderson* (1942), AC 243 (H.L, United Kingdom). It has been used to describe the Indian Supreme Court recently; see Alok Prasanna Kumar, "More Executive-Minded than the Executive: The Supreme Court's Role in the Implementation of the NCR," *National Law School of India Review* 31 (2019): 203; A. G. Noorani, "Judicial Strictures," *Frontline*, April 22, 2011, https://frontline.thehindu.com/the-nation/article30175139.ece.

173. See, on this increasing practice at the Supreme Court, Gautam Bhatia, "A Petty Autocracy: The Supreme Court's Evolving Jurisprudence of the Sealed Cover," *Indian Constitutional Law and Philosophy*, November 17, 2018, https://indconlawphil.wordpress.com/2018/11/17/a-petty-autocracy-the-supreme-courts-evolving-jurisprudence-of-the-sealed-cover/ ; Peter Ronald deSouza, "The Question of the Sealed Envelope," *The Hindu*, September 2, 2016, https://www.thehindu.com/opinion/lead/opinion-on-black-money-case/article6584159.ece#.

174. "Siddique Kappan Case | Kerala Union of Working Journalists to Use Arnab Goswami Case as Precedent," *The Hindu*, December 2, 2020, https://www.thehindu.com/news/national/kappan-case-sc-questions-locus-standi-of-journalists-union/article33230292.ece.

175. See, e.g., Rohit De, "Constitutional Antecedents"; Madhav Khosla, *India's Founding Moment: The Constitution of a Most Surprising Democracy* (Cambridge, MA: Harvard University Press, 2020).

176. Rohit De, "Constitutional Antecedents," 18; Hanna Lerner, "The Indian Founding," 60–61. Lerner describes this as "adopting an incrementalist approach based on creative use of constitutional language."

177. *Constituent Assembly Debates*, vol. I (9 December 1946) 1.1.24, as cited in Union of India v. V. Sriharan, (2016) 7 S.C.C. 1, para 39 (Supreme Court of India).

178. Ibid.

3

The Persistence of the AFSPA

ANUBHA BHONSLE

Introduction

It was at the first session of the Constituent Assembly of India in December 1947 that India's first defence minister, Sardar Baldev Singh, introduced the Armed Forces (Special Powers) Bill.[1] "Th[e] ordinance [giving additional powers to the armed forces] expires early in January or sometime in the middle of February and if we [Parliament] do not pass the Bill, the ordinance will lapse, and the armed forces will find themselves in a difficult position. It is for this reason that this Bill is placed before the house so that we do not have to resort to an ordinance again," he said on December 11, 1947.[2]

Singh's reasons centered on the communal riots that had broken out in Punjab, where the administration had collapsed and the police had failed to perform its duties, in some cases refusing to work. "We [the Indian government] sent a large number of troops, but the presence of troops there did not improve the situation much. It was not on account of the inadequacy of the troops, but because the troops were spread over the whole of that part of the country and under the laws then prevailing, they were not in a position to take any action," Singh said.[3]

Also on Singh's mind while moving the bill for adoption was the deteriorating situation in the United Provinces, Bengal, and Assam, where too the provincial governments had asked the Government of India to extend the provisions of this ordinance. "So, at present the position is that this ordinance is in force in four provinces of India. Under this Bill we will be taking power which will apply to the whole of India, but it will be open to the provincial governments to enforce this Bill in any way they like," he assured the house.[4]

On several occasions during the debate, Singh admitted that the bill may appear "drastic" but emphasized that it contained checks and balances: the armed forces could not use their powers under this legislation unilaterally, and the provincial government had to declare the region a disturbed area first. "Some honourable members may have a feeling that perhaps we will go on extending it beyond one

Anubha Bhonsle, *The Persistence of the AFSPA* In: *Internal Security in India*. Edited by: Amit Ahuja and Devesh Kapur, Oxford University Press. © Oxford University Press 2023. DOI: 10.1093/oso/9780197660331.003.0003 year or even later. I can assure the house that we have absolutely no such desire and it will be extended only if the communal situation does not improve," Singh had said in response to concerns and questions from members like K. Santhanam, who wanted to know: "If the Bill is so essential and inoffensive why should it be only for a year?"[5]

The vocabulary, arguments, and concerns surrounding the Armed Forces (Special Powers) Act (AFSPA) today remain strikingly similar to the fears anticipated and voiced by many of independent India's earliest lawmakers. Even in 1947, legislators were concerned that the "black bill"[6] was close to martial law. The defence minister admitted as much to the assembly when he said, "Short of martial law, this is the only alternative that we can resort to [in order to tackle communal disturbances]," to which Dr. P. S. Deshmukh responded, "This is very little short of martial law."[7]

A Permanence of the Temporary

Originally intended to be a temporary measure but now almost as old as independent India, the "very little short of martial law" bill first came into being as four different ordinances, drawing provisions from the Armed Forces Special Powers Ordinance of 1942[8] promulgated by the British to quell the Quit India Movement. In 1958, the central law, the Armed Forces (Special Powers) Act, was promulgated. It has since then been extended, used, abused, deified, and crucified in equal measure, but never repealed. The five words—Armed Forces (Special Powers) Act—are rarely used in the expanded form. The acronym AFSPA often stands for a "state of exception" that allows sweeping powers in "disturbed areas." These powers can go from search, seizure, and arrest, to the right to shoot to kill and conduct operations.

How can a law, virtually in continuous existence since 1958 in large parts of the country, be described as an "exception"?[9] Just as how can states with democratically elected governments and operational institutions be designated as disturbed areas for years on end? A conversation about AFSPA can invoke a stiffening of posture among Army men and a sense of despair among those who live under it. The chasm between those who see the act as holding drastic, unbridled powers that make a mockery of individual rights and dignity and those convinced that the powers are essential, moral, and have not been unnecessarily used has only hardened with time. In between lies the economy of AFSPA that has thrived even as insurgencies have reduced, violence has decreased, and ceasefires have tenuously held.

In this chapter, I explore how AFSPA is imposed and withdrawn, and the circumstances that lead up to both. I attempt to map the internal security challenges that lead to the deployment of the Army in areas, the role of the civilian government in asking, allowing boots on the ground and their return to barracks. The AFSPA is a small, compact law with just seven sections. The precursor to invoking the AFSPA is a powerful notification, the Disturbed Areas Act (DAA) 1976. I attempt to unpack how and why the DAA is extended without much contention or debate, and who out of the Center and states holds the cards.

As outlined in a chapter in this volume by Amit Ahuja and Srinath Raghavan, domestic roles for the military are ordered and monitored by civilian leaders. They are not autonomous choices of the armed forces, but militaries are not entirely without agency in this decision. I explore this argument in the context of AFSPA and the deployment of the military in the erstwhile state of Jammu and Kashmir, Manipur, and Nagaland where levels of violence, counterinsurgency operations, peace agreements, and demand for armed forces by civilian authorities have varied at different times, but what has remained more or less constant is the AFSPA.

The question that follows is, has the AFSPA been effective and allowed the armed forces to wipe out insurgencies, or at least bring down violence to a level that allows other institutions to play their role and govern effectively? The answer is both yes and no. The Army's counterinsurgency record can be considered a successful one. Insurgencies have been reversed in states, but that has not been on account of the AFSPA alone. Ground situations have changed considerably many times over, but that has not necessarily led to the Army's exit. I explore why that is so. In some insurgency-affected regions it is the political leadership that has shirked its responsibility of steering a political solution. In others, the armed forces have taken on a wider sphere of responsibilities deepening their role and influence in governance. In still others, it is an ironic interplay where nearly everyone benefits from a long, stretched insurgency where there is neither war nor peace, the enemy has not been defeated but neither has it run away, where the AFSPA feeds insurgents and vice versa, and a state of emergency is the rule, not the exception.[10]

Chapter 1 (by Amit Ahuja and Devesh Kapur) and Chapter 8 (by Amit Ahuja and Srinath Raghavan) explore how a prolonged deployment of the Army—enabled by AFSPA—can distort the choice of strategy in counterinsurgency operations, mar the professionalism of the forces, and undermine the local police and law enforcement agencies. I join the dots to see how this overarching presence lasting decades—enabled by the AFSPA—impacts the local population that is living under the shadow of the gun. Eventually all that is left is the gun, and generations live under its nozzle. The legitimacy that a man in uniform hopes to command can be slowly dented. Ahuja and Raghavan argue that a small percentage of the country's population has been subjected to military operations. Had this footprint been more expansive, public trust in the military would have been the casualty.

I rely on deep background interviews with serving and retired military personnel, government officials, and ground reportage in Jammu and Kashmir, Manipur, and Nagaland to understand this persistent use of the AFSPA and the inability to consider its withdrawal in a consistent manner. Most conversations with serving military personnel veer on how the moral, legal, and quantum/method of force to be used in a counterinsurgency operation is best left to the Army. It should not be the subject of armchair moralizing. It would be impossible for the Army to discharge its duties if soldiers were to be interrogated for their actions in the line of duty, they argue. Safeguards and legal protection to effectively operate under these circumstances without fear of retribution for legitimate actions is an absolute right, they say in unison. It is hard to argue with that, but the question arises: how does the Army maintain its legal and moral authority in the conduct of counterinsurgency operations and what happens when there is a misuse? In principle, the AFSPA does not give blanket immunity. "Rogue actions" must be dealt with as per the law of the land, which includes military law. Does this happen in letter and spirit? Several officers have referred to severe repercussions on the careers of individuals caught in "rogue operations," but very little is known or made public about the precise nature of measures imposed by the military. This often brings the legitimacy of the military justice system and the sanctioning authority (the government) into question. Even after years of documented abuse under the patronage of the AFSPA, justice has rarely been seen to be done. I devote a section—Justice in the Times of the AFSPA—to understand how allegations against military men are investigated and how the Center decides to allow or deny prosecution of Army men. The former has never happened. As Raeesa Vakil argues in her chapter in this volume on "Internal Security and India's Constitution," even when matters reach the highest court of the land, laws like the AFSPA operate in the field of legal exceptionality, often allowing security institutions to function outside the framework of law and guarantees of individual dignity.

In conclusion, I examine whether the AFSPA has helped a complicated counterinsurgency environment or if its overarching powers have further polarized and traumatized every landscape it has touched. The AFSPA remains sheltered despite high-powered recommendations for its repeal and a shadow of human rights violations. Could the AFSPA ever go, either by being repealed or just by ending up being moot if its footprint decreases? Has it outlived its utility? Are many ills today hiding in the guise of the AFSPA? Even among those who argue that AFSPA must go, the dilemma often is about what would replace it. What is often missed in this is the legacy of impunity the law has hardened into the system and the mindsets of those who rule and are ruled, thus creating a different set of rules, expectations, and justice. Unless we understand this, we get the story wrong and fail to see why a dark law continues to govern many parts of India.

Withdrawing the AFSPA

The AFSPA was withdrawn from Tripura in 2015 after being in force in the state for a just over eighteen years. After 2010, Tripura saw a rapid decline in militancy and witnessed the surrender of hundreds of militants. The ruling Left Front, led by then Chief Minister Manik Sarkar, in power in Tripura since 1993, had the support of the opposition parties that were also in favor of the withdrawal of the AFSPA. The best testament to the decline of violence in Tripura was the over 84 percent voter turnout in the 2014 Lok Sabha election—one of the highest in the country. When AFSPA was withdrawn, Sarkar said, "In view of the significant taming of terrorism in Tripura, the council of ministers . . . decided to withdraw the AFSPA from the entire state. . . . The security forces recently exhaustively reviewed the law and order situation in the state. . . . However, the security forces would be watchful over the situation."[11]

In March 2022, in a significant move the central government announced a reduction in the disturbed areas under AFSPA, thereby reducing its footprint from three states. The government said it was withdrawing the disturbed areas tag entirely from 23 districts in Assam; and partially from seven districts in Nagaland, six districts in Manipur, and one district in Assam. AFSPA remains very much in force in other parts of these three states as well as in parts of Arunachal Pradesh and Jammu and Kashmir.[12] I examine how and what allowed for the withdrawal of the AFSPA from some areas.

The decline in violence and the reversal of key insurgencies is vital to the decision. In Tripura, this was achieved not on the back of the AFSPA alone. Multiple factors were responsible, including coordinated policing and combat operations, effective diplomacy, and changing political realities in neighboring countries like Bangladesh and Myanmar, which made governments less inclined to harbor anti-India rebels, and also a political will across party lines to do so. All this together created an environment ripe for the possibility of removal of the AFSPA and the Army.

In 2018, the AFSPA was withdrawn from Meghalaya and its area of operation in Arunachal Pradesh was restricted. These areas had lived with the AFSPA for twenty-seven years. It was first imposed in 1991, fearing a spillover of violence from Assam-based outfits like the United Liberation Front of Asom (ULFA). In this case it was done in a staggered manner. Ministry of Home Affairs (MHA) officials who briefed this author, among other journalists in March and April 2018, explained how 40 percent of Meghalaya was under the AFSPA, including a 20 km stretch that bordered Assam, until September 2017. A review was held in consultation with the state government when the 20 km stretch was reduced to 10 km. A decision to revoke the AFSPA was taken at another review meeting, the official said.[13] A significant improvement in the security situation in the state and no spillover from Tripura were among the reasons. "All on board," the official had said when asked if this was a unanimous decision among all stakeholders.

Unlike Meghalaya, in August 2004, when the AFSPA was withdrawn from seven Assembly constituencies of the Imphal municipal area, it followed unprecedented protests over the custodial rape and brutal killing of Thangjam Manorama by the Assam Rifles. One of the most painful protests involved twelve elderly women, *Imas* or mothers, disrobing themselves in front of the Kangla Fort in Imphal carrying a banner saying, "Indian Army Rape Us." For three months after these protests, the troops remained at their posts. No operations were allowed. A month after the iconic protest, the state government withdrew the Armed Forces Special Powers Act (AFSPA) from seven assembly constituencies. While the Center and the Army remained opposed to the move, the massive protests forced the Ibobi Singh–led Congress government in the state to make this concession. The caveat was always hanging. Under Section 3 of the Act, the Center could reimpose the AFSPA if it was deemed fit.[14] The Congress-led UPA government at the Center did not do so. At the time, the general belief was that this was the beginning of the end of the AFSPA from Manipur. That too did not happen.

For a few years after the move, the areas from where the AFSPA was withdrawn in Imphal saw high levels of state and non-state related violence, prompting the chief minister to issue repeated warnings of reimposing the Act, but not acting on it.[15] Pradeep Phanjoubam, editor of the *Imphal Free Press*, says this belied a widely held public perception that the violence endemic in Manipur society was conditional to the existence of the AFSPA, or that once the stick (AFSPA) would go away, everyone would behave on their own.[16] Another perception was that a decline in violence, which may be one metric to consider, automatically translates into the withdrawal of the AFSPA. The Act continues in Manipur even though law and order has improved as claimed by successive governments. The 2022 decision to reduce the disturbed areas in Manipur and thus AFSPA came after eighteen years and excluded just fifteen police station areas from six districts of the state.

Disturbed Areas, Forever

Former home secretary Gopal Krishna Pillai believes that "a part often missed in the debate on AFSPA is the Disturbed Areas Act, which lays the ground for the enforcement of AFSPA. It is a powerful notification. It is meant to be a limited operation. How can a state be called a disturbed area for decades? If the law and order in a state is disturbed or remains broken down for decades, then something is amiss."[17]

The power to declare an area "disturbed" lies with the government (state or central), which decides whether the use of armed forces in the aid of civil power is essential. While state governments can suggest whether the DAA is required or not under Section (3) of the Act, their opinion can be overruled by the governor or the Center.

It is a cat-and-mouse game often played between the Center and states when it comes to the DAA notification and naming a state a "disturbed area." Nagaland has often felt that its opinion in this matter is reduced to a mere formality, while Manipur has often accepted the tag without major discomfort even as its chief ministers made public comments about the withdrawal of the AFSPA.

The Ministry of Home Affairs (MHA) under the Center issues periodic "disturbed area" notifications to extend the AFSPA for Nagaland and Arunachal

Pradesh. Notifications for Manipur and Assam are issued by their respective state governments.[18]

The Center has been extending the law in Nagaland for years despite the state government and legislative assembly recommending against it. "Law and order is a state subject. When the Nagaland cabinet says 'no' [to the extension of AFSPA], why does the centre not accept it," said Imkong L. Imchen, MLA of the Naga People's Front.[19] Siding with the opposition legislator, Chief Minister Neiphiu Rio told the house that the union home minister always seeks the state government's suggestion "just as a formality" before extending the law. "Every time a suggestion is sought, the state cabinet discusses the matter and tells the centre that there is no need to extend AFSPA or the Disturbed Areas Act," Rio said.[20] Yet the Center goes ahead.

In December 2021, the aftermath of an operation by the Indian Army's 21 Para Special Forces near the village of Oting in the Mon district of northern Nagaland went horribly wrong. It led to the death of six coal miners who were returning home and another seven civilians and a soldier in subsequent violence.

Residents of Oting barred men in uniform from entering the village, a move more symbolic than legal, though this author learned that no security-related movement had taken place until the start of 2022. Voices for the withdrawal of the AFSPA grew once again. Chief ministers of Nagaland and Meghalaya, both allied to the BJP (the party ruling the Center), demanded that the Act be withdrawn. "Oting was a misuse and abuse of AFSPA," Rio said.[21] The Nagaland legislative assembly unanimously demanded the withdrawal of the AFSPA from the North East and specifically from Nagaland.

By the end of the month, the MHA had extended the AFSPA in Nagaland through a DAA notification stating that "in such a disturbed and dangerous condition the use of armed forces in aid of the civil power is necessary,"[22] a line repeated in DAA notifications on Nagaland for years. In Oting, it was clear though civil powers had not been aware that an operation like in Oting was to be undertaken by the armed forces.

The central government though made one major overture. For the first time since it came to power it constituted a panel to review the withdrawal of the AFSPA in Nagaland and subsequently took the decision to reduce the disturbed areas tag from fifteen police stations in seven districts of Nagaland. Mon district where the botched up operation took place continues to be under AFSPA. Nevertheless, this was the first panel since 2005 when the Congress-led UPA government constituted the Justice Jeevan Reddy Committee to investigate the AFSPA. That report, which recommended the AFSPA be repealed, gathered dust for years before it was officially rejected in 2015 by the Narendra Modi government. A Union Home Ministry official who was part of the decision to form the latest panel spoke to the author in January 2022 in New Delhi and mentioned how there were moves in the past to discuss reducing the AFSPA's footprint, but they failed because the governments of Manipur and Assam resisted the move and a change in status quo.

Who decides that a state is a "disturbed area" and armed forces are needed in aid of the civil administration? Nagaland has often claimed that it is not a disturbed area. The Center believes it is. Each time the matter comes up, it has been settled in favor of the Center and the AFSPA. It has never escalated or gone to court. "For their own reasons, approaching the apex court, while peace talks are on, with a framework agreement, they [Nagaland] are unlikely to do that," Pillai said.[23]

In the case of Manipur, the state and the Center have more or less tangoed step for step on the disturbed area declaration and the AFSPA. The Manipur government has barely offered any resistance, renewing the provision for years in a bureaucratic fashion with nothing changing except the date, year after year.[24,25]

A notification like the DAA, which essentially indicates that a democratically elected government and all its arms such as the police have failed and is now incumbent on the Army to do the job while suspending fundamental freedoms in its midst, has rarely troubled Manipur's political class.[26]

In 2021, Chief Minister N. Biren Singh said that his government was urging the Center to withdraw the AFSPA as the law-and-order situation in the state had improved considerably.[27] Even so, the state continued to issue notifications extending the AFSPA in Manipur. In the last forty years, the Center has never issued any notification under the Act for Manipur,[28] which brings to scrutiny the public position taken by political leaders. A former Supreme Court judge, Justice Madan Lokur, writes, "on a different subject the Supreme Court has held that the issuance of repeated ordinances would be a fraud on the Constitution. This logic should apply to repeated declarations of an area as 'disturbed area' being a fraud of AFSPA."[29]

Until 2018, these notifications published in the *Gazette of India* specified reasons and details, like the number of incidents, and insurgent groups operating in the area. It stopped, perhaps because the same text was being copied and pasted every six months. "Possibly because it's done with no application of mind. You don't want to be hauled up," Pillai said.[30]

While the "disturbed" area tag is a precursor to the AFSPA, it also facilitates more funds from the Center and could be one of the reasons why states continue with its application despite changed ground realities. In September 2011, shortly after retirement, Pillai spoke at a lecture on India's mistakes in Manipur. He spoke of a "collective depression" on account of the manner in which the merger of Manipur was affected, and also the delay in granting statehood. Among the things he recounted was that he had rarely heard anyone—MPs, MLAs, or even the chief minister of the state—talk about the issues and daily problems Manipur faces when they came for meetings at the Home Ministry. "If everything else was within manageable limits, violence was more or less controlled, they talked only about money," he said.[31]

Since 1995, the Center has been implementing the Security Related Expenditure (SRE) scheme for all North East states except Mizoram and Sikkim. The Center reimburses 90 percent of the expenditure incurred by states on security-related items including logistics to the Central Armed Police Forces (CAPF) and the Army, maintenance of designated camps of insurgent groups with which Suspension of Operation (SoO) agreements have been signed, and stipends to surrendered militants. In the last seven years the reimbursement under the SRE scheme has touched INR 1925 crore.[32]

How then can the AFSPA be withdrawn? I ask a former home ministry official in-charge of the North East, Ravi [name changed]: "With honesty and account-ability, and a realisation that the buck will stop with you when they go," he said.[33]

In the section that follows, I intersect ground realities and counterinsurgency op-erations in three AFSPA regions—Jammu and Kashmir, Manipur, and Nagaland—to understand why the armed forces, the third main stakeholder in any decision on the AFSPA, remain vociferously against its withdrawal. Jammu and Kashmir has a separate J & K Armed Forces Special Powers Act 1990, but the playbook has fa-miliar notes.

AFSPA: State versus Center

In Jammu and Kashmir, where the Army's operations have been twofold—addressing counter-infiltration from Pakistan (which continues to this day) and counterinsurgency in the hinterland (which has considerably reduced)—the Army opposed any modicum of withdrawal, even when the state government felt it could handle the situation.

As chief minister from 2009 to 2015, Omar Abdullah made several attempts to lift the AFSPA from the state. He encountered stiff resistance from the Army, polit-ical play from the People's Democratic Party (PDP), and no major support from the ruling Congress Party. In July 2009, the Indian Army opposed the proposal that the AFSPA be lifted from some relatively violence-free districts like Srinagar, Budgam, Jammu, and Kathua. The move would fritter away the hard-earned gains made with the backing of the law, the Army said,[34] adding that their convoys going up to the Line of Control passed through Srinagar and intermediate areas where military installations and lines of communication are spread. They would need the Act if they came under attack, which they did.

Designating areas as under-AFSPA and non-AFSPA would be counterproduc-tive, the Army said, to undertake seamless operations and would leave military as-sets in non-AFSPA areas vulnerable. The Manipur experience of 2004 is often cited, where the revocation of the Act led to more violence in the non-AFSPA areas.

At several unified command meetings in Srinagar, which Abdullah chaired as chief minister, he asked for an objective look with the understanding that if the situ-ation required the Army to intervene, they could make a temporary sort of return to that. The warning often was that should a need be felt to reimpose the Act, it would be at grave political cost and may far outweigh the option of not revoking it in the first place.[35]

In that period, whenever the issue came up, the Cabinet Committee on Security left the decision to the unified command. "There was no appetite to change the status quo among anyone, even lower down the hierarchy. No one was prepared to take the political risk of disagreeing with the armed forces, especially if things went south. We did push them saying it would be an incentive for the civil administration, especially in districts where there were no incidents. It would be a positive signal for the political process. But no one was ready to overrule. The Army had the veto here," says a retired home ministry official.[36]

Former Union home minister P. Chidambaram admitted deferring to the Army in this matter, although he and the CM (Omar Abdullah) were in favor of dilution of the AFSPA.[37]

The Army's stand over the years has remained similar. "There cannot be islands of peace [in the disturbed valley]. The military requires the provisions that enable it to act. Without these provisions, the Army will be handicapped," former Northern Army Commander Lt. General K. T. Parnaik said in November 2011.[38] Commanders who served in Kashmir often make the case that reduced violence is seen for lasting peace. They argue that while the situation has shown improvement several times over, trends have reversed. Instead of political processes taking over, the relative peace is used to generate momentum for revocation of the AFSPA.

"What's failed in Kashmir is the political battle, more so from 2010. The Army has done its job at least three times since its deployment in Jammu and Kashmir. There has been an opening [to withdraw the AFSPA], multiple times," says Lt. General Haracharanjit Singh Panag (Retd.), Former Northern Army Commander,[39] who believes the AFSPA could be removed from parts and remain in force in a 15–20 km belt along the Line of Control. The Jammu and Kashmir police, he argues, was competent enough to do the job while the Army could focus on infiltration across the Line of Control.

"While that is true, they [the Army] did [bring the situation under control], in my entire tenure, I have never heard the Army ever say, 'I think it's time for us to go. Our job is done here,'" a former home ministry official told this writer, further underlining how the Army's presence in counterinsurgency duties as a near permanent fixture needs to be looked at when talking about the AFSPA.

The number of terrorists active in the Valley today is around 250 to 300. However, the pattern of the insurgency and its trademark tool—terrorism—have changed, with far more potent dimensions of civil disobedience, stone pelting, mass agitations, and radicalization. All of these have challenged the security forces more than the terrorism they were originally called out to quell, which in the process placed them in direct conflict with citizens. Amit Ahuja and Srinath Raghavan explain in this volume how the widespread and prolonged use of military in internal security duties impacts their ethos and perception and distracts them from their core mission of defense of the state from external threats.

Counterinsurgency, Far from Lofty Ideals

Counterinsurgency by nature is a messy, chaotic affair. It aspires to win the loyalty of the population through security and governance. In reality, it is far more complex, unpleasant, grubby, and less grandiose. It can descend into intense violence even with the best intentions, or cave into an "ugly stability"[40] through repression, bribery, accommodation, betrayal, and negotiation.

The reasoning for why the armed forces must replace civil agencies is often that violence from insurgent groups needs to be met with some amount of restorative counter-violence (from the state) to ensure the security of the population. The state's own police forces may be overwhelmed as it is actively negotiating with insurgent groups, and the government needs the military in proximity even if operations are restrained.

While violence has reduced in many states, a complex and confusing peace process has see-sawed over the years, keeping the Army tethered to a landscape that is neither at war nor at peace. Military men often talk about the irony of being deployed to neutralize insurgents only to get them to the talking table, or of their men upholding a ceasefire whose geographic validity is deliberately kept ambiguous.

The Manipur government insists that the central government's ceasefire with the main Naga group, the Nationalist Socialist Council of Nagaland-Isaac Muivah (NSCN-IM), does not extend beyond Nagaland into Manipur. This, even though camps of the NSCN-IM (referred to as "taken note of camps") exist in Manipur. On the other hand, the NSCN-IM contends that the ceasefire is "without any territorial limits," applicable to all places where the Naga group is active. While saying so, they often reiterate the 1988 statement of the Atal Behari Vajpayee government's interlocutor for peace talks, Swaraj Kaushal,[41] who said, "Wherever they [the NSCN] are, we observe ceasefire, even abroad. . . . It covers Delhi and even Paris." Officially, there is no ceasefire but a tacit agreement that Indian security forces would not bother Naga militants in Manipur as long as they stay put in the "taken note of camps."

"This arrangement, official or unofficial, has ensured relative peace. . . . If the government concedes officially that there is no ceasefire in Manipur, they will be forced to act against the NSCN-IM, which will hurt the peace process," said Lt. General D. S. Hooda (Retd.),[42] who commanded the Army's 57 Mountain Division (2009–2011), which spearheads counterinsurgency operations in Manipur.

Over the years, as military operations have given way to negotiations, an umbrella architecture of militarization has remained. New Delhi's strategy of sometimes letting insurgent groups stagnate in peace or playing the waiting game has meant that the Army's presence has been routinized.

"They have come to be involved in tasks relatively messier, more pedestrian, and possibly handle-able by others," says a retired Home Ministry official.[43] Overseeing the suspension of operation (SoO) agreements with armed Kuki groups, a task with little overt insurgent activity, is one such example. Once a SoO agreement is inked with an insurgent group, a set of ground rules govern cessation of hostilities. The insurgent group moves into a designated camp, paid for by the government, where they can be monitored. Ten-odd weapons are allowed to be held by their cadre; the rest are secured under double-barrel locks inside camp premises. The government's idea is that SoO agreements, a stipend of a few thousand rupees per cadre, and the promise of a political dialogue can keep things under control; and they do. It then becomes the Army's job to manage these men, prevent assimilation of this cadre with rival groups, and prevent extortion and clashes. The Army keeps an eye on them but rarely overtly fights them. A quasi-peace persists.

"The Army is pulling various levers in a messy conflict. When we came, the politician-insurgent-police nexus was indistinguishable. How is it fathomable that we can operate here without legal protection when so many technically non-state actors are within and outside?" asks an officer in the Army's 57 Mountain Division.[44]

He recounts recent violence to explain why the AFSPA is vital to their freedom of action. In June 2015, a convoy of the Indian Army's Dogra regiment was ambushed. Eighteen soldiers died. "Their bodies were found charred in their last actions," the officer adds. The attack, carried out by the proscribed NSCN-Khaplang, is one of the deadliest attacks on the Indian Army in decades. The external threat on both borders means insurgent groups operating inside are working with elements outside and can orchestrate terrorist actions in other parts of the country. Counterinsurgency operations, he argues, are small, proactive, and swift. Information must be acted on with little time to await clearances.

Six years later, in November 2021, a convoy of the Assam Rifles was ambushed in Manipur's Churachandpur district, killing a battalion commander, his wife, son, and four other soldiers. The attack was carried out by the People's Liberation Army of Manipur and a lesser-known Naga outfit. Later in the year, soldiers allegedly opened unprovoked fire on a pickup truck carrying local coal miners back to their village in Nagaland's Mon district, killing six of them. Those opposing the Act argue this blanket cover provided by the AFSPA incentivizes collateral damage and lazy soldiering. If soldiers get away with murder, they can never befriend the locals without whom it is impossible to generate credible intelligence to avoid something like the first attack.[45]

"If we want to continue like this, we can go on forever. In many North Eastern states, I see no reason why AFSPA should not go," says Panag.[46] The prolonged deployment of the Army—for which the AFSPA is an enabler despite the changed ground situation—is one major problem. "There is no articulation of a time-bound use of the security forces or even a defined, stated political end for which they are being called in. In the absence of this clarity, they stay. The longer their deployment 'after the crisis is over' the more complicated life becomes without them," Panag adds.[47]

A few years after their counterinsurgency role in Jammu and Kashmir fell into place, the Army began a civic affairs program, Operation Sadhbhavana. The initial aim was to prevent insurgency from spreading to the Ladakh region and the focus was on developmental activities and maintaining a symbiotic relationship. As the years progressed, the Army took on a larger role in planning, providing technical solutions, supervising projects, and moving beyond being a facilitator between state administration and locals. Slowly, the program came to be identified with every facet of public life. "Schools, hospitals, appointment of teachers, contractors, schemes, prizes, expenditure, secret service funds, all come with the Act. There is a patronage and a vested interest that comes about," says the retired Home Ministry official.[48]

Contrary to Jammu and Kashmir and the North East, in areas affected by left-wing extremism, once referred to as the biggest threat to internal security,[49] deployment of the Army was seen as a misapplication of the military. The task was left in the hands of specialized police units and the central armed paramilitary forces like the Central Reserve Police Force (CRPF), which made it clear that the force did not need protection under the AFSPA, arguing that Section 197 of the CrPC gave them all the protection they needed.[50] Army chiefs serving and retired opposed bringing in the Army in anti-Maoist operations. "Deploying the Army is not the answer. If armed forces are deployed there [in Maoist-hit areas], they will shoot our own citizens. This would tarnish the reputation and image of the Army," former Army General and Union Minister V. K. Singh said.[51] Many other political stakeholders echoed these sentiments. "The Constitution does not allow deployment against our own people, and neither does my heart. For the sake of argument, if the Army is deployed, the issue can be solved in four hours. But this should never happen," Chhattisgarh Chief Minister Raman Singh said.[52]

"Imagine what this means and translates [into] for the people in states like Manipur, or Jammu and Kashmir, where Army and AFSPA is the rule of thumb," Babloo Loitongbam, executive director of Human Rights Alert, had said.[53]

Justice in the Times of the AFSPA

When it started out in 2009, the Extrajudicial Execution Victims Family Members (EEVFAM) was an oddly named collective documenting testimonies of alleged human rights violations in Manipur. The documentation included atrocities by security forces and non-state actors. In 2012, the organization, along with Human Rights Alert, filed a public interest litigation (PIL) in the Supreme Court asserting that 1,528 civilians, including 98 children, were killed in Manipur between 1979 and 2012. These deaths they claimed were cold-blooded murders—extrajudicial executions.

A year later, in response to the petition, a Supreme Court–appointed committee headed by retired Supreme Court Judge Santosh Hegde reached Imphal to inquire into the first six cases—seven deaths—from the dossier. A hotel banquet room served as the Commission's office where witnesses, family members, policemen and women, Manipur Police commandos, and district magistrates appeared. The Assam Rifles, the central armed paramilitary force that works in counterinsurgency operations with the Army in Manipur, had requested that testimonies of their personnel be recorded in Delhi since they were posted in different parts of the country. The Justice Hegde Commission submitted its report to the Supreme Court later in 2013 saying that all six cases the commission had investigated were fake encounters. The Commission noted how periodic reviews justifying the continuance of the AFSPA had been given the go-by, and the continuous imposition of prohibitory orders under Section 144 as well as the continuance of the AFSPA made a "mockery of the law."[54]

While this set in motion a process of judicial scrutiny and accountability, the constitutional validity of the AFSPA was not up for debate. The Supreme Court had already upheld it in prior cases and refined the application of the Act by issuing guidelines and incorporating the commandments issued by the chief of Army staff in its orders. Raeesa Vakil, in her chapter in this volume on "Internal Security and India's Constitution," explains how these guidelines (dos and don'ts for the armed forces to follow in disturbed areas) proposed by the Government of India have been subsequently cited by the Government of India as protection when it was found that security forces were responsible for custodial deaths in the AFSPA areas. She elaborates how when it comes to national security laws like the AFSPA, the Supreme Court has consistently interpreted the Constitution in a manner prioritizing public order over the liberty of an individual.

Technically speaking, the AFSPA does not grant blanket immunity. Violations in conflict areas may be the result of legitimate and good faith actions. These have the protection of the AFSPA. Violations could also stem from legitimate actions that are overzealous or do not follow the rules of engagement. These do happen when force has to be used against terrorists who intermingle with people and enjoy their tacit or coerced support. Such violations also get the protection of the AFSPA from prosecution in civil courts but are dealt with under military law. It is the third kind of violation caused by rogue actions that do not have the armor of the AFSPA, in principle. Prior sanction of the government is required for the accused officer to be prosecuted in a civil court.

To date, no soldier has been prosecuted in a criminal court for an alleged offense committed under the AFSPA. As of 2021, no government had sanctioned prosecution in a single case over the previous sixty-three years.[55] The government received fifty requests since 1990 from Jammu and Kashmir alone for permission to prosecute security force personnel. Forty-seven were denied permission and three were pending, as of 2018.[56] The lack of prosecution sanction by the government in effect grants carte blanche immunity to the armed forces. Six decades of the Act have passed without any set procedures, norms, and criteria followed in deciding prosecution sanction under the AFSPA.[57] "If there is no SOP for grant of prosecution sanction in India as far as the military is concerned, then I feel that such a procedure must be laid out for the sake of objectivity, along with defined timelines. Other departments do have a procedure for grant of sanction for prosecution of government servants," says Navdeep Singh, an advocate at the Punjab and Haryana High Court and former officer of the Indian Territorial Army who specializes in military law and service matters.

The AFSPA protects us from vexatious and mischievous litigation in counterinsurgency landscapes where the nexus between the insurgent and other stakeholders is often unclear, say the forces. They point to the military justice system and swift disciplinary action under the court-martial system as sufficient safeguards. Panag says, "there is no carte blanche, no absolute impunity, and rogue actions of soldiers have to be dealt with as per the law of the land—which includes military law."[58]

Officers with tenures in the Kashmir counterinsurgency say they always insist an FIR is filed in cases of death caused by security forces. While the police and Army run parallel investigations, in cases where only the police investigation finds an offense has been committed, the Army informs the court of its own inquiry and invokes the AFSPA. In most cases, the matter ends there. Very rarely do matters come to head, like in the highly politicized 2010 Machhil encounter. Five Army personnel convicted by a general court-martial for the death of three civilians were sentenced to life imprisonment, dismissed from service, and lodged in different prisons across the country. The Armed Forces Tribunal later suspended their sentences.

Even though affected parties can seek information under the RTI Act to the extent permissible, military measures imposed on offenders remain out of the public eye. "Bad faith acts are not protected. Measures are taken when actionable information on any such infraction is provided to the higher-ups. But there is a requirement of more transparency and moral courage, as is expected in the highest traditions of the Indian military,"[59] says Navdeep Singh.

Internally there could be repercussions on the careers of individual soldiers. Publicly, though, the majority of human rights violation cases (96 percent) are termed false by the Human Rights Cell of the Army headquarters.[60] Created in 1993, it was upgraded to a directorate in 2019 and appointed a major general–rank officer to head it in 2020. Of the seven complaints of human rights violations received against the Army in 2020, none was found true. Of the twenty-six complaints of human rights violations registered against the Army in 2019, one was found to be true. In 2018, all forty-two complaints received were deemed false.[61]

Questions arise whether the military justice system is a valid arbiter, especially in cases related to the AFSPA violations. Worldwide, the military justice system is not pressed into service everywhere to punish military personnel for offenses in operational areas, says Singh. In certain nations, a hybrid system is followed, while in others, offenses are only tried in regular courts and military courts have been abolished. The idea that "human rights, including soldiers' rights" is not a bad term and all must strive to uphold them, is currently of the utmost importance.[62]

A trust deficit looms large vis-à-vis the AFSPA, even though the forces' own track record on human rights has improved. Retired Home and Defence Ministry officials with whom the author spoke suggest that the imagery of the armed forces in civilian courts does no good to anyone, certainly not "morale of the forces," a phrase often used by military commanders as well whenever the topic comes up.

For those like Loitongbam fighting the EEFVAM case in the Supreme Court, the military justice system has not delivered. "In our experience, military courts have consistently failed to act when they should have. It is a bit late to claim military jurisdiction for human rights violations of civilians, as most of the country has moved to the jurisdiction of the civilian court," he says, citing the example of the investigations by the CBI in the EEVFAM case and the inherent double standards. "When the CBI investigation clearly establishes the fact of committing murder, the Union of India has denied prosecution sanction in several cases. In the present EEVFAM case being heard in the Supreme Court, there are cases where, in the same operation, police personnel are indicted but the Army personnel are not, due to lack of prosecution sanction under AFSPA," says Loitongbam.[63]

Conclusion: AFSPA and Impunity

Three committees, including one headed by former Supreme Court judge B. P. Jeevan Reddy—perhaps the most significant attempt to change the status quo on the AFSPA—have recommended its repeal. But the AFSPA has remained. Formed in the aftermath of a powerful protest movement sparked by the abduction, rape, and murder of Thangjam Manorama in Manipur, the Jeevan Reddy Committee's report lay unattended for years in the face of a strong push from the security establishment not to accept any of its recommendations. In March 2015, the Ministry of Home Affairs recommended a rejection of the report to the Cabinet Committee on Security, headed by Prime Minister Narendra Modi. In 2019, the Press Information Bureau said there is no proposal to repeal the Armed Forces (Special Powers) Act 1958. That the AFSPA will continue to be part of the internal security landscape for the foreseeable future is not lost on even its most vocal critics. "The total uprooting of the draconian law does not seem to be on the horizon yet," says Loitongbam, who believes that the Supreme Court intervention along with civil society activism related to the AFSPA have brought down cases of wanton killings. "If it is repealed, the AFSPA is likely to be made more draconian," says retired Lt. General Panag.

Several chapters in this volume have unlayered the dimensions and impact of using the military in internal security challenges. The AFSPA is a centerpiece in the counterinsurgency vocabulary. The debate on the need for the AFSPA in internal security situations and its efficacy in containing these challenges have not moved much since the matter first came up in Constitutional Assembly debates. But its continuous use in diverse situations has given us enough markers to see it for what it is.

The AFSPA was enacted with the specific purpose of ensuring that employment of armed forces in internal security situations was legal and effective. It empowered military men lower in the command hierarchy to exercise their discretion in the use of force. This assumed a degree of responsibility on the part of the commander as an outcome of training and experience. The violence to follow was assumed legitimate, in service of resolving the conflict and creating public order.

Within this paradigm, the military considers the AFSPA to be an effective and necessary tool. Whether the same could have been achieved without the AFSPA cannot be entirely and reasonably assessed given the complexity of judgment and stakeholders. Military men who spoke to me for context stress how the AFSPA has received more than its fair share of attention, and that the efficacy of AFSPA is not just in operations that go haywire, but also in those that are successful. The former obviously makes it to the headlines. Contrary to popular understanding, they say the AFSPA is not a mindset built into every operation. Military strategy in counterinsurgency is its own beast. The mere presence of the AFSPA does not lead to laxity though slackness, if any, while pursuing legitimate goals can be protected by the AFSPA.

In the situation we find ourselves in, it can be concluded that the military has played a vital role and without it, India's internal security challenges would not have been met. Without the AFSPA, the military could not have been employed.

Could the AFSPA have been judiciously imposed and also judiciously employed? The answer is part political, and a definite yes. The AFSPA assumes that the situation requires use of force beyond armed policing, which is the invocation of the Disturbed Areas Act. This law has moved beyond just being an enabler for security forces. Its motivations today lie elsewhere: a lack of political imagination, an architecture of militarization, and applying the exceptional lens to sensitive regions in the periphery. Militarization of the periphery shrinks democratic space and gives rise to further patterns of abuse. The AFSPA's prolonged use in the North East of India is highly questionable, and both central and state leaderships over the years can be blamed for this status quo. The political economy of an insurgency and the political economy of the AFSPA often run parallel. Both need a gun to look down the barrel of another gun for their survival.

Any law is as good as its employment to uphold constitutional values, where those empowered to use force do so discriminately and under the highest levels of provocation. If found guilty of indiscriminate use of force, those in question would submit themselves to values of justice and empathy. It is in this regard that the AFSPA has been a dark blot, breaking a bond between a citizen and men in uniform. When one hears about lines being crossed and rights violated, there is an expectation that wrongs will be righted. The mere acknowledgment that wrongs have been committed and need to be remedied have been hard to come by. The military is held on a pedestal. What could have remained aberrations if justice was done and seen to be done have turned into deep violations because of a stubborn resistance to submit to justice, review, and empathy. Some practices have come to be accepted as part and parcel of internal security challenges. There is a judicial tolerance for it, and a broad political and media acceptance for it.

Even the AFSPA may not be considered the problem sometimes, as provisions of the law do not give impunity to military men who kill in cold blood. Where then does the problem lie? Not all injustices in these landscapes have begun or will end with the AFSPA. At the heart of it is a culture of impunity that the AFSPA has cemented into the landscape where it operated. Impunity, not just as a legal term, means "freedom" of state or non-state actors to inflict harm and loss without fear of consequence. But impunity works at multiple and mutually reinforcing levels. Impunity is understood as a systematic exemption of punishment or a denial of redress. Impunity allows a casual acceptance of the inevitability of loss of life, or that mistakes are made in a righteous war. Or that there is a hierarchy of more or less legitimate killings. Or even a broader, more tragic explanation, is that violence against some is not really considered an aberration of law, but almost a necessary feature. Whether the AFSPA goes, stays, or is reviewed or reduced, these scars of impunity are likely to persist.

Notes

1. Full text of the 1947 debate on Armed Forces (Special Powers) Bill in The Constituent Assembly of India (Legislative) Debates, Vol II, First Session, 29 November to 10 December 1947. Available at https://www.humanrightsinitiative.org/download/CAL-debates-1947-AFSPAdiscussion1.pdf; last accessed on December 25, 2021.
2. Constituent Assembly of India (Legislative) Debates, 1732. Available at https://www.humanrightsinitiative.org/download/CAL-debates-1947-AFSPAdiscussion1.pdf; last accessed on December 25, 2021.
3. Constituent Assembly of India (Legislative) Debates, 1732. Available at https://www.humanrightsinitiative.org/download/CAL-debates-1947-AFSPAdiscussion1.pdf; last accessed on December 25, 2021.
4. Constituent Assembly of India (Legislative) Debates, 1732. Available at https://www.humanrightsinitiative.org/download/CAL-debates-1947-AFSPAdiscussion1.pdf; last accessed on December 25, 2021.
5. Constituent Assembly of India (Legislative) Debates, 1745. Available at https://www.humanrightsinitiative.org/download/CAL-debates-1947-AFSPAdiscussion1.pdf; last accessed on December 25, 2021.

6. Constituent Assembly of India (Legislative) Debates, 1749. Available at https://www.humanrightsinitiative.org/download/CAL-debates-1947-AFSPAdiscussion1.pdf; last accessed on December 25, 2021.

7. Constituent Assembly of India (Legislative) Debates, 1747. Available at https://www.humanrightsinitiative.org/download/CAL-debates-1947-AFSPAdiscussion1.pdf; last accessed on December 25, 2021.

8. (The) Armed Forces (Special Powers) Ordinance, 1942, *Gazette of India*, Extraordinary, August 15, 1942. Available at https://web.archive.org/web/20131030035512/http://indianarmy.nic.in/Site/RTI/rti/MML/MML_VOLUME_3/CHAPTER__01/452.htm; last accessed on January 20, 2022.

9. Pratap Bhanu Mehta, "Repealing AFSPA Will Not Weaken, Only Strengthen Constitution," December 10, 2021. Available at https://indianexpress.com/article/opinion/columns/repealing-afspa-will-not-weaken-only-strengthen-constitution-7663144/; last accessed on January 20, 2022.

10. Anubha Bhonsle, Introduction to *Mother, Where's My Country?* (New Delhi: Speaking Tiger, 2016).

11. "Tripura Withdraws AFSPA from State after 18 Years," *Business Standard*, May 28, 2015. Available at https://www.business-standard.com/article/news-ians/tripura-lifts-afspa-as-terrorism-ebbs-115052701148_1.html; last accessed on December 25. 2021.

12. "Notifications for Disturbed Areas in North eastern states under AFSPA issued by Central government," Ministry of Home Affairs, Government of India, March, 31, 2022. Available at https://www.mha.gov.in/commoncontent/armed-forces-special-power-act-1958; last accessed on September 5, 2022.

13. Rahul Tripathi, "AFSPA Revoked from Meghalaya, Eight Police Stations in Arunachal Pradesh," *The Indian Express*, April 24, 2018. Available at https://indianexpress.com/article/india/afspa-removed-from-meghalaya-eight-police-stations-in-arunachal-pradesh-5148386/; last accessed on December 25, 2021.

14. "AFSPA to Be Withdrawn from Parts of Manipur," *Zee News*, August 12, 2004. Available at https://zeenews.india.com/news/nation/afspa-to-be-withdrawn-from-parts-of-manipur_172713.html; last accessed on December 25, 2021.

15. "Manipur May Reimpose the Act," *India Today*, March 18, 2008. Available at https://www.indiatoday.in/latest-headlines/story/manipur-may-reimpose-armed-forces-special-powers-act-23733-2008-03-18; last accessed on December 25, 2021.

16. Pradip Phanjoubam, "Hunter Gatherer: AFSPA Reflects the Poverty of Liberal Imagination," July 16, 2012. Available at https://www.news18.com/blogs/india/pradip-phanjoubam/hunter-gatherer-afspa-reflects-the-poverty-of-liberal-imagination-10876-747009.html; last accessed on December 1, 2021.

17. Interview with Gopal Krishna Pillai, Former Home Secretary, New Delhi, 2020/21. (All interviews in this chapter were conducted by the author.)

18. "Notifications on Armed Forces Special Powers Act, 1958." Ministry of Home Affairs. Available at https://www.mha.gov.in/commoncontent/armed-forces-special-power-act-1958; last accessed on January 1, 2022.

19. Press Trust of India, "Nagaland Assembly Members Raise Concern over AFSPA Extension," *Outlook*, February 13, 2020. Available at https://www.outlookindia.com/newsscroll/nagaland-assembly-members-raise-concern-over-afspa-extension/1733523; last accessed on December 1, 2020.

20. Press Trust of India, *Outlook*, February 13, 2020. Available at https://www.outlookindia.com/newsscroll/nagaland-assembly-members-raise-concern-over-afspa-extension/1733523; last accessed on December 1, 2020.

21. "Oting Incident Was a Misuse and Abuse of AFSPA: Nagaland CM Neiphiu Rio," *The Times of India*, December 9, 2021. Available at https://www.indiatoday.in/india/story/oting-incid

ent-was-a-misuse-and-abuse-of-afspa-nagaland-cm-neiphiu-rio-1886171-2021-12-09;   last accessed on January 1, 2022.

22. "Ministry of Home Affairs Notification Extending AFSPA in Nagaland," *The Gazette of India*, December 30, 2021. Available at https://static.pib.gov.in/WriteReadData/specificdocs/documents/2022/mar/doc202233134101.pdf; last accessed on January 20, 2022.

23. Interview with Gopal Krishna Pillai, Former Home Secretary, New Delhi, 2020/21.

24. Manipur Government Notification, December 31, 2018. Available at https://www.indiac ode.nic.in/handle/123456789/1527?sam_handle=123456789/1362;   last   accessed   on December 1, 2021.

25. Manipur Government Notification, December 8, 2021. Available at https://www.mha.gov.in/sites/default/files/AFSPAManipur_22122021.pdf; last accessed on January 1, 2022.

26. Anubha Bhonsle, *Mother, Where's My Country?* (New Delhi: Speaking Tiger, 2016), 27.

27. Jimmy Leivon, "Govt Urging Centre to Withdraw AFSPA from Manipur, Says CM Biren Singh," *The Indian Express*, February 5, 2021. Available at https://indianexpress.com/article/north-east-india/manipur/govt-has-been-urging-centre-to-withdraw-afspa-from-manipur-says-cm-biren-singh7174949/; last accessed on October 1, 2021.

28. "Center Extends AFSPA in Nagaland for Six More Months," *The Hindu*, December 30, 2021. Available at https://www.thehindu.com/news/national/afspa-extended-in-nagaland-for-6-more-months/article38068888.ece; last accessed on January 1, 2022.

29. Justice (Retired) Madan B Lokur, "AFSPA: The Misuse of Power," Economic & Political Weekly, December 25, 2021. Available at https://www.epw.in/journal/2021/52/comment/afspa-misuse-power.html; last accessed on January 4, 2022.

30. Interview with Gopal Krishna Pillai, Former Home Secretary, New Delhi, 2020/21.

31. "Manipur, The Way Out." Available at https://www.youtube.com/watch?v=KCt87g_AFX4.

32. "Reimbursement of Security Related Expenditure (SRE) Scheme for North Eastern States." Available at https://www.mha.gov.in/sites/default/files/NE_Reimbursement_SRE_25022 022.PDF; last accessed on August 18, 2022.

33. Personal interview with the former Home Ministry official, New Delhi, January 2022.

34. Rajat Pandit, "Army Opposes AFSPA Withdrawal in J&K," *The Times of India*, July 8, 2009. Available at https://timesofindia.indiatimes.com/india/Army-opposes-AFSPA-withdrawal-in-JK/articleshow/4751094.cms; last accessed on December 1, 2021.

35. Major General (Retd) Umong Sethi, "Armed Forces Special Powers Act—The Way Ahead," IDSA Monograph Series No. 7, 2012. Available at https://idsa.in/monograph/ArmedForc esSpecialPowersActTheDebate; last accessed on December 1, 2021.

36. Personal interview with retired Home Ministry official, New Delhi, 2019.

37. "Wanted to Remove AFSPA but Army Opposed: Chidambaram," *Firstpost*, February 6, 2013. Available at https://www.firstpost.com/india/wanted-to-remove-afspa-but-army-opposed-chidambaram-616406.html; last accessed on December 1, 2021.

38. Murali Krishnan, "Indian Generals Opt to Preserve Shoot, Arrest and Search Powers," *Deutsche Welle*, November 11, 2011. Available at https://www.dw.com/en/indian-gener als-opt-to-preserve-shoot-arrest-and-search-powers/a-6657064; last accessed on December 1, 2021.

39. Interview with Lt. General (Retired) Haracharanjit Singh Panag, Chandigarh and New Delhi, 2020/2021.

40. Paul Staniland, "Counterinsurgency Is a Bloody, Costly Business," *Foreign Policy*, November 24, 2009. Available at https://foreignpolicy.com/2009/11/24/counterinsurgency-is-a-blo ody-costly-business/; last accessed on December 1, 2021.

41. Arunabh Saikia, "Decoding the Naga Ceasefire: Where Is It Really Applicable?" *Scroll*, June 2, 2019. Available at https://scroll.in/article/925052/decoding-the-naga-ceasefire-where-is-it-really-applicable; last accessed on September 1, 2021.

42. Saikia, "Decoding the Naga Ceasefire."

43. Personal interview with retired Home Ministry official, New Delhi, 2020/2021.

44. Personal interview with Army official on condition of anonymity, citing service rules.

45. Subir Bhaumik, "Playing with Fire," *The Telegraph Online*, December 31, 2021. Available at https://www.telegraphindia.com/opinion/playing-with-fire-counter-insurgency-operations-in-indias-northeast/cid/1845369; last accessed on January 2, 2022

46. Interview with Lt. General (Retired) Haracharanjit Singh Panag, Chandigarh and New Delhi, 2020/2021.

47. Interview with Lt. General (Retired) Haracharanjit Singh Panag, Chandigarh and New Delhi, 2020/2021.

48. Personal interview with retired Home Ministry official, New Delhi, 2020/2021.

49. Press Trust of India, "Naxalism Biggest Threat to Internal Security: Manmohan," *The Hindu*, New Delhi, May 24, 2010. Available at https://www.thehindu.com/news/national/Naxalism-biggest-threat-to-internal-security-Manmohan/article16302952.ece; last accessed on September 1, 2021.

50. Rakhi Chakrabarty, "Don't Want Armed Forces Special Powers Act Shield: CRPF Brass," *The Times of India*, May 17, 2012. Available at https://timesofindia.indiatimes.com/india/Dont-want-Armed-Forces-Special-Powers-Act-shield-CRPF-brass/articleshow/13178962.cms; last accessed on September 1, 2021.

51. "Don't Use Army against Maoists, Says V K Singh," *Hindustan Times*, April 15, 2015. Available at https://www.hindustantimes.com/india/don-t-use-army-against-maoists-says-vk-singh/story-sN5SEneHhCdDxmbLbRXbpL.html; last accessed on September 1, 2021.

52. Sagnik Chowdhury, "Chhattisgarh: Army Can Solve Naxal Issue in Four Hours, but My Heart Won't Allow It, Says Raman Singh," *The Indian Express*, May 12, 2015. Available at https://indianexpress.com/article/india/india-others/army-can-solve-naxal-issue-in-four-hours-but-my-heart-wont-allow-it-says-raman-singh/; last accessed on September 1, 2021.

53. Interview with Mr. Babloo Loitongbam, New Delhi, 2021.

54. "Continued AFSPA, CrPC Section 144 Make a Mockery of the Law," *The Indian Express*, July 22, 2013. Available at https://indianexpress.com/article/news-archive/web/continued-afspa-crpc-section-144-make-a-mockery-of-the-law/; last accessed on September 1, 2021.

55. Sanjoy Hazarika, "63 Years Later, India Must Repeal AFSPA," *Hindustan Times*, December 7, 2021. Available at https://www.hindustantimes.com/opinion/63-years-later-india-must-repeal-afspa-101638886750673.html; last accessed on January 1, 2022.

56. A. G. Noorani, "The Wrongs in Kashmir," *Frontline*. Available at https://frontline.thehindu.com/the-nation/article24561017.ece; last accessed on December 1, 2021.

57. Nidhi Sharma, "There Are No Set Procedures or Norms to Sanction AFSPA Cases: Defence Ministry," *The Economic Times*, July 26, 2020. Available at https://economictimes.indiatimes.com/news/politics-and-nation/there-are-no-set-procedures-or-norms-to-sanction-afspa-cases-defence-ministry/articleshow/77186823.cms; last accessed on December 1, 2021.

58. Interview with the Lt. General (Retired) Haracharanjit Singh Panag, 2020/2021.

59. Interview with Advocate Navdeep Singh via email, 2021.

60. See investigation of allegations: "Human Right Cell and Handling of Human Rights Violation Cases in the Army," December 31, 2011. Available at https://indianarmy.nic.in/Site/FormTemplete/frmTempSimple.aspx?MnId=WDib66JZKfwQIYafz8bTHg==&ParentID=I7kH/Zw1krhHe0wFtRkRAQ; last accessed on January 1, 2022.

61. "Army Got Seven Complaints of Human Rights Violations in 2020, None Found to Be True: Shripad Naik," *The Economic Times*, March 8, 2021. Available at https://economictimes.indiatimes.com/news/defence/army-got-7-complaints-of-human-rights-violations-in-2020-none-found-to-be-true-minister-of-state-for-defence-shripad-naik/articleshow/81396142.cms; last accessed on January 1, 2022.

62. Interview with Advocate Navdeep Singh via email, 2021.

63. Interview with Mr. Babloo Loitongbam, New Delhi, 2020/2021.

4

Role of the MHA in Internal Security

SHAKTI SINHA

The Ministry of Home Affairs (MHA) is the Indian state's primary instrument for ensuring the country's internal security. This chapter examines the internal security role of the MHA and its evolution over the years. The chapter argues that while the expansion of the MHA's ambit comes across as ad hoc and episodic, a certain internal logic and consistency marks this approach, irrespective of the ruling dispensation at the Center.[1]

The Indian Constitution obligates the central government to ensure that the governance of every state is carried on in accordance with its provisions. India's asymmetrical federalism better places the central government fiscally, and in terms of residual powers, than do its counterparts in the states. These two features have enabled considerable accretion to the role and powers of the MHA over the decades.

Second, the MHA's size—both budget and personnel—has grown massively, especially since the 1980s. The growth of its role and responsibilities has not been driven by any master plan or even a strategic vision, but rather has been episodic and reactive. Two examples are illustrative. Though law and order is a state subject, the meager investments by states in their police forces have led to a massive growth in the Central Armed Police Forces (CAPFs)—the executive arm of the MHA which was primarily created to support the state governments. Similarly, the establishment of the Central Industrial Security Force (CISF), one of India's largest CAPFs, in 1969 precipitated political contestation when the left-dominated governments of Kerala and West Bengal refused to comply with the MHA's directions on the handling of strikes by central government employees in their states. The creation of most CAPFs follows a similar logic, driven by quick reactions to unforeseen developments without necessarily exploring alternate options. The creation and expansion of the CAPFs exemplifies a core argument of this chapter: the evolution of the MHA is a textbook example of mission creep.

The third feature underlying the growth and changes in the roles and responsibilities of the MHA is the Indian state's predisposition to prioritize order over individual liberty (discussed further in Raeesa Vakil's chapter in this volume).

Shakti Sinha, *Role of the MHA in Internal Security* In: *Internal Security in India*. Edited by: Amit Ahuja and Devesh Kapur, Oxford University Press. © Oxford University Press 2023. DOI: 10.1093/oso/9780197660331.003.0004

This approach, running across the political spectrum, has never been articulated as a coherent policy choice, which is why it is not possible to categorize it as a strategy; it is best described as reflecting deep-rooted fears in the Indian polity about vivisection and possible loss of independence. The primacy of state security has implied that normal laws cannot be allowed to impede steps to safeguard sovereignty. The use of preventive detention laws, which allows for incarceration without following rule-of-law processes, as well as giving security forces almost limitless immunity while dealing with insurgencies, reflects this attitude. On the other hand, when armed insurgent groups have accepted the inviolability of the Indian Constitution, the state has shown flexibility in accommodating demands, reflected in the creation of new states, devising innovative administrative arrangements such as autonomous districts and councils, and providing large financial resources. But overall, individual liberty is curtailed if it is seen as an obstacle in defending the territorial integrity and sovereignty of the Indian state.

It needs to be emphasized that the MHA has other major functions besides internal security. These include the administration of Union Territories, the co-ordination of Center-state relations, disaster management, census operations, national honors, implementation of the Official Languages Act, and freedom fighters' pensions. However, this chapter focuses only on its internal security functions, which also constitute the core of its responsibilities.

Functions of the MHA

The MHA occupies a prime position among all ministries in the Government of India, second only in importance to the Prime Minister's Office (PMO). This is true even despite the fact that its role is anomalous in federal polity, as noted above. The roles and functions of the MHA have evolved, reflecting changing political dynamics, national priorities, the evolution of specialized agencies and ministries in the government, and the clout of individual home ministers.

The Indian Constitution vests in the federal government unusual powers of supervision over the functioning of the state governments. Article 355 asks the central government "to ensure that the government of every State is carried on in accordance with the provisions of this Constitution." If the MHA concludes that the executive power of any state is lax in ensuring "compliance with the laws made by Parliament and any existing law which apply to that State," then under Article 256, the Government of India (GOI) has the powers to give "such directions to a State as may appear" necessary for that purpose. In the event the GOI concludes that governance in a state "cannot be carried on in accordance with the provisions" of the Constitution, it can dismiss the state government (under Article 356) and take over direct administration. The state then temporarily comes under "President's rule," with the MHA supervising on behalf of the central executive. While these provisions have been much misused in the past, they have been curbed since the landmark Bommai judgment of the Supreme Court in 1994. However, in cases of breakdown of public order, this remains a potent latent power exercisable by the central government.

The MHA combines most functions of the interior ministries in continental Europe minus the direct control of civil police common in centralized states. This includes certain functions of the attorney general of the United States in the MHA's judicial responsibilities, including bilateral/multilateral treaties on mutual assistance, extradition, and a key role in the appointments of judges of the high courts and the Supreme Court, etc. It sits on judgment over such laws passed by state legislatures, which the federally appointed governors, otherwise titular, can refuse to assent to on grounds of legal flaws, and refer to the president.

Critically, as the nodal ministry for internal security, the MHA frames and oversees the implementation of preventive detention laws and other special legislation that allow the government to designate organizations as "unlawful" or declare an area as "disturbed," allowing the security organs of the GOI to operate with much greater latitude than what a normal rule-of-law situation would allow. For example, federal sanction is required to prosecute any alleged violation of law by a member of the armed forces, including killings. Similarly, it exercises a degree of control over civil society by vetting their eligibility for receiving foreign funds through its superintendence of the Foreign Contribution Regulation Act (FCRA).

The MHA has also emerged as an important source of financial support for states' police forces to build capacity and enhance their effectiveness, given persistent low levels of spending by state government on police. The MHA also reimburses most costs incurred by states in their anti-insurgency operations and its research arm disseminates information on different aspects of policing. Crucially, cadre management of the premier police personnel belonging to the Indian Police Service (IPS), including their deployment in the GOI, and their professional training is under the MHA. The MHA also has an infrastructure of specialized laboratories and support training institutions in investigation, forensics, civil defense, prison management, fire services, and civil defense that are meant to support state police forces.

However, the locus of the MHA's powers lies in its surveillance and coercive instruments. Its foremost surveillance instrument is the Intelligence Bureau (IB), the government's internal intelligence establishment, spread across the country. Its local units, the Subsidiary Intelligence Bureau (SIB), maintain close relations with state police forces, sharing intelligence and often help coordinate actual operations (Saikat Datta's chapter in this volume discusses the IB in more detail). The IB is also extensively used by the government to open channels of communications with insurgent groups. In fact, IB often carries out the actual negotiations, with the bureaucratic and political element entering only when sufficient progress is achieved, allowing the state to break off if positive outcomes look doubtful. Unfortunately, on occasion, the IB has also been used for negotiations with armed insurgent groups, bypassing the MHA itself.

The MHA has other coercive instruments as well arising from its direct control over federal investigative agencies like the Narcotics Control Bureau (which was previously under the Ministry of Finance) and the National Investigation Agency (NIA), which deals with terrorism cases and was established in the wake of the Mumbai terror attack in November 2008.

The kinetic fist of the MHA's coercive powers is vested in its gendarmerie responsibilities. By 2020, the MHA had built a corps of seven separate CAPFs, with just under a million personnel—a more than sixfold increase from approximately 150,000 in 1970. While the CAPFs are examined in detail in the chapter in this volume by Yashovardhan Azad, it is important to note that their deployment to combat insurgencies and help maintain public order has become the norm. States ask for CAPF deployment since they have not invested sufficiently in building up their own forces, and even these personnel are poorly trained and armed. Another unstated reason is that CAPFs are seen as nonpartisan with no local interests. The GOI has had a consistent view that in the appointment to sensitive posts like governor, non-locals are preferred for senior civil service positions and other key posts. CAPFs fit this bill precisely. They are recruited from all over the country, with emphasis in recent years on increased representation from insurgent-prone areas, as a means to providing employment to youth.

The MHA is the second largest civilian ministry in terms of employees (after Railways), with 0.956 million people in position as of March 1, 2020, representing 30.5 percent of the 3.13 million civilian personnel in position across all ministries and departments.[2] According to data from the Seventh Pay Commission, from 2006 to 2014, "all ministries with the exception of the Ministry of Home Affairs (MHA), witnessed a decrease in employees. The number of MHA employees (including the paramilitary forces) went up by 32 percent, during this period."[3] The trend began in the 1980s and has continued for nearly four decades. Similarly, if one looks at the staffing pattern of the ministry itself, it is the largest in terms of the number of senior officials (e.g., secretaries, special secretaries, additional secretaries, and joint secretaries).

However, it is not size alone that matters when it comes to perceived hierarchy. More often than not, a political heavyweight has been the minister-in-charge of the MHA, frequently second in the ruling dispensation and a putative prime minister (e.g., Sardar Patel, Govind Ballabh Pant, Lal Bahadur Shastri, Gulzari Lal Nanda, Y. B. Chavan, Charan Singh, Gyani Zail Singh, P. V. Narasimha Rao, S. B. Chavan, L. K. Advani, P. Chidambaram, Rajnath Singh, and Amit Shah). In fact, twice when an incumbent prime minister died in office, the home minister was sworn in as the prime minister until a new prime minister was chosen by the ruling party.

For these reasons, the MHA retains its primacy in the GOI among ministries, although its powers have been circumscribed in several instances. There was a short period during the Janata Party government at the Center (1977–1979), when there was a conscious attempt at reduction of responsibilities (following the excesses of the Emergency). Crucially, however, even as the MHA has won many battles, it has lost others.

Since the 1970s, the PMO has seen its powers expand from coordination of ministries to leadership over many aspects of policymaking and executive action, including the MHA. In 1968, the MHA suffered a big setback when a separate external intelligence (RAW) was created by moving the unit out of IB, upgrading it, and making it directly responsible to the prime minister. Similarly, the separation of department of personnel from the MHA meant that the power of determining sizes of ministries and recruitment of personnel moved away to the Ministry of Personnel (now Ministry of Personnel, Public Grievances and Pensions), which was created in 1970. In the process, the MHA also lost control over the Central Bureau of Investigation (CBI), the federal anti-corruption and criminal investigation and prosecution agency.

The CBI, often seen as a part of the MHA since it is staffed by police officers, reports to the Ministry of Personnel, which falls under the prime minister. The reason behind this is more political than administrative. The CBI was created to prosecute corrupt federal civil servants, and once Personnel was hived off from MHA in 1970, it moved out of the latter. However, as CBI's role has expanded allowing state governments to refer major corruption cases in their states, often involving political big wigs, housing it in the MHA would have made the ministry extremely powerful. Except for a short period (2003–2004) when L. K. Advani was deputy prime minister and held the Personnel portfolio, CBI has stayed with the prime minister as minister in charge of Personnel. The present arrangement means that the CBI, contrary to public perception, is less micro-managed than if it were with the MHA. This does not detract from the fact that the CBI has been used as an instrument to settle political scores, but that extends to carrying out raids only. Its low success rate in prosecution, including in high-profile cases, shows the limits of its coercive powers or perhaps its limited investigative competence.

Lastly, V. P. Singh as prime minister separated Jammu and Kashmir from the MHA and appointed the Railway Minister George Fernandes to look after the subject. Later, even when the home minister looked after the subject, the department retained its identity as a separate entity until it recently merged with the MHA. On the other hand, Advani succeeded in bringing the Sahastra Seema Dal, a CAPF, under his ministry's ambit from the Cabinet Secretariat, which works directly under the prime minister. Similarly, in his time, disaster management also moved to MHA from ministry of agriculture. Later, when P. Chidambaram was home minister, the Narcotics Control Bureau (NCB) was moved to the MHA from the Finance Ministry.

There have been exceptions, with the home minister not always enjoying the power that are commensurate with his office.[4] During the Emergency, Minister of

State (MOS) of the MHA Om Mehta effectively ran the ministry, not Home Minister Brahmananda Reddy. During the V. P. Singh government, though the home minister was Mufti Mohammad Sayeed, his MOS Subodh Kant Sahay not only handled Ayodhya matters, but also Punjab, Jharkhand, and the North East. Rajesh Pilot, as communications minister, was "quasi-officially" dealing with Kashmir matters bypassing the HM and the MHA. Pilot also made policy announcements on Punjab, Bodoland, Ayodhya, Jharkhand, etc. by taking orders from the prime minister directly.

The overall trend toward an increase in MHA's responsibilities, initiatives, and resources, notwithstanding, it forms part of a complex network of federal government instruments of internal security. Some of this capacity is under the MHA, while other portions are located in the Ministries of Finance, Personnel, Defense, and the Cabinet Secretariat. The country's external intelligence outfit, the Research and Analysis Wing (RAW), is part of the Cabinet Secretariat, and is coordinated through the National Security Council (NSC), along with other agencies like IB. While the NSC is technically a part of the Cabinet Secretariat, it works under the national security advisor, who is a part of the PMO.

Perceived Threats to National Unity

The upheaval of Partition, the challenges of integrating princely states, and the insurgency meant that territorial unity could not be assumed, and thus preserving it became an abiding concern of the Indian state. These concerns soon led the government to place limits on freedom of speech as well as the use of preventive provisions of the Code of Criminal Procedure to "bind" down potential mischief makers to good behavior. The bureaucratic agent of the GOI to implement these measures was the MHA.

Preventive Detention and Limits to Liberty

Indian states used criminal laws to check what was termed as "anti-State" behavior. When courts struck down such laws, the government introduced in the interim parliament a preventive detention law, which after passing became the National Security Act 1950, the first piece of legislation adopted after the coming into force of the Constitution. While it was to be valid for one year, it was regularly extended, and besides a brief period between 1978 to 1980, India has always had preventive detention laws that have allowed keeping a person in custody without charges or recourse to robust judicial processes.[5] Specific detention laws dealing with maintenance of internal security, safety of public infrastructure, advocating secession, terrorism, etc. are also in the statutes.

The National Security Act was followed by the First Amendment. Ironically, it was legislated by the interim parliament, which as the constituent assembly had adopted the very constitution that it now amended. Unlike the First Amendment in the United States, which guarantees the freedom of expression, the reverse happened in India, an indication of the Indian state's apprehensions regarding the balance between individual liberty and public order. Article 19 of the Constitution guarantees freedom of speech and expression. However, its sub-clause allowed the state to impose restrictions, initially on grounds of "libel, slander, defamation, contempt of court or any matter which offend against decency or morality or which undermines the security of the state or tends to overthrow the state." Existing legislations at the time restricted fundamental freedoms of speech and expression (e.g., pre-censorship of publications, on grounds of maintenance of public order, securing public safety). These were challenged and reached the Supreme Court, which ruled that expressions like "public order" and "public safety" had much wider connotations than "security of the state."[6] These acts were accordingly stuck down as *ultra vires* of the Constitution. The GOI decided to meet this legal challenge by a constitutional amendment that brought in two more grounds allowing the imposition of restrictions, namely, friendly relations with foreign states and public order.[7]

Skepticism of Foreigners

Independent India looked upon foreigners with a fair amount of skepticism. As early as 1949, the MHA decided that it was "necessary to establish a means to check against the infiltration of Chinese and other foreign nationals." However, it agreed to give certain exemption to Tibetans, Nepalese, and Bhutanese.[8] With the signing of the "Agreement between the Republic of India and the People's Republic of China on Trade and Intercourse between Tibet Region of China and India 1954," India accepted Tibet as part of China, and some exemptions given to Tibetans under the passport rules were withdrawn. Significantly, the MHA has continued to categorize Tibetans and Chinese separately.

Though India passed a Citizenship Act only in 1955, the MHA prescribed a registration process for foreign residents at the outset (excepting diplomats and their families). The numbers of foreigners registered (by nationality) were detailed in the MHA's annual reports. Subsequently, since 1968, the MHA has listed registered foreigners under two categories: missionaries and others.

In 1961, the MHA issued the Foreigners (Registration of Activities) Order (1962), as shadows loomed over the Himalayan borders with Tibet. Consequent to the 1962 war with China, the Indian government detained most resident Chinese (around 3,000), including Indian citizens of Chinese origin, and interned them in a camp in Rajasthan, akin to the internment of people of Japanese origin in the United States during World War II. Furthermore, India issued a constitutional order under Article 359 "suspending the right of any person who is a foreigner, or a person not of Indian origin, to move any Court for the enforcement of the rights conferred by Articles 21 and 22."[9] While the detainees were released between 1965 and 1967, an entire community was deemed a threat to national security, even though some had moved to India over a century prior, married locally, and had no connections to China.[10]

Concerns about foreign funds directed to individuals and organizations, "other than in the course of ordinary business transactions,"[11] led the MHA to introduce the Foreign Contribution (Regulation) Bill in 1973, which targeted political parties. Parliament approved this legislation during the emergency when the Foreign Contribution (Regulation) Act (FCRA) came into effect in 1976.[12] Total non-business foreign exchange receipts in 1968 were estimated at just Rs. 24 crores; by 2004–2005, the amount received had gone up to Rs. 6,256 crores and in 2018–2019 to Rs. 20,011 crores.[13] The law was subsequently amended in 1985, 2010 (in response to protests against the Kudankulam nuclear power plant), 2015, and 2020. The most recent changes reflect an increasingly securitized approach to foreign funding, leading thousands of NGOs to forgo the license (and much needed revenues).

Insurgencies

While the GOI's internal security doctrine is discussed in detail elsewhere in this volume (see chapters by Paul Staniland and Sushant Singh), the focus here is on the MHA's role in the context of insurgencies in four different contexts: North East, Punjab, Jammu and Kashmir, and left-wing insurgency.

The manner in which the GOI dealt with the Naga insurgency—a twin-track approach combining armed response with political outreach—became the template for other insurgencies in the region. Nehru's focus remained the integrity of the Indian Union, which necessitated a refusal to allow any region, whether Nagaland or elsewhere, to secede. Nehru was initially against a separate state of Nagaland, as it "would be a risk in the frontier region." An unsettled frontier was viewed as a threat to the security and integrity of India. However, when faced with rising tribal aspirations, Nehru's commitment to a political solution led to a willingness to change governing structures within the Indian Union.

The Naga Hills district was separated from Assam, and after an accord with the Naga People's Convention, the new state of Nagaland came into existence on December 1, 1963.[14] Its formation violated the twin criteria of a common linguistic community and of economic viability recommended by States Reorganization Commission (1955).[15] Since then, Nagaland has seen elected state governments, several agreements between the GOI and Naga insurgents, and splits in insurgency and intra-insurgent violence. Throughout this period, the MHA, and not the state government, has been the primary agent of the GOI dealing with demands raised by insurgent groups, since the latter does not have the power to change the constitutionally mandated administrative and political arrangements. The MHA's consistent strategy throughout has been the adoption of political solutions within the Indian Constitution but without compromising sovereignty, backed by substantial flows of development funds, unconnected to the levels of violence, or prevalence of ceasefire.

The MHA's playbook for other insurgencies in the North East—in Manipur, Lushai Hills district of Assam (now Mizoram), Assam (ULFA, Bodo rebels, and various groups in Karbi Anglong), Tripura, and Meghalaya—has been broadly similar. Initially, the local authorities failed to assess the depth of the movement or scale of violence that would erupt. This would be followed by the deployment of the Army. Later, the CAPFs would be used extensively in anti-insurgency operations, even as lines of communications were opened with rebel groups. Often the groups splintered between pro-talks and anti-talks factions, the former sometimes promoted by intelligence agencies. There have been, and continue to be, different levels of agreements—ceasefire, suspension of operations, etc.—between the government and these insurgent groups. The sharp decline in violence over the last decade might appear to vindicate the twin approach of a heavy security footprint combined with political engagement and economic development programs. However beneath the surface, calm, strong tensions persist, especially in places like Manipur. And the Naga imbroglio endures as Naga demands infringe on the territorial integrity of other states in the region.[16]

Punjab

The rise of extremist violence in Punjab possibly posed the most serious threat to the Indian state. It began as demand for greater autonomy to states, but was soon enmeshed in Sikh extremism that used violence and selective assassinations to press its demand for a separate sovereign Sikh state, Khalistan. Initially, the movement was seen as an attempt by the Union Government led by Indira Gandhi through her home minister, Giani Zail Singh, to outflank the Akali Dal, the Sikh political party closely identified with Sikh temporal institutions. But it badly backfired, resulting in an almost complete breakdown of state authority in Punjab. This led the MHA to enforce the disturbed areas laws in Punjab in 1983, which allowed special courts to be set up and speedily try militancy-related cases.[17] The government implicitly accepted that the troubles in Punjab had their roots in dissatisfaction with Center-state relations, and in 1983, the MHA set up the Sarkaria Commission "to examine and review the working of the existing arrangements between the Union and States in regards to powers, functions and responsibilities in all spheres and recommend such changes or other measures as may be appropriate."[18]

The attempt to replicate the North East playbook, however, fell apart in 1984. Confronted with the limitations of a demoralized state police and ineffective CAPFs already deployed in the state in large numbers, the GOI called in the Army to flush out Jarnail Singh Bhindranwale, who had emerged as the leader and voice of Sikh militancy, and his armed militants from the Golden Temple, Sikhism's holiest shrine, where the latter had taken refuge. This action and the resultant death toll—a thousand dead inside the temple, including 150 from the Indian Army—would have serious ramifications. Later that year, Prime Minister Indira Gandhi was assassinated by two of her own Sikh bodyguards. Sikhs in Delhi and other parts of North India were then targeted by mobs, often led by politicians, resulting in the deaths of about 3,000 people, almost all Sikhs.[19] These events continue to cast a dark shadow, and have vitiated India's relationship with the Sikh diaspora.

With the crisis threatening to spiral out of control, the MHA declared several organizations unlawful under the Unlawful Activities (Prevention) Act (UAPA) (1967),[20] a legislation enacted when there was no real threat to the country's sovereignty. In addition to the application of UAPA, the MHA pushed two Punjab-focused legislations: the Terrorist Affected Areas (Special Courts) Act (1984) and the Terrorist and Disruptive Activities (Prevention) Act (TADA) (1985). The latter defined terrorist acts, laid down stringent punishment, and provided for a special machinery for speedy disposal of cases. It lapsed in 1995.

The GOI tried different approaches, including the appointment of well-regarded police officers from outside the state as police chiefs and the massive deployment of CAPFs. But success was achieved only when the locus of these efforts shifted from Delhi to Punjab with an elected government in the state and a resuscitated state police entrusted with the task of fighting the militants and the MHA providing CAPFs in support. Aggressive police tactics, criticized for often disregarding legal norms, together with a combination of local political, administrative, and social factors, contributed to the collapse of the Khalistan movement and particularly its reliance on terrorist violence.

Jammu and Kashmir

Kashmir is a case of armed "conflict within states [that] can continue for decades without any serious prospect of victory or settlement."[21] Compared to the insurgencies of the North East and Punjab, the international dimension of the insurgency in Kashmir, particularly the role of Pakistan, is manifest.

Jammu and Kashmir's (J&K) political development within the Indian political system was sui generis, allowing the state legislative assembly the final say in accepting specific provisions of the Indian Constitution, national laws, and even the jurisdiction of apex institutions like the Election Commission and the comptroller and auditor general. As with Punjab, a series of egregious political missteps by the central government in a border state where a hostile neighbor was itching to fish in troubled waters ignited an insurgency and led to the collapse of the state machinery.

As the insurgency raged, the state was initially directly administered by the central government, with the Army and CAPFs in the lead as the state's police force crumbled. However, the security forces' initial adherence to legal procedures when dealing with militants was weak at best, and there were substantial human rights abuses that shed a harsh light on the CAPFs' discipline and training. The absence of local police also meant that credible intelligence was often lacking.

The security forces gradually brought the situation under control, with a considerable decline in violence from 2006 onward. However, in the absence of a viable political settlement and continued abetment from Pakistan, periodic upsurges of violence have continued, although the share of civilian casualties has continued to decline.

On August 5, 2019, the GOI attempted to break the stalemate by effectively abrogating Article 370, bifurcating the state into two Union territories: Ladakh and Jammu & Kashmir. The exercise was initiated and shepherded by the MHA without involving other ministries or government agencies since secrecy was key to its implementation.[22] While this has changed the political dynamics and underscores the MHA's preeminent role in the government's internal security agenda, the implications for the region are too early to tell as deep alienation in the Kashmir Valley continues.

Assam

The sensitivity of the Indian state to the borders in the East and its impact on security are not limited to insurgency-affected areas like Nagaland; these concerns were far more acute when it came to borders with East Pakistan. Here, instability arose not because of ungovernable spaces but as a result of the cross-border flows of people. The Partition initially saw relatively lesser Hindu minorities flow into India from East Pakistan (compared to the deluge from West Pakistan). However, soon the province saw large-scale violence targeting Hindus, which led to substantial refugee flows to West Bengal and Assam. The sustained migration, or what the GOI called "infiltration," led to fears of demographic changes in Assam, fueling tensions in that state. Under pressure to act, the GOI established four Tribunals "for more effective disposal of the cases of Pakistani migrants in Assam in 1963."[23] A year later, the MHA reported that cases of 32,645 persons of which 32,022 were held to be of Pakistani origins had been referred to tribunals.[24]

The problem of illegal migration festered and precipitated the student-led Assam agitation in 1979. The security situation in Assam deteriorated so rapidly that the January 1980 Lok Sabha elections could not be held in the state except for the two Bengali-dominated constituencies of the Barack Valley. Allegations that electoral rolls were defective as millions of "illegal aliens" were registered as voters made it impossible to hold elections in the rest of the state. Led by the All Assam Students Union (AASU) and the All Assam Gana Sangram Parishad (ASGP), the one-point agenda of the agitation demanded the identification and deportation of all illegal migrants with a cutoff date going back to 1951.

Over the next years, the deteriorating law-and-order situation led the GOI to make several decisions that significantly altered its role in internal security with a lasting impact on Center-state relations. Reversing the decision of the short-lived Janata Party government that had reduced the strength of the CAPFs, the MHA decided to add more battalions to the Border Security Force (BSF) to enhance border management and coordinated increased investments in border infrastructure (more posts, border fencing, and roads). The GOI also decided to introduce photo identity cards for voters in Assam and other states of the North East.[25]

The MHA took on a new responsibility: making arrangements for Internally Displaced Persons (IDPs) in Assam, as people fled their homes and villages and took shelter in camps elsewhere in the state and in West Bengal. The new Illegal Migrants (Determination by Tribunals) Act 1983 brought back special tribunals "to determine in a fair manner the question if someone was an illegal migrant." To try to ensure neutrality, judges appointed to the tribunals were from outside Assam.[26]

These efforts culminated in the signing of a tripartite memorandum of settlement, popularly referred to as the Assam Accord, on August 15, 1985, between the GOI, the leaders of the agitation (AASU and ASGP), and the government of Assam. The GOI committed to detecting and deporting foreigners who entered Assam after a cutoff date and substantially improve border management, specifically that the "international border shall be made secure against future infiltration by erection of physical barriers like walls, barbed wire fencing and other obstacles at appropriate places."[27] The state government committed to registering all births and deaths, to preventing foreigners from acquiring immovable property, and to protecting government and community lands from encroachment, as well as the use of constitutional, legal, and administrative safeguards "to protect, preserve and promote the cultural, social, linguistic identity and heritage of the Assamese people."[28]

Despite the accord, Assam saw the outbreak of extensive terrorist activity with the rise of an armed separatist group, the United Liberation Front of Assam (ULFA), with ties to other militant groups in the North East that set up sanctuaries in Bangladesh and Myanmar. It took almost two decades, an extensive deployment of the Indian Army and the CAPFs, the promulgation of the Armed Forces Special Powers Act (AFSPA), and closure of ULFA camps in Bangladesh before the situation limped back to normal, when a tripartite agreement on suspension of operations was signed between the GOI, the government of Assam, and ULFA in 2011.[29]

The Indian state's response in Assam was distinctive in two significant ways. First, it led to the practice of Unified Command to combat insurgencies because of the deployment of the Army extensively. Though the structure was formalized only in 1997, civil-military cooperation was established across all levels.[30] While this structure was in operation in Jammu and Kashmir, the context was considerably different. In the latter, it was a military-led effort combating an externally aided and directed insurgency. Assam was more like Punjab with the state police force an integral part of the anti-insurgency operations since the Army and CAPFs only operated in select areas. Unlike Jammu and Kashmir, where for long periods during which counterinsurgency operations was dominant and the state was directly administered by Delhi with the state governor (often a retired senior army general or policeman taking the lead), Assam mostly had elected governments, except for a brief interregnum.[31] The local political leadership therefore took ownership of the unified command mechanism and viewed it a success.[32]

Moreover, unlike other insurgencies in the country, the state government took the lead in directly opening lines of communications to the insurgent group (ULFA). Successive state governments launched two amnesty schemes for surrendered insurgent cadres, with generous financial payouts funded by the central government, but developed and operated by the state government. However, these led to perverse outcomes with state politicians using surrendered ULFA (SULFA) "to further partisan political interests and, on the other, as a weapon in transient and often extra-constitutional counter-terrorism operations . . . to attack ULFA, settle political scores and intimidate rivals."[33] Despite funding the amnesty schemes, the MHA had limited control over the surrender policy, finding the results as "not very encouraging."[34]

Left-Wing Extremism

India has a long history of armed uprisings and violence led by different factions of the Communist Party. In the immediate post-independence period, the Communist Party of India (CPI) launched an armed struggle in Telangana, which was suppressed by the Indian state. In 1967, with both the CPI and the breakaway Communist Party of India (Marxist) in power in West Bengal, an extreme faction of the latter inspired by Mao Zedong, broke away and formed the Communist Party of India (Marxist-Leninist) (CPI) (ML). The CPI (ML) soon launched an armed struggle, which came to be known as the Naxalite movement. Targeted killings of landlords and other "class enemies" began in North Bengal and spread to urban areas. Operation Steeple Chase, a joint operation of the Indian Army and the police, broke the back of the Naxalite movement in mid-1971, and over the next three years (1972–1975), the state government, assisted by central security forces, doused the urban embers of the movement. But the movement reappeared in the states of Bihar, Odisha, Madhya Pradesh, and Andhra Pradesh by the early 1980s.[35]

In the next decade, Naxalite violence (or Left-Wing Extremism [LWE], as categorized by the MHA) surged, with around 500 extremists, security forces, and civilians killed annually. Unlike the other insurgencies, the MHA saw LWE more the result of economic backwardness rather than as a political issue. But it was slow to address this because economic planning and development were state subjects and a responsibility of the Planning Commission. However, with time, this approach changed, with the MHA taking the lead in formulating a "Backward District Initiative."

By the early 2000s, LWE had spread across the middle of the country, and by the end of the decade, there was a "red corridor" from Nepal, through Bihar, Jharkhand,

Odisha, and Chhattisgarh to Andhra Pradesh, afflicting over a hundred districts. The Naxalites took advantage of the forested border regions of many of the states, set up camps in these weakly administered areas, and conducted operations across state boundaries.[36]

The MHA played a central role in the Indian state's response. It began to compile much more detailed reports, deployed CAPFs in the LWE-affected states, designed and funded ambitious development programs as well as increased assistance to states to improve general police infrastructure, and ramped up the numbers of well-trained and equipped special forces. The situation turned around, and at the time of writing, while LWE violence exists in pockets, the movement's potential to run a parallel state in "liberated zones" had substantially weakened. Total casualties had fallen to a third of the peak levels in the mid-2000s.

Internal Fissures and Terrorism

Communal Riots

One of the most pernicious stains on the Indian body politic has been the persistence of inter-community or communal violence. The toxic atmosphere that preceded Partition and the horrific violence that accompanied it has continued to impact long after independence.

The first major communal riot in independent India was in Jabalpur (Madhya Pradesh) in 1961 where fifty-five people died.[37] In December 1963, a theft at the Hazarat Bal incident in Srinagar led to large-scale communal violence in East Pakistan. As hundreds of thousands of refugees streamed into West Bengal and Assam, communal incidents erupted in Eastern India, especially in the three cities of Kolkata, Rourkela, and Jamshedpur. Communal violence increased over the decade but moderated in the early to mid-1970s. However, over a quarter century from the late 1970s to 2002, India witnessed its worse communal violence. While somewhat less virulent, this violence has continued to be endemic. The fact that the national capital, which has India's best equipped police force, saw communal riots in February 2020, leaving fifty-three dead, on the heels of the visit of the US president with security measures at their peak, amply demonstrates that communal violence in India is manifestly political.[38]

At one level, the ubiquity of communal violence lays bare the inadequacies of state police forces. However, to the extent that the police are subservient to their political masters, the problem is much deeper. After the first major eruptions of communal violence in 1961, the GOI set up the National Integration Council (NIC) "to find ways and means to combat the evils of communalism, casteism, regionalism, and narrow-mindedness, and to formulate definite conclusions in order to give a lead to the country."[39] The NIC was moderately active (meeting sixteen times between 1962 and 2013), forming subcommittees, engaging with civil society, commissioning studies, and debating and recommending legal changes in criminal and election laws.[40]

The MHA also began convening regular meetings of state chief ministers and occasionally of state home ministers to discuss the handling of communal riots. Often, extensive guidelines were finalized at such meetings and sent to all chief ministers on how to prevent and control communal violence. However, such high-level meetings slowly died out beginning in the 1990s and they have not been convened for many years (the NIC has not met since 2013). Although law and order is a state subject and the core responsibility for preventing and managing communal violence lies with the states, the MHA, alarmed by spiraling communal violence, in 1992 formed a specialized force, the Rapid Action Force (RAF), from existing battalions of the CRPF, to handle riots and communal violence (discussed further in the chapter by Nirvikar Jassal and Hanif Qureshi in this volume).

While large-scale communal conflagrations have ebbed, violence persists as more localized riots. The core challenge is—and in many ways has always been—political. Whether it is delays in the deployment of security forces, their conduct, or holding security forces and rioters (especially from the majority community) accountable, the record of the Indian state—both central and state governments—is sordid. If the roots are political, so are the solutions. Bureaucracies like the MHA are the agents and not the principal.

Jihadi Terrorism

The events of 9/11 were a searing reminder to the world of the dangers posed by jihadi terrorism, whose ravages have afflicted numerous countries around the world, including India. Indeed, given the size of its Muslim population, democratic mobilization, real and perceived discrimination, communal tensions and violence, and cross-border machinations from Pakistan, the rise of jihadi terrorist groups in India is unsurprising.[41] The most powerful and violent of these groups has been the Indian Mujahideen (IM).

While the IM started making claims for terror attacks only from 2007, elements that formed the core of the IM, mostly from the Students Islamic Movement of India (SIMI), carried out such attacks from 2002.[42] Initially, while SIMI believed that establishing an Islamic state (Khilafat) was the duty of every Muslim, it officially abjured violence. However, increased communal tensions in the 1990s, the 1993 Mumbai bombings that killed 260 people, and the 2002 Gujarat riots radicalized a section of Muslim youth and reaffirmed the beliefs of SIMI radicals that they must defend the Muslim community and avenge the attacks. There were also local factors, like the existence of fertile grounds for Islamic radicalism in the city of Hyderabad, which contained groups who had not reconciled Hyderabad's accession to independent India.[43]

Between 2002 and 2013, IM carried out twenty attacks on civilians, causing about 750 deaths. While the number of attacks has been relatively modest, the human, cognitive, and political impact of the attacks have been substantial. Like multiple other jihadi terrorist groups, IM organized itself around small, independent cells spread across the country. This would have made it more difficult to neutralize, but it often drew from the ranks of Muslim criminal gangs, allowing state police, especially in Mumbai and Delhi, to penetrate IM and bust key cells. The importance of local police, particularly at the beat level in maintaining links with the community, helped control these groups.[44] The challenge faced by the Indian state from jihadi terrorists also forced a level of cooperation between MHA agencies (especially IB and NIA), India's external intelligence agency (RAW), and police of different states.

While the IM was gradually marginalized, the relative lull in the activities of jihadi terrorist groups does not mean that the danger is over. Easy access to digital media has led to a shift to online radicalization of middle-class youth, especially in southern states and West Bengal. While there have been some successes by law enforcement agencies in preventing the radicalization of vulnerable youth, the MHA has done poorly in developing systemic de-radicalization programs or addressing the root causes of disaffection.

Border Security

Border control has become a major preoccupation of countries around the world and has emerged as a core preoccupation of the MHA. As Yashovardhan Azad details in his chapter in this volume, the MHA-controlled CAPFs guard India's borders. In recent years, the MHA has driven the policy of gradually hardening India's borders with Bangladesh and Pakistan with barbed wire fencing, lighting, sensors, etc. In addition, a realization that lack of development in the remote Himalayan border areas could pose security issues led to a gradual buildup of development schemes in border districts. In the mid-1980s, in response to the challenge of infiltration of terrorists from Pakistan, the MHA initiated the Border Area Development Programmed (BADP) covering the western border (Punjab, Rajasthan, Gujarat) and, subsequently, the eastern border with Bangladesh in the 1990s. Between 2014–2015 and 2018–2019, the annual disbursement to states under BADP averaged Rs. 900 crore.[45]

One component rolled out in 1987 in response to persistent infiltration from across the border with Pakistan was a scheme to issue identity cards in four border districts of Rajasthan, followed by similar pilots in the border districts of Gujarat and Punjab.[46] Subsequently, ID cards were issued to residents of border areas of Assam, Meghalaya, Tripura, and Mizoram, with costs borne by the GOI.[47] These were the precursors of ID schemes, such as Aadhaar and the National Register of Citizenship (NRC), whose roots lay in decisions taken over the decades to tackle the perceived threat to national security from unchecked illegal migration (North East) and infiltration by terrorists (on the western border).

The challenges of the management of India's borders with Bangladesh and Pakistan were assessed quite differently by the MHA. In the former, an influx of illegal migrants, who could potentially cause social disruption with consequent negative implications for internal security, was seen as the main problem.[48] In the latter, infiltration by terrorists and smuggling of arms, ammunition, and drugs were the main concern.[49] In contrast, the India-Tibet (China) and Indo-Nepal borders were seen to have little internal security implications. But this was not so for the Indo-Bhutan border since for a long time, ULFA maintained sanctuaries and camps in Bhutan.[50] Although a formal articulation only found place in the MHA Annual Report of 2008–2009, after it created a department of Border Management, a strategy based on this assessment had been under implementation for decades.

The horrendous sea-borne terrorist attacks on Mumbai, referred to as 26/11, exposed deep flaws in the security of India's coastal borders and in federal-states coordination. The botched response revealed systemic dysfunctions in intelligence assessment and response mechanisms. The absence of a single chain of command meant that vital assets like the Anti-Terrorist Squad (ATS) and quick response teams (QRTs) sent by MHA were underutilized.[51] The MHA was in effect missing in action at a time when the country was under attack, and it exposed the sorry state of state-level policing and federal-state security coordinating mechanisms.

Ironically, the GOI had launched a centrally assisted Coastal Security Scheme, a major program of financing state coastal police assets in 2005, but like many such programs its progress had been desultory.[52] Post-Mumbai, in addition to changes in responsibilities allocated to the Navy and Coast Guard, there have been concerted efforts to better prepare coastal states and union territories, but how well the system would respond to another such attack is unclear.[53]

The MHA's Coordinating, Leadership, and Financing Roles in Internal Security

The MHA plays a critical role in coordinating federal-state discussions on internal security. There are three extant platforms besides the NIC that bring the GOI and state governments together to discuss internal security. At the top political level, there are meetings of chief ministers normally called by the prime minister and occasionally by the home minister. While handling communal riots was the earlier priority, it has since shifted to discussing Left Wing Extremism (LWE), jihadi terrorism, coastal security, and border management. However, there is no fixed periodicity to these meetings. In the immediate aftermath of the Mumbai attacks of 2008, there was a spurt of such meetings for about a year, but this has become relatively moribund since then.

The most regular and substantive mechanism is the annual meetings of state inspectors general of police that is convened and chaired by the IB director, seen as the country's top policeman. These meetings last three to four days, and generally the prime minister and the home minister attend some sessions. For example, eighty-four agenda items were discussed in the March 17–20, 1986, meeting, and both the prime minister and home minister attended one session each.[54] In contrast, during the fifty-third annual meeting of the directors/inspectors general held on December 20–22, 2018, the prime minister was present on the last two days and the home minister on all three days, along with the ministers of state and home secretary.[55]

Another platform that often passes under the radar is the regular meetings of the different zonal councils under the purview of the interstate council. These five zonal councils, grouped geographically, are chaired by the Union home minister, and attended by state chief ministers and administrators of UTs. These councils meet to discuss issues of regional importance and administrative steps to address them. While development issues have typically dominated the agenda, these are increasingly discussed in the context of internal security. For instance, the twenty-first meeting of the central zonal council in September 2018 discussed measures to increase density of roads and upgradation of existing roads, assistance required to combat LWE, and connected with this, leveraging Mahatma Gandhi National Rural Employment Guarantee Act (MGNREGA) to create community assets in Bastar.[56]

Strengthening State Police Forces

In the first decade after independence, the MHA collected data on the strength of states' police forces but could do little with it. It did, however, extend technical support in training and procuring communications equipment. Early on, the MHA identified inadequate housing as a major factor for low police morale in states, and in 1956, it started a small loan scheme for police housing, with states required to contribute on a matching basis. This has continued since, but at a slow pace.[57]

Concerned that states were not allocating enough budgetary support to the police, various finance commissions, starting with the Seventh Finance Commission (1979–1984), began recommending grants to states for enhancing resources for their police forces, whether increasing personnel, police stations, equipment, or housing.

However, in 2014, after the Fourteenth Finance Commission increased the share of block grants to states from 32 percent to 42 percent, many centrally sponsored schemes like "Police Modernization" were initially dropped since the Union Government had less resources available for it. But the MHA fought for its restoration arguing that states would not use this bonanza to increase expenditures on police and it would undermine the MHA leverage over states.[58] The MHA prevailed. While it had already been providing funds for LWE affected States, these increased under its Security Related Expenditure Scheme to strengthen Special Forces and Special Intelligence Branches and Special Infrastructure Scheme for infrastructure like rural roads and bridges, mobile towers and fortified police stations.[59]

The funds provided by the MHA to states to help improve their police forces totaled 12,473 crores in financial year 2019–2020. About a third of this was for police force modernization and for police infrastructure, and 7 percent each for women's safety and development of border areas.[60] However, according to one analysis, over five years from 2012 to 2017, less than half (48 percent) of the overall modernization budget was utilized by states, in part because they could not come up with matching funds.[61]

With state governments relying on CAPFs for combating insurgencies in their states, the question of who would pay for these costs became more pressing. When states could not pay the charges for deployment of CAPFs, the MHA designed a scheme called Security Reimbursement Expenditures (SRE) to defray the costs. The amounts involved are substantial, with Rs. 7,402 crores disbursed to J&K over thirty years (1989–2019) and Rs. 4,146 disbursed to seven North East states (2001–2019).[62]

This commitment to strengthening state police forces notwithstanding, state police forces continue to be undermanned, under-equipped, poorly trained and badly managed.[63] Interestingly, for more than half century, the MHA has strongly internalized the belief that inadequate development and poverty are the main causes of insurgencies and breakdown of public order. The prescription, therefore, was development. Hence, in addition to general schemes for assistance and modernization of the state police forces, the MHA decided in 1971–1972 to pay special attention "to the solution of specific problems in particular areas," beginning with a study of the dacoit-dominated Chambal Valley (encompassing parts of Madhya Pradesh, Uttar Pradesh, and Rajasthan). While it recommended measures for strengthening police personnel and equipment, it concluded that a long-range and lasting plan that generated economic growth was a more permanent solution to the dacoity problem.[64]

Although the plan was not followed through, it became a template for handling future insurgencies in addition to parallel political processes and counterinsurgency operations. In districts identified as affected by LWE, considerable resources were spent to promote economic development through investments in social and economic infrastructure. Once elected state governments became the norm again in Jammu and Kashmir from late 1996, each prime ministerial visit to the state meant the announcement of a big economic package.

Similarly, agreements on Gorkhaland, on Bodoland, in Tripura, or with the various insurgent groups in Assam, led to the establishment of new institutional arrangements such as autonomous district councils. All these political settlements put together by the MHA, were underpinned by funding support from the GOI.

This approach of the MHA, unlike security-oriented ministries elsewhere, can be located in its structure and mandate. While the MHA's staffing norms have changed over the years, its middle and senior management has historically been dominated by members of the Indian Administrative Service (IAS), rather than the IPS. During the early part of their careers, IAS officers are tasked with both promoting development and maintaining public order simultaneously and are more prone to link the two. But the emphasis on development as the panacea to all internal problems facing the country has been deeply internalized across the system, even in the police forces. Additionally, given the parlous condition of public finances of state governments, the MHA's ability to bring finances on the table over and above what states receive under federally mandated devolution strengthens its hand in negotiations with state governments and insurgent groups looking for a settlement. However, given state governments' weak implementation capacities—which shows up in the list of incomplete projects year after year—the "development dividend" in insurgency-hit areas has also been low.

The danger of the MHA's predominance is exemplified by the challenges posed by LWE, which has led to a perception that "the Naxal problem" is a MHA problem. The perennial deployment of CAPFs in LWE districts since 2006, together with the increased role of intelligence-based inter-state operations, undermined the Naxal tactics of locating themselves in border-straddling states and operating across state boundaries. However, this has created a sort of moral hazard in that even though CAPFs are in principle temporarily deployed for combatting LWEs, state governments have become excessively reliant on them and do not release them easily. This takes away the incentive for states to invest more resources in building the capacities of their own police forces and is de facto ceding power to the central government.

There are two other areas where the MHA plays an important coordination role: providing security for elections and management and settlement of interstate border conflicts. The MHA protects parliamentary and state assembly elections from violence. The Election Commission of India (ECI) works closely with the MHA to coordinate the movement and deployment of CAPFs from one region to another during the different election phases. The 2019 parliamentary election, for example, was organized over forty days in seven phases and involved multiple deployments of over 300,000 CAPF personnel.

The MHA also facilitates the management and settlement of inter-state boundary disputes. Occasionally, these turn violent, as was the case in July 2021, when six police personnel died and seventy were injured in a clash between police forces from Assam and Mizoram. When violence is imminent, or actually occurs, the MHA deploys CAPFs as a neutral force to keep the peace. The MHA also works with states to set up a dialogue to manage these disputes.

New Capabilities and Challenges

The greater complexity of internal security challenges and the weakness of state police forces have meant that the MHA has gradually emerged as the key actor setting the national internal security agenda. It began with the MHA analyzing communal riots, commissioning studies, organizing conferences of state chief ministers, and prescribing how states should preempt riots. As internal security challenges within states grew, their manifest inability to meet them led to increasing reliance on the central government. In the aftermath of the Kargil War (1999), the intelligence failures led to the establishment of the Multi-Agency Centre (MAC) to bring together national and state intelligence agencies on a common platform with access to a substantial digital database. Subsidiary MACs function at the state and local levels.

Subsequently, as terrorist threats grew, the National Investigation Agency (NIA) was established in 2008 as a specialized investigative and prosecuting agency, given limitations in state police capacities and complex inter-state and international linkages. Its ambit has since expanded, and it has developed surveillance capacities. The NIA has been particularly successful in busting jihadi terrorist modules with international links.

A parallel attempt to set up an integrated intelligence master database to enhance the country's counterterrorism capabilities, called the National Intelligence Grid (NATGRID), initially fell afoul of another major challenge: bureaucratic turf battles. NATGRID aimed at collecting and integrating data from twenty-one different government agencies and leveraging big-data analysis. It was subsequently resuscitated and is currently located in the MHA to manage turf issues, but appears likely to ultimately migrate to IB.

The rapid growth of IT has inevitably led to a new security battleground, cybersecurity. The MHA houses the India Cybercrime Coordination Centre, or IC4, which commenced operations in January 2020. It serves as the nodal point to deal with cybercrime and involves many agencies cutting across ministries (e.g., MHA, National Security Council Secretariat).

The capabilities of several of these agencies are untested. The skill and capacity limitations in areas like cybercrime are manifest. These new challenges should, in fact, force the MHA to rethink its staffing policies. Civil service officers, whether belonging to the Indian Administrative Service or the Indian Police Service, have limitations in acquiring the new skill sets. The levels of domain expertise required is unavailable in-house, barring a few individuals, and requires changes in hiring policies and organizational hierarchies. This is one internal security challenge where India needs to move out of the civil service paradigm, hire the best that the market can offer, change remuneration norms, and partner with the private sector to build necessary capabilities to improve security.

The Way Forward

Numerous government reports have proposed that public order and police, which is List II State List of Schedule VII of the Constitution, should be moved to List III, that is, the Concurrent List. This proposal is misconceived. While the Constitution may be quasi-federal, the critical role of the states should not be underestimated. The Constitution gives the central government sufficient powers to deal with any issue of national security, external or internal, and even deploy its forces against the will of a state, although such "forceful" deployment has never occurred.

The local police are, and should remain, the first responder. Punjab would not have been brought back from the brink without restoring the primacy to state police forces. Even in 26/11, those security forces who were killed or who captured the lone surviving attacker belonged to the state police. While the GOI, particularly the MHA, can play a supportive role in supplementing operational capacities, it is imperative to have strong capacity at the first responder level. Some states have developed operational capacities by developing elite units, (e.g., in dealing with LWE). It is more important that the MHA and the states work toward developing vertical integration with both operational and intelligence synergies.

States sometimes feel that the MHA is interfering since law and order as well as crime are state subjects. Why should internal security be treated differently? The reality is that the changing security environment that India faces has a fair degree of transborder characteristics. The weakness of states' police forces, the blurring—indeed interconnectedness—of lines between certain types of crime, particularly inter-state and transnational crime (drugs, gun running, counterfeit currency, etc.) and internal security, mean that co/joint responsibility between the Center and states is not a matter of choice.

India could be moving to a stage where the Government of India establishes a Central Law Enforcement Agency, using Entry 1, to deal with what can be described as federal offenses (e.g., terrorism, hijacking, arms running, drugs trafficking). In such a case, various legislations like TADA, NSA, UAPA, POTA, etc. could come within its ambit. States had objected to the MHA setting up a National Counter-Terrorism Centre (NCTC), viewing it as an encroachment on their responsibilities. With different political parties ruling in different states and at the Center, political resistance is not surprising.

It has been argued that since internal security has become such a complex subject, requiring specialized knowledge and treatment, it should form a separate ministry. However, creating another ministry risks creating another silo and more turf battles. Instead, the MHA should be restructured by shedding many of its functions that are peripheral to its core responsibilities and more professionalized staffing with much greater specialization from middle management upward. With insurgency-related violence levels declining, the continued increase in the strength of the CAPFs should be reviewed. Instead, building up state government capacities is vital since their police force operates within, and near, local communities, and are best placed to identify and address budding problems. But long-term success lies in prevention, and a leaner but focused MHA that also curbs itself would make for a more effective MHA.

The debates on internal security, like those on national security or even public health, are dominated by insiders, but in reality, we are all stakeholders. There is a need to go beyond insularity in diagnosis. Accepting that operational issues are best left to professionals, the societal aspects of internal security are critical. A gargantuan system, which has developed and grown episodically with inadequate capacities to tackle emerging challenges, needs to get out of both business-as-usual and crisis-mode approaches and develop a more focused, preventive, and integrated approach to enhance the security of its people.

Notes

1. Mr. Shakti Sinha sadly passed away after completing a draft of this chapter. After discussions with Mr. Sinha's family, the draft was lightly edited by Amit Ahuja and Devesh Kapur and has been approved by his family.
2. Department of Expenditure, Ministry of Finance, "Annual Report on Pay and Allowances of Central Government Civilian Employees, 2019–20," https://doe.gov.in/sites/default/files/Annual%20Report%202019-20.pdf.
3. PRS Legislative Research, "Vital Stats: Overview of Central Government Employees," December 8, 2015, https://prsindia.org/files/policy/policy_vital_state/1449721528~~Vital%20Stats-%20Overview%20of%20Central%20Government%20Employees.pdf.
4. According to Subroto Mitra, for the optimal functioning of the MHA, the Prime Minister, Home Minister, and the Home Secretary must have a good working relationship. The poor relationship shows up in a stark manner in moments of crises, which end up getting mishandled. See Subroto Mitra, *Governance by Stealth: The Ministry of Home Affairs and the Making of the Indian State* (New Delhi: Oxford University Press, 2021).
5. Rachit Garg, "Preventive Detention Laws in India," iPleaders, November 12, 2020, https://blog.ipleaders.in/preventive-detention-laws-india/#:~:text=The%20rules%20laid%20down%20in,passed%20after%20independence%20in%201950.
6. The three epochal cases were *Romesh Thapar v. State of Madras; The Superintendent, Central Prison, Fatehgarh v. Dr Ram Manohar Lohia;* and *Brij Bhushan v. State of Delhi.*
7. Tripurdaman Singh's outstanding work, *Sixteen Stormy Days: The Study of the First Amendment to the Constitution of India* (New Delhi: Vintage 2020), brings out the full dimensions of the debate and process. An unpublished piece by Ratika Gaur on legal discourse and the limits of Indian rationality in the public sphere added to my understanding.
8. MHA, *Annual Report, 1950–51*, Government of India, New Delhi.
9. MHA, *Annual Report, 1962–63*, Government of India, New Delhi.
10. Neither the central governments nor civil society have acknowledged this shameful episode, best captured in Joy Ma and Dilip D-Souza's *The Deoliwallahs: The True Story of the 1962 Chinese-Indian Internment* (New Delhi: Macmillan, 2020).
11. MHA, *Annual Report, 1970–71*, Government of India, New Delhi, ii.
12. OZG Documentation Centre, "The Foreign Contribution (Regulation) Act," *FCRA*, October 1, 2011, https://fcraonline.in/2011/01/08/the-foreign-contribution-regulation-act-1976/.

13. Government of India Ministry of External Affairs, *LOK SABHA unstarred question no. 457, To be answered on the 15th September, 2020.*

14. Minodhar Barthakur and Deryck O. Lodrick, "Nagaland," *Encyclopaedia Britannica*, July 9, 2020, https://www.britannica.com/place/Nagaland; J. C. Johari, "Creation of Nagaland: Triumph of Ebullient Infra-Nationalism," *Indian Journal of Political Science* 36, no. 1 (1975): 13–38, http://www.jstor.org/stable/41854650.

15. "Reorganisation of States: The Approach and Arrangements," *Economic Weekly*, October 15, 1955, https://www.epw.in/system/files/pdf/1955_7/42/reorganisation_of_statesthe_approach_and_arrangements.pdf.

16. Rahul Karmakar, "The Hindu Explains: What Has Made the Naga Peace Wobble," *The Hindu*, August 16, 2020, https://www.thehindu.com/news/national/other-states/the-hindu-explains-what-has-made-the-naga-peace-process-wobble/article32364459.ece.

17. MHA, *Annual Report, 1983–84*, Government of India, New Delhi, 5.

18. MHA, *Annual Report, 1983–84*, 56.

19. "Sajjan Kumar: Milestone Conviction over 1984 Sikh Killings," *BBC News*, December 17, 2018, https://www.bbc.com/news/world-asia-india-46589391.

20. MHA, *Annual Report, 1984–85*, Government of India, New Delhi, 3.

21. Eric Hobsbawm, *Globalisation, Democracy and Terrorism* (London: Abacus, 2007), 25.

22. Discussions with certain key individuals involved in the process.

23. MHA, *Annual Report 1963–64*, Government of India, New Delhi.

24. MHA, *Annual Report 1964–65*, Government of India, New Delhi.

25. MHA, *Annual Report 1980–81*, Government of India, New Delhi, 13–15.

26. MHA, *Annual Report 1983–84*, Government of India, New Delhi, 6–7.

27. Government of Assam, *The Assam Accord*, https://assamaccord.assam.gov.in/portlets/the-assam-accord.

28. Government of Assam, *The Assam Accord.*

29. "Tripartite Agreement Signed with ULFA," *The Hindu*, September 3, 2011, https://www.thehindu.com/news/national/tripartite-agreement-signed-with-ulfa/article2421033.ece.

30. Bhashyam Kasturi, "Unified Command HQ in Counter Insurgency and Role of Intelligence in J&K," *Indian Defense Review* 16, no. 1 (2001), https://www.satp.org/satporgtp/publication/idr/vol_16(1)/Bhashyam.htm.

31. The author was witness to Assam Governor Lt. Gen. SK Sinha (Retd.) giving the then prime minister a detailed briefing on the Assam situation, April 1998.

32. "Assam's Unified Command Structure One of the Best: CM," *Times News Network*, May 25, 2013, https://timesofindia.indiatimes.com/city/guwahati/Assams-unified-command-structure-one-of-the-best-CM/articleshow/19182075.cms.

33. Ajai Sahni and Bibhu Routray, "SULFA: Terror by Another Name," *Faultlines: Writings on Conflict & Resolution* 9, no. 1, 2001, https://www.satp.org/satporgtp/publication/faultlines/volume9/Article1.htm.

34. MHA, *Annual Report 1999–2000*, Government of India, New Delhi.

35. MHA, *Annual Reports, 1981–82 to 1991–92*, Government of India, New Delhi.

36. Rustom K. Nanavatty, *Internal Armed Conflict in India: Forging a Joint Civil-Military Approach* (New Delhi: Pentagon Press, 2013), 48.

37. Violette Graff and Juliette Galonnier, "Hindu-Muslim Communal Riots in India I (1947–1986)," *Mass Violence and Resistance—Research Network, Science Po*, July 15, 2013, https://www.sciencespo.fr/mass-violence-war-massacre-resistance/en/document/hindu-muslim-communal-riots-india-i-1947-1986.html; Violette Graff and Juliette Galonnier, "Hindu-Muslim Communal Riots in India—II (1986–2011)," *Mass Violence and Resistance—Research Network, Science Po*, 2013, https://www.sciencespo.fr/mass-violence-war-massacre-resistance/en/document/hindu-muslim-communal-riots-india-ii-1986-2011.html.

38. "What Are Delhi Riots 2020," *Business Standard*, https://www.business-standard.com/about/what-is-delhi-riots-2020.

39. MHA, *Background Note on National Integration Council*, https://www.mha.gov.in/sites/defa
    ult/files/NICBackG-171013.pdf.
40. MHA, *Annual Report, 1969–70*, Government of India, New Delhi, 81–84.
41. Farzana Sheikh, *Making Sense of Pakistan* (London: Hurst & Co, 2009). Sheikh makes a
    powerful argument that the "loss" of power in India was a powerful driving force behind the
    sense of deprivation felt by Muslim Indians and their demand for a separate country, since
    in an independent, democratic India, the Muslims would be a permanent minority. Several
    communiqués of Indian jihadi groups mention this perceived loss.
42. This section is largely drawn from V. S. Subrahmanian, Aaron Mannes, Animesh Roul and
    R. K. Raghavan, *Indian Mujahideen: Computational Analysis and Public Policy* (Springer, 2013).
43. Discussions with a senior police officer, long associated with de-radicalization.
44. Discussions with a senior police officer. He pointed to specific cases where families tipped off
    the police about their sons' changed behavior patterns, and sought police help in counseling
    the potential recruits, including by co-opting local imams.
45. Discussions with a senior police officer, 3.33
46. MHA, *Annual Report 1987–88*, Government of India, New Delhi, 27.
47. MHA, *Annual Report 1991–92*, Government of India, New Delhi, 13–14.
48. MHA, *Annual Report 2008–09*, Government of India, New Delhi, para 3.6–3.9.
49. MHA, *Annual Report 2008–09*, para 3.10–3.21.
50. MHA, *Annual Report 2008–09*, para 3.41–3.42.
51. Pradhan, Ram. "The 26/11 Terrorist Attack in Mumbai: A Critical Analysis of the Modus
    Operandi and Operation," in Dhruv Katoch and Shakti Sinha, eds., *Terrorism Today: Aspects,
    Challenges and Responses*, (New Delhi: Pentagon Press, 2016).
52. MHA, *Annual Report 2008–09*, Government of India, New Delhi, para 3.43–3.44.
53. MHA, *Annual Report 2018–19*, Government of India, New Delhi, para 3.38.
54. MHA, *Annual Report, 1986–87*, Government of India, New Delhi.
55. MHA, *Annual Report, 2018–19*, Government of India, New Delhi, para 2.117.
56. MHA, *Annual Report, 2018–19*, Government of India, New Delhi para 4.15–4.16.
57. MHA, *Annual Report, 1979–80*, Government of India, New Delhi.
58. Discussions with a top MHA official who was involved in this decision.
59. Government of India, Ministry of Home Affairs, Rajya Sabha Starred question no.*81,
    February 9, 2022. https://www.mha.gov.in/MHA1/Par2017/pdfs/par2022-pdfs/RS09022
    022/81.pdf.
60. MHA, *Accounts*, personally accessed.
61. Atman Mehta, "Indian Police Forces Short of Communications, Transport, Weapons but Not
    Money," *Indiaspend*, August 23, 2019, https://www.indiaspend.com/indian-police-forces-
    short-of-communications-transport-weapons-but-not-money/.
62. MHA, *Annual Reports, Annexure V (2012–13)*, Government of India, New Delhi, Para 2.41;
    and MHA, *Annual Reports, Annexure V (2018–19)*, Government of India, New Delhi.
63. Nanavatty, *Internal Armed Conflict in India*, 75.
64. MHA, *Annual Report, 1971–72*, Government of India, New Delhi, 20. The total estimated
    expenses for all the schemes that it recommended was Rs. 250–300 crores to be spent over five
    to seven years.

5

Public Finances of Internal Security in India

NIRVIKAR SINGH

In many respects, internal security, or law and order, represents a classic public good, in the economist's use of the term: goods that are non-rival and nonexclusive. However, internal security does not fall as clearly into this category as national defense: all citizens of a country are protected together and fairly equally by secure borders, but internal security can be more of a local good. Also, citizens may hire private security to protect their property, either individually or in local associations. In either case, there is some exclusion of other citizens. Nevertheless, internal security has a significant public good aspect, since policing, prisons, and courts are typically funded and provided by government entities, even when private provision is an option.[1] Hence, the public finances of internal security are an important aspect of government, particularly since law and order underpins almost every aspect of economic activity, in addition to their intrinsic benefits.

International comparisons of public spending rely on the Classification of Functions of Government (COFOG), where "public order and safety" is one of ten main categories or divisions of government spending.[2] The data may be for all levels of government ("general government"), for the central government only, or for both central and subnational (state and/or local) governments. "Public order and safety" includes a variety of services: police, fire protection, prisons, courts, research and development, and miscellaneous administration. This disaggregation is available for many European countries, as well as the United States, but not for most nations.

Overall, in 2010, India spent 2.29 percent of GDP on public order and safety,[3] of which slightly over half was subnational expenditure.[4] To benchmark India against other large countries, for Brazil public order and safety spending by the central government was 1.13 percent of GDP in 2018, and for the Russian Federation, it was 2.06 percent. In the latter case, another 0.14 percent of GDP was spent by state governments.[5] Overall, China spent 1.53 percent of GDP in 2017 (1.3 percent of GDP subnationally), and the United States spent 1.99 percent of GDP in 2018

Nirvikar Singh, *Public Finances of Internal Security in India* In: *Internal Security in India*. Edited by: Amit Ahuja and Devesh Kapur, Oxford University Press. © Oxford University Press 2023. DOI: 10.1093/oso/9780197660331.003.0005

(1.7 percent subnationally).[6] Globally, at the high end, a few countries spend in the range of 3–5 percent of GDP, but most are in the range of 1–2 percent of GDP.[7]

When the data allow disaggregation of "public order and safety," the comparison of spending on two key aspects of internal security, police and prisons,[8] is revealing. For the decade from 2007 to 2016, the European Union and the United States each spent about 1.2 percent of GDP on police and prisons, but in the EU, police accounted for over 80 percent of that total, versus 60 percent in the United States.[9] Given the United States' exceptional rates of incarceration, its high level of spending on prisons is unsurprising, but what is noteworthy is the lower level of spending on police. This suggests that spending levels themselves provide limited information: for example, they may not capture the militarization of US police forces. In any case, India's expenditure pattern is more similar to that of the EU: spending on police is 1.085 percent of GDP, or 1.123 percent if prisons are included.[10] Public spending on prisons is therefore a very small fraction of India's spending on the police. In the rest of this chapter, we focus on spending on the police, setting aside spending on prisons.

As noted, India's spending on public order and safety is roughly equally split between the national and subnational governments. The relevant subnational level is India's states: local government has a very minor role in any kind of public spending. India is formally a federal system, with constitutionally assigned responsibilities for the national government, state governments, and—to some extent—local governments. These responsibilities sometimes overlap, either de jure or de facto. This blurring of authority is particularly evident in matters of internal security. In the case of law and order, constitutional assignments define functions such as the police as a state subject, rather than as a national responsibility, but the reality is more complicated.[11] Some of the complications are explicitly associated with the structures of fiscal (as opposed to political) federalism in the country, because subnational governments rely extensively on fiscal transfers from higher levels of government. Another complication in the case of internal security is the use of military and paramilitary organizations controlled by the national government for internal security tasks in addition to national defense.[12] Hence, examining the public finance aspects of internal security in India requires considering several different categories of expenditure.

In recent years, India's central government has been spending about 13 percent of GDP, and running a fiscal deficit of between 3 and 4 percent of GDP.[13] The aggregate expenditure of the states has constituted about 15 percent of GDP (including local government expenditure, which is very small), and their aggregate fiscal deficits have recently been about 3 percent of GDP. These are approximate figures, and vary from year to year. They do not take account of off-budget items, such as losses of public-sector enterprises. The key points to note are that India's government is relatively small, and that the national and state governments are roughly equal in their overall spending, although the patterns of expenditure differ between the two levels, reflecting differing constitutional responsibilities. Also, the figures do not reflect the large transfers from the Center to the states, comprising constitutionally mandated tax sharing as well as discretionary—often earmarked—transfers.

Within this overall context, we provide an overview and analysis of India's public spending on internal security, especially in the category of police services.[14] In the next section, we describe and evaluate the central government's spending on internal security, its levels, patterns, and, where possible, its outcomes. In the subsequent section, we perform a similar analysis for the states, focusing especially on variation across the states, and trying to understand possible sources of inter-state differences in spending on internal security. The next section offers some broader discussion and analysis of the public finances of internal security, also relating it to spending on external security and, briefly, to private sector provision of internal security. The chapter ends with a summary conclusion.

Central Government

Although law and order is a state subject according to the Indian Constitution, language in that document (and underlying political and economic rationales) also makes internal security an important item of central government expenditure. Central government spending on internal security is controlled by the Ministry of Home Affairs (MHA). The expenditure of the MHA is just under 5 percent of total central government expenditure, of which almost all (close to 95 percent) is on internal security. Indeed, "Police" is a separate expenditure head in the central government accounts. To put this into perspective, interest payments constitute about 30 percent, and defense, including pensions and civil defense, accounts for about 20 percent. Spending on internal security is less than that for rural development or public distribution of food, but greater than for health or education.

Expenditure on the police comes under twenty-two different headings, but by far the bulk of it is on various Central Armed Police Forces (CAPFs), with another half-dozen significant expenditure categories (Table 5.1). The first column of the table has the serial numbers assigned to those categories in government accounts. The twenty-two categories cover a miscellany of specialized and auxiliary functions, including criminology and forensics, tracking of foreigners, education and training, protection for VIPs, central police organizations, women's safety, cybercrime, and so on: these and other spending heads have all been aggregated in Table 5.1 under "Other." It is difficult to assess the optimality of these allocations, or the organizational structures that the categories represent, but we return to such issues in the penultimate section.

One noteworthy item is the expenditure on the Delhi Police. Delhi, as the National Capital Territory (NCT), has an elected legislature, but the NCT government has no control over the police force in its jurisdiction. Hence, even micro-level

Table 5.1 **Central government spending on police by category (in %)**

		2017–18 Actuals	2018–19 Budget	2018–19 Revised	2019–20 Budget
1	Central APFs	70.8	71.4	73.3	73.0
2	Intelligence Bureau	2.3	2.1	2.2	2.4
5	Delhi Police	8.0	7.9	7.8	7.6
11	Border Infrastructure & Mgt.	2.5	2.0	2.2	2.2
12	Police Infrastructure	5.6	5.4	5.2	4.8
20	Research	3.8	3.8	2.3	2.5
21	Modernization	3.1	3.6	3.5	3.5
	Other	3.9	3.7	3.6	3.9
	POLICE TOTAL	100.0	100.0	100.0	100.0

Source: Calculated from various Union Government Budget documents, available at https://www.indi abudget.gov.in/previous_union_budget.php. The figures reported here include revenue as well as capital expenditure.

decisions with respect to the Delhi Police, such as the efficacy of traffic lights in the city, are governed by the MHA and scrutinized by the national Parliament. The raison d'être for this assignment of authority includes direct control of protection of the nation's core institutions, but also political calculations with respect to managing popular protests in the capital.

Spending on the CAPFs, as a large proportion of central police expenditure, deserves to be broken down further. The largest share goes to the Central Reserve Police Force (CRPF, about 32 percent in 2018–2019), followed by the Border Security Force (BSF, 27 percent) and the Central Industrial Security Force (13 percent).[15] The Indo-Tibetan Border Patrol and Assam Rifles each account for close to 9 percent of the CAPF total, with the Sashastra Seema Bal (also border-focused, but designed to provide armed support to the Research and Analysis Wing, a national intelligence agency) at 7 percent. Finally, the National Security Guard, a counterterrorism unit, accounts for the remainder of CAPF expenditure.[16] Hence, the CAPFs have a mix of internal and external security responsibilities among the individual organizations, though in practice there is a blurring of boundaries between these two functions.[17] Importantly, the bulk of the spending in all these categories, whether the police overall, or the individual CAPFs, is on personnel, with infrastructure categories being partial exceptions. Close to 90 percent of spending on the police is revenue expenditure—dominated by personnel costs—as opposed to capital outlays.

The possible efficacy of central spending on the police and related internal security may be gleaned from parliamentary committee reports that analyze and comment on the Demand for Grants. This is the formal request for budget appropriations that each central ministry or department submits for the annual budgeting exercise, which culminates in a finance bill. For example, the most recent parliamentary committee report (at the time of writing) commented on the need for modernization and technology upgrading, as well as adequate capital spending in general, with implications or sometimes explicit concerns that budgeted amounts were insufficient.[18] Another concern—an example of a broader issue with the operations of the government—was the failure to spend on capital projects in a timely manner. These committee reports are surprisingly detailed and specific with respect to issues such as unfilled vacancies, working conditions, women's representation in the police forces, and specific deployments of technology and infrastructure.

Initial comments and recommendations by the parliamentary committee are followed by responses from the MHA, and follow-up reports discuss the nature of these responses.[19] Again, there is great specificity and detail, but the true issues may be deeper underlying problems of the processes of government operations, rather than the specificities discussed. There are many mechanisms in place to ensure that funds are spent as intended, and that capital projects are well-executed without undue corruption, and it may be that these procedural checks slow down spending. Naturally, it is difficult to offer evidence on the actual degree of corruption, if any, in these kinds of spending. What is missing from these documents, and perhaps outside their scope, is any strategic analysis of the optimality of the allocation of funds across purposes, or of whether the expenditures achieve stated goals. One can infer a broad impression of reasonable functioning, based on general crime statistics or law-and-order data, but no more than that.

An annual report, Data on Police Organizations, published by the Bureau of Police Research and Development (BPRD) in the MHA, provides additional data on human resources, including the number of personnel at different levels of various police organizations; numbers of police stations, training institutes, laboratories, and types of equipment; and enumeration of internal proceedings against police personnel, as well as commendations.[20] However, in recent years, these documents do little more than counting, with almost no assessment of trends, patterns, or outcomes.[21] This is arguably a general problem with government expenditure in India, where many numbers are tracked, but the data are not distilled in a way that would allow for strategic assessment.

Two relatively recent changes in these reports are also worth noting. The 2015 report (reporting data as of January 1, 2015) was the last to include data on crime statistics, including crimes under the Indian Penal Code as well as Special and Local

Laws. This section of the report also provided data on disposition of cases and the performance of state and regional Forensic Science Laboratories. Crime data, including disposition of cases, are alternatively available in annual reports from the National Crime Records Bureau (ncrb.gov.in), which has existed since 1986.[22] Second, 2017 was the last year of these reports including data on what are termed "Agitations," including their number, type (e.g., communal, student, labor, etc.) and resulting casualties (both civilians and police). These data are not obviously available elsewhere in an integrated form.[23] It is notable that both types of data have been removed from the Data on Police Organizations annual report, despite the report's continuing goal of compiling data that would be useful to policymakers and to citizens.

State Governments

As noted earlier, law and order is a state subject according to India's constitutional assignments. Total police expenditure by the states in recent years has been about 20 percent higher than central expenditure, and—similar to the Center in proportion—between 4 and 5 percent of total state expenditures. However, as one would expect, the patterns of expenditure are different at different levels of government. There is also a great deal of variation across the different states, which reflects significant heterogeneity in the states and their experiences of managing internal security. We explore some of these aspects of state government spending on internal security in this section.

According to figures from January 2019, the sanctioned strength of all state police forces in India was about 2.6 million, of which about 1.7 million were Civil Police, 0.3 million were District Armed Police, and 0.6 million were State Armed Police.[24] However, because of vacancies, the actual numbers of police were about 20 percent lower overall, roughly uniformly across all the three categories. For comparison, the sanctioned strength of all the CAPFs was about 1.1 million, with a vacancy rate of close to 10 percent. However, the expenditure on the state police forces in 2017–2018 was only about 30 percent higher than the expenditure on the CAPFs, implying that spending per employee was considerably higher at the Central versus the state level. This is consistent with differences in pay scales, cost of perquisites, seniority structures, and skills or specialization. It is difficult to identify the individual contributions of these factors, but all of them are plausible explanators of differences in spending per employee.

One can reasonably infer that the bulk of spending by states on their police forces was for personnel and related operational costs. Expenditure on training is broken out in BPRD reports, and has been just over 1 percent of their total expenditure on the police. Expenditure on modernization has been slightly higher than on training, at 3 or 4 percent of total police expenditure, though this includes modernization grants from the central government, in addition to allocations from the states' own budgets. Modernization in this context refers to improvements in physical infrastructure and equipment, especially for specialized functions such as dealing with terrorism, and therefore it presumably complements the objectives of expenditures on training, though those also include physical infrastructure such as training facilities. Next, we illustrate some of the variation across states in terms of patterns of expenditure on the police.

Table 5.2 uses figures from the RBI database on state finances and central budgetary documents to calculate the ratio of expenditure on police to total revenue expenditure for 2017–2018 (leftmost column of numbers).[25] Using this ratio, the percentage for all states is about 4.7 percent, but there is considerable variation across the states. Recall that the figure for Delhi is misleadingly low, because of central control of the NCT's police services.

The seven North Eastern states (Arunachal Pradesh, Assam, Manipur, Meghalaya, Mizoram, Nagaland, and Tripura) all have high percentages, as one might expect for a region that has had a mixed relationship with the "mainstream" of the idea of India as a nation, resulting in frequent internal conflict. So also does Jammu and Kashmir, for somewhat similar reasons.[26] One can understand the high percentage for Jharkhand as a consequence of being a state with both a large tribal population and Maoist unrest.[27] Perhaps the most surprising figure is for Punjab: although it is a border state, there are dedicated central police forces for border protection, and it is not peripheral in the same way as the North East. A plausible conjecture is that relatively high spending on police in Punjab is a long-tailed legacy of the unrest of the 1980s and early 1990s. There are no other obvious patterns, such as a correlation with per capita state incomes, although the percentages seem to be lower for southern and eastern states (excluding the North East from the latter category).

Figure 5.1 displays patterns of police expenditure as they relate to the income levels of the states. The horizontal axis measures Net State Domestic Product (NSDP) per capita, and the vertical axis has state police expenditure per capita. To display a readable graph, the smaller North Eastern states with high police expenditures have been omitted, as have Jammu and Kashmir, and the small states of Goa and Sikkim, which are outliers in terms of per capita NSDP. Punjab's outlier status among the included states, which represent almost all of India's population, is clear from the graph. There is an expected positive relationship between per capita income and police expenditure, but it is quite weak. One can conjecture what other factors may influence where individual states lie relative to some average relationship, such as size (since there may be scale economies) or higher proportions of non-mainstream populations (leading to greater ethnic conflict), or stronger civil society institutions (reducing the need for public-order aspects of policing).[28] However, these explanations may not fit other states, and a detailed analysis of each state would be required to further understand the patterns in Figure 5.1.

Table 5.2 **Police expenditure as a percentage of different expenditure categories**

State	2017–18 Police/Rev Exp (%)	2017–18 Police/Soc Serv (%)	2007–08 Police/Soc Serv (%)	2017–18 Police/Devt (%)	2007–08 Police/Devt (%)
All States	4.70	118.57	115.90	29.39	23.46
Andhra Pradesh	3.72	155.84	684.88	34.11	15.26
Arunachal Pradesh	8.06	102.72	82.98	33.22	17.49
Assam	6.59	128.39	367.08	49.77	59.28
Bihar	5.59	134.72	163.89	21.95	22.26
Chhattisgarh	5.46	115.75	66.97	31.65	16.23
Goa	4.63	74.68	63.23	28.99	15.16
Gujarat	3.75	64.99	55.07	17.40	15.73
Haryana	4.88	112.70	83.90	27.39	23.77
Himachal Pradesh	3.88	92.46	42.58	29.44	18.41
Jammu & Kashmir	11.75	172.52	88.91	50.35	37.64
Jharkhand	7.77	258.92	65.97	35.50	26.06
Karnataka	2.96	48.65	62.21	14.22	16.08
Kerala	3.49	248.23	598.10	41.15	56.77
Madhya Pradesh	3.96	96.19	91.77	17.08	15.49
Maharashtra	4.65	495.19	398.23	43.55	26.53
Manipur	13.17	184.04	69.00	92.41	26.01
Meghalaya	7.71	180.00	106.59	69.51	44.66
Mizoram	7.07	79.24	139.72	25.92	27.89
Nagaland	12.89	270.43	139.65	130.33	59.39
NCT Delhi	0.10	2.25	1.04	1.17	0.19
Odisha	4.14	70.74	92.69	14.40	21.99
Puducherry	3.10	167.98	82.67	58.83	20.69
Punjab	8.40	572.57	290.65	241.57	69.27
Rajasthan	3.19	64.53	37.76	23.19	18.98
Sikkim	6.83	53.05	54.69	20.90	19.69

Table 5.2 **Continued**

State	2017–18 Police/Rev Exp (%)	2017–18 Police/Soc Serv (%)	2007–08 Police/Soc Serv (%)	2017–18 Police/Devt (%)	2007–08 Police/Devt (%)
Tamil Nadu	3.41	121.13	126.27	29.61	21.77
Telangana	5.79	173.43	N/A	21.19	N/A
Tripura	11.08	122.02	95.39	69.38	38.98
Uttar Pradesh	5.25	120.11	152.15	38.45	19.64
Uttarakhand	5.55	148.58	71.18	31.57	14.63
West Bengal	3.80	70.42	193.27	29.16	56.52

Source: Calculated from RBI database on state finances.

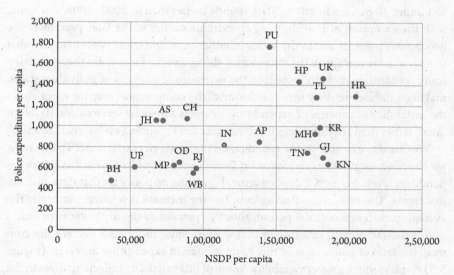

Figure 5.1 Per capita NSDP and police expenditure (Rs.), 2017–2018
Source: Calculated from Union Budget documents, National Census data, and BPRD (2019). Population figures were interpolated where needed.

For example, Mangla (this volume) provides a detailed, albeit qualitative, analysis of the institutions and functioning of the police in Madhya Pradesh.

Another way of comparing the states in terms of their spending on police is to relate that expenditure to other categories. Table 5.2 (second numerical column) displays police expenditure calculated as a percentage of social services spending, again for 2017–2018, using the RBI state finances database. For all states combined, total spending in the two categories is very similar (the ratio is close to 100 percent), but this masks considerable variation across the states. Punjab is an outlier once more, but there is no clear pattern among the other states, in terms of geography or income level. We also calculate the same numbers for a decade earlier, 2007–2008. These percentages are displayed in the third column. The value for Andhra Pradesh is not directly comparable to the later year, since 2007–2008 is before its bifurcation, but the percentage is much higher than for either Andhra Pradesh or Telangana in 2017–2018. Comparing the other states across the two years, while the All-India average is very similar, there is wide variation between the two years in terms of relative spending by individual states on police versus social services. Nor is the ranking of the states according to this measure consistent across the two years.

The rightmost two columns of Table 5.2 report the results of similar calculations, but replacing social services with development expenditure as the comparison category. Development spending is greater than expenditure on social services, so the All-States average for police expenditure relative to development expenditure was just under 30 percent in 2017–2018, slightly higher than in 2007–2008. But again, with the exception of Punjab being an extreme outlier in the later year, there are no obvious patterns across the states in either year, and there is no evidence that there is a stable ranking of the states across the two years. Essentially, there are many sources of variability with respect to the expenditure patterns of individual states, making it difficult to draw firm conclusions. The comparisons may say more about the instability of patterns of expenditure by states for social services and development, rather than anything definite about state level spending on internal security.[29]

We can also examine states' spending on police services over time. To illustrate, we choose a single state, and focus on Punjab because of its salience in police expenditure levels. Figure 5.2 displays annual spending on police for that state, in nominal terms. There are some fluctuations, but the increase is relatively smooth. The average growth rate over the period, about 12 percent, is slightly lower than India's nominal GDP growth rate during that span of time, about 13.5 percent. By contrast, the ratio of police expenditure to development expenditure over time (Figure 5.3) displays much greater variability. Some of this variability reflects changes in the nominal growth rate of police expenditure, which was higher in the mid-2000s. But a likely explanation is the differing nature of expenditure commitments. Internal security is a basic public good, and spending on personnel, in particular, is locked in by political and managerial considerations that make retrenchment of personnel infeasible or undesirable. By contrast, development expenditure is a more flexible and heterogeneous category, and likely to be where states adjust their spending, based on fiscal pressures.[30] We conjecture that similar factors are at work for other states, and that the time series patterns observed for Punjab would be found in other cases.

We round out the discussion of patterns of state spending on police by illustrating differences in states' spending on modernization and training (Figures 5.4 and 5.5). The states are ranked by percentage, and the All-India figure provides a reference

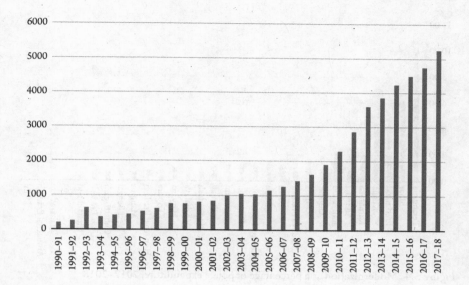

Figure 5.2 Annual police expenditure in Punjab (Rs. crore), 1990–1991 to 2017–2018
Source: Calculated from RBI database on state finances

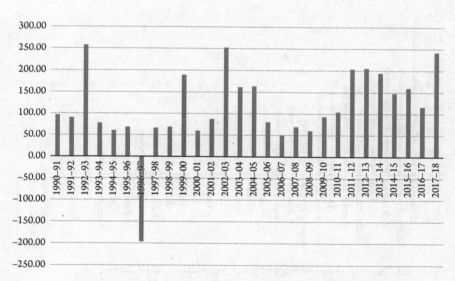

Figure 5.3 Annual police expenditure in Punjab as a percentage of development expenditure, 1990–1991 to 2017–2018
Source: Calculated from RBI database on state finances

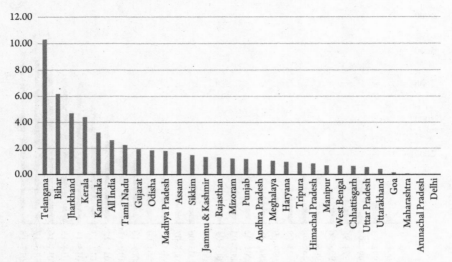

Figure 5.4 Modernization as a percentage of police expenditure, 2017–2018
Source: BPRD annual report, 2019.

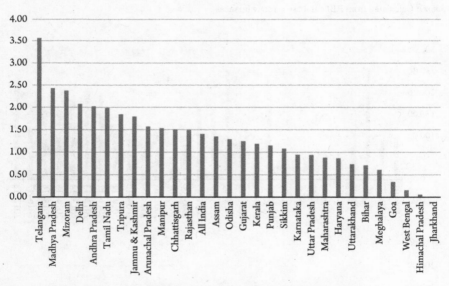

Figure 5.5 Training as a percentage of police expenditure, 2017–2018
Source: BPRD annual report, 2019.

point. The calculations are based on slightly different reporting than the previous figures, so the numbers are not completely comparable to those discussed earlier for modernization and training. They are the same magnitude for training, but somewhat lower for modernization. For both categories, Telangana is an outlier, easily explained by its recent creation as a separate state, which presumably led to additional expenditures on establishing its own independent police forces. Referring back to Table 5.1, Telangana's expenditure on police in 2017–2018 was higher than that of Andhra Pradesh or other southern states: that difference is heightened for the categories of modernization and training.

Aside from the outlier case of Telangana, the distribution of relative spending across states is more skewed in the case of modernization than for training, possibly reflecting the less routine, or more discretionary nature of the former. One aspect of parliamentary committee discussions of spending on police, albeit at the central level, is that there are varying degrees of absorptive capacity among different police organizations. Similarly, there may be differences among the states in terms of how well they are able to plan and execute certain types of expenditures. On the other hand, the fact that Bihar and Jharkhand had high relative spending on modernization in 2017–2018 may be driven by greater need, coinciding with an effort to tackle that need, rather than good absorptive capacity. Also noteworthy is that the ranking of states by relative spending on modernization is quite different from the ranking by training expenditure. It may be that constraints on managerial attention in the police organizations, or in political and bureaucratic oversight, make modernization and training substitutes in any given fiscal year, rather than complements. A final observation from Figures 5.4 and 5.5 is that Punjab, despite its relatively high total police expenditure, is below average in the expenditure proportion devoted to modernization and training, though not an outlier. Again, detailed state-level case studies would be required to explain the variations across states.

Assessment

Given all the variables that are in play, it is difficult to be too conclusive with respect to India's public spending on police. However, one can make some broad observations to begin with. India's spending on public order and safety in relation to its GDP is typical of other large countries, and not out of line with the great majority of countries. Compared to many other large countries, India's public spending on policing appears to be more balanced between the central government and subnational governments, reflecting the federal structures devised in the nation's constitution. Of course, formal accounting does not necessarily reflect real authority, as the Chinese case—in which subnational spending on public security strongly reflects national priorities—might suggest. India's balance between spending on internal and external security also seems to be reasonable, though it is difficult to say what would be an optimal combination.[31]

Turning to the specifics of India's case, central-level spending on internal security receives a considerable amount of scrutiny from the relevant parliamentary committee, as well as from within the MHA. This is understandable in terms of the importance of internal security from a national perspective, given independent India's history of insurgencies and "agitations," as well as more recent instances of terrorism. It is difficult to say whether the processes of interlocution lead to significantly better strategic outcomes, but there is a salience to the subject at the national level. Indeed, as noted earlier, this salience is visible in the MHA's annual report, which emphasizes dealing with terrorism and left-wing extremism.

As also previously noted, data on agitations seem to be more difficult to find than in the past. Looking at the data we have, the BPRD report for 2005 tells us that there were 37,745 agitations in 2004. Similar numbers were recorded for the next four years, although each of the five years had missing data for different states each year. In 2009, the reported number had risen to 56,445, though this may be partly because fewer states' numbers were missing. In 2016, the last year for which the data is available in BPRD reports, the number had doubled to 115,837. As one might expect, there is considerable year-to-year variation in the distribution of these protests across states, and this, along with concentration of protests around specific issues, would argue for a central role in this aspect of law and order. One analysis identifies higher literacy as being positively associated with larger numbers of protests across the states.[32] Certainly, what has happened after 2016 is consistent with that characterization. Aggregate data on public expenditure on police from 1990–1991 to 2017–2018 suggest that the new century saw this spending (both central and state level) rising faster than expenditure on defense, especially in the past few years.[33] Again, many complex factors are at work here, but these data, on police spending and protests, may be hinting at strains in the Indian fabric, even though total spending on internal security remains in line with many democratic countries, including much richer ones.[34]

At the level of the states, assessing the situation with respect to public spending on security is even less clear. States are responsible for delivery of a wide variety of public goods or merit goods, and analyses of state public finances tend to focus on areas such as health, education, and, more generally, development-related expenditures. Another issue of concern has been fiscal deficits at the state level, since these are seen as more difficult to manage and control than central fiscal deficits (although the latter have also received significant attention). In these discussions, law and order repeatedly tends to get put on the back burner. Certainly, this seems to be the case with the judiciary at all levels, where little progress has occurred in improving its functioning and reducing backlogs, despite lengthy reports with detailed recommendations.[35] Modernizing legal codes and police procedures also seem to receive inadequate attention. These are issues that do not necessarily need large investments from public budgets, but they do require prioritization and managerial and political attention. The most topical example of these inadequacies has been the police response to the coronavirus lockdown in March 2020, especially in northern cities, where police displayed some degree of brutality, or at least incomprehension with respect to their required duties. However, even day-to-day functioning with respect to criminal investigations, traffic control, and preventive maintenance of public security is arguably in need of improvement—although this might be said of almost all government activities in India. One might argue that training expenditures are generally too low, reflecting hierarchical structures in which proper training of the numerous lower ranks is almost ignored (Mangla, this volume).

In the case of policing, there is one obvious outcome variable that can be considered in assessing the effectiveness or impact of spending on the police, namely crime rates. Since crimes vary greatly in character, violent crime seems to be a particularly relevant, more homogeneous category. Figure 5.6 plots 2017–2018 rates of violent crime against per capita public expenditure on police, for the same set of states as in Figure 5.1: that is, we have omitted Goa, Sikkim, Jammu and Kashmir, and the smaller North Eastern states, for reasons given earlier. In fact, all those omitted North Eastern states have relatively high crime rates. In the graph, Assam is clearly an outlier, with a crime rate more like those of its neighbors. Punjab is also an outlier, in this case because of its high police expenditure.[36] Studying the rest of the scatter diagram, there does not appear to be any strong relationship between police expenditure and violent crime. This should not be surprising, since the causality can run in both directions, with different implications for the sign of the relationship: if higher police spending reduces crime, there would be a negative

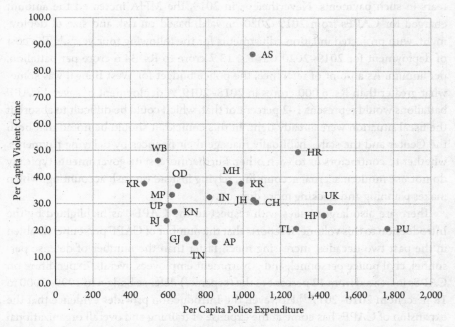

Figure 5.6 Per capita police expenditure and violent crime, 2017–2018
Source: BPRD (2019) and NCRB website

relationship, whereas if high crime rates bring forth greater police spending, the relationship would be positive.[37] Analyzing causality also involves considering several
other social factors, and leads to a challenging empirical exercise. The United States
has been the focus of much of the empirical research, but contentious issues remain,
and solid conclusions are lacking.[38] Indian data do not seem to have been subject to
the same level of scrutiny, though Prasad does a causal analysis that finds economic
liberalization leading to lower murder rates, while police strength has no significant
effect.[39]

Returning to general questions of effectiveness of state government spending,
one symptom of the inadequacy of state capacity with respect to internal security is
the handling of extraordinary circumstances such as agitations (discussed earlier in
the aggregate). As in one example, in 2017–2018, there was a dispute between the
West Bengal government and the central government with respect to the deployment of CAPFs within the state.[40] The situation involved an agitation for a separate
state (Gorkhaland), and was precipitated when the Center moved to withdraw 700
CAPF personnel from Darjeeling. The West Bengal government obtained a stay
order from the Calcutta High Court, but this was set aside by the Supreme Court
of India.[41]

Aside from deeper issues of authority and responsibility in an abnormal security
situation, fiscal issues were also at stake. Deployments of CAPFs require payments
from the states to the central government, but there is apparently a problem of arrears in such payments. Nevertheless, in 2019, the MHA increased the amount
charged for CAPFs from 2019–2020 onward, based on risk and size of deployment, with projected inflation adjustments for the following four years.[42] The cost
of deployment for 2019–2020 was Rs. 13.7 crore to Rs. 34.6 crore per battalion,
per annum. As a point of reference, the police budget for West Bengal was somewhat greater than Rs. 6,000 crores in 2018–2019. A deployment of several CAPF
battalions would represent 1–2 percent of that, which could be difficult to absorb if
the fiscal situation were already tight. In this context, it should be noted that both
the Center and the states habitually manage their finances by delaying payments,
whether to contractors or to each other. Furthermore, state governments typically
do not use modern accrual accounting, relying instead on cash accounting, which
makes planning and tracking more difficult.

There are also larger issues with respect to the CAPFs, as highlighted by the
Introduction to this volume. It reports that the number of CAPF personnel doubled
in the past two decades, increasing much faster than the number of defense personnel, civil police personnel, and government employees overall. Expenditure on
CAPFs increased from 12 percent of the (separate) defense budget in 1999–2000 to
18 percent in 2016–2017.[43] However, the Introduction provides evidence that the
expansion of CAPFs has come at the expense of training and overall organizational
quality. More important, it argues that the expansion of the CAPFs has negative
implications for federalism, as well as for Indian democracy more generally. Some

of this shifting balance is reflected in public expenditure data: from 2011–2012 to 2015–2016, the ratio of CAPF expenditure to aggregate police expenditure of the states remained between 47 and 48 percent, but thereafter has regularly exceeded 50 percent.

With respect to federal division of responsibilities, Devesh Kapur argues that India's states have been "abdicating their constitutional responsibilities on law and order," suggesting underinvestment and politicization.[44] The states' nominal expenditure on police grew more slowly than aggregate state expenditure from 2011–2012 to 2015–2016 (63 percent versus 74 percent), though there has been a slight reversal of this trend in the following four years.[45] Politicization of the bureaucracy is a pervasive problem in India, but the state's monopoly on law and order makes politicization of the police particularly dangerous. Indeed, India's defense forces have been considered to be a shining exception to the problem of politicization, which has even crept into the conduct of the judiciary. The problem of underinvestment is also part of a larger fiscal story: two decades ago, worries about subnational fiscal deficits led to attempts to increase fiscal discipline at both the national and subnational levels. A seesaw struggle between Center and states has also manifested itself in the conduct of intergovernmental transfers and in the tax system.[46]

Therefore, the shift toward central paramilitary police forces, at the expense of internal security expenditures by the states, is part of a larger and very complicated narrative of Indian federalism, both fiscal and political. In this context, Kapur's concern about increased militarization of internal security also deserves discussion. To the extent that CAPFs take on tasks that might otherwise be forced on the military (which has happened often in India), the defense forces are protected against politicization and being turned on by the country's own citizens. But if an expansion of CAPFs represents a stealth method for achieving this purpose, it is also a matter of concern for Indian democracy.

A subtler issue is the choice between central and state armed police forces (rather than between CAPFs and civil police at the state level). Kapur's point about militarization would also apply to state armed police, but one might argue that accountability and external control are potentially stronger at the state level, simply because the monopoly power over violence at the subnational level is more circumscribed.[47] The examples of conflicts over deployments and costs discussed earlier in this section are indicative of the complicated issues that are embedded in the federal structure of India's internal security institutions.

We close this section with some observations on private security expenditures. The number of private security workers has been growing rapidly, faster than, for example, health workers and teachers (Nath and Jayadev, this volume). One could argue that this rapid growth is an indicator of ineffectiveness or inadequacy of public spending on internal security. However, private security functions are not perfect substitutes for public policing, and the disproportionate growth of private

security employment and spending may, to a considerable extent, reflect a higher income elasticity of demand for certain kinds of protective services versus traditional
public policing.

Of course, when wealthy neighborhoods erect entry gates with private guards,
they directly substitute for police patrols in those localities. As Bowles and Jayadev
argue in the US context, this kind of substitution is a consequence of increasing
economic inequality, and the growth of employment and spending for private security in India may also be partly a similar phenomenon, although the evidence is
inconclusive (Nath and Jayadev, this volume).[48] This is part of a broader concern,
where privatization or marketization of certain kinds of public goods may have undesirable consequences for more fundamental goods—in this case, equal treatment
under the law.[49]

Conclusion

Analyses of public finance in India have a rich history, especially within the context of the complexities of India's federal system. Much of the attention has been
focused on the various components of the intergovernmental transfer system, on
the intricacies of the tax system, and on the allocations and outcomes of spending
on health, education, and welfare payments. The public finances of internal security
have received relatively little attention. This paper has attempted to redress that im-
balance and provide an initial overview of this issue.

Despite domestic law and order being constitutionally assigned to the states,
there is enough leeway in the document to allow the national government to play
a significant role in policing. This role has been increasing over time, as measured
by the allocation of resources within government budgets. While there is considerable detailed oversight of central spending on internal security, in practice there
are weaknesses in the structure and operations of central armed police forces. At
the central level, there are also numerous specialized functions beyond day-to-
day policing, including various kinds of intelligence and cybersecurity services,
but it is difficult to assess their functioning as it relates to the efficacy of government budget allocations. One can at least say that fears of terrorism have increased
spending on these kinds of security functions.

At the state level, there is considerable variation among the states in terms of
expenditure on internal security, which is dominated by day-to-day policing at
that level. States also vary greatly in their spending on modernization and training,
though with a seeming bias toward underspending (Mangla, this volume). It is difficult to discern patterns in states' police spending, beyond the inertia of maintaining
spending on personnel. One exception is that North Eastern or other "peripheral"
states typically spend higher proportions of their budgets on internal security. These
states also have higher crime rates, though the direction of causality from crime to

police spending still has to be established. In the rest of India, there is no clear relationship between police spending by states and rates of violent crime.

The government's monopoly on violence makes the issue of spending on internal security an important one, from the perspective of citizens' rights and welfare. Militarization of internal security, as evidenced in increased central government spending relative to other categories, is a major concern in this context. A subsidiary issue is the federal dimension of this militarization, which is complicated by continued evolution of federal structures of taxation, intergovernmental transfers, and fiscal deficits at the national and subnational levels. At a more basic level, the professional qualities and effectiveness of public policing in India (which includes militarization as one dimension) are difficult to establish based on public expenditures alone, though spending on specific areas such as modernization and training are indicative. Here, there is a potential concern that substitution of private security workers for public policing may not only magnify inequalities, but also undermine the culture of police organizations as providers of public services. Of course, this is a challenge for many branches and functions of government, not just those organizations that provide security. If one thinks of ideal bureaucracies as navigating between the Scylla of private profit and the Charybdis of politicization, perhaps public policing in India as a provider of internal security, like its counterpart institutions that provide external security, has not done too badly, but challenges are ever present. Certainly, considerable additional research is needed on all these issues.

Notes

1. The justification for non-market provision comes from free-rider problems that arise in the case of public goods, requiring funding through taxes rather than voluntary payments. Potentially, governments can contract with private organizations for actual provision of the internal security services, even if they are taxpayer-funded, such as the use of private prisons in the United States. However, there is no obvious case for private provision in the absence of competition to drive efficiency. Competition might be achieved with periodic contract bidding, but that can create other incentive problems. Private organizations can also easily diverge from social goals of equal treatment that are ideally embedded in the culture of government. For different aspects of these issues, see Albert O. Hirschman, *Exit, Voice, and Loyalty* (Cambridge, MA: Harvard University Press, 1970); George Akerlof, "Loyalty Filters," *American Economic Review* 73, no. 1 (1983): 54–63; and Elizabeth Anderson, *Value in Ethics and Economics* (Cambridge, MA: Harvard University Press, 1995).
2. Other categories include defense, social protection, education, and general public services.
3. All these data are from https://data.imf.org/regular.aspx?key=61037799.
4. Later years' data are available in this database for each of the categories, central and subnational, though not both for the same year.
5. In Brazil's case, there is no corresponding data on state level spending. The problem may be one of classification. For 2015, a Brazilian study reported total "public security" spending of about 1.3 percent of GDP, but reported much lower federal spending, not matching international data sets: see https://agenciabrasil.ebc.com.br/en/direitos-humanos/noticia/2016-11/public-security-spending-brazil-insufficient-expert-says. The definition of "public

security" used there may not be as comprehensive as what is included in "public safety and order."

6. Adrian Zenz, "China's Domestic Security Spending: An Analysis of Available Data," *China Brief* 18, no. 4 (2018), https://jamestown.org/program/chinas-domestic-security-spending-analysis-available-data/, reports a slightly higher number, 1.62 percent of GDP. He emphasizes the growth of China's spending on internal security, its concentration in the Tibet Autonomous Region and Xinjiang, and the absence of certain kinds of security expenditure from the government figures.

7. There is considerable variation in the component breakdown of totals, and countries also vary greatly in their spending on defense, making it difficult to conclude too much from broad comparisons, without detailed investigation of institutions. For example, the United Kingdom spends more on public order and safety than Israel as a percent of GDP (1.83 percent vs. 1.65 percent in 2018), but much less on defense (1.89 percent vs. 5.52 percent). Similarly, for Pakistan, central government spending was only 0.33 percent of GDP in 2015 (data on subnational spending are not available), but its defense spending was 2.55 percent of GDP, considerably higher than India (1.58 percent) for the same year. Ahuja and Kapur (this volume) provide broader global context for India's approaches to internal security.

8. Daniel Bier, "Police vs. Prisons in the US and Europe," *The Skeptical Libertarian*, 2019, https://blog.skepticallibertarian.com/2019/01/09/charts-police-vs-prisons-in-the-us-and-europe/, describes the salience of these two categories: "There are two basic ways for the government to deter crime: increase punishment (more prison) or increase the probability of punishment (more police)." Spending on social protection and welfare can also be important, though not a deterrent in the sense of punitive action. For example, the United States spends more than double per prisoner what it spends per student for public K–12 education (https://knoema.com/infographics/odgnikf/education-vs-prison-costs-in-the-united-states), and more than double on public order and safety than what it spends on welfare programs. E. Saez and Gabriel Zucman, *The Triumph of Injustice: How the Rich Dodge Taxes and How to Make Them Pay* (New York: W. W. Norton, 2019).

9. These data are from Bier, "Police vs. Prisons in the US and Europe." The difference is starker when expressed as a ratio of police to prisons, 5 to 1 for Europe versus 1.5 to 1 for the United States. As Bier shows, there is almost no overlap in these ratios for the individual European nations and the individual states in the United States.

10. These figures are from Amit Ahuja and Devesh Kapur (this volume) and are based on Indian government data.

11. M. Govinda Rao and Nirvikar Singh, *The Political Economy of Federalism in India* (New Delhi: Oxford University Press, 2005), discuss the organizational aspects of the police in India from a federal perspective, and in relation to other components of the law-and-order functions of the government. Beyond the use of defense personnel for internal security, the issue of who controls the police is complicated by the structure of the Indian Police Service (IPS) as an "All-India" cadre, with close ties to the preeminent Indian Administrative Service (IAS), which has dual allegiance to state—each IAS officer is assigned to a home state, where they begin their career—and national governments—where senior officers typically serve. David H. Bayley, *The Police and Political Development in India* (Princeton, NJ: Princeton University Press, 1969), is a seminal account of these structures. M. Govinda Rao and Nirvikar Singh, *The Political Economy of Federalism in India* (New Delhi: Oxford University Press, 2005), also discuss issues of (improper) politicization of the police, and possibilities for internal and external accountability. Mangla (this volume) details many of these institutional issues.

12. Indeed, the Central Reserve Police Force (CRPF) was established before the Indian Constitution was put into effect, and it is now one of several paramilitary or police-like security forces directly funded and controlled by the national government. The CRPF and similar central forces are discussed later in this chapter, and in Azad (this volume).

13. These numbers are derived from various budget documents of the national government, available at https://www.indiabudget.gov.in/previous_union_budget.php. The Covid-19 pandemic has altered these and other government expenditure and deficit figures temporarily but dramatically: it is difficult to estimate the longer run implications.

14. Nath and Jayadev (this volume) examine private as well as public provision of internal security or protective services. Private provision of security is mostly beyond the scope of this chapter, although it can represent a substitution of the market for inadequate governance: we consider it briefly in the penultimate section. The growth of private provision of education in India is a significant example of such substitution.

15. The CRPF was created in 1939, as the Crown Representative's Police, and took its current name in 1949. Its original mission was to directly buttress British colonial power, and to support the princely states that were also subject to the British.

16. Another central police force, the Indian Railway Protection Force Service, is controlled by the Ministry for Railways.

17. This blurring extends to the military, which has been used for internal security at various points in independent India's history. The BSF was created in 1965 after a war with Pakistan, to strengthen border security by replacing local police forces and the CRPF in tasks like patrolling the border. Presumably this was seen as more of a "policing" function than "fighting," which is the military's job, but as the term "paramilitary" implies, even that distinction is not a hard and fast one.

18. Parliament of India, Parliament of India, Rajya Sabha, *Two Hundred Seventeenth Report: Action Taken by Government on the Recommendations/Observations Contained in the Two Hundred Ninth Report on Demands for Grants (2018–19) of the Ministry of Home Affairs*, Department-Related Parliamentary Standing Committee on Home Affairs (New Delhi: Rajya Sabha Secretariat, 2019).

19. For example, see Parliament of India, Parliament of India, Rajya Sabha, *Two Hundred Seventeenth Report* (New Delhi: Rajya Sabha Secretariat, 2019).

20. These reports are available as pdf files at https://bprd.nic.in/content/62_1_DataonPoliceOrganizations.aspx. They are also available in print: for example, Bureau of Police Research and Development, *Data on Police Organizations (As on January 01, 2019)*, BPR&D, Ministry of Home Affairs (New Delhi: BPR&D, 2019).

21. For a discussion of the BPRD, as well as other institutional characteristics of policing in India, see, for example, Arvind Verma, *The New Khaki: The Evolving Nature of Policing in India* (Boca Raton, FL: CRC Press, 2011).

22. The NCRB also maintains detailed prison statistics for the nation. Matching its relatively low spending on prisons, India's incarceration rate is also low in global comparisons (34 per 100,000 according to latest data). The US rate is the highest, at 655, but again, it is difficult to draw meaningful conclusions just from cross-country variations. For example, the rates in Costa Rica (374) and New Zealand (199) are higher than for China (121). See https://www.prisonstudies.org/highest-to-lowest/prison_population_rate for a full country list.

23. The data were compiled by the BPRD from reports submitted by the states, so presumably they are available in state police documents. The most recent MHA annual report provides statistics on violent "Left Wing Extremist" incidents, and terrorist incidents, but not "Agitations" in general Government of India, Ministry of Home Affairs, *Annual Report 2018–19* (New Delhi: MHA, 2019). It is likely that political protests in India in 2019 associated with the Citizenship Amendment Act led to very high numbers of what would come under "agitations."

24. The numbers reported here are derived from those in Bureau of Police Research and Development, *Data on Police Organizations (As on January 01, 2019)*, BPR&D, Ministry of Home Affairs (New Delhi: BPR&D, 2019).

25. See https://www.rbi.org.in/Scripts/StateStatisticsFinances.aspx.

26. The similarity here is at the abstract level of periphery vs. Center, since the details of the history of Jammu and Kashmir and its characteristics are quite different from the North East. In

2019, the status of Jammu and Kashmir was drastically altered, being split into two parts, with both new components becoming Union Territories.

27. By contrast, the ratio for Chhattisgarh (another, nearby, state with a large tribal population) is not as high. I am grateful to the editors of this volume for help in understanding this comparison, which illustrates the difficulty of pinpointing general causes for differences in internal security spending across states.

28. Assam, Chhattisgarh, and Jharkhand all fit that classification. In particular, Himachal Pradesh and Uttarakhand are both relatively small states. Karnataka and Tamil Nadu might fit this description.

29. A detailed analysis of differences in patterns of expenditure across states is beyond the current scope, but it is worth remarking that there do not seem to be many systematic or comprehensive studies of why states spend differently on health, education, or other sectors.

30. The negative development expenditure reported for Punjab in 1996–1997 is likely an accounting artifact, but we do not have an explicit explanation.

31. Furthermore, spending totals may convey limited information. Returning to an earlier example, the United States spends proportionately less than the EU on police, but its police forces are much more heavily armed, to the point where even everyday policing has a paramilitary feel: this feature of US policing became particularly obvious in 2020, during protests against racial injustice.

32. Prabhpreet Singh Sood and Prince Singhal, "Protests Rose by 55% in India from 2009 to 2014—and Literate States Led the Charge," *Scroll.In*, December 2, 2016, https://scroll.in/article/822918/protests-rose-by-55-in-india-from-2009-to-2014-and-literate-states-led-the-charge.

33. These data are from government budget documents and were provided to me by the editors. Ahuja and Kapur (this volume) discuss many of the issues of types and effectiveness of spending, and broader questions of governance and state action, that are touched on in the current section.

34. The analysis in this chapter has focused on expenditure. Airport security is an example where dedicated revenue is generated from fees, and although it goes into the central budget, rather than being earmarked for security expenses, overall, revenue and expenditure approximately balance: see Government of India, Ministry of Civil Aviation, *Lok Sabha Unstarred Question No. 2359, CISF Security at Airport* (New Delhi, 2020). I am grateful to Devesh Kapur for raising the issue and providing the source. Another revenue source associated with policing is traffic fines. These revenues accrue to the state government, although the central government has some power to set levels of fines. It did so in 2019, raising traffic fines substantially. This was intended to promote safety rather than generate revenue. Data on traffic fine revenue are spotty, but do not seem to be a significant amount for most states. At the same time, there may be unintended incentive effects from changing the levels of fines, because of the possibility of bribery or extortion. Also, some countries implicitly generate significant revenue by using prison labor, but this is not the case for India.

35. For example, see Government of India, Ministry of Home Affairs, *Committee on Reforms of Criminal Justice System, Report Volume I* (New Delhi: MHA, 2003), what is commonly known as the Malimath Committee Report, as well as an analysis by Dilip Mookherjee, *The Crisis in Government Accountability: Governance Reforms and Indian Economic Performance* (New Delhi: Oxford University Press, 2004); Amnesty International, *India—Report of the Malimath Committee on Reforms of the Criminal Justice System: Some Observations* (2003), available at https://www.amnesty.org/en/documents/ASA20/025/2003/en/, offers a critique of human rights aspects of the report and its recommendations in that dimension.

36. A similar pattern is in data from 2011–2012, with Punjab again an outlier.

37. There are many other considerations, including reporting, numbers, density and deployment of police personnel, and intrastate variation. See Prasad Kislaya, "A Comparison of Victim-Reported and Police-Recorded Crime in India," *Economic and Political Weekly* 48, no. 33

(2013): 47–53, for a detailed discussion. Arvind Verma, Hanif Qureshi, Michael Frisby, and Alok Mohan, "How Real Is the Crime Decline in India?" *Economic and Political Weekly* 54, no. 45 (2019): 37, empirically buttress the case that declining crime rates in India are not the result of manipulation in police reporting, and they speculate about causal factors, but without formal data analysis for such factors.

38. See Vanessa Barker, "Explaining the Great American Crime Decline: A Review of Blumstein and Wallman, Goldberger and Rosenfeld, and Zimring," *Law & Social Inquiry* 35, no. 2 (2010): 489–516, for one recent assessment.

39. Interestingly, Punjab is an influential outlier, and Prasad's results on police strength change if its data are included. Prasad Kislaya, "Economic Liberalization and Violent Crime," *Journal of Law and Economics* 55, no. 4 (2012): 925–948.

40. The discussion here is based on Press Trust of India, "Central Forces Can't Substitute State Police: MHA to States," *Economic Times*, 2018, available at https://economictimes.indiati mes.com/news/defence/central-forces-cant-substitute-state-police-mha-to-states/articles how/61133432.cms?from=mdr. I am grateful to Devesh Kapur for pointing me to this issue and the references cited.

41. This sequence of events can also be considered as an illustration of successful operation of a federal system, with the Supreme Court handling a disagreement over powers of the two major levels of government.

42. See IndoAsian News Service, "Pay More for Paramilitary Deployment: MHA to States," *Economic Times*, 2019, available at https://www.indiatvnews.com/news/india/pay-more-for-paramilitary-deployment-mha-to-states-555652, for the source of these numbers and discussion of the policy change.

43. Devesh Kapur, "The Worrying Rise of Militarisation in India's Central Armed Police Forces," *The Print*, November 29, 2017, available at https://theprint.in/opinion/worrying-rise-militar isation-indias-central-armed-police-forces/19132/.

44. Kapur, "The Worrying Rise of Militarisation in India's Central Armed Police Forces."

45. However, in this latter period, expenditure on CAPFs was increasing even faster.

46. In addition to Rao, M. Govinda, and Nirvikar Singh, *The Political Economy of Federalism in India* (New Delhi: Oxford University Press, 2005), see Y. V. Reddy and G. R. Reddy, *Indian Fiscal Federalism* (New Delhi: Oxford University Press, 2019), for more recent developments.

47. This is also a contestable proposition. Citizens subject to local injustices can move to a different jurisdiction, but mobility can be constrained, and inequalities might be more severe at the local or subnational level. Indeed, the latter was the basis for B. R. Ambedkar arguing for a more centralized constitution than some other leaders of the Indian independence movement would have desired. See Rao, Govinda, and Singh, *The Political Economy of Federalism in India*, for further background and discussion.

48. Samuel Bowles and Arjun Jayadev, "One Nation under Guard," *Opinionator, New York Times*, February 15, 2014, https://opinionator.blogs.nytimes.com/2014/02/15/one-nat ion-under-guard/. For further detailed discussion, the reader is referred to Nath and Jayadev (this volume). Note that recent reports of the ratio of public to private security employment in India appear to undercount the number of public police personnel—see FICCI, *Private Security Industry, Job Creation and Skill Development: A Report* (New Delhi: FICCI, 2018), as well as its sources—and also may overstate the number of private security workers. Even with these corrections, India has a higher ratio of private to public security workers than many countries. Some writings highlight the fact that this ratio is greater than one, but that by itself does not seem to be critical since, as noted, private security functions are not all perfectly substituted by public policing.

49. See Elizabeth Anderson, *Value in Ethics and Economics* (Cambridge, MA: Harvard University Press, 1995). In this context, the uncritically positive approach to private security services as a generator of employment in publications such as the FICCI report, and pressures to classify private security services as "para police," Asit Manohar, "Grant Para Police Status to Private

Security Sector: Interview with Kunwar Vikram Singh," *The Day After*, 2018, https://web.
archive.org/web/20200813141542/https://www.dayafterindia.com/2018/01/01/grant-
para-police-status-private-security-sector/, are worrying, because they potentially undermine
basic notions of equal citizenship. See also Claire Provost, "The Industry of Inequality: Why
the World Is Obsessed with Private Security," *The Guardian*, 2017, https://www.theguard
ian.com/inequality/2017/may/12/industry-of-inequality-why-world-is-obsessed-with-priv
ate-security, which emphasizes how income and wealth inequality drives private security
spending and undermines basic qualities of citizenship.

PART II

INTERNAL SECURITY

Doctrine and Strategy

6

India's Internal Security in Comparative Perspective

PAUL STANILAND

There are a number of valuable overviews of political violence and internal security in India.[1] Rather than repeating the same exercise, this chapter seeks to identify a set of patterns in how Delhi manages, manipulates, and represses non-state violence. I examine several themes: the variation in responses across political context, the management of borderlands, the links between multilevel governance and violence in electoral politics, and the profoundly uneven nature of state coercive and infrastructural power.

In doing so, I try to answer a set of questions: What is India's internal security doctrine? What are the range and balance of punitive as well as accommodative strategies that the state has used to respond to insurgencies? What have been the ideational influences on this doctrine? Have the guiding principles evolved? How does India's security doctrine compare to other democracies? How successful has this doctrine been in achieving a Weberian monopoly of state violence?

There is no formal government internal security doctrine that spans the various kinds of conflict we see in India, from insurgency to party-linked violence.[2] Instead, I offer a set of claims about patterns of state response to the existence of non-state armed actors that we can view as a "de facto" set of rules.[3] I argue that the use of both force and accommodation varies by political context (with minority religious armed groups being the most intensely targeted), the type of conflict and violence being faced (insurgencies as opposed to election-linked specialists in violence), and geographic location. Nationalist ideas matter at the macro-level, helping to determine which groups and conflicts are seen as worthy of high-cost repression and sustained efforts at violence monopolization, and which can instead be managed in a fairly loose and flexible way. The goals of violence are also crucial for determining the political threat perceived, with anti-state insurgencies receiving a much different response than the murky world of electoral violence, private armies, and thugs. Border areas receive particular attention, contributing to an interesting blend

Paul Staniland, *India's Internal Security in Comparative Perspective* In: *Internal Security in India*. Edited by: Amit Ahuja and Devesh Kapur, Oxford University Press. © Oxford University Press 2023. DOI: 10.1093/oso/9780197660331.003.0006 of hardline suppression in some areas with the creation of buffer zones and even toleration of cross-border insurgents in others. There is incredible heterogeneity in responses to organized political violence in India, rather than a set single approach.[4]

In addition to exploring variation within India, I use comparisons with other countries, especially India's regional neighbors. We see that some of the patterns I identify in India can be found, in some form, elsewhere, while we also see very important differences that help to more clearly identify where "Indian exceptionalism" makes sense and where India is essentially just like other countries. I conclude by outlining the implications in thinking about state power and political order in India. Profound imbalances in how state power has been developed and the variations in state-society relations across space, community, and level of political authority hold implications for what to expect as the Indian state both grows in power and wealth, and faces new challenges.

Internal Security: Setting the Stage

Internal security is a capacious term. Here I limit its usage to primarily focus on the management of armed actors pursuing some nominal political goals; private security arrangements, policing of law and order, incarceration practices, and "normal" criminality. Other hugely important topics are admittedly left out, and exploring them may complicate or overturn the picture I paint here. These are of course enormously important in shaping broad perceptions of security and insecurity among citizens, and deserve careful research. This understanding of "internal security" is limiting but also provides a clarity of focus.

As a result of this choice, I examine three broad sets of armed actors: insurgents, counterinsurgent militias, and disciplined political parties that operate in consistently "militarized" electoral contexts. I also refer to the amorphous networks that are linked to political parties but not formally incorporated into them, but these tend to be localized, diffuse, and harder to study as coherent organizations interacting with state power.[5] Their "latency" makes them difficult to systematically map out over time.

A large number of avowedly anti-state rebel groups have emerged in India, stretching back to the scattered CPI revolt of 1948–1951, through first the Naga and then the Mizo insurgencies in the 1950s and 1960s, the first wave of Naxalism in the late 1960s, the expansion of conflict in the North East from the late 1970s in Manipur, Assam (in several parts of the state), and Meghalaya, the Punjab insurgency in 1980s, the ongoing Kashmir insurgency since the late 1980s, and the revivification of Naxalite mobilization in central India over the last twenty years. It is difficult to think of a more extensive and complex wave of insurgencies over such long periods of time in a non-failed state—Myanmar, for instance, has had a much weaker state overall yet much greater political instability.[6]

This landscape of violence allows us to see patterns precisely because there are so many cases of open anti-state insurgency to examine. There are certainly other countries with many insurgencies, and others with far higher levels of violent crime, but India combines a huge number of rebel groups with a fairly powerful central state and a political system that, for the most part, is unaffected by peripheral insurgencies.

There is another set of insurgents who have operated out of Indian soil. While Pakistan is by far the most promiscuous supporter of transnational insurgents in South Asia, India has also engaged in this activity at various times. India has backed insurgents fighting in Sri Lanka, East Pakistan, Bangladesh, and Burma/Myanmar.[7] In some cases, this support is intended to affect substantial change in a target country (i.e., the Indo-Lanka Accord and liberation of Bangladesh); in others, like links with the Shanti Bahini and some ethnic minority groups fighting Burma's Tatmadaw, a more limited-aims, defensive logic is held.

Pro-state, but non-state, militias in counterinsurgency contexts are less common in India than in some other contexts, in part because of the substantial coercive capacity of the central state and the creation of local defense organizations under formal state auspices (like Village Defence Committees). Yet we do see some variant of this organizational form, in two varieties. The first are "flipped" militants who end up working with the government after fleeing fratricidal fighting or being coerced into cooperation. The "Ikhwans" in Kashmir and Revolutionary Government of Nagaland in Nagaland (from 1968 to 1973) are prominent examples.[8] In Punjab, a more localized variant occurred, with small bands allegedly working under state direction.[9]

The second pattern involves state- or politician-backed creation of armed actors. The Salwa Judum in Chhattisgarh is a clear example of paramilitarism originated in part from mobilization by "mainstream" actors rather than insurgents changing sides.[10] Murkier is the rise of the "senas" in 1980s and 1990s Bihar, arising from a complex blend of caste conflict, anti-Naxal reaction, and local efforts at political entrepreneurship;[11] they exist in a grim space in between counterinsurgency, social conflict, and electoral violence.

Finally, political parties have long-standing links to violence and actors capable of violence.[12] This takes multiple forms, which can be difficult to systematically measure. The most "visible" are political parties that are known to have cadres who act as specialists in violence integrated into the party. West Bengal and Kerala are both states in which comparatively ideological and organized parties engage in quite violent political competition. The CPM's notorious dominance of West Bengal from 1977 to 2011 was preceded by Congress, which militarized in particular during the late 1960s and early 1970s (in part in response to Naxalite attacks, and in part in response to intense party competition). The Trinamool has now absorbed many of the CPM's specialists in violence, with the BJP making a play as well more recently.

The more difficult to observe, but more common, arrangement is looser. As Paul Brass has famously outlined, "institutionalized riot networks"[13] exist in many Indian cities, with informal links among politicians, criminals, party and social organization activists, and often bureaucrats and police. They can be summoned into action in moments of political expediency or periods of polarization, often at a highly localized level. Over the last two decades, we appear to have seen a shift from high-profile, very intense, riots and pogroms (like Gujarat in 2002) toward much smaller-scale instances of lynching and vigilantism, which tend to be policed at the state level with less central involvement (i.e., CRPF deployments or President's Rule).

Internal Security Strategy in Counterinsurgency

One of the standard assessments of Indian counterinsurgency suggests that there is a pattern to counterinsurgency (COIN) operations: first, a display of force, followed by movement toward mainstream politics and incentives for armed actors to move into elections. There is certainly truth to this characterization; India's electoral system has much more malleability and space for co-optation than the likes of Suharto's New Order in Indonesia or Thailand's Deep South. There is also a consistent application of force in the early days of an insurgency: Nagaland in the mid-1950s, Mizoram in 1966, Kashmir in 1990, and Assam in 1990–1991 all saw major applications of repressive force.

Yet there are serious limits to stopping at this as a description of Indian counterinsurgency.[14] We also need to take seriously the political stakes of conflicts as a variable that helps to guide state responses: in some places at some times, the state is much more repressive and motivated than others. Punjab and the first wave of Naxalite insurgency saw delays in concerted crackdowns, and the Kashmir conflict has attracted far more sustained repressive attention than the long second wave of the Naxal insurgency (i.e., pre-2004). In Nagaland, we have seen rounds of ceasefires (the Naga Peace Mission, then the post-1997 Suspension of Operations agreements) rather than concerted repression.

The nature of electoral co-optation also varies across cases. Nagaland has seen limited movement from open rebellion to successful electoralism; groups that changed sides, most notably the Revolutionary Government of Nagaland in 1973, have been rewarded with government posts and patronage, but have not launched successful major political parties. In Kashmir, for a variety of reasons, rebel-to-politician transitions have been rare and tenuous. Mizoram obviously offers a radical contrast, with the Mizo National Front becoming a top-tier state party, but this is very far from the modal trajectory for most rebel leaders: even if co-opted, they are more likely to end up in a small and marginal party or as a low-level cadre rather than front-line leader, never truly enter electoral politics, or find a role in the state apparatus other than offering a reprise of Laldenga's path.

This empirical record suggests a more complex and contingent approach than relying on the "iron fist in a velvet glove" summary of Indian counterinsurgency doctrine. For a state without a total monopoly of violence (itself often the outcome of centuries of state-building or cataclysmic revolutions), choices need to be made about how to allocate coercive, economic, and political resources. This is certainly true for India; though by no means a weak state, it cannot flood every nook and cranny of the country with highly trained, well-resourced security forces to enforce total compliance with state goals. Even in much richer countries, including the United States, selective enforcement, variation in capacity, and differing responses to different kinds of threats and armed groups are very common, so it should be no surprise to see the same in India.[15]

Most important, I argue that political stakes differ across conflicts in important ways. Given this broad context, factors like external support and contingent leadership can certainly also matter, but there is a deep structure to internal security practices built around the core political battles that have shaped colonial and independent India.[16] This helps us understand why internal security shows substantial continuities over time in India: unlike the more fluid and malleable world of international affairs, the basic cleavages of domestic politics are comparatively "sticky," even if they vary in salience or predominance over time.[17]

The greatest threat to Indian nationalism is perceived to come from armed religious minorities making demands in part or entirely on a religious basis. Though the Congress and BJP have differed in their views of Hindu majoritarian violence, they converge on seeing Sikh and Muslim armed mobilization as distinctively dangerous, with grim echoes of Partition. For Congress, the prospect of a multi-religious India hinges on not allowing minority separatism, while the BJP adds to this project its own goal of a hegemonic Hindu role within state and society.[18]

The most intensive counterinsurgency operations have occurred in Kashmir and Punjab, with large-scale, sustained deployments of forces aimed at re-monopolizing state violence (amid credible allegations of substantial rights abuses). There was a longer delay in moving toward a full-scale crackdown in Punjab than Kashmir because of the rather odd political origins of the insurgency (in political manipulations aimed at the Akali Dal),[19] but by the late 1980s a large-scale, full-throated security footprint was in place. In Kashmir, an initial period of disarray and disorganization was more quickly resolved in a huge and ongoing application of coercive power.[20] In both cases, counterinsurgency was aimed at area domination, close integration of central and state security forces, limited to no serious negotiation with insurgents over the core politics at play, and a relatively high degree of elite consensus about the need to respond by crushing the insurgency.

These cases both touch on two core triggers for a clampdown. First, both were revolts at least in large part along religious minority cleavages (Sikh, Muslim, though overlain with other cleavages). Under the dominant nationalism reigning at the time of their onset, both represented challenges to the idea that a multi-religious, secular India could exist, and thus were highly threatening, especially given the history of Partition, as well as concerns about Sikh separatism that Nehru and Patel worried about in the late 1940s.[21] Second, both movements had support from Pakistan's security apparatus, especially Kashmiri militants.[22] For fairly obvious reasons, and intertwined with the ideological-historical factor above, this heightened threat perceptions and encouraged a vigorous security response. These were high-priority, high-salience internal conflicts that saw large-scale, long-term resource applications.

Other factors have undoubtedly also contributed to the distinctive nature of these conflicts. Attacks on Delhi and Mumbai were carried out by armed groups operating in Kashmir, and also in border states. These add to the political stakes and salience of these conflicts, which take on a central position in India's internal security.

The political stakes of other conflicts have been lower, though far from irrelevant. Both leftist and linguistic claims are more easily accommodated within Indian politics than minority religious cleavages, and so armed groups mobilized on that basis see overall less intense repression and more ambiguity in their relationship to the state. While the Naxal conflict has unquestionably seen moments of serious resource application (1971–1972 in West Bengal and post-2009), there have been much longer stretches of containment and comparative neglect.[23] The Indian political system has allowed a substantial degree of permeability for left-wing political forces that make even radical leftist mobilization more potentially manageable than avowed religious-minority claims.[24] Furthermore, the geographical and social distance of the Naxalite movement from the centers of economic, state, and political power in India render them of less pressing interest to security managers. There has been much less effort devoted to thoroughgoing violence monopolization: rather, serious repression has been brought to push the movement back to a level in which containment is possible, with a long-term goal of slowly rolling back, isolating, and eventually fragmenting the movement rather than shattering it with rapid, high-intensity hammer blows.

In the North East, with its blend of tribal and linguistic armed groups, we see the most initial applications of large-scale force scaled back into a blend of containment, negotiations, ceasefires, and sporadic—though important—government offensives.[25] Nagaland and Mizoram are the classic cases here, but we also see some similar dynamics in Tripura, Meghalaya, and Assam: even when there haven't been the full-scale peace deals like in Mizoram, smaller deals and side-switching by factions and defectors have regularly occurred.[26] There have undoubtedly been serious counterinsurgency operations and ongoing security force attention to armed groups, but not at a scale or intensity comparable to Kashmir/Punjab. These are dramatically more heterogeneous conflict contexts, with more fluidity and "gray zone"[27] armed groups and group-state interactions.

The North East is a place apart politically with low-salience conflicts on the Indian national stage. While Delhi cares about maintaining territorial integrity and avoiding disintegrative challenges to central power, these insurgencies are not existential threats. Even Pakistani (before 1971), Bangladeshi, and Chinese external support for armed groups (especially Nagas) have not triggered the same threat perceptions as Pakistani involvement in Punjab and Kashmir.[28] In the North East, cross-border backing and sanctuary seem to be seen as part of the game, rather than a signal of irreconcilable political aims. The Indian political system has extensive mechanisms for managing linguistic and tribal political demands, which are the dominant cleavages among North East insurgencies, so there is greater flexibility for accommodative approaches.

What are some other factors that can influence overall internal security posture? The nature of state party systems and state-level politics in general may make incorporation easier. In the North East, party systems tend to be very fluid and fractious, with relatively easy "new entry" compared to Punjab and Kashmir. This has made meaningful electoral transition quite easy for some groups/factions/leaders in the North East, though the extent of real rebel-to-party transitions across India is much lower than some commonly accepted wisdoms would suggest. There is some evidence that former Naxalites in northern India have been able to move into low-level electoral politics, with southern India by contrast seeing more reintegration into communities and civil society organizations than parties.[29]

Patronage opportunities are also an element of counterinsurgency management. We see some direct cash payments to defecting rebels (as well as alleged rebels who do not seem to have actually been hardened fighters), employment in state bureaucracies, and murkier forms of sustenance gathering (such as allegations about surrendered ULFA members acting as bodyguards and enforcers in 1990s/early 2000s Assam). Some armed groups under ceasefire are able to continue extracting resources without state repression, which is a kind of indirect, tolerated form of patronage politics. This is especially noteworthy in Nagaland under its long ceasefire periods.

This suggests a key ideological element to the management of internal security: some armed groups are simply much more threatening than others, as a reflection of dominant understandings of nationalism by Indian governments.[30] Interestingly, there has been some stability over time in how governments have viewed linguistic and tribal claims; even Modi's BJP does not seem to have changed these "rules": for instance, it has pursued peace agreements with Naga and Bodo insurgents. Where there is an ideological change is in the meaning of Muslims and Kashmir. While the Congress regimes were deeply threatened by Kashmiri insurgency and worried about the communal cleavage as a potential source of disintegration, the BJP is equally threatened but for somewhat different reasons. Rather than seeing Kashmir as a test of secularism, the BJP claims to see it as the cutting edge of an Islamist wave, a land that has been colonized by Islam, and a direct proxy contest with Pakistan. A hardline stance ensues, and is likely to become more pronounced as the BJP consolidates its power.

What then can we say about Indian COIN posture? There is not a single set of procedures that are mechanistically applied across contexts, even when the same bureaucracies and leaders are in charge of responses. Political stakes are central to the variation in response, with a smaller and more contingent role for state-level patronage and party system dynamics. Sometimes the iron fist dominates; sometimes the velvet glove makes a rapid appearance; in some cases, the state is more distracted than motivated to pursue either.

How does this pattern compare to India's neighbors and to other democracies? The pattern is a reverse of Pakistan's, where Islamist groups are treated with far greater ambivalence and variation than the hardline stance adopted toward ethno-separatist groups. In Burma and Sri Lanka, the "sons of the soil" majoritarian nationalism makes ethno-linguistic separatism much less politically amenable to compromise and accommodation than in India, which has very different rules for managing language politics than its neighbors.[31]

There are no obvious comparisons for India in the broader democratic world: the Philippines is perhaps the closest in facing a variety of domestic insurgencies across a huge geographic space; Indonesia has many similarities but most of its insurgencies arose and endured under the authoritarian New Order; Sri Lanka, Israel, Colombia, and Turkey (during its democratic phase) all primarily faced one insurgent group or type of insurgency. That said, there seems to be an unusual amount of flexibility in responses to separatism in India along linguistic and tribal lines, which is likely due to the highly effective constitutional provisions for managing remarkable diverse social cleavages.[32] The potential for movement into something approximating "mainstream" politics in India is also somewhat unusual, compared to the highly rigid lines of southeastern Turkey or West Papua; that said, conflicts in Aceh, Mindanao, and Karachi have seen similar fluidity and ambiguity, so India is not unique, but it is part of a fairly small subset of countries. The long-running ceasefires in the North East are not unique, but they are also not common practice.[33]

The picture here is therefore a bit mixed: India is not unique and does not have a distinctive single doctrine it pursues, but its particular blend of both policies and diverse insurgencies makes it quite unusual, with few obvious comparison cases. This relates to my broader argument: governments' internal security policies largely reflect their ideological predisposition.

Federalism and Electoral Violence

Though counterinsurgency does involve state governments and state police forces, it tends to be dominated by the Center. A very different world of internal security exists in the world of electoral politics. Armed actors—often quite murky and opaque—are part of the internal security landscape in a number of states, as well as in cross-state national movements.

There are several forms such violence (or its threat) can take. At the local level, Paul Brass's "institutionalized riot networks" link specialists in violence to politicians and bureaucrats. These networks and arrangements are often hard to identify ex ante, liable to shift and transform, and often function as part of "normal" crime and politics, but can become activated or newly salient in the runup to riots or other forms of clashes, or displays of street power. The management of these networks can be highly localized by local police, district magistrates, and politicians, or attract the attention of state-level politicians and bureaucrats higher up in the administrative chain. Short of massive riots, it is less likely to attract serious intervention from Delhi, though the Center will often track sensitive areas. These actors and contexts are central to the usually localized urban communal riots that have attracted so much attention in the study of political violence in India.[34]

As we scale up, we move into state-level political parties that have a track record of incorporating violence and its threat into their party structures and activities. Kerala (despite its otherwise rather idyllic qualities) and West Bengal have developed perhaps the most institutionalized armed parties in India. The BJP, Trinamool, and CPM are major players in these violent electoral politics (though Congress was a key pioneer of this approach in early/mid-1970s West Bengal), and campaigns can see some strikingly high levels, and brutal forms, of violence. Party cadres can be directly involved in violence. Maharashtra and Bihar have also seen periods and forms of this kind of more organized, party-linked violence—the Shiv Sena in the former and the caste-based *senas* in the latter (some of which had links to politicians).[35] In contrast to communal riots, this mixture of bullets and ballots has received surprisingly little attention.

From a central internal security perspective, both militarized elections and communal riots are not considered anti-systemic, unlike even very small or marginal insurgencies. The risks to the broader internal security setup can come in at least two forms: first, a total breakdown in law and order can trigger central intervention if it appears that the state government is unable to manage the situation, and, second, the diffusion of violence across borders can risk "waves" of violence that have All-India implications.[36] The latter is especially relevant to communally sensitive violence, which can spread rapidly in periods of high political tension. Communal riots have generally triggered these interventions; despite high levels of violence in Kerala and West Bengal, it has been grimly "structured" within mainstream politics rather than leading to uncontrollable spirals that impel intervention. State governments are captured by parties, with the security apparatus politicized and directed in alignment with the wishes of its ruling party or coalition. These cases are strikingly under-studied in the literature—there is far more work on riots than on party armies.

Finally, we see All-India parties and movements, especially on the Hindu nationalist right, that can be involved at the local and state level, but also coordinate nationally in mobilization campaigns. The classic case here is the set of mobilizations by the BJP and its affiliate Sangh Parivar organizations in the late 1980s and early 1990s around the Ram Janmabhoomi issue: this was a national campaign rather than a highly localized brushfire.[37] The crackdown on the RSS and removal of several state governments after the 1992–1993 riots across India showed how these issues can rise to the level of requiring a vigorous central response, which occurred under a Congress government.

What should we make of this? The first point to note is that there is far less active central involvement in managing this kind of violent or coercive politics. Despite sometimes quite severe conflict (especially in periods in West Bengal and Bihar), this violence is funneled through mainstream electoral politics and thus is politically categorized in very different ways than is insurgent violence. Political meaning is central here: many of the small insurgencies in the North East (and even Kashmir is quiet years) generate far fewer dead bodies than a bad election year in West Bengal, but generate radically different government responses.

The second point is that these dynamics are not unique to India, which suggests some interesting bases for comparative studies across countries.[38] Karachi and periods of politics in Pakistan's Punjab saw this entangling of electoral mobilization and party politics with violence. Politics in post-democratization Bangladesh very closely resembles the model of party-linked violence we see in parts of India: the Awami League and Bangladesh National Party both have used substantial violence while manipulating and politicizing the state apparatus.[39]

Finally, the involvement of violence in mainstream politics suggests a crucial caveat on the meaning of "legitimate" in the Weberian conception of the legitimate monopoly of violence—the definition of legitimate violence varies across and within countries. What would be seen as shockingly unacceptable in Japan or Ghana may be part of the standard rules of the game in Côte d'Ivoire or India. Just as with the long-running ceasefires with ethno-tribal separatists in the North East, India shows slack and flexibility with some kinds of armed actors, even as it is unwilling to tolerate others.

Borderlands and Buffers

Many of the internal security challenges the Indian state deals with occur in border zones, and these take on a particular significance compared to those in the interior. They are primarily insurgencies, though in the North East they blend into militia politics and criminality. How has the Indian state managed these zones of geopolitical importance?

In line with its COIN posture, the Punjab and Kashmir conflicts saw high levels of effort aimed at sealing off the border and Line of Control from infiltration from Pakistan. Though obviously never perfect given geography, these were extremely sustained efforts at clearly, forcefully creating sovereign divisions.

Matters have been distinctively more ambiguous in the North East. While, eventually (after a long period of avoiding major infrastructure that could be used by China in an invasion), there were major efforts to build up a coherent border presence with China, the borders with Bangladesh and Myanmar have been more fluid and permeable. This does not mean there are not large-scale and expensive efforts to fence and manage these border zones, but they have not involved the resource investments or political attention as in Punjab and Kashmir.

Illicit economies, flows of people, and areas of weak state presence are all far more common in the North East. Not only have separatist insurgents been backed by Myanmar, China, and Bangladesh at different points, but India has been involved in some degree of toleration/support for insurgents targeting Bangladesh and Myanmar as well, creating more of a two-way street than in Kashmir/Punjab conflicts.[40] The terrain is extremely daunting, but not obviously worse than substantial parts of the LOC and LAC, and therefore this fluidity at least partially reflects the more peripheral politics of the region.

The border variable also affects the deployment of forces. The Army is used in border zones, as is the Border Security Force (BSF). The Central Reserve Police Force (CRPF) is deployed across a whole variety of conflict environments, from preemptive stationing near areas of potential communal violence (the Rapid Action Force) to Naxal-affected areas to the North East and Kashmir. While the border overlaps with other crucial cleavages, it also has a strategic importance of its own that creates other motivations and constraints.

The Indian State

India is neither a high- nor low-capacity state, in comparative perspective. Yet "medium capacity"[41] doesn't tell us an enormous amount about what capacities it has and lacks. In the area of internal security, there is a large amount of coercive capacity: the MHA's paramilitary forces alone are larger than most nations' entire militaries, in addition to the Army and state-level police. While the training and resources available to different security forces within India varies dramatically, there is no plausible comparison to the classic "weak states" that are the focus of so much attention in political violence research.[42]

Yet both as a matter of resource constraints and political choice, decisions need to be made about how to deploy this capacity. I have argued in this chapter that politics is essential to making sense of internal security. The nature of Indian nationalist projects, even despite the shift from Congress to BJP dominance, has made some political cleavages much more sensitive and difficult to manage than others. Claims made on the basis of language and tribe, while certainly not uncontroversial or apolitical, have been easier to accommodate than claims along the religious (especially Muslim or Sikh) political dimension. There have also been changes as Hindu

nationalism has risen, with even greater space for Hindu vigilantism and armed intimidation, and a further increase in suspicion and repression of Muslims.[43]

In comparative perspective, this focus helps us understand what is and what is not
exceptional about India—unlike Pakistan and Sri Lanka, which have approached
ethno-regional movements with far more iron fist than velvet glove (or any kind of
glove). Similarly, there has been a comparatively flexible approach to the hard left,
with pathways into mainstream politics at least possible, in sharp contrast to the
New Order or Ne Win's Burma, which also wiped out the more moderate, parliamentary left. Just as research on communal riots has emphasized, to understand the
Indian state's resource deployments and implementation of formal doctrines and
ostensible policy statements, we need to think carefully about the political goals and
incentives of governments.

These politics are not all that is at stake, of course: electoral incentives dominate
in state-level militarized politics, the distinctive attributes of border zones induce
particular considerations, there is a general desire to avoid radically destabilizing
disorder that creates a "ceiling" on tolerating or fostering violence, and a whole variety of bureaucratic and economic dynamics also matter. I have sketched out some
of these factors above, and their importance is undeniable.

Yet a focus on high politics and nationalist projects makes sense of both variation
across space even under the same leaders and security institutions, and changes over
time. It helps us understand the priorities of the Modi government as it has established national political dominance. While anti-Naxal policy and strategies in the
North East (including a deal with the NDFB and a long-ongoing process with the
NSCN-IM, plus smaller Naga groups) have shown some degree of flexibility and
malleability, the approach to Kashmir has further hardened from an already tough
state posture under previous governments (the INC had its own reasons to hold
the line on Kashmir): the Hindu-Muslim cleavage, layered atop and intertwined
with the history of Partition and India-Pakistan tensions, gives Kashmir a particular
salience and place in the BJP's politics. Beyond Kashmir, the rise of social contention and violence aimed at Muslims and the various classes deemed to be traitors to
the nation (liberal university campuses above all) is the kind of outcome that more
narrow explanations of internal security focused on organizational structures, bureaucratic doctrines, or regime type, struggle to explain.

Finally, how might we characterize success and failure in India's approach to
these issues? India has avoided any successful secessions, its state has grown increasingly powerful in terms of coercive capability, and political violence over the last
two decades has dropped substantially. The coercive core of the Indian state has
grown notably, with massive increases in the size of the CAPFs in particular, making
the costs of both starting and sustaining major rebellion increasingly daunting.[44]
Similarly, there has been notable expansion in other sinews of state capacity, such
as roads and mobile connectivity, that seem likely to further augment state reach.
The state has successfully consolidated control of India's political heartland and

the level of anti-state violence has largely trended down over the last decade and a half: compared to the period from the late 1980s through early 2000s, the state is ascendant versus its challengers.

At the same time, a number of these conflicts endure despite this massive increase in state power, even at a much lower level of violence, absorbing substantial resources from a government and society with many other pressing needs. Importantly, the major surge of insurgency that rose in the 1980s emerged in part from government policies, complicating a simple story about changes in state capabilities over time: there has not been a straightforward linear trend since independence. The threat of resurgent conflict continues, and there is always potential for a spark of communal conflict to flare into something larger. Moreover, the human cost of conflict suppression has also been high—extrajudicial killings, torture, sustained crackdowns, and other limitations of rights have been common. It is difficult to offer any simple takeaway—there have been major successes, but also real failures, both of which provide insights into what drives patterns of state response to armed groups.

Notes

1. Bidisha Biswas, *Managing Conflicts in India: Policies of Coercion and Accommodation*, repr. ed. (Lanham, MD: Lexington Books, 2015); William Gould, *Religion and Conflict in Modern South Asia* (New York: Cambridge University Press, 2012), http://pi.lib.uchicago.edu/1001/cat/bib/11830557; Bethany Ann Lacina, *Rival Claims: Ethnic Violence and Territorial Autonomy under Indian Federalism* (Ann Arbor: University of Michigan Press, 2017).
2. For an excellent overview, see Amit Ahuja and Devesh Kapur, "The State and Internal Security in India," in this volume.
3. This approach is inspired by Paul R. Brass, *Language, Religion and Politics in North India* (London: Cambridge University Press, 1974).
4. Sushant Singh explores the practical implementation of these policies in "India's Internal Security Doctrine in Practice" in this volume.
5. Paul Brass, *The Production of Hindu-Muslim Violence in Contemporary India* (Seattle: University of Washington Press, 2003); Ashutosh Varshney, *Ethnic Conflict and Civic Life: Hindus and Muslims in India* (New Haven, CT: Yale University Press, 2002).
6. Martin J. Smith, *Burma: Insurgency and the Politics of Ethnicity*, 2nd ed. (London: Zed Books, 1999).
7. Avinash Paliwal and Paul Staniland, "Strategy, Secrecy, and External Support for Insurgent Groups," working paper (2020).
8. Paul Staniland, "Between a Rock and a Hard Place: Insurgent Fratricide, Ethnic Defection, and the Rise of Pro-State Paramilitaries," *Journal of Conflict Resolution* 56, no. 1 (February 2012): 1640.
9. C. Christine Fair, "Lessons from India's Experience in the Punjab, 1978–1993," in *India and Counterinsurgency: Lessons Learned*, ed. Sumit Ganguly and David P. Fidler (London: Routledge, 2009), Chapter 8.
10. Nandini Sundar, *The Burning Forest: India's War in Bastar* (New Delhi: Juggernaut Books, 2016).
11. Ashwani Kumar, *Community Warriors: State, Peasants and Caste Armies in Bihar* (London: Anthem Press, 2008).

12. An excellent review overview of this literature is Sarah Birch, Ursula Daxecker, and Kristine Höglund, "Electoral Violence: An Introduction," *Journal of Peace Research* 57, no. 1 (January 2020): 3–14.

13. Brass, *The Production of Hindu-Muslim Violence in Contemporary India.*

14. Paul Staniland, "Internal Security Strategy in India," *India Review* 17, no. 1 (January 2018): 142–158.

15. Joe Soss and Vesla Weaver, "Police Are Our Government: Politics, Political Science, and the Policing of Race–Class Subjugated Communities," *Annual Review of Political Science* 20, no. 1 (2017): 565–591.

16. Steven I. Wilkinson, "Which Group Identities Lead to Most Violence? Evidence from India," in *Order, Conflict, and Violence*, ed. Stathis Kalyvas, Ian Shapiro, and Tarek Masoud (New York: Cambridge University Press, 2008), 271–300; Paul R. Brass, *Language, Religion and Politics in North India* (London: Cambridge University Press, 1974); Varshney, *Ethnic Conflict and Civic Life.*

17. Pradeep K. Chhibber and Rahul Verma, *Ideology and Identity: The Changing Party Systems of India*, repr. ed. (New York: Oxford University Press, 2018); Milan Vaishnav, ed., *The BJP in Power: Indian Democracy and Religious Nationalism* (Washington, DC: Carnegie Endowment for International Peace, 2019).

18. Paul Staniland, "Militias, Ideology, and the State," *Journal of Conflict Resolution* 59, no. 5 (August 2015): 770–793, https://doi.org/10.1177/0022002715576749.

19. Mark Tully and Satish Jacob, *Amritsar: Mrs. Gandhi's Last Battle* (London: J. Cape, 1985).

20. Sumantra Bose, *Kashmir: Roots of Conflict, Paths to Peace* (Cambridge, MA: Harvard University Press, 2003); Ahsan I. Butt, *Secession and Security: Explaining State Strategy against Separatists* (Ithaca, NY: Cornell University Press, 2017).

21. Paul Staniland, *Ordering Violence: Explaining Armed Group-State Relations from Cooperation to Conflict* (Ithaca, NY: Cornell University Press, 2021).

22. Butt, *Secession and Security.*

23. A long-run study of variation in the success of the Naxalite movement can be found in Kanchan Chandra and Omar García-Ponce, "Why Ethnic Subaltern-Led Parties Crowd Out Armed Organizations: Explaining Maoist Violence in India," *World Politics* 71, no. 2 (April 2019): 367–416.

24. Bidyut Chakrabarty, *Communism in India: Events, Processes and Ideologies* (New York: Oxford University Press, 2014).

25. Subir Bhaumik, *Troubled Periphery: Crisis of India's North East* (Los Angeles: SAGE, 2009); B. G. Verghese, *India's Northeast Resurgent: Ethnicity, Insurgency, Governance, Development* (Delhi: Konark Publishers, 1996).

26. M. Horam, *Naga Insurgency: The Last Thirty Years* (New Delhi: Cosmo Publications, 1988); Marcus Franke, *War and Nationalism in South Asia: The Indian State and the Nagas* (London: Routledge, 2009); Åshild Kolås, "Naga Militancy and Violent Politics in the Shadow of Ceasefire," *Journal of Peace Research* 48, no. 6 (November 2011): 781–792, https://doi.org/ 10.1177/0022343311417972; Shalaka Thakur and Rajesh Venugopal, "Parallel Governance and Political Order in Contested Territory: Evidence from the Indo-Naga Ceasefire," *Asian Security* 15, no. 3 (September 2019): 285–303; Sanjoy Hazarika, *Strangers of the Mist: Tales of War and Peace from India's Northeast* (New Delhi: Viking, Penguin Books India, 1994).

27. Javier Auyero, *Routine Politics and Violence in Argentina: The Gray Zone of State Power* (Cambridge: Cambridge University Press, 2007).

28. For a granular study of some of these cross-border dynamics, see Subir Bhaumik, *Insurgent Crossfire: North-East India* (New Delhi: Spantech & Lancer, 1996).

29. Rumela Sen, *Farewell to Arms: How Rebels Retire without Getting Killed* (New York: Oxford University Press, 2021).

30. On variation in nationalist projects, see Maya Tudor and Dan Slater, "Nationalism, Authoritarianism, and Democracy: Historical Lessons from South and Southeast Asia,"

Perspectives on Politics 19, no. 3 (September 2021): 706–722; Scott Straus, *Making and Unmaking Nations: War, Leadership, and Genocide in Modern Africa* (Ithaca, NY: Cornell University Press, 2015); Stephen E. Hanson, *Post-Imperial Democracies: Ideology and Party Formation in Third Republic France, Weimar Germany, and Post-Soviet Russia* (Cambridge and New York: Cambridge University Press, 2010).

31. Staniland, *Ordering Violence.*

32. Alfred Stepan, Juan Linz, and Yogendra Yadav, *Crafting State-Nations: India and Other Multinational Democracies* (Baltimore: Johns Hopkins University Press, 2011).

33. Kolby Hanson, "Good Times and Bad Apples: Rebel Recruitment in Crackdown and Truce," *American Journal of Political Science* 65, no. 4 (October 2021): 807–825.

34. Steven I. Wilkinson, "Riots," *Annual Review of Political Science* 12, no. 1 (2009): 329–343.

35. On the Shiv Sena, see Thomas Blom Hansen, *Wages of Violence: Naming and Identity in Postcolonial Bombay* (Princeton, NJ: Princeton University Press, 2001).

36. The standard intervention in these cases is a determination that the state has lost control of law and order and requires central rule until new elections can be held.

37. Christophe Jaffrelot, *The Hindu Nationalist Movement in India* (New York: Columbia University Press, 1996).

38. For instance, Ward Berenschot, "Patterned Pogroms: Patronage Networks as Infrastructure for Electoral Violence in India and Indonesia," *Journal of Peace Research* 57, no. 1 (January 2020): 171–184.

39. On these cases, see Laurent Gayer, *Karachi: Ordered Disorder and the Struggle for the City* (Oxford: Oxford University Press, 2014); Vali R. Nasr, "International Politics, Domestic Imperatives, and Identity Mobilization: Sectarianism in Pakistan, 1979–1998," *Comparative Politics* 32, no. 2 (2000): 171–190; S. Mahmud Ali, *Understanding Bangladesh* (New York: Columbia University Press, 2010); Ali Riaz, *Bangladesh: A Political History since Independence,* Sew edition (London: I. B. Tauris, 2016).

40. Bhaumik, *Insurgent Crossfire;* Paliwal and Staniland, "Strategy, Secrecy, and External Support for Insurgent Groups."

41. Shivaji Mukherjee, "Why Are the Longest Insurgencies Low Violence? Politician Motivations, Sons of the Soil, and Civil War Duration," *Civil Wars* 16, no. 2 (April 2014): 172–207.

42. See, for instance, Philip Roessler, *Ethnic Politics and State Power in Africa: The Logic of the Coup–Civil War Trap* (Cambridge and New York: Cambridge University Press, 2016).

43. Milan Vaishnav, ed., *The BJP in Power: Indian Democracy and Religious Nationalism* (Washington, DC: Carnegie Endowment for International Peace, 2019).

44. Paul Staniland, "Political Violence in South Asia: The Triumph of the State?," Carnegie Endowment for International Peace, https://carnegieendowment.org/2020/09/03/politi cal-violence-in-south-asia-triumph-of-state-pub-82641, accessed October 20, 2020.

7

India's Internal Security Doctrine in Practice

SUSHANT SINGH

Internal security in one part of the country or another has been a constant challenge for India since its independence from the British in 1947, when some militant armed group attempted to secede from India. Indian officials, justifiably, claim that despite "a million mutinies," no attempt by any rebel group has succeeded so far and that this should be taken as evidence of a successful internal security strategy pursued by the government. Strategies have varied over time and regions, but they all fall within the constant doctrine for ensuring internal security against armed rebel groups.

Even though a doctrine has been often dismissed as being "the last refuge of the unimaginative," it provides the fundamental set of principles that guides various stakeholders as they pursue internal security objectives.[1] They are principles that have been successful under many conditions in the past, but are not limiting; they must provide a basis for incorporating new ideas, technologies, and organizational designs. Essentially, a doctrine is not merely a prescriptive belief system; it has to be authoritative and a starting point for addressing new problems.

But a doctrine cannot give context to itself. The cultural, political, social, and environmental factors are necessary to create context, and understanding the doctrine requires an understanding of context. That makes any doctrine a challenge to produce, and an internal security doctrine more so, because the belief system underlying the document will have to be *perforce* political. Nevertheless, an internal security doctrine is an important document that serves as a guide to institutionalized thinking and points to a whole-of-government approach, which can help align the energies of different stakeholders toward the fulfillment of a political goal.

In India, the government has not put out any formal document enunciating its doctrine for internal security; the only institution to do so has been the Army. This, coupled with the fact that the Army is used as an instrument of last resort in a situation and is primus inter pares among all the stakeholders, has placed the Army's

Sushant Singh, *India's Internal Security Doctrine in Practice* In: *Internal Security in India*. Edited by: Amit Ahuja and Devesh Kapur, Oxford University Press. © Oxford University Press 2023. DOI: 10.1093/oso/9780197660331.003.0007 view at the center of the discourse. However, based on the strategies followed in various regions that have produced internal security challenges, a fair assessment can be made of the doctrine in practice and the variations in its implementation.

This chapter argues that the internal security doctrine, as practiced, seeks a political resolution, without affecting the integrity of the country and within the constitutional framework. This means isolating the armed rebels from the people and targeting them. This has to be done by using minimum force so as to win the hearts and influence the minds of the general populace. The security forces are provided special legal protection to prevent targeted harassment by rebel groups. The armed forces have to work closely with the civil administration for developmental work to win the people over, which also helps restore civilian control over the area as violence declines.

Though there are variations in implementation, they have not changed the underlying tenet of the doctrine, which is to use military means in a calibrated manner for a political resolution of the problem. Though the degree of repression and the degree of cooperation with each rebel group differ on a case-to-case basis, the deployment patterns, methods for conducting operations, the tempo of operations, and tasks given to units are all geared toward reasserting government control over territory and population.

This chapter looks at the Indian internal security doctrine in theory and in practice, the variations in its implementation, the role of the Army and other stakeholders, and the limitations of the doctrine, and finally it gazes into trends for the future. It does not go into a comparative study with other global experiences of internal security challenges in democratic societies.

The Doctrine on Paper

The Indian government has never publicly articulated an internal security doctrine and there is no evidence that any such formal document exists. That such a doctrine ever existed informally is also a questionable assumption, because that suggests a certain amount of deliberation and institutionalization at the highest levels of the government, which has not been evident so far. There has also been no formal document placed in the public domain by the Central Armed Police Forces (CAPF), more commonly known as the paramilitary forces, or the state police departments that have participated in the internal security campaigns.

Even as cyberspace has become an important domain for malevolent domestic actors, India's existing cybersecurity policy makes no mention of any policy to prevent or repel such domestic actors.[2] Various other ministries of the government, whether it is the Information and Broadcasting Ministry which deals with communication strategy, or the Rural Development Ministry which deals with development of rural areas, have also been silent on any internal security strategy. Even the limited number of documents, speeches, and policies from the Home Ministry that refer to internal security deal mostly with the threat posed by the Maoists in tribal areas of some central Indian states.

This is due not only to lethargy of the government or its agencies but also because of practical reasons of the complex human and social phenomena in internal security, which cannot be dealt with by a broad set of general principles. Moreover, understanding context is an important factor in internal security situations because the principles codified in the doctrine, which are based on past experiences, may not be relevant to situations in the future. Also, a political document that deals with internal security can only follow a formal articulation of a national security strategy document, which has not seen the light of the day despite multiple false starts.[3]

Interviews with a cross-section of retired bureaucrats and police and military officers have confirmed that a formal internal security doctrine neither exists nor has been debated in the past three decades. When pressed to name at least one document, most government officials refer to the 2001 report by the Group of Ministers (GoM) chaired by the then Home Minister, L. K. Advani. That GoM had four task forces, which included one dealing with internal security, headed by N. N. Vohra, former home secretary and principal secretary to the prime minister.

The terms of reference of the task force included an assessment of "the national level threats to internal security, such as insurgencies, terrorism, left wing extremism, drug trafficking and religious fundamentalism and to recommend appropriate measures for tackling them" and an examination of "the role and responsibility of MHA and State Governments."[4]

A section in Chapter 2 of the GoM report provides a brief overview of the ongoing internal security challenges such as in Jammu and Kashmir, Punjab, the North East, and Left Wing Extremism, while Chapter 4 of the report includes recommendations for the government. At no place is there a clear articulation of the underlying philosophy for defeating internal security challenges, but a couple of dictums in Chapter 4 are still noteworthy. "The Constitution of India provides the basis for the rule of law in the country," the report asserts in Paragraph 4.4, adding: "The supremacy of the Constitution therefore has to be upheld by all the three wings of the Government i.e. the legislature, the executive and the judiciary."

In Paragraph 4.3, it unambiguously states that "the paramount importance of maintaining the civil face of Government, even while the Armed Forces of the Union are deployed in aid of civil authority, cannot be over-emphasised." It expands on the premise in Paragraph 4.18: "The reins of Government must, of course, never be handed over to the Armed Forces. The civil face of governance must remain visible at all levels, even in situations of militancy and terrorism. The Armed Forces of the Union can be used only in aid of civil power and not in supercession of it."

It states in Paragraph 4.10 that "the Ministry of Home Affairs (MHA) has the nodal responsibility for maintenance of internal security in the country" and mentions in the same spirit in Paragraph 4.56 that "the ultimate objective should be to entrust Internal Security (IS)/Counter Insurgency (CI) duties entirely to CPMFs and the Rashtriya Rifles, thus de-inducting the Army from these duties, wherever possible."[5]

Even though a doctrine cannot be crafted from these dictums, three principles are evident: (1) the Constitution is not suspended during internal security operations; (2) the civil administration remains supreme in all cases, with the armed forces only in its aid; and (3) central police forces should replace the Army in all internal security duties. This document is nearly two decades old but these principles, though not followed fully since, remain the benchmark for the government to aspire to. A formal internal security doctrine would have been more comprehensive and done this job even better.

Military's Doctrine

In this vacuum, the Army has taken the lead in establishing a formal document. Many observers reckon that the inspiration for such a public document came from the deep American involvement in counterinsurgency operations in Iraq and Afghanistan that was dominating global military discourse. The Indian Army was keen to showcase its experience and prowess in similar duties and put out its Doctrine for Sub-Conventional Operations (DSCO)—originally in 2006 and a revised version in 2013—while Sub-Conventional Operations also find a place in the Indian Army Doctrine (2010) and in the Joint Doctrine of the three defense services (2017).[6]

A review of these doctrines shows that the armed forces define sub-conventional warfare as "a politico-military confrontation between contending States or groups, below conventional war and above routine peaceful competition among States. Proxy war is being waged against India, by an inimical adversary, engineered through hybrid elements." By only highlighting the proxy war, the doctrine seems to shift the blame for any rebellion on inimical foreign states, and takes the focus away from the process of political accommodation to overcome local disaffection and demand for development. At another level, this is understandable as the focus of the armed forces is on the external adversary, which lends them to view every internal security challenge through the external prism.

Joint Doctrine goes on to prescribe that "countering this proxy war mandates concomitant capabilities and establishment of a robust Counter Infiltration and Counter Terrorism Grid. Counter Proxy war is being waged through a number of means viz political, economic, social, cultural, psychological, informational and military. In combating Low Intensity Conflict (LIC), the Military dimension is not dominant, as in conventional war, but supportive—it is low profile, restrained and people-friendly nature."

That the military dimension is not dominant but supportive is emphasized by the DSCO, which essentially captures lessons from India's long history of fighting insurgencies inside its own borders that the Army wishes to institutionalize. It outlines central concepts and operational approaches for the Army, wherein the military's function is to facilitate conflict resolution by reducing the level of violence to the point where the political process can begin. This is stated up front in the foreword of DSCO, penned by the then Chief of Army Staff: "The overall concept of sub conventional operations by security forces revolves around an endeavor to restore a sense of normalcy from where the civilian authority can assume its responsibility."

Without diluting the importance of these formal military documents, it needs to be emphasized that these articulations are limited to the authority of armed forces and do not have the imprimatur of either the political leadership or the government, especially the Home and Defense ministries.[7] They do not refer to the role of other agencies, such as the state police, the CAPFs, and the local administration, except for providing help to the Army to complete its task. The Army-centric view places this doctrine at a variance with the 2001 GoM report on internal security, which has civilian administration and the Home Ministry at the center of internal security operations. These documents, nevertheless, provide an important basis to formulate the internal security doctrine followed in practice.

An Informal Doctrine

Any discussion on India's informal internal security doctrine begins invariably with the case study of Mizoram, before moving to Punjab. Both these cases are examples of a successful counterinsurgency campaign that led to elimination of militancy and the state's return to constitutional democracy. The two cases are vastly dissimilar but their success makes it easier for the experts to talk about them. Moreover, as Paul Staniland reminds us in this volume, India has avoided any successful secessions, its state has grown increasingly powerful in terms of coercive capability, and political violence over the last two decades has dropped substantially.

When asked to define the informal internal security doctrine followed by India, most policymakers find it hard to go beyond the obvious truisms. Almost everyone contends first that India believes in finding a political solution to all grievances and wants rebels to give up the path of violence and join the political mainstream. The second truism is about the inviolability of India's territorial boundaries and its sovereignty, wherein all concessions are possible within the purview of the Constitution and without any foreign mediation. The third prong is the use of security forces to suppress violence, which is solely done with a view to restore civil administration and clear the path for an early resumption of democratic politics. The fourth line is about the employment of security forces, who follow the policy of "iron fist in a velvet glove" and attempt to "win the hearts and influence the minds" of the civilian population by limiting the use of violence, but still need legal protection. The fifth argument is about the inevitability of the success of the Indian state—it will outlast any rebel group.

Like all clichés, these points contain some truth in them even though they flatten out any nuance in the argument. These need to be examined in light of the historical facts to frame any informal doctrine, and track its evolution. Some of the arguments listed above can be combined and a few discarded to provide a three-point doctrine. As we will see later, this only provides an idealized view of how India manages its internal security, while the reality is far removed.

It can be safely said that the essence of India's internal security doctrine is to find a political solution to accommodate the demands of the rebel group, without affecting the territorial integrity and constitutional framework of the country. India has historically made major concessions—from creating new states (like Nagaland) to integrating rebel leaders in mainstream politics (Laldenga in Mizoram)—to arrive at a political solution. The nature of these concessions and their process depends on contextual, geographic, ethno-religious, and strategic dimensions, but the fundamental aim of the government remains unaltered, even in long-standing insurgencies such as Nagaland and Kashmir.

The focus on arriving at a political solution perforce calls for an early revival of the civil administration and resumption of democratic politics. Elections are seen as a marker of democracy and were conducted during some of the toughest periods of anti-India movements in Assam, Nagaland, Sikkim, and Kashmir. Even a weak democratically elected government is seen to be better and more representative than the central rule, echoing the primacy of India's liberal constitutional values, which are seen to be the biggest attraction for the country's diverse population staying together.

The next dictum flows from the previous. If finding a political solution lies at the core of the guiding philosophy, it necessarily warrants that minimum force be used against the armed rebels. It also means that force be used only when absolutely necessary to contain the violence, and not as a punitive measure. This principle was established by India's first prime minister Jawaharlal Nehru when he sent the Army to fight the Naga insurgents in the mid-1950s.[8] The Army sought the use of airpower and heavy weaponry but it was rejected by Nehru, establishing a precedent that has been followed since (apart from a couple of aberrations). In Manipur in 1966, airpower was used to restore an adverse situation, but was denied by the government until the 1980s. Heavy weaponry was used inside the Golden Temple in Amritsar during Operation Bluestar in June 1984. These exceptions prove the norm.

While rebuffing the Army's demand, Nehru emphasized the political nature of the Naga problem, arguing that the Nagas had never developed a sense of Indian nationalism because they had been kept isolated from the rest of the country by British colonial rule.[9] Thus, the Naga alienation was understandable, and their identity within the Indian nation needed to be developed gently. Even though Nehru emphasized that the unity and integrity of the country was inviolable, he suggested a carefully moderated policy that emphasized the need for understanding the context of the Naga rebellion, and a strategy that sought political accommodation rather than military victory. Nehru reminded the Army that the Nagas were fellow-countrymen who had to be won over, not suppressed. Though there were rumblings within the Army about being forced to fight with one hand tied behind their backs, the Army accepted these political limits on the use of force.[10]

Having been established in the early years of independent India and reinforced since, these basic tenets of the internal security doctrine are informally understood and have been imbibed by all stakeholders. They have broadly remained unchanged as part of the Indian state's grand political strategy since its independence from the British in 1947. The constancy of these tenets, however, does not dilute their evolution over the last seven decades. These underlying tenets have often been tailored to respond differently to each insurgency, depending on the geography, the character of the rebel group, its political demands, its ethno-religious nature, the threat perception, and the foreign support provided to the group.

For instance, while the Indian state demonstrates a high degree of resolve to establish total state dominance in Jammu and Kashmir, it is comfortable sharing political authority with rebel groups in Nagaland. In other areas such as Manipur and in central India, the political aim is to keep a lid on violence below a politically acceptable threshold. The balance between the degree of repression and the degree of cooperation with each group is a political calculation which changes with time, even if these groups are of comparable military power.[11]

That being said, whether a rebel group has to be subjugated, pacified, or eliminated has depended on one thick red line: secession is taboo. As long as a rebel group insists on seceding from India or moving out of its constitutional ambit, the security forces understand—even if they are not told so explicitly—that the group has to be eliminated. Often, when put under consistent pressure by the security forces over a duration of time, these groups open a backchannel for negotiations with the government and no longer insist on their demand for secession. That is a signal for the security forces to take the foot off the pedal, as the state finds means of political accommodation with the group while ensuring that the violence is contained below a certain acceptable threshold.[12]

The choice between suppression of violence and the elimination of the rebel group determines the concept of operations by the forces. From small-team operations based on specific intelligence to targeting top leaders and other linchpins of the group, the security forces shift their focus toward prevention of violent incidents through area domination by extensive patrolling and by creating company-sized camps at various locations. The larger aim is to create an environment in which civilian administration can resume functioning, and the political process restarts.

To be able to swiftly move between these two options suggests a very high degree of calibration and control over the quantum and nature of violence that can be brought upon by the forces. This is a product of multiple factors, foremost being the limitations imposed on the violence ab initio, which abjured the use of artillery, heavy weaponry, or airpower against the rebel groups. It means that the calibration of violence has to be done by the Army within a limited spectrum, without any overt signaling by its leadership.

The Army's Role

The Indian Army developed its approach by studying Mao Zedong's theory of insurgent warfare and the British theory of counterinsurgency drawn from their experience in Malaya.[13] It initially gave primacy to isolating the insurgents and maintaining control of operations. Since quick fights with insurgents did not allow support to reach a unit in contact, the Army only began sending units on patrol that were durable enough to sustain a fight on their own with guerrillas. This led to the practice of keeping most operations at company-level units.

The Army thus focused on the organization, leadership, tactics, bases, funding, and external support of the rebel groups as a security measure, with an aim to either militarily decimate the group or bring violence down to politically acceptable levels. This was done by establishing local intelligence networks, either through the local police and government officials or by creating its own "sources." In some cases, the Army also attempted to either split the most dominant group or helped raise friendly counterinsurgent groups to bring the situation under control at the earliest. But it simultaneously followed an interlinked task of isolating the armed rebels from the larger population. Popularly called the "iron fist in a velvet glove" or "winning the hearts and influencing the minds of the local population," it was articulated unambiguously by the then Chief of Army Staff in the 1950s in Nagaland:

> You must remember that all of the people in the area in which you are operating are fellow Indians. They may have different religions, may pursue a different way of life, but they are Indians and that very fact, that they are different and yet part of India is a reflection of India's greatness. Some of these people are misguided and have taken to arms against their own people, and are disrupting the peace of this area. You are to protect the mass of people from these disruptive elements. You are not there to fight the people in the area, but to protect them. You are fighting only those who threaten the people and who are a danger to the lives and properties of the people. You must do therefore everything possible to win their confidence and respect and to help them feel they belong to India.[14]

However, this did not mean that the Army was drawn in to fight against the rebel groups without any additional legal protection. Despite strong parliamentary arguments against a tough legal provision to shield the Army's actions, the government did pass the colonial-era ordinance passed during the Quit India movement of 1942 into a more stringent Armed Forces Special Powers Act or AFSPA.[15] Enactment of the AFSPA, and its companion, the Disturbed Areas Act, has become a precursor to the deployment of the Army to a state but its draconian provisions have also become a lightning rod for political grievances among wide swathes of population in these disturbed areas.

Even with all the legal protections within its own territory, the situation was complicated for the Army because many of the rebel groups had safe bases in neighboring countries, just across the border. In some cases, such as Myanmar, it was due to the lawless nature of the bordering areas, but in others like Pakistan and China, it was a policy of these countries to keep India unbalanced.[16] At times, the Army would launch operations in lawless areas such as in Bhutan, but eventually it needed diplomatic and political engagement for these countries to stop providing active support to rebel groups.[17] The creation of Bangladesh in 1971 resolved this problem to a great extent but it still needed a friendly government in Dhaka to stop providing shelter to the groups from North Eastern states. In Myanmar, the Army worked with the Myanmar Army to launch joint or coordinated operations and deny the rebels these safe spaces.[18] The government believed that it was better placed to deal with them once they were on Indian territory.

Working with the local population meant that the Army had to operate in tandem with the civilian administration, and civil-military cooperation at a local level became an integral part of the strategy. Even though the presence of civilian government was often limited in far-flung areas, the government did not try to replace them with the Army—the gaps in their capacities were nevertheless filled by the Army.[19] This provided the added advantage of moving swiftly toward restoration of civil control after the security operations had sufficiently isolated and weakened the armed rebels.

The role of the state police, once the Army moved in, was of a supporting nature in internal security as it had already been overwhelmed by the armed rebels. But it remained the major provider of intelligence to all the security forces and used the space created by the Army's actions against the rebels to regain its primacy in law and order. The CAPFs, though under the Union Government, often acted as additional forces for the state government, working closely alongside the state police. As the situation came under control, the states created their own armed police units, which were a more militarized version of the police and deployed along with the Army. The police then comprised those who did the routine policing duties and those who performed the specialized task of dealing with armed rebels.

Essentially, the Army, with its strong public image, often gained primacy over the state police and the CAPFs, which had to play a supporting role in most aspects. When tensions erupted between the two sides, the Army usually got its way. A long-standing view in the Army about the supremacy of the elected political leadership meant that the political view prevailed, eventually preventing any differences from becoming disputes.[20]

Another factor that allows the Army to quickly shift gears is its vast experience of counterinsurgency campaigns of various types in different theatres. Aided in good measure by a highly disciplined organization that functions under the directive style of command, the soldiers are cognizant of the changing nature of counterinsurgency operations where different kinds of tasks require different types of operations.[21] By reducing the tempo of operations, deployment patterns, and changing KRAs for military units, the leadership can direct the military means to be quickly in tune with the political ends.

This relationship between the political ends and the military means has not always been smooth. Political leadership has always been concerned that the Army would not be sufficiently sensitive to political considerations, and it was expressed loudly in Parliament during the debates in the 1950s. Institutionally, the Army sees itself as an instrument of last resort which comes in to fix things when they have been mishandled by the political setup and administrative machinery creating conditions for an insurgency. There has been a vigorous debate within the Army about its employment in counterinsurgency duties vis-à-vis its primary role of defending against an external aggression.[22] In the early years, counterinsurgency was seen as a task that the Army wanted to forsake in favor of its more conventional role.

However, the fusing of a low-intensity conflict on the Line of Control with Pakistan along with the militancy in Kashmir, as both India and Pakistan became nuclear weapon states, has turned the view toward counterinsurgency as a part of the Army's duties—so much so that military leadership has started articulating "a two and a half front challenge" for the Army, the half front referring to the Kashmir insurgency.[23]

It is also reflected in the creation of dedicated counterinsurgency force within the Army, the Rashtriya Rifles (RR).[24] The original purpose of the RR appears to have been to create a new paramilitary force but one stiffened with Army officers, which would relieve the army of its counterinsurgency burden. But it eventually ended up as a force with more than sixty battalions owned, manned, and controlled by the Army, defeating its original purpose. It provided the Army with additional manpower through fresh recruitment, which allowed the Army's standard units and formations to move away from counterinsurgency to conventional warfighting duties. Even though a permanent government sanction for these RR units does not exist, they are now deeply entrenched in the system with no talk of their partial or full disbandment.

Other Stakeholders

The political leadership at the national level plays the most important role in dealing with a rebel group once the situation becomes serious enough to warrant induction of central forces or the Army. It is preceded by the enactment of the Disturbed Areas Act and the AFSPA, and the state government is often replaced by central rule until a semblance of order is restored. In many cases, the Center sends retired generals as governors who can work in close coordination with the Army when the state is under central rule. The local military commander also has a formal role as a security advisor to the state government, but does not take orders from the state government, and follows the existing command-and-control structures of the Army.

The central political leadership usually appoints a pointsman—a senior politician, a minister, a retired intelligence official, or a retired bureaucrat—to deal with the situation in the state.[25] Such an appointment has to be politically empowered to be effective and can often get caught in the overlapping jurisdictions between the ministries of defense and home, the Army, the intelligence agencies, the office of the National Security Advisor, and the ruling party. The role of the pointsman is more as a coordinator and advisor to the political leadership, while allowing opening of backchannels of communication with various actors in the strife-ridden state.

The role of the intelligence agencies assumes its greatest importance as situations worsen in the state, and local policing mechanisms fail. They are supposed to provide direct inputs to the central government and also help the Army conduct targeted military operations against the rebel leaders. The most important input provided by the agencies is of the assessment of the situation, which helps the political leadership decide on the manner of dealing with the rebel group. These inputs essentially translate into specific political goals, for which the military means and intelligence agencies themselves are employed. With their proximity to the political leadership and connections with the rebel groups, the intelligence agencies at the national level often act as the most important and powerful advisors to the central government.

In association with the security forces, the intelligence agencies have been at the forefront of creating, fostering, and sustaining friendly insurgent groups (Ikhwan ul Muslameen in Kashmir or Salwa Judum in Chhattisgarh) to diminish and damage the major rebel groups, unencumbered by legal restraints imposed on the forces. Most of these experiments have delivered short-term results but have been catastrophic failures in the long run, further denting the credibility of the Indian state in the minds of the affected population. Similarly, these agencies have also tried to raise new political parties, or support existing political groupings, to muddy the political landscape or to get favorable electoral outcomes during polls, but have had mixed results.

India has a large strength of central armed police forces that are inducted in support of the local police, but operate under the state government. As the Center takes direct control of the situation, the paramilitary forces become a part of the unified command structure of the state but also have direct lines of communication with the union home ministry. The state police, the central forces, and the Army are often given separate roles as per their capability and strength, but also conduct joint operations as jurisdictions and areas of interest often overlap. A sharp increase in the number of central armed police forces has not changed their role in counterinsurgency, with their extensive commitments in central India against the Maoists, and frequent rotations for other activities such as the conduct of assembly and parliamentary elections across the country.

India has been fortunate in that most insurgencies have been localized in a single state, with only minimal or no overlap with neighboring states. As law and order is a state subject in India's federal structure, the state police forces would be challenged if the rebels were moving across state boundaries. The successful run of the Maoists in central India was due to their presence across the states of Chhattisgarh, Odisha, and Jharkhand, which leveraged this fault line of federalism. It was eventually overcome by a strong coordination from the Union home ministry and a heavy influx of central forces.

The civil administration, after a state is placed under central rule, emerges as the only vehicle of undertaking development activities that help win the population over. Though the Army units have also started undertaking limited developmental activities under various schemes, the final aim is to restore the authority and primacy of the civil administration. Since civil officials often come under pressure from rebel groups and find it hard to operate in an environment of total administrative and political breakdown, the Army finds it frustrating to work with officials. The Indian experience shows that even when violence has been suppressed or militant groups decimated, the decapacitated administrative machinery is unable to revive itself and establish its authority. In such a situation, it is often left to the restoration of a political setup through democratic means to make the civilian setup effective and responsive to the larger demands of the public.

After having established the political process and revived the administrative machinery, the biggest challenge for the Army is to decide on an appropriate time to exit from the counterinsurgency theater. A premature exit may lead to a revival of the insurgency, while delaying that decision could mean that the Army becomes part of the local political economy and is bogged down by a secondary task at the cost of its primary role. The local administration and the state governments are often happy to keep the Army around, even though the situation may not warrant it fully, and a risk-averse central government is likely to oblige the state. The lack of an exit plan has been the biggest lacuna in the counterinsurgency doctrine of the Army, as seen in practice and in implementation.[26]

Limitations

Every doctrine has its inherent limitations due to the difference in the context of various situations where it is applied, but those limitations are more pronounced in the case of an internal security doctrine because of its complex interplay of ideas, policies, principles, and stakeholders. As Paul Staniland notes in Chapter 6, the empirical record suggests a more complex and contingent approach than relying on the "iron fist in a velvet glove" summary of the Indian counterinsurgency doctrine. In India's case, an absence of a formal document makes the situation worse, whereby personalities and ideologies shape the implementation of the doctrine to a given situation. It is not surprising, then, that India's internal security policies have witnessed slower shifts than its external security policies, notwithstanding the links between foreign policy and internal security.[27]

Unlike the clamor for a national security doctrine, there has been no public demand for the government to issue an internal security doctrine.[28] It has been raised neither by think tanks, public intellectuals and subject matter experts, nor by political leaders. As Staniland observes in Chapter 6, India is not unique and does not have a distinctive single doctrine it pursues, but its particular blend of both policies and diverse insurgencies makes it quite unusual. Preparing an official doctrine would thus require extensive discussions between various institutions and ministries, and that whole-of-government thinking would then be reflected in the document. It would then push various agencies and ministries to formulate their laws, policies, programs, and SOPs as per the overarching doctrine. A lack of doctrine is explicable, but a lack of formal and institutionalized deep deliberation on the subject, given the nature of the threat spectrum, has troubling implications for the future as the nature of internal security challenges becomes more complex, diffused, and intertwined with other security challenges: external, cyber, economic, and ecological.

In the absence of a formal articulation, the Army has stepped in to fill the breach by releasing its doctrine. For obvious reasons, it has placed the Army at the center of the doctrine, with everyone else playing only supporting roles. This has also been translated into real-life situations on the ground, where the Army is employed only as a matter of last resort and remains the most respected institution. An ideal doctrine would replace the centrality of the Army with political direction, providing guidance to all the stakeholders.

It is often said that the shortcomings of a system are often blamed on a doctrine, for any document is only as good as those implementing it. The success in Mizoram and the failure in Nagaland both flow from the same unofficial doctrine. Successful examples are often attributed to the doctrine, and there is an incentive to persist with the doctrine even where it is not effective. After more than six decades in Nagaland and three decades in Kashmir, the doctrine is still followed. However, as it is not formalized, it is often misinterpreted as a doctrine of patience and stamina—of wearing the rebels out. It is an inversion of the expression attributed to a captured Taliban fighter about the Western forces in Afghanistan: "You have the watches, but we have the time."[29] In India's case, it doesn't matter who has the watches; it is the Indian state that has the time.

For the general populace, there are implications of prolonged exposure to counterinsurgency. Multiple generations have been exposed to cordon-and-search operations and restrictions in Nagaland, Manipur, and Kashmir. There is a parallel in economics regarding the trade-off between consumption and investment. More consumption today leaves fewer resources for investment, which in turn leads to less consumption tomorrow. India's current approach of wearing the rebels out may ensure order and security today, but it sows seeds of insecurity tomorrow as new generations of alienated youth come of age. A modern doctrine would identify specific benchmarks that would mark the end of a long, attritional security-centric approach in a theater lest it turn counterproductive.

There is a fundamental question thrown by this quest of framing an informal internal security doctrine that is beyond the scope of the chapter. The increasing perception of insecurity at the level of the individual and the family is a recognized phenomenon, while India has expanded its internal security apparatus, as seen by a massive increase in CAPFs. It seems that internal security remains a purely state-centric concept in practice, which undervalues the need to be more responsive to individual and family concerns. As Devesh Kapur and Amit Ahuja ask in the Introduction to this volume, security is a means to an end. The question is, What is the end here? The trade-off between order and liberty is especially important in a democracy, and even more so if marginalized communities have to bear the brunt of the costs of curtailment of liberties.

Shifts in Trends

India's journey of tacking its internal security challenges across time and geographies displays three trends for the future. These trends also serve as a warning, as much as they reinforce the need for a formal internal security doctrine.

The first is the widespread acceptance in the government about the necessity of using military force as an integral part of counterinsurgency campaigns, but there is a lack of recognition that use of force against its own people needs to be limited. The counterinsurgencies in India seem to have moved from a people-centric approach—arrived at after the brutalizing experience of village regrouping programs in Nagaland and Mizoram in the 1960s, which was exemplified by the creation of the National Human Rights Commission in 1993 and issuance of ten commandments of the Chief of Army Staff in the late 1990s—to a completely territorial approach in some cases.[30] This shift was most visible in Kashmir after 2014. It means an unhealthy reliance on the use of force as an end in itself, without any political endgame in sight. As Amit Ahuja and Srinath Raghavan note in this volume, Army units are evaluated more on the number of insurgent kills and the kinetic operations undertaken than on their record of preserving peace and winning over the population. The security apparatus in India has become better at controlling violence in insurgencies but the relative peace is no longer translating into a political settlement.[31] So far, the use of force had to be carefully modulated for it to be effective in the fulfillment of political goals, which were negotiations and concessions, without compromising India's territorial integrity or constitutional framework.

Second, it is clear from the Indian experience that the changing nature of Indian politics is affecting the way in which the security forces are approaching counter-insurgency campaigns. The nationalistic rhetoric and an uncompromising major-itarian view seem to have seeped into security forces.[32] This could possibly alter its professional character, changing its approach in fighting the counterinsurgency campaign in places like Kashmir and Nagaland. The long-standing limitations on the use of heavy force domestically could then be lifted when faced with a serious challenge from the rebels, especially with foreign support. It buttresses the argu-ment made by Ahuja and Raghavan in this volume that for the sake of the health of civil-military relations and the military's preparedness for its primary role—protection from external threats—the Indian military's internal security posture has to be reduced, not expanded.

Finally, the Indian doctrine carries a bias toward kinetic options rather than leveraging a full spectrum of grand strategy of all the tools at the state's disposal. Falling violence is being matched by an increasing militarization of the security approach. The strategy and tactics, as evident in practice, reflect a bias toward militarizing what should essentially be a political, social, commercial, cultural, and psychological action.[33] These are significant changes in character and direction, explored in other chapters of the volume. India needs a formal document from the government laying out the broad contours of its internal security doctrine that acknowledges and incorporates these shifts.

If the question is whether India should have an internal security doctrine, the answer is obviously yes. But if the question is whether India will have an official internal security doctrine, the most likely answer is no. Maintaining ambiguity is an integral component of statecraft, and no political leadership wants to get its hands tied by a formal articulation of such a doctrine. Even with an informal doc-trine in practice, this leads to loss of institutionalized memory and relearning of lessons, but that is a price the government is willing to pay to retain its flexibility in decision-making.

Conclusion

Insurgencies are also fought with ideas, not just guns. There are hardly any deliberations on non-coercive aspects of countering insurgencies, which are often fought in remote border areas. In such a scenario, it is incumbent upon academics and think tanks to capture the informal doctrine, as practiced, and critically analyze the dictums in the hope that various stakeholders—and most important, the Indian people—will benefit from the discourse.

Notes

1. The quote is often attributed to Former US Secretary of Defense Jim Mattis.

2. There is a new National Cybersecurity Strategy 2020–2025 document that is awaited from the government. It is expected that there would be a detailed exposition of securing India's cyberspace in the document.

3. There have been three known attempts in the recent years to produce a national security strategy document for India, in 2007, 2015, and 2019. It was also included in the charter of duties of the Defence Planning Committee, when it was formed under the chairmanship of NSA Ajit Doval in 2018. All these attempts have not yielded any result so far.

4. Annexure D to the Report of the Group of Ministers on National Security, 2001 (available at vifindia.org).

5. Report of the Group of Ministers on National Security, 2001 (available at vifindia.org).

6. Doctrine for Sub-Conventional Operations, HQ ARTRAC, Shimla, India, December 2006; Doctrine for Sub-Conventional Operations (revised), HQ ARTRAC, Shimla 2013; Classified document, a revised version of the Indian Army Doctrine issued in 2004; and Joint doctrine for the Indian armed forces, HQ IDS, New Delhi April 2017.

7. The formulation of these doctrines is usually done through consultative means, but the groundwork is often done by Army Training Command, which takes the lead, along with the Army Headquarters where the final approval is given. None of India's military service doctrines have been formally approved by the defense ministry, limiting them to just being service-specific manuals without any government backing.

8. Jawaharlal Nehru's letter to Chief Minister of Assam, B. R. Medhi, May 1956. Also see Rajesh Rajagopalan, "Insurgency and Counterinsurgency," *India Seminar*, 2009.

9. Rajagopalan, "Insurgency and Counterinsurgency". Also see Samanth Subramanian, "The Long View: AFSPA's Bitter Roots," *India Ink, New York Times*, November 12, 2011.

10. Rajesh Rajagopalan, *Fighting Like a Guerrilla: The Indian Army and Counterinsurgency* (New Delhi: Routledge, 2008).

11. Paul Staniland, "Internal Security in India," *India Review* 17, no. 1 (2018): 142–158.

12. Ibid., 147–148.

13. Daniel G. Hodermarsky, "Lessons from India's Counterinsurgency Campaign in Jammu and Kashmir," Monograph 2013-02, School of Advanced Military Studies, United States Army Command and General Staff College, Fort Leavenworth, Kansas.

14. Rajesh Rajagopalan, *Fighting Like a Guerrilla*, 11.

15. Srinath Raghavan, "Military Needs and Societal Values," *The Hindu*, November 10, 2014.

16. Rajeev Bhattacharyya, "Rebel Camps in Myanmar: Will They Hamper the Act East Policy?," in *Mainstreaming the Northeast in India's Look and Act East Policy*, ed. Atul Sarma and Saswati Choudhury (Singapore: Palgrave Macmillan, 2018), 121–126.

17. M. S. Prabhakara, "Crackdown in Bhutan," *Frontline*, January 16, 2004.

18. "India and Myanmar Forces Coordinate to Destroy NE Insurgent Camps across Border," *The Indian Express*, June 16, 2019.

19. Arpita Anant, "Counterinsurgency and 'Op Sadhbhavana' in Jammu and Kashmir," IDSA Occasional Paper No. 19, 2011.

20. Steven Wilkinson, *Army and Nation: The Military and Indian Democracy since Independence* (Ranikhet: Permanent Black, 2015).

21. V. R. Raghavan, "Military and Internal Security: The Indian Experience," in *Internal Security in India: Issues, Structures, Approaches*, ed. Shrikant Paranjpe (Mumbai: Indus Source Books, 2014), 68–72.

22. "Our Only Allegiance Is to Constitution: Army Chief," *Business Standard*, January 12, 2020.

23. "Indian Army Prepared for a Two and a Half Front War: Army Chief General Bipin Rawat," *The Indian Express*, June 8, 2017.

24. Nitin Gokhale and S. K. Chatterji, *Rashtriya Rifles: Home of the Brave* (New Delhi: Bloomsbury India, 2017).

25. "PMO Overrules Home Ministry, Appoints JIC chief RN Ravi as Naga Interlocutor," *The Times of India*, August 29, 2014.

26. Samir Srivastava, "Indian Army in Counter Insurgency Operations: Search for That Elusive End State," www.claws.in (accessed on July 21, 2020).

27. Better relations with the United Arab Emirates, Bangladesh, and Myanmar in recent years have helped in garnering intelligence about malevolent actors, but these countries are no longer safe havens for insurgents and their leadership, as in the past.

28. Arun Prakash, "Needed: Policy, Not Reaction," *The Indian Express*, February 18, 2019.

29. Sami Yousafazai, "10 Years of Afghan War: How the Taliban Go On," *Newsweek*, October 2, 2011.

30. The dividing line between the two approaches cannot be very sharply defined, but there was a written and spoken commitment of the political and military leadership that the idea was to win over the population and not merely to get control of the territory. Even those commitments were no longer being made after 2014, particularly in Kashmir with the most prominent active insurgency in India during the last two decades.

31. The example of Kashmir is the most significant in this regard. While the number of gun-wielding militants had come down to around 200 in the second decade of this century, there has been no concomitant decrease in the security forces or the security-centric approach of the Indian state. After the constitutional changes of August 2019, the government has repeatedly told Parliament that there has been a marked decline in the number of terror incidents, infiltration attempts, deaths of security forces personnel, and other indicators of violence, but this has not led to the opening of political negotiations and engagement with the other side.

32. Sanjiv Krishan Sood, "India's Armed Forces Are Losing Their Political Neutrality—Putting National Security at Risk," *Scroll.in*, May 25, 2019.

33. Raman Raghu, "India Needs to Reboot Its Counter-Insurgency Doctrine," *Hindustan Times*, July 15, 2019.

PART III

INTERNAL SECURITY

The State's Coercive Capacity

8

The Military in Internal Security

AMIT AHUJA AND SRINATH RAGHAVAN

Militaries are the final guarantors of a state's sovereignty. They are traditionally trained to protect the state from external threats. Still, across a large part of the world, including India's immediate neighborhood, militaries have emerged as prominent actors in securing the state internally. Many of these militaries have fought against left-wing, ethnic, and religious insurgencies as well as criminal and drug cartels. Militaries in Mexico, Columbia, the United Kingdom, Nigeria, Kenya, Turkey, Thailand, and Indonesia, among others, have also fought bloody counterinsurgencies on their own territory. Almost every country in the Indian subcontinent, including Pakistan, Bangladesh, Nepal, Burma, and Sri Lanka, has deployed its military in domestic counterinsurgency operations.

In this chapter, we focus on counterinsurgency, which is the Indian Army's most consequential internal security mission. The Indian Army has significantly expanded its counterinsurgency capacity, and of all its internal security tasks, it makes the largest claim on the army's resources.[1] According to government figures, between 1947 and 2018, the army lost a total of 8,772 personnel in internal security and counterinsurgency operations.[2] By way of comparison, the army met with a combined total of 13,946 fatalities across five inter-state wars, counterinsurgency operations in Sri Lanka, and the military mobilization following the attack by Pakistani militants on the Indian Parliament in 2001.[3] Although the army has been fighting against insurgencies since the 1950s, its share of internal security fatalities among total conflict fatalities increased sharply between the two periods 1947–1990 and 1991–2018 (see Figure 8.1). This shift highlights the growing prominence of the army's internal security role in recent decades.[4] Prolonged and substantial counterinsurgency engagements, often lasting decades, have shaped the army's ideational and organizational character.

Three arguments emerge from our analysis of the army's use in internal security. First, continuity and change characterized the Indian Army's role in internal security after 1947. The colonial military was the guarantor of British rule in the Indian subcontinent.[5] As much as a third of it was assigned to domestic security tasks.[6]

Amit Ahuja and Srinath Raghavan, *The Military in Internal Security* In: *Internal Security in India*. Edited by: Amit Ahuja and Devesh Kapur, Oxford University Press. © Oxford University Press 2023. DOI: 10.1093/oso/9780197660331.003.0008

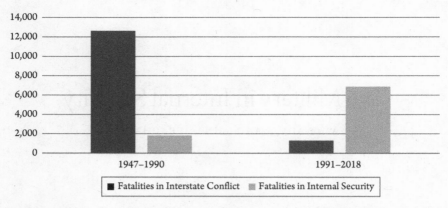

Figure 8.1 Share of army's internal security fatalities among total conflict fatalities, 1947–1990 and 1991–2018

Source: National War Memorial website, https://nationalwarmemorial.gov.in/, and government figures provided in response to questions asked in the parliament.

Notwithstanding the expansion of the Indian Army during World War II, the post-colonial state inherited an army which, besides fighting wars, was also well-drilled in maintaining law and order. Traumatized by the partition of the subcontinent and the accompanying violence, driven by the need to politically integrate the country, and facing a number of insurgencies, the postcolonial state came to prioritize the preservation of national unity and territorial integrity. It did not hesitate to use the military to this end. After 1947, the civil-military ideational and institutional framework began to change. The leaders of the freedom movement, who were at the helm of the postcolonial state, sought more than the political control prioritized by their colonial predecessors; they valued popular legitimacy.

Second, conventional wisdom holds that shifts in India's security policy are mostly crisis-driven. The evolution of the army's counterinsurgency forces suggests that this does not apply to internal security, especially in the face of long internal conflicts. A lengthier time horizon enables institutional learning and policy shifts, albeit slowly. Since the 1980s, the army's counterinsurgency engagements have increased sharply and, instead of adopting a one-size-fits-all approach, it has arrived at different approaches for different theatres. It created the Rashtriya (National) Rifles (RR), the world's largest counterinsurgency force, while also expanding the Assam Rifles (AR), a paramilitary force it has administered since 1962. The RR evolved to counter the Kashmiri insurgency, whereas the AR force's structure was oriented to tackling the insurgencies in the North East. In both sites of counterinsurgency, continuity, interoperability, and pre-deployment training emerged as important principles.

Third, judged from a purely military standpoint, the army's counterinsurgency record has been viewed as a success story. It has fought numerous domestic insurgencies and has been able to reduce the level of violence in all of them. The army's prolonged counterinsurgency role has, however, exacted a heavy price. It has arguably distorted civil-military relations, endangered the army's professionalism, and undermined military effectiveness in confronting external threats and securing India's foreign policy goals. Decades-long counterinsurgency engagements have normalized the militarization of society and the use of draconian laws that violate fundamental civil rights. Its prominence notwithstanding, the army's counterinsurgency role is perceived as a distraction among its officers.

Why do states across the world turn to their militaries, their last line of defense, for their internal security needs? Experience points to several reasons.

First, the military is used when states face well-armed and well-trained insurgencies that overwhelm their police forces. In some instances, the police may even defect and side with the insurgents. The state is then compelled to turn to its military, its most potent instrument of coercion, to impose its writ and preserve its territorial integrity.

Second, civil disturbances and natural calamities test state capacity. In such instances, the military is called to aid the civil authority because it is perceived as a more neutral, less politicized, and a better trained organization compared to other state instruments like the police. In countries where militaries enjoy a great deal of public respect, politicians may prefer to use them in a crisis to protect and enhance their own reputations.

Third, militaries are trained to work in mission mode under any condition and for prolonged periods. They can mobilize faster because they have the logistical skills and assets to move manpower and materials swiftly. They possess a robust communications system as well as a clear chain of command. A military has engineering and medical resources it can deploy to augment and scale up state administration. It can install bridges, build levees, and restore electricity and communication grids swiftly. Militaries can also build and staff hospitals as well as distribute critical drugs and food. States often turn to their militaries as first responders when faced with the challenges of humanitarian assistance and disaster relief.

Militaries, thus, perform a broad set of internal security roles. The military's role in internal security is observable in low-income countries as well as in developed countries.[7] When the external environment is benign, an internal security role potentially allows the military to make claims on budgetary resources, expand its size, and enhance its reputation.[8]

The Indian Military's Internal Security Role

The postcolonial Indian state began to use the military for a wide range of consequential internal security roles soon after independence.[9] Departing British rulers allowed the princely states, indirectly governed by them, to join either India or

Pakistan. Most princely states complied with the directive to choose a side, but a few prevaricated, resisted, or came to be claimed by both countries. The Indian government then turned to its armed forces to compel the accession of certain princely states to the Indian Union.[10] In 1961, Indian armed forces also intervened to end Portuguese rule in the territories of Goa, Daman and Diu. In addition to the first Indo-Pakistan war in 1948–1949, these interventions burnished the nationalist reputation of the military, which was the face of British colonial power until 1947.

Gradually, counterinsurgency emerged as a major focus of the military. Until 2017, 30 percent of the Indian Army's infantry was deployed to fight insurgencies while 30 percent was recuperating and training for the same task.[11] The army is frequently called in aid of civil authority too.[12] It has been asked to quell riots and public violence in thousands of instances across the country,[13] and has suppressed mutinies in the police and paramilitary forces.[14] Additionally, the military is called in aid of civil administration during natural calamities: floods, earthquakes, and pandemics. Its responsibilities include search-and-rescue operations, delivery of medical and food aid, restoration of infrastructure, and provision of security.[15] If required, it also builds airfields, roads, and bridges. When natural calamity or political conflict shuts down public services, the state asks the military to restore them.

The remainder of the chapter first traces continuity and change in the Indian Army's internal security role as it transitioned from a colonial to a postcolonial state institution. Next, it discusses the key innovations in counterinsurgency warfare in recent decades by examining two counterinsurgency forces: the Rashtriya Rifles and the Assam Rifles. The penultimate section evaluates the costs of the army's involvement in internal security. The final section offers concluding observations.

Continuity and Change in the Army's Role in Internal Security

Independent India inherited a well-honed apparatus for maintaining internal order and security from the colonial state. Notwithstanding the strains imposed by Partition and the massive ethnic cleansing that accompanied it, the Indian state and its security apparatus managed to impose order and stability in large swathes of its territory. Yet, as a legatee of the nationalist movement, the postcolonial state also functioned in a democratic and liberal constitutionalist context. In consequence, the ideational and institutional framework in which the Indian state conceived of internal security had elements of continuity and change vis-à-vis the colonial inheritance.

Historian Ranajit Guha has aptly characterized the colonial state as a "dominance without hegemony"—an entity that relied more on coercion than persuasion throughout its existence. Starting from its origins in military conquest, the army raised in India remained the sword arm of the colonizers. The centrality of the military underscored the endemic internal security challenges confronting the colonial state. Between 1783 and 1900, there were no fewer than 110 instances of agrarian disturbances, ranging from localized riots to large-scale rebellion.[16]

Counterinsurgency, by the same token, remained a central task of the Indian Army. Thus, the Government of India frankly stated in 1881 that "the Indian Army is required to maintain internal tranquility rather than for employment against external foes."[17] Indeed, the mature colonial state had to regularly confront internal security challenges: occasional rural insurgencies in the mainland, regular tribal revolts in the North West Frontier, and above all, the novel problems posed by mass nationalist mobilization and communal riots.[18] These called for the development of a new ensemble of doctrine, tactics, and training—one that was bequeathed to independent India.[19] A closer examination of these constituent elements will help understand continuity and change between late colonial and early independent India in maintaining internal security.

In the decades following World War I, the employment of the army in internal security duties was governed by three broad principles: deterrence, minimum use of force, and robust civil-military cooperation. There was no written doctrine, nor were these principles static. Yet they featured prominently in the discourse of internal security. Let us start with deterrence. The military was believed to have a deterrent effect on the native population. The Internal Security Instructions of 1926 maintained that "the civilian authorities have the right when they have reason to think that a disturbance is likely to occur which will be beyond the powers of police to control, to call in the aid of the military to prevent disturbances from coming to a head."[20]

The postcolonial state, by contrast, regarded the military as the last resort—to be deployed only when controlling a riot or insurgency was clearly beyond the capabilities of the local administration and police. This is evident in the reluctance to call in the military during communal riots even when troops are stationed nearby. In insurgencies, the army has seldom been deployed in the early stages. This approach stemmed from two broader changes after independence. The postcolonial state laid claim to the allegiance of the people and sought more than their submission. It wanted hegemony and not just dominance—as a democratic state it sought active consent rather than mere acquiescence owing to coercion. Second, the army's primary task was defense against external aggression, especially in the context of the territorial disputes with Pakistan and China. Indeed, when these became pressing in the 1960s, the Indian government raised central armed police forces exclusively for internal security duties.

On the other two doctrinal principles—minimum force and civil-military cooperation—there was much continuity between the late colonial and independent Indian state. The notion of minimum force gained currency after the Jallianwala Bagh massacre in Amritsar in 1919, when an army detachment was ordered to fire on unarmed civilians, leaving 379 dead and over a thousand wounded.[21]

A booklet *Duties in Aid of the Civil Power* issued in 1923 stated: "The degree of force to be used is to be just so much and no more than is essential to deal with the immediate situation."[22] This was enforced by a series of oversight mechanisms, the most important of which was the practice of instituting an official inquiry whenever the military resorted to force. Yet the principle was periodically violated, especially in dealing with rebellions and insurrections.

During the Quit India revolt of 1942, the largest uprising since 1857, the Raj jettisoned the idea of minimum force: aircrafts were used to machine-gun large crowds; gas and mortar shells were fired at protestors and rebels.[23]

Civil-military cooperation was considered axiomatic in dealing with internal security problems, though it was also important in controlling the use of force. The district magistrate and the commissioner of police worked closely with the local military commander in drawing up contingency plans and carrying out rehearsals. A uniform riot control drill was instituted and practiced. This required a magistrate to be present alongside the commander of a military detachment, and the former had to sign a form authorizing the use of force before the latter could issue a public warning to disperse and instruct his troops to fire below the knee-level. Again, under the pressure of circumstances these formalities were at times dispensed with. During the 1942 rebellion, the government introduced the Armed Forces (Special Powers) Ordinance, which allowed orders for the use of force to kill to be given by an officer of the rank of captain or above. The requirement of authorization by a civilian official was practically done away with.[24] These practices were, however, carried over into the postcolonial period and remain a feature of riot control in contemporary India.

Prior to 1919, insurgencies were usually dealt with by martial law, which implied the absence of any law. The principal advantage was that it established unity of control. By placing the civil machinery under the military and by granting the latter draconian powers, rebellion could be easily subdued.[25] However, after the Amritsar massacre, the government became wary of giving the military complete control. Instead, it chose to introduce martial law ordinances, which retained the powers of the civil administration. A system of unified command was improvised.

During the Mapilla revolt of 1921 in the Malabar province (now in the state of Kerala), the Malabar Force headquarters included civilian officials and the local police.[26] In handling the Saya San revolt of 1930–1931 in Burma, civilian and military officials cooperated closely at all levels.[27] In its early counterinsurgency campaigns in the North East, the Indian government sought to use similar arrangements. The weaknesses of local police and administration, however, left the military in the driver's seat. In 1958, the Indian government got the Parliament to enact the Armed Forces Special Powers Act (AFSPA). This legislation was modelled on the Armed Forces (Special Powers) Ordinance of 1942 but was modified for a counter-insurgency context. In particular, the new law authorized even non-commissioned officers to issue orders to use lethal force.

The principles and tactics evolved for internal security were incorporated into professional military education in the British Indian Army. Officers attending the British Army Staff College in Camberley had to undergo a module on the Army in India. "Duties in Aid of the Civil Power" was one of the six topics it comprised.[28] The Staff College at Quetta also emphasized this subject.[29] The Senior Officers school in India imparted advanced training on internal security.[30]

In contrast, internal security—especially counterinsurgency—did not feature prominently in military curricula for decades after independence. Given the commitment to counterinsurgency operations over these years, its neglect in professional military education is striking. In 1967, the army established the Jungle Training School in Meghalaya. Subsequently this was moved to Mizoram and rechristened Counterinsurgency and Jungle Warfare School (CIJWS). The establishment of this school, however, served to move counterinsurgency to the margins of military education. It is instructive to contrast CIJWS with the army's commando wing in Belgaum. While every infantry officer, as well as several from other arms, had to undergo commando training, CIJWS was not mandatory and was largely for officers and men deployed in counterinsurgency duties. Not until the 1990s did internal security regain its prominence in military education. A recent study of the Defence Services Staff College notes that over the past two decades, internal security accounts for 20–30 percent of the curriculum.[31]

Counterinsurgency Forces

The Indian Army has fought more insurgencies and for longer durations than any other contemporary army. It has been fighting Naga rebels since 1956, in addition to having fought the Mizo rebels between 1966 and 1986. In 1971, it participated in an operation to crush the Maoist "Naxalite" rebellion in Eastern India.[32] In the late 1970s, other insurgencies began in the states of Manipur and Tripura. In the 1980s and 1990s, it was involved in fighting Sikh rebels in Punjab, Tamil guerrillas in Sri Lanka, Kashmiri separatists in Jammu and Kashmir, and a wide variety of insurgent groups in the North East. With the exception of the war against the Tamil guerrillas in Sri Lanka, the Indian Army has never undertaken a counterinsurgency campaign outside the borders of India.[33]

The army's expanding counterinsurgency engagement over the decades is reflected in the sharp increase in the fatality figures, as outlined in Figure 8.1. Between 1947 and 1990, the army lost 1,902 personnel in internal security operations. But, over the next two decades, it lost another 6,206 personnel in these operations.

Like other major armies, the Indian Army has a conventional war bias.[34] However, with an increase in its counterinsurgency role, the army has learned by experience and experimentation. Where rebel groups have found shelter and support in states bordering India, the army has developed a significant infrastructure to interdict the infiltration of insurgents. In Jammu and Kashmir, it has fenced the border and created a security grid to block the traditional routes of infiltration from Pakistan. The army has also undertaken retaliatory cross-border raids against rebel groups in neighboring countries as outlined by Sushant Singh in his chapter in this volume. Besides fighting insurgencies directly, the army extends training support to counter-insurgency forces drawn from the Central Armed Police Forces.[35]

The army also undertakes nonmilitary counterinsurgency measures across the different theaters. These include People Control Measures and Military-Civic Measures. The former are used to physically isolate the insurgent from their support base. These may involve relocation and resettlement of a population, conducting a census, monitoring the flow of finances and people, and electronic and digital sur-veillance. These tend to be unpopular and can easily further alienate the civilian population. Military-Civic Actions are undertaken to build goodwill among the civilian population by carrying out developmental activities and welfare services. Ideally these should be carried out in collaboration with civil administration and involve a degree of public ownership. This is often not the case. Instead, army units end up repurposing their personnel and resources to sustain these activities.

The decline in insurgency-related violence as noted in the Introduction to this volume attests to the army's fulfillment of its mandate. In Kashmir, where the army has the largest counterinsurgency presence, it has been able to limit insurgency to a few districts of the state, and it has reduced the number of active insurgents from approximately 2,000 in the early 2000s to 150 in 2022. Similarly, in the North East theater, the army has been able to control and reduce the levels of violence.

The Indian Army has, for the most part, avoided the use of heavy weapons, in-cluding artillery and airpower, in its counterinsurgency operations. It has also refrained from displacing local populace after attempting strategic hamletting in Nagaland and Mizoram.[36] Across the conflicts, its gains, however, have been limited to containment of violence. These have led to political settlements only in a few instances. In some cases, its actions have in fact further alienated already disaffected populations.

The army's approach toward counterinsurgency has remained manpower-intensive with limited reliance on technology. The emphasis remains on an area-saturation ap-proach that aims to increase the ratio of security forces to insurgents first to 19:1 and then to 30:1.[37] That said, the army's wide-ranging counterinsurgency experience has produced organizational as well as tactical innovations, including two distinct theater-specific counterinsurgency forces, RR and AR, in which continuity, interoperability, and familiarity with the context are emphasized. As frontline counterinsurgency forces, the RR and AR have won a large number of gallantry awards.[38]

Rashtriya Rifles (RR)

By the 1990s, the army's nationwide counterinsurgency role increased sharply, and the total requirement approached 160 battalions by 1998. This meant that

45 percent of the total 356 combat battalions at that time came to be earmarked for counterinsurgency even as there was no reduction in the demand for the army's conventional readiness.[39] Recognizing the need for a dedicated counterinsurgency force, the army conceptualized the RR in the late 1980s. It was hoped that such a force would be officered by the army and largely draw on the lateral entry of active-duty Central Armed Police Forces (CAPF) personnel and army veterans. By the time the first RR units were raised in the early 1990s, this plan could not be executed.[40] The RR, therefore, sourced its officers and ranks from within the army. Initially, an RR battalion was built from different regiments. Observing cohesion and administrative problems, the army discontinued this practice, and the bulk of a battalion, four out of six companies, came to be drawn from one regiment. An RR battalion is unlike any other infantry battalion in the army. RR is the only organization where troops from the infantry and other arms and services operate under a single banner.[41] Each battalion has a strength of 1,200 troops and an RR tenure lasts for thirty months.[42] By contrast, the US military's counterinsurgency tours in Afghanistan and Iraq lasted for up to only twelve months.[43] The infantry component comprises 60 percent of the troops in the six rifle companies. Personnel from other arms, including field artillery, armor, air defense artillery, and engineers are also present in each of the rifle companies. Most of India's infantry regiments are affiliated with RR battalions.

The RR experiment began with six battalions in 1990. By 2005, it had grown tenfold, becoming the fastest-growing army organization in independent India. Initially, the army deployed three of these in Punjab and three in Kashmir. Later, the government approved more battalions for Kashmir. In 2020, the RR has sixty-five battalions with a total strength of 75,000 personnel. The RR's role is currently confined to Jammu and Kashmir.[44]

Battalions are controlled by brigade-level sectors that, in turn, form part of division-strength formations called Forces. Presently, five such division-strength formations exist: Delta (Doda) Force, Victor (Valley) Force, Kilo (Kupwara) Force, Romeo (Rajouri) Force, and Uniform (Udhampur) Force. The RR is led by a major-general ranked officer and is currently headquartered in Udhampur.[45] It is funded by the Ministry of Defence under a special line item.

The RR units form a part of a security grid that performs a counterinsurgency and counterinfiltration role. An army unit's counterinsurgency tour is for a limited duration. When a unit rotates out, the area knowledge and intelligence networks it has produced during its tenure are lost.[46] Since RR battalions remain stationed in the same area, with only a select number of its personnel rotating in and out at any given time, it is able to develop and retain area awareness and intelligence networks that are crucial to counterinsurgency.[47] The terrain is well known, the human intelligence sources are more loyal, the standard operating procedures are easier to follow, and lessons of the past are always applicable to the same ground.[48]

In Jammu and Kashmir, the army has worked closely with CAPFs and the police force. Interoperability of different security forces has been a fundamental challenge across counterinsurgency theaters.[49] The army assumes command much to the chagrin of the other security forces. The CAPFs argued that because the RR was raised as a domestic counterinsurgency force, its units should be placed under the CAPF command structure. This policy was resisted by the army. But since the RR units are drawn from the army, interoperability problems between the RR and the regular army are relatively infrequent. The RR units form part of regular infantry formations just as an RR Sector HQ can have regular infantry units placed under it. The continuity enabled by the RR format gradually improved the army's interoperability with the paramilitaries and the police with better intelligence sharing and coordination during operations.

Counterinsurgency deployment requires orientation of troops to operate among civilian populations besides familiarity with the local context. RR troops are mostly non-Kashmiris.[50] To improve the effectiveness of RR units, the army established Corps Battle Schools (CBS) for both the 15 and 16 Corps. Pre-induction training is mandatory for all RR personnel. It lasts for six weeks—four weeks at the CBS and two additional weeks in the unit. The CBS are critical for ensuring continuity and understanding the mission, the ethos of the Force, and the ramifications of various actions.

Initially, the RR units faced administrative and cohesion-related troubles; however, the army worked its way out of these problems. The RR battalions were deployed extensively and experienced combat against hardened insurgents. In the early years, these units suffered significant casualties. In response, the army scaled up the forces and the RR grew into a substantial and specialist force.

Unlike an infantry unit, an RR unit faces no personnel shortage because soldiers and officers are not rotating in and out for courses or training.[51] The RR units have their own distinct traditions and insignias. Postings with an RR unit are coveted. A successful RR tenure gives an officer an edge over his peers in promotion board assessments. As more RR commanding officers populated the higher ranks, the respect and weightage of the RR tenure increased. The RR tenure is purely operations-focused, and this alone guides a unit's activities. An infantry officer who had served with an RR unit explained, "Naturally, my life and those of my men is in greater danger during an RR posting, but there is the reward of capturing or eliminating terrorists . . . there is a promise of contact and action." He went on to explain that it is a tenure devoid of the unnecessary distractions of army life. There is much greater (operational) focus and higher camaraderie.[52] Another officer from the armored corps put it differently, however: "For those of us not from the infantry, an RR tenure gives us the bragging rights that we are as good as if not better than infantry officers at commanding infantry troops."[53]

The RR represents an organizational success for the army. In the 1960s, the army had repurposed a few infantry units to fight insurgencies in the North East. These units had felt downgraded and suffered morale problems. By the early 1970s, the experiment was discontinued. The RR's superior institutional design, rapid scaling-up, and its prominence in the army enabled it to avoid a similar fate.

The sharp decline in insurgency-related violence in Kashmir, and an improvement in CAPF and police capacities, has made it possible for the government to consider drawing-down the strength of RR units. As a part of the rationalization of its total troop strength the army is currently reviewing two proposals to cut down the size of the RR. One will reduce the number of RR battalions. The other will reduce the size of a battalion from six to four companies.

Assam Rifles (AR)

India's earliest insurgencies appeared in the North East states. The AR has played a prominent role in counterinsurgency warfare in the region. The unit traces its origins to a force set up by the colonial government in 1835, making it India's oldest paramilitary force.

In 1947, the AR had five battalions. By 1960, the number had increased to seventeen, and it currently stands at forty-six. The Assam Rifles is made up of sixty-six thousand personnel. As the RR's predecessor, the AR offered a workable model of a counterinsurgency force. In some respects, the two organizations are similar, but in many others they are different.

The AR is jointly controlled by the Ministry of Defence (MoD) and the Ministry of Home Affairs (MHA), with the latter financing its budget. The AR's operational control was transferred from the Ministry of External Affairs to the army after the defeat against China in the 1962 war.

An AR battalion is organized like a regular infantry battalion and comprises four rifle companies, but these battalions are not affiliated to the army's infantry regiments. In the past, emphasis was on recruiting Nepali and Indian Gorkhas, locals from Nagaland and Assam and also other hill people from Garhwal, Kumaon, and Himachal. Today, the recruitment occurs on an all-India basis and 20 percent of the intake is reserved for the North East. Approximately 70 percent of AR officers are deputed from the army, while the rest come from within the AR.[54] AR personnel retire at sixty years—as in the CAPF—unlike in the army where enlisted men can retire as early as thirty-five.

The AR headquarters are in Shillong, the capital of the North East state of Meghalaya, and the force is headed by a lieutenant general–ranked officer.[55] It has three Headquarters Inspectorate Generals: North, South, and East located at Kohima (Nagaland), Imphal (Manipur) and Srikona (Assam) respectively. These are commanded by major general-ranked officers. Under these are the twelve sector headquarters commanded by brigadiers. The forty-six battalions falling under these sectors are commanded by colonels. All AR officers don police ranks.

In addition to the counterinsurgency role assigned to thirty-two battalions, the AR provides aid to civil authority and fourteen AR battalions are tasked to guard India's 1,000-mile-long border with Myanmar. Army officers speak highly of their tenure with AR. However, officers do not covet a tenure with AR as much as one with an infantry or an RR unit. In an AR unit, army officers command *jawans* who are older and not from the army. Besides, the nature and intensity of the insurgency varies from state to state in the region. In many instances, since the state is actively negotiating with or hopes to reach out to insurgent groups, counterinsurgency is more constrained.[56] The AR tenure, then, offers fewer opportunities for obtaining the gallantry medals and career rewards as compared to an RR posting. The AR is also different from the other CAPFs administered by the MHA, which are officered by Indian Police Service officers alongside the force cadre. The AR cadre who rise to officer's rank undergo training with the army at the Indian Military Academy in Dehradun. The army officers try to reproduce the regimental ethos, which emphasizes strong officer-men relations, adding to its cohesion and *esprit de corps*.[57] Training levels also tend to be higher in the AR as compared to other CAPFs.

The AR has now begun to add women in its ranks as well. It is hoped that such a step will enhance its outreach to the local population during counterinsurgency, improve interaction especially with women and children, and advance AR's human rights record.[58] On this front, it is different from the RR where induction of women officers and soldiers is yet to occur.

The AR puts its troops through a counterinsurgency training program. Today, the AR draws troops from within and outside the region. Since the AR operates mostly within the North East states, those troops who are from outside serve long tenures in the region and get accustomed to its culture and ethnic diversity. AR units therefore tend to be more sensitized to the local context as compared to the regular infantry.

In the past, the AR battalions were deployed in a fixed location. Now, the unit moves to a different location in the region, following a three-year tenure in a site. The movement of battalions allows units to recover from challenging deployments. But with rotation, the benefits of continuity are lost.

Both the RR and the AR are supported by regular army formations in their counterinsurgency operations. Since the AR is mostly officered by the army, it has been able to achieve high levels of interoperability with it, while at the same time retaining its paramilitary character. The AR has been used during India's wars with China and Pakistan. It was also deployed in Sri Lanka and subsequently in Kashmir. The government is currently reviewing a proposal to merge AR with the Indo-Tibetan Border Police, a CAPF, and transfer the operational control of the AR to the MHA. If approved, these changes will see the departure of army officers and dilute the AR's paramilitary character, thus diminishing AR's interoperability with the army. The MHA is also eager to press AR into regular CAPF duties, such as securing India's elections. While the AR performs these duties in the North East region, it has been reluctant to take on this role elsewhere. The uncertainty around the AR's role highlights a longstanding problem for the organization. Jointly run by the MOD and MHA, the organization lacks a coherent voice to consistently advocate for its long-term interests.

Diminishing insurgencies and falling violence across the North East has resulted in the withdrawal of the army from counterinsurgency to a great extent. Besides the AR, until 2020, eighteen army brigades supported the counterinsurgency operations in the North East. The internal security responsibilities in the region will now be spearheaded by the AR.

In some respects, the army's extensive engagement with counterinsurgency through its units, the RR, and the AR, has had its unintended benefits. An inadvertent benefit of a counterinsurgency tenure is the exposure of gaps in an individual's or a unit's training. An NCO illustrated this point during an interview, "I was a part of a raiding team. I was assigned the rocket launcher(RL). I was not confident with the weapon because I was not trained well on it. On that day, fortunately, we did not have to use the RL. I told the senior JCO about my concern. When we came out of the counterinsurgency tenure, the unit sent me on a course to master the RL."[59] Officers pointed to other benefits of counterinsurgency tenures. The deployment tested the training of officers and units by putting them in unanticipated and uncertain positions. A number of officers wanted to go back for more counterinsurgency tours. It became a mechanism for identifying the most driven officers, one retired army commander explained. Counterinsurgency involves small team operations in which an officer and his men are in a small tight interdependent group. Officers pointed out that such experiences are good for unit cohesion. The officer gets a sense of the quality of the men he is commanding and they get to assess the leadership of the officer.

Governments in India have widely used the military to provide internal security. To its credit, the military has mostly proven to be effective in adapting to the varied demands of this role. Still, any benefits of the military's role in internal security must be considered in the light of the many adverse effects flowing from it. We explore these in the next section.

Consequences of Military's Use in Internal Security

The Indian military's experience points to two broad kinds of detrimental effects. The first concerns governance and the second relates to the erosion of the army's organizational capacity and effectiveness. They suggest that the armed forces as well as the rest of the state may be paying a considerable and unnecessary price for the Indian state's substantial reliance on the military for internal security.

Endangering Civil-Military Relations

There are two views on the effects of the military's internal security role on civil-military relations. One suggests that military intervention requires two prerequisites—a crisis and the absence of institutionalized civilian control over the military.[60] A different view contends that the military's involvement in internal security begins to repurpose the state instrument of violence into an instrument of governance. This dilutes the civilian-military institutional boundary. The broader the sphere of responsibilities civilians and the military consider appropriate for the armed forces, the greater the danger of the military's involvement in politics.[61]

Thus far, civilian governments in India have weathered many crises successfully. A popular mandate renewed through free and fair elections has enabled the civilian governments to maintain control over the military. In India there is no instance of an actual, attempted, or planned military coup. But a coup represents the extreme form of civil-military breakdown.[62] A deterioration of civil-military relations is visible in other forms.[63]

Two examples are illustrative. First, in insurgency-affected states, the military's role in governance has been normalized. When deployed to fight insurgencies, the army operates under nominal civilian oversight. The army is occasionally able to sideline the state governments, albeit with the central government's approval. Both serving and retired military personnel have been given executive positions in insurgency-affected regions.[64] The central government has appointed retired army officers as governors and to government panels in insurgency-impacted states. In the late 1990s, the army mooted a plan for its serving officers to be appointed as deputy commissioners and commissioners in the states' administration.[65] The central government, however, rejected this proposal. The army has also been involved in conducting elections in insurgency-affected areas. This role has not always been benign. In 1996, with the blessing of the central government, the army interfered with the elections in parts of Jammu and Kashmir. In 2002, the chief election commissioner had to warn the security forces against similar involvement.[66]

Second, the military and not the civilians hold the veto on the withdrawal of AFSPA. As Anubha Bhonsle shows in this volume, AFSPA has continued despite demands for its revocation by state-level and national leaders.[67]

Over a period of time, the army may have become a victim of its own success in dealing with counterinsurgency. Its ability to control and reduce the levels of violence in insurgency-affected regions has diminished the urgency of the crises and enabled the political leadership to shirk the responsibility of exploring political solutions. Such a situation only prolongs the army's role in internal security.[68] The use of the armed forces for tackling myriad problems incentivizes underinvestment in civilian bureaucratic capacity. The military is then the first force to be pressed into service in a crisis instead of being the last resort. The unit commanders who we interviewed reminded us that they were the face of the state on the ground in their respective sectors. They helped with provision of essential public services like schooling, health, electricity, and weather-related emergencies. But, one officer's comment captured the dilemma this type of engagement produces. He said, "What happens when we are withdrawn?"[69]

A widespread internal security role has far-reaching effects for the military too. It endangers cohesion, threatens the public perception of the military as a neutral institution, undermines professionalism, and distracts the military from its core mission of protecting the state from external threats.

Threat to Cohesion

An ethnically diverse military's actions in polarized contexts threatens trust among organization personnel belonging to different groups. In extreme instances, a breakdown of trust can result in insider attacks as well as acts of mutiny. When militaries are deployed for policing duties, they face the danger of importing social conflicts into the organization. The army's long counterinsurgency tenures have produced both types of effects.

When the army carried out Operation Blue Star against Sikh militants in Amritsar's Golden Temple complex in 1984, a number of Sikh troops belonging to different regiments mutinied. The units that deserted were 3 Sikh, 8 Sikh, 9 Sikh, 18 Sikh, 14 Punjab, 166 Mountain Regiment, 171 Field Regiment, and 196 Field Regiment. Putting down these rebellions cost many lives, and almost 2,800 personnel were arrested and charged with mutiny. These events damaged relations between Sikh and non-Sikh officers.[70] Within the army, the Sikh mutiny is viewed as one of the most painful and embarrassing moments in its history.[71] In analyzing the extent and roots of the mutiny, Tully and Jacob bluntly defined the army's conundrum: "How many more times can the Indian Army be used to put out the fires of religious, communal and caste hatred before it too becomes consumed in their flames?"[72] It is relevant to note that despite these challenges the army recruits personnel from insurgency-prone areas and has successfully deployed these local soldiers in counterinsurgency tours in their home regions.

The Erosion of Neutrality

Internal security roles can alter the military's image of neutrality and erode its legitimacy in the eyes of citizens in a multiethnic and multireligious society. So far, this damage has been limited because less than 5 percent of India's population lives in the North East, Jammu and Kashmir, and Punjab. A small percentage of the country's population has therefore been subjected to the military operations in their cities and villages. Had this footprint been more expansive, it would have undoubtedly dented the larger public trust in the military.

Take the long and costly counterinsurgency in Kashmir. A substantial part of the force has served in the region since 1989. As the Kashmiri insurgency took a pronounced Islamist turn, officers and soldiers have begun to adopt a religious lens to understand the conflict. A recently retired general with multiple tenures in the Kashmir valley noted, "We are increasingly viewed as a Hindu army occupying a Muslim land. Our units, jawans and officers face hostility from people who increasingly fight us in the name of their religion. They cannot remain unaffected. Such a turn threatens the army's secular tradition."[73] In contrasting the army's neutral image with the police force's more communal one, General Zameer Uddin Shah notes: "The police officers become communalized because of prolonged exposure to communal trouble. It is essential that the armed forces are kept insulated from prolonged exposure to internal disorder. . . . They should also, at the earliest, be relieved from internal security in Jammu and Kashmir."[74]

Threat to Professionalism

The doctrinal emphasis on winning the "hearts and minds" of the local population notwithstanding,[75] in keeping with its training, the army views insurgent kills and seizure of arms in counterinsurgency theaters as an important metric of success. Metrics for measuring public confidence as well as peace are poorly developed, and improvements in these indicators are seldom rewarded. Emphasis remains on kinetic operations and the use of force.[76] The commanding officers are strongly encouraged to demonstrate effectiveness and win recognition for the battalion to climb steep career pyramids. Together these incentivize the use of force.[77] Occasionally, captured insurgents are eliminated in fake encounters, as well as innocent civilians are killed and weapons are planted in false flag operations.[78]

Moreover, counterinsurgency tenures grant officers authority to operate poorly supervised budgets, resulting in instances of misappropriation of funds. Sometimes, these misdemeanors are brought to light and the army acts against the guilty officers and unit. However, in many cases, either the criminal activity escapes scrutiny or the army does not act because of insufficient evidence.[79] Still, the prevalence of such behavior begins to corrode the army's professional ethos and undermines the organization's discipline as well as morale.[80] Discussing this concern, a brigade commander noted, "The problem with corruption is not what the public thinks of us. The bigger problem is what we think of each other. Once you lose the respect of your men and fellow officers, how do you go into battle with them? They will not trust you."[81]

Distraction from the Core Mission

"Slowly, the Indian Army has turned into a counterinsurgency army. This should be a cause for worry," a brigadier who rose to be a corps commander in the Northern Command had observed during an interview in 2016.[82] The military's core mission is the defense of the state from external threats. Counterinsurgency and interstate wars require very different mindsets, weapon systems, and training of the force.[83] In an interview, an NCO outlined the difference in the two deployments,

"The heavy weapon systems, the volume of fire, the training of the enemy that we confront in war are entirely different from what we face in counterinsurgency. Counterinsurgency can keep a soldier on his toes, but it is not training for (conventional) war."[84]

A counterinsurgency military awards and promotes its personnel based on an operational performance in a low-intensity conflict context. Counterinsurgency tours have shaped an entire generation of officers who are rising through the army presently. As these counterinsurgency specialists rise in the institution, they shape the training, approaches, and orientation for the future generation of officers.

The infantry has dominated counterinsurgency to a greater degree than would be the case during conventional warfare. It has suffered the bulk of casualties and has won most of the gallantry awards. Counterinsurgency's prolonged nature has therefore raised and sustained the profile of the infantry officer within and outside the army, an elevation paid for in blood.[85] This change contributed to the institutionalization of infantry's higher share in the promotions to top ranks (colonel and above), a stage at which the promotion pyramid gets particularly steep.[86] Such a lopsided promotion policy has angered officers belonging to other combat and noncombat branches.[87] The shift in the infantry's status is reflected in the selection of the Chief of Army Staff (COAS). Among the last ten appointments since 2000, seven have come from infantry. By contrast, among the twenty-one previous heads of the army since independence, twelve were from the infantry. When the government picked General Bipin Rawat above more senior generals as COAS in December 2016, it justified the decision by emphasizing his superior counterinsurgency experience.[88] Both the superseded generals were not from the infantry.[89]

Besides potentially hurting cohesion, this inadvertent effect of counterinsurgency is consequential because infantrization of the top ranks can promote groupthink among those who are responsible for the army's preparation for confronting present and future threats. It can also unnecessarily restrict the talent pool available to the army to develop solutions to its pressing challenges.

Currently, if we add the recruitment, training, and arming costs of the army to the benefits extended to serving and retired personnel, the army soldier is financially the most expensive counterinsurgent available to the state. From an economic perspective, the deployment of the army against far less expensive insurgents over decades-long internal wars represents inefficient use of scarce resources and undermines the defense from external threats. If we add the recruitment, training, and arming costs of the army to the benefits extended to serving and retired personnel, the army soldier is financially the most expensive counterinsurgent available to the state. Had the counterinsurgency wars been shorter and the manpower commitment to them smaller, its effect on the force would have been less pronounced.

India is surrounded by two revisionist powers: China and Pakistan. Both countries make substantial claims on Indian territory; China on Ladakh and Arunachal Pradesh and Pakistan on Jammu and Kashmir. The China threat is unprecedented.

For the first time in its history as a modern state, India shares a border with a hostile superpower. The Indian military continues to fall behind China's expanding conventional military power and has struggled to deter the PLA's growing intrusions into Indian territory.[90]

The dominant counterinsurgency posture may have distracted the army from deterring military intrusions. According to defense analyst Ajai Shukla, the Pakistani intrusion in Kargil in 1999 went unchallenged until it was too late because the 15 Corps responsible for monitoring the region was deployed in counterinsurgency. Similarly, the 14 Corps facing the Chinese intrusion in 2020 could not easily draw on the Northern Command's reserve formations, which are often committed to counterinsurgency operations in the Kashmir valley.[91]

Substantial counterinsurgency commitments, which are typically manpower-intensive, also constrained the army's ability to downsize to release resources for modernization.[92] With a fall in insurgency-related violence, downsizing is under consideration in 2022. Finally, these commitments have made India reluctant to defend its own sphere of influence in South Asia.[93] Taken together, these outcomes highlight how a prolonged counterinsurgency engagement impedes the military's ability to fulfill its core mission of defending the state from external threats.

For decades, the Indian state has underinvested in building capacity to face external threats. Freeing up resources to enhance India's military capacity and focusing on converting military capacity to military power has become necessary.[94] In this regard, counterinsurgency forces should not be viewed as reserves for conventional war. The experience of units that were shifted from counterinsurgency into conventional operations during the Kargil conflict made it obvious that reorientation for regular warfare requires both training and time.[95] The military's officer corps is conscious of this distraction. Out of the fifty-six members of the 2017 DSSC course who responded to a survey, 75 percent agreed or strongly agreed with the statement "Counterinsurgency tasks distract from the military's primary mission of external defense." Only 16 percent disagreed.[96] In a survey of 615 retired army officers conducted by one of the authors in 2013, respondents were presented with a proposition that prolonged involvement with counterinsurgency has been beneficial for the Indian Army. Only 25.37 percent of respondents either strongly or somewhat agreed with it. A majority, 64.5 percent of respondents, either strongly or somewhat disagreed.[97]

Conclusion

India's conception of its vulnerabilities has mostly been domestic. They are physical, proximate, and visceral. The trauma of Partition embedded a permanent fear of centrifugal forces and national unity became a primary objective of the Indian Constitution.[98] The army, which partly inherited its internal security role from its colonial sire, was thus destined to continue its domestic engagement.

When India's internal security situation deteriorated sharply during the 1980s and 1990s, the state turned to the army to bear a greater burden of managing violence and imposing order. Unrest in sensitive border states like Jammu and Kashmir, Punjab, Nagaland, and Assam directly impacted the military's effectiveness in performing its primary security role. To restrict its exposure to counterinsurgency and retain its capacity to fight conventional wars, the army raised the RR and supported the expansion of the AR. Still, since the 1990s, counterinsurgency has shaped the army in profound ways.

The Indian military and political leadership must understand the limitations of the military's use in containing internal threats—not least because today India also faces unprecedented external challenges. It has to contend with an intimidating and rising China on its eastern flank and a hostile Pakistan to the west. Other organizations could replace the military for internal security duties, but no such alternatives are available to counter external threats. The Indian state must accurately assess the financial and security costs of deploying the army so widely. It is not possible to withdraw the army entirely from internal security responsibilities, yet the army's role must be seriously reconsidered. On the one hand, the effectiveness of the police and CAPF should be improved. On the other, the prolonged use of force to tackle fundamentally political conflicts should be re-evaluated. A sizable drop in insurgency-related violence in the past decade, as noted in the Introduction, presents an opportunity to make these changes.

State-making is an inherently violent process, and the experience of the Indian state is not all that different from Western states except in one respect: the violence accompanying state-building in India is taking place under conditions of universal franchise.[99] Domestic insurgencies are difficult to fight because excessive use of violence against citizens can be counterproductive. At the same time, controlling violence cannot be the only or the dominant measure of successful conflict resolution. Possessing the world's largest counterinsurgency force can hardly be a matter of pride for a democratic state. Nor can a mere transfer of counterinsurgency responsibilities from the MOD to the MHA, or from the army to the CAPFs, constitute progress. In a democracy, violence cannot be the primary mode of exercising political control. We know that the state is supposed to wield a monopoly over violence, that security is its primary responsibility, and that order is a prerequisite for economic and social development.[100] But order maintained only through violence or the threat of violence is not legitimate. Political resolution of internal conflicts in a just and timely way is the ultimate source of India's internal security.

Notes

1. Outside Indonesia and Nigeria, few states' militaries have had such prolonged and widespread exposure to domestic counterinsurgency.

2. Data from the National War Memorial website, https://nationalwarmemorial.gov.in/.

3. Anit Mukherjee, "A Name upon a Grave," *The Caravan*, January 31, 2014, https://caravanm agazine.in/perspectives/name-upon-grave. The list of external conflicts include: the 1947–1948 Kashmir war, the 1962 Sino-Indian war, the 1965 and 1971 India-Pakistan wars, the 1987–1990 Sri Lanka operations, the 1999 Kargil war, and the 2001–2002 mobilization along the India-Pakistan border known as Operation Parakram. It does not include fatalities in cross-border firing or related operations along the borders with Pakistan and China respectively.

4. This change since 1990 is also reflected in the gallantry medals awarded to the army. A larger proportion are awarded for the internal security operations.

5. Rob Johnson, "The Indian Army and Internal Security: 1919–1946," in *The Indian Army in the Two World Wars*, ed. Kaushik Roy (Boston: Brill, 2012).

6. Gyanesh Kudaisya, "'In Aid of Civil Power': The Colonial Army in Northern India, c. 1919–42," *Journal of Imperial and Commonwealth History* 32, no. 1 (June 2004): 41–68.

7. Ajay Madiwale and Kudrat Virk, "Civil-Military Relations in Natural Disasters: A Case Study of the 2010 Pakistan Floods," *International Review of the Red Cross* 93, no. 884 (December 2011): 1085–1105; Derek Lutterbeck, "Between Police and Military: The New Security Agenda and the Rise of Gendarmeries," *Cooperation and Conflict* 39, no. 1 (2004): 45–68.

8. David Pion-Berlin and Harold Trinkunas, "Democratization, Social Crisis and the Impact of Military Domestic Roles in Latin America," *Journal of Political and Military Sociology* 33, no. 1 (Summer 2005): 5–24.

9. Both the Navy and the Air Force perform critical internal security roles. Since the Indian Army is the largest branch at 1.2 million strong, it ends up carrying the bulk of the burden of the internal security, including counterinsurgency, aid to civil authority, and disaster relief operations.

10. The armed forces were involved to force a merger with India in the western state of Junagadh in 1947, the central state of Hyderabad in 1948, and in the northern state of Jammu and Kashmir in 1947 and 1948. For the military's role in securing the political integration of India, see Arjun Subramanian, *India's Wars: A Military History, 1947–1971* (New Delhi: HarperCollins, 2016), 104–195.

11. Correspondence with Ajai Shukla.

12. For the list of reasons for which the government can turn to the military to aid civil authority, see: The Government of India, "Instructions on Aid to the Civil Authorities by the Armed Forces 1970," *Ministry of Defence Publication*.

13. Prominent among these are the army's deployment to suppress nationwide Hindu-Muslim riots in 1992, the pogrom against Sikhs in Delhi in 1984, and against Muslims in Gujarat in 2002. It was deployed in Haryana to quell public violence during the Jat agitation in 2016 and in the North East states of Tripura and Assam to discourage protests against the Citizenship Amendment Act in 2019.

14. Including the Bihar police in 1946, the Uttar Pradesh provincial armed constabulary in 1973, and the Central Reserve Police Force and elements of the Central Industrial Security Force in 1979.

15. The Indian military acted as the backbone of state administration during the earthquakes in Maharashtra in 1993 and in Gujarat in 2001. It administers flood relief activities every year in the flood-prone parts of the North East. Recently, it provided flood relief in Uttarakhand in 2013, in Kashmir in 2014, and in Maharashtra, Karnataka, Kerala, and Tamil Nadu in 2019.

16. Ranajit Guha, *Dominance without Hegemony: History and Power in Colonial India* (Cambridge, MA: Harvard University Press, 1998); Guha, *Elementary Aspects of Peasant Insurgency in Colonial India* (Durham, NC: Duke University Press, 1999), 2.

17. Cited in David Omissi, *Sepoy and Raj: The Indian Army, 1860–1940* (London: Palgrave Macmillan, 1994), 199.

18. On insurgencies in the North West Frontier, see T. R. Moreman, *The Army in India and Development of Frontier Warfare, 1849–1947* (London: Palgrave Macmillan, 1998).

19. Srinath Raghavan, "Protecting the Raj: The Army in India and Internal Security, c. 1919–1939," *Small Wars & Insurgencies* 3, no. 16 (2005): 253–279.
20. Quoted in Memo by Home Department, October 14, 1930, R/2/628/166, Asian & African Collections (AAC), British Library, London..
21. Kim A. Wagner, *Amritsar 1919: An Empire of Fear and the Making of a Massacre* (New Haven, CT: Yale University Press, 1919).
22. Duties in Aid of the Civil Power, 1923, WO 32/297, The National Archives, London.
23. Srinath Raghavan, *India's War: The Second World War and the Making of Modern South Asia* (New York: Basic Books, 2016), 273–274.
24. Raghavan, *India's War*, 272–273
25. Charles Gwynn, *Imperial Policing* (London: Macmillan, 1934), 16–17.
26. Government of India to India Office, August 26, 1921, L/P&J/6/1782; "The Mapillah Rebellion and Malabar Operations 1921/22," Mss Eur F161/167,AAC; W. St. J. Carpendale, "The Moplah Rebellion 1921–22," *Journal of the United Services Institute of India* 56, no. 242 (January 1926): 76–94.
27. Gwynn, *Imperial Policing*, 114
28. Text of Lecture, Brigadier Sir John Smyth Papers, Box 5, File 3, Imperial War Museum (IWM), London.
29. John Ewart, "Police Work in India," *Journal of the United Services Institute of India* 68, no. 290 (January 1938): 28–29.
30. Text of Lecture, Smyth Papers, Box 6, File 7, IWM.
31. David O. Smith. *The Wellington Experience: A Study of Attitudes and Values within the Indian Army* (Washington, DC: Stimson Center, 2020), 88–89.
32. Sidin Vadukut, "A Reason to Pause in Sukma," *Mint*, April 28, 2017, http://bit.ly/3dmUqFa.
33. Rajesh Rajagopalan, "Innovations in Counterinsurgency: The Indian Army's Rashtriya Rifles," *Contemporary South Asia* 13, no. 1 (October 2004): 25–37.
34. See Rajesh Rajagopalan, *Fighting Like a Guerrilla: The Indian Army and Counterinsurgency* (New Delhi: Routledge, 2008).
35. For example, retired counterinsurgency specialists like Brigadier Basant Ponwar, now Inspector General Ponwar—were tapped to train the state police forces of Chhattisgarh (and of surrounding states) at a makeshift jungle warfare college in Kanker. He was Commandant CIJWS before taking up this assignment.
36. This is in sharp contrast to counterinsurgency tactics used by armies in Sri Lanka, Pakistan, Myanmar, or the US global war on terror, which have produced a large number of internally and externally displaced persons.
37. See Rostum Nanavatty, *Internal Armed Conflict in India* (New Delhi: Pentagon Press, 2013), 80–83.
38. PTI, "Army's Elite Counter-Insurgency Unit Rashtriya Rifles Turns 25 Tomorrow," *The Economic Times*, July 11, 2018, https://bit.ly/337TeAE; Deeptiman Tiwary, "Explained: Assam Rifles' Dual Control Structure, and Its Role," *The Indian Express*, December 7, 2021, https://indianexpress.com/article/explained/explained-assam-rifles-dual-control-structure-role-nagaland-violence-7658329/.
39. Rajesh Rajagopalan, "Innovations in Counterinsurgency: The Indian Army's Rashtriya Rifles," *Contemporary South Asia* 13, no. 1 (October 2004): 25–37.
40. This was primarily owing to the administrative and financial challenges of recruiting ex-servicemen and seconding personnel from other CAPF as well as standardizing their pay and entitlements (including operational allowances) vis-à-vis serving army personnel.
41. "Rashtriya Rifles Have Come a Long Way since Its Inception," *Force*, March 11, 2019, https://bit.ly/3g9CGM4.
42. As opposed to a typical battalion, which has 840 men.

43. Short tenures hurt counterinsurgency in both theaters. See Mike Jason, "What We Got Wrong in Afghanistan," *The Atlantic*, August 2021, https://www.theatlantic.com/ideas/archive/2021/08/how-america-failed-afghanistan/619740/.

44. Until recently, the RR fulfilled two-thirds of the army's counterinsurgency requirement in J&K. The other one third was met by regular infantry units.

45. The HQ only handles administration. Operational decisions are taken at the level of Force HQ and Corps HQ.

46. See Anit Mukherjee, "India's Experience with Insurgency and Counterinsurgency," in *The Routledge Handbook of Asian Security Studies*, ed. Sumit Ganguly, Andrew Scobell, and Joseph Liow (London and New York: Routledge, 2009), 66–86.

47. Occasionally, RR units are moved when there is a breakdown of a relationship between the unit and the local population. Human rights violations often trigger such breakdowns.

48. Syed Ata Hasnain, "Rashtriya Rifles: The Story of Independent India's Finest Military Experiment," *Swarajya*, July 23, 2017, https://bit.ly/309qCVr.

49. According to Routray, outside the experience in Punjab, interoperability among security forces has always been a problem resulting in poor coordination and competition. See Bibhu Prasad Routray, "India's Internal Wars: Counterinsurgency Role of Central Police Forces," *Small Wars and Insurgencies* 24, no. 4 (2013): 648–668.

50. Three out of the sixty-five units affiliated with the RR are made up of recruits from Jammu and Kashmir; two from JAK LI and one from JAK RIF. The JAK LI units are 50 percent Muslim and personnel from the regiment are attached to many RR units to assist in operations.

51. The ready availability of personnel also ensures that *jawans* can avail of their full quota of leave in a timely way, a significant determinant of morale.

52. Interview conducted in December 2019. The same officer also noted that these comments should not take away from the stress of RR tenures, especially at the peak of counterinsurgency in the late 1990s and early 2000s.

53. Interview conducted in July 2020.

54. 900 army officers serve with the AR. All command positions above the battalion level are held by army officers.

55. AR is the only Central Para Military Force which has its headquarters away from New Delhi. For coordination with Ministry of Home Affairs, the Force maintains a Liaison Office in New Delhi.

56. For example, in the North East, the Indian state has not forced insurgents to disarm or stop collecting taxes after entering into a peace deal with them. See Anubha Bhonsle, *Mother, Where's My Country? Looking for Light in the Darkness of Manipur* (Delhi: Speaking Tiger Limited, 2016).

57. The AR unit may not reflect the same bond between officers and enlisted men as an infantry unit; however, these bonds are stronger than a CAPF unit.

58. On how female soldiers improve effectiveness of counterinsurgency forces, see Synne L. Dyvik, "Gender and Counterinsurgency in Woodward," in *The Palgrave International Handbook of Gender and the Military*, ed. Rachel and Claire Duncanson (London: Palgrave Macmillan, 2017), 319–334.

59. Interview conducted in July 2022.

60. Alfred Stepan, "The New Professionalism of Internal Warfare and Military Role Expansion," in *Authoritarian Brazil: Origins, Policies and Future*, ed. Alfred Stepan (New Haven, CT: Yale University Press, 1973), 47–65; Claude E. Welch, *Civilian Control of the Military: Theory and Cases from Developing Countries* (Albany: State University of New York Press, 1977).

61. Peter D. Feaver, "Civil-Military Relations," *Annual Review of Political Science* 2, no. 1 (June 1999): 211–241.

62. Pion-Berlin and Trinkunas, "Democratization, Social Crisis and the Impact of Military Domestic Roles in Latin America."

63. For how this process operates in the North East states, see Sanjib Baruah, *In the Name of the Nation: India and Its Northeast* (Stanford, CA: Stanford University Press, 2020).

64. For the effect of counterinsurgency on civil military relations in India, see Ayesha Ray, *The Soldier and the State in India: Nuclear Weapons, Counterinsurgency, and the Transformation of Indian Civil-Military Relations* (Los Angeles: SAGE Publications, 2013).

65. Sawhney and Wahab, "The Threats Have Changed and the Indian Army Needs to Change Too," *Force India*, December 28, 2021, https://forceindia.net/indian-military/indianarmy/at-the-crossroad/.

66. James Lyngdoh, *Chronicles of an Impossible Election: The Election Commission and the 2002 Jammu & Kashmir Assembly Elections* (Mysuru, India: Penguin Books, 2004).

67. Srinath Raghavan, "Soldiers, Statesmen, and India's Security Policy," *India Review* 11, no. 2 (May 2012): 116–133.

68. See Ali Ahmed, "Internal Security Crises in Punjab, Kashmir and Jaffna: The Power of Moderation," *South Asian Survey* 17, no. 2 (August 2012): 295–311.

69. Interview conducted in July 2022.

70. The discord spread as far as the Defence Services Staff College in Wellington. See David Smith, *The Wellington Experience: A Study of Attitudes and Values within the Indian Army* (Washington, DC: Stimson Center, 2020).

71. Amit Ahuja, "India," in *Religion in the Military Worldwide*, ed. Ron E. Hassner (Cambridge: Cambridge University Press, 2013).

72. Mark Tully and Satish Jacob, *Amritsar: Mrs Gandhi's Last Battle* (New Delhi: Rupa Publications, 1985), 197.

73. Interview conducted in March 2019.

74. Lt. Gen. Zameer Uddin Shah, "Indian Army Should Be Relieved from Internal Security in J&K. It Goes against Secular Ethos," *The Print*, November 6, 2019, https://bit.ly/335J4QQ.

75. Vivek Chadha, "'Heart as a Weapon': A Fresh Approach to the Concept of Hearts and Minds," *Institute for Defence Studies and Analyses Policy Brief* (November 2011).] in keeping with its training, the army views insurgent kills and seizure of arms in counterinsurgency theaters as an important metric of success.

76. Smith, *The Wellington Experience*, 85.

77. These observations should not be interpreted to mean that army officers are bloodthirsty hunters. In fact, many officers we interviewed were deeply empathetic to the misery of the Kashmiris caught between the insurgents and counterinsurgents.

78. See Kishalay Bhattacharjee, *Blood on My Hands: Confessions of Staged Encounters* (Noida, Uttar Pradesh: HarperCollins Publishers India, 2015).

79. Lt. Gen. Harcharanjit Singh Panag, "'Booze Brigadier' to egg & tent scams: Indian military must check falling standards in ethics," *The Print*, May 30, 2019, https://theprint.in/opinion/booze-brigadier-to-egg-tent-scams-indian-military-must-check-falling-standards-in-ethics/242994/.

80. See Alok Asthana, "Rewarding Major Gogoi for Using a Human Shield Is against the Army's Moral Fabric," *The Wire*, May 26, 2017, https://bit.ly/39FRgIE.

81. Interview conducted in September 2018.

82. Interview conducted in September 2016.

83. Sawhney and Wahab, "The Threats Have Changed and the Indian Army Needs to Change Too."

84. Interview conducted in June 2022.

85. The Kargil operations in 1999 also raised the relative status of infantry and artillery because the other combat branches did not get to participate in a meaningful way.

86. Combat arms dominate the top ranks of the army. Changes triggered by the Kargil Review Committee shortened the command tenures of infantry and artillery officers as compared to officers from other combat and noncombat branches. With command exit driving promotions, the infantry benefited immensely. Since 2009, approximately 60 percent of promotions to rank of the colonel have gone to the infantry even though it forms 37 percent of the Indian Army.

87. They have taken the government to the Supreme Court, and the Armed Forces Tribunal has even called such a practice as malicious.

88. See Sandeep Unnithan, "New Chief on the Block," *India Today*, December 22 2016, https://bit.ly/3jTegsE.

89. The appointment of General Manoj Pande, the current army chief marks a clear departure from this trend. He belongs to the corps of engineers, and he is the first officer to hold this office from outside the combat branches.

90. Krishn Kaushik, "The Army Is Cognizant of the Challenge It Faces. See Disputed Border with Nuclear Neighbours, Proxy Wars Stretching India's Security Resources, Says Army Chief," *The Indian Express*, February 4, 2022, https://indianexpress.com/article/india/naravane-india-defence-security-conflicts-army-7754946/.

91. Ajai Shukla, "Let the Army Prove Its Worth," *Business Standard*, July 16, 2020, https://bit.ly/2X6eSRM.

92. Harsh V. Pant and Kartik Bommakanti, "India's National Security: Challenges and Dilemmas," *International Affairs* 95, no. 4 (July 2019): 835–858.

93. Neil Devotta, "Is India Over-extended? When Domestic Disorder Precludes Regional Intervention," *Contemporary South Asia* 12, no. 3 (January 2003): 365–380.

94. Pravin Sawhney and Ghazala Wahab, *Dragon on Our Doorsteps: Managing China through Military Power* (New Delhi: Aleph Book Company, 2017).

95. See Harinder Baweja, *A Soldier's Diary: Kargil the Inside Story* (Delhi: Roli Books, 2018), who identifies one such unit, 14 J&K Rifles.

96. Smith, *The Wellington Experience*, 102.

97. The survey was conducted in Chandigarh, Pune, Delhi, NOIDA, Mau, and Secunderabad. The survey sample was developed using the stratified random sampling method.

98. See Uday Mehta, "Constitutionalism," in *The Oxford Companion to Politics in India*, ed. Niraja Jayal and Pratap Mehta (New Delhi: Oxford University Press, 2010), 15–27.

99. For the use of military in internal armed conflict in the United States, see Robert Coakley, *The Role of Federal Military Forces in Domestic Disorders, 1789–1878* (Washington, DC: Center of Military History, US Army, 1988); Clayton Laurie and Ronald Cole, *The Role of Federal Military Forces in Domestic Disorders, 1877–1945* (Washington, DC: Center of Military History, US Army, 1997); and for Britain, see Anthony Babington, *Military Intervention in Britain: From the Gordon Riots to the Gibraltar Incident* (London: Routledge, 1990).

100. This argument linking order and economic development has been made most forcefully by scholars of Africa. See Robert Bates, *When Things Fell Apart: State Failure in Late-Century Africa* (Cambridge: Cambridge University Press, 2008).

9

Role of Central Armed Police Forces (CAPF) in India

YASHOVARDHAN AZAD

From fighting terrorists in the rugged and hostile terrains of Kashmir to leading the charge against lethal Maoists in the dense jungles of the Red Corridor, patrolling the barren salt deserts of Kutch, protecting nuclear installations, space establishments, airports, seaports, controlling riots and sectarian violence, ensuring fair conduct of elections, and coming to the aid of civilians in times of disaster—the CAPF of India perform myriad, crucial functions as the backbone of internal security and act as a key pillar of its law enforcement and management. The CAPF send their contingents under the UN missions to various countries where they are greatly in demand for their discipline and commitment to duty. Their total strength of around 964,000 men and women exceeds the military manpower of many a small nation and constitutes almost 80 percent of Indian Army's strength, with matching fire-power when deployed at the borders.

This chapter focuses on four areas. First, it gives a profile of each CAPF, outlining its multifarious duties and the work environment. Second, the deployment pattern is delved in detail, to show how diversion from its main task impacts morale and efficiency. Third, an assessment of CAPF performance in each theater of operation is undertaken, and finally, the conclusion covers a range of issues from the rationale of increasing numbers in the CAPFs to the need for bringing them under the ambit of Right to Information Act.

Under Article 355 of the Indian Constitution, it is the duty of the Union to protect the various states in the country against external aggression and internal disturbances, and to ensure that the governance in each state is carried out in accordance with the provisions of the Constitution. This article enables the union to come to aid of the states facing threats from terrorism, insurgency, and left-wing extremism (LWE). Law and order, being a state subject under the Constitution, is managed by the states on their own. The Center directs the CAPFs to assist the states, whenever help is sought.

Yashovardhan Azad, *Role of Central Armed Police Forces (CAPF) in India* In: *Internal Security in India*. Edited by: Amit Ahuja and Devesh Kapur, Oxford University Press. © Oxford University Press 2023. DOI: 10.1093/oso/9780197660331.003.0009

As Sushant Singh clarifies in Chapter 6, India has no formal document articulating its internal security doctrine. However, during the hearings of the Estimates Committee of Parliament in 2018, the Ministry of Home Affairs (MHA), Government of India, listed out four major areas of threat to internal security:

1. Terrorism in the hinterland
2. Cross-border terrorism in Jammu and Kashmir
3. Left-wing extremism in certain states
4. Insurgency in the North East

These are the main spheres of CAPF deployment. In addition, CAPFs assist various states in handling law-and-order situations, conducting elections, providing security to vital installations, and disaster relief.

Profiles and Tasks

There are seven Central Armed Police Forces (CAPFs) in India—Assam Rifles (AR), Central Reserve Police Force (CRPF), Indo-Tibetan Border Police (ITBP), Border Security Force (BSF), Central Industrial Security Force (CISF), National Security Guard (NSG), and Seema Sashastra Bal (SSB).

Assam Rifles (AR)

Assam Rifles is the oldest, created during British Rule in 1835 as a militia called the "Cachar Levy" to protect British tea estates and their settlements against tribal raids. Renamed as "Frontier Force," it was merged with the Assam Military Police in 1870 and took part in World War I in the Middle East. Due to the war experience under the British Army, it was conferred upon the title of Assam Rifles in 1917. Presently, it has a twofold task—guarding the Indo-Myanmar border spread over 1,631 km, and carrying out counterinsurgency operations in the North East (NE), comprising eight states of India. All senior positions of the Assam Rifles are held by Army officers.

Central Reserve Police Force (CRPF)

The CRPF came into being as the Crown Representative Force in 1939 and was used in the states exclusively on the British Political Agent's orders to quell law-and-order disturbances. It acquired its new name after the enactment of the CRPF Act of 1949. It is the largest CAPF, with a total strength of approximately 313,000 men and women divided in 246 battalions. Its task, as laid out in its official website, is to maintain rule of law, public order, and internal security. It is deployed all over the country and engaged in multifarious duties from counterinsurgency, anti-militancy and anti-Naxalite operations, to VIP security and, above all, handling law-and-order incidents in various states. The CRPF has specialized units in the form of Rapid Action Force (RAF) and Commando Battalions for Resolute Action (CoBRA), meant for quelling communal disturbances and countering Maoist insurgency, respectively. States demand increasing numbers of CRPF companies to assist them in maintenance of law and order, which puts the force under great strain, stretching its resources to the maximum.

Indo-Tibetan Border Police (ITBP)

The ITBP was raised in 1962 in the wake of the Chinese armed intrusion in the North Eastern Frontier Agency (NEFA) and Ladakh. With a total manpower of around 89,000 divided in sixty battalions, it is deployed from Karakorum Pass in Ladakh to Jacep La in Arunachal Pradesh, covering a stretch of 3,488 km. Some of the border posts manned by its men on the Indo-China border are at formidable heights from 9,000 to 18,700 feet. Being a specialized mountain force, most of its officers and men are trained mountaineers and skiers. The force is also used for rescue and relief operations in the country. The ITBP has a Water Wing, which guards the riverine borders of the Himalayan region, including the sensitive Pangong Lake in Ladakh, the Brahmaputra region in Arunachal Pradesh, and the Indus in Jammu and Kashmir (J&K).

Border Security Force (BSF)

The Border Security Force, the world's largest border-guarding force, has 250,000 personnel arranged in 186 battalions. It was raised in 1965 and is deployed along the Indo-Pak and Indo-Bangladesh border, covering a distance of 6,386 km. It patrols segments of the Line of Control (LOC) in J&K under the operational control of the Army. While guarding the border and checking cross-border infiltration, it also monitors transnational crimes along the border. It is armed with powers under Criminal Procedure Code (CrPC), Customs Act, Passport Act, and Dangerous Drugs and Opium Act. BSF is often deployed for counterinsurgency and internal security duties and forms a part of the Indian contingent to UN missions every year.

Central Industrial Security Force (CISF)

The CISF was raised in 1969 to guard central government industrial complexes in the country. Presently, it provides security to major critical installations of the country, including nuclear, space, and power stations as well as airports, seaports, heritage monuments including the iconic Taj Mahal and Red Fort, and sensitive government office complexes in the capital. It has created a special unit specializing in VIP security and provides security cover to selected threatened individuals under X, Y, and Z categories. It also provides security to some important private sector units on payment and the Delhi Metro Rail Corporation. The Fire Wing of the CISF pitches in during major fire outbreaks. The CISF has a current strength of approximately 145,000 to attend to its wide range of duties.

National Security Guard (NSG)

The NSG formed in 1984 is a counterterrorism force comprising both Army and police officers, with a total strength of 7,000. Its commandos are in readiness to be deployed for counter-hijacking, bomb disposal, post-blast investigations and hostage rescue acts. NSG hubs are situated in Mumbai, Kolkata, Chennai, and Hyderabad to reach the affected areas in the shortest possible time. It is modeled after the GSG 9 Germany and SAS UK.

Seema Sashastra Bal (SSB)

The SSB, earlier known as the Special Service Bureau, became a border-guarding force in 2001 after the Kargil War. It has a manpower strength of around 99,000 to guard the Indo-Nepal (1751 km) and Indo-Bhutan borders (699 km). Its deployment is along the international border in the states of Himachal Pradesh, Uttar Pradesh (UP), Uttarakhand, Bihar, and West Bengal.

Training

Each CAPF has its own training institutions and programs tailored to the needs of the rank and file and the nature of jobs they perform. The training of AR personnel is on the Army pattern. NSG personnel go through an arduous basic training course followed by an advance one. Being an anti-terrorist force, the commandos go through regular drills of anti-hijack, hostage rescue, bomb disposal, close quarter battle and hand-to-hand combat. Joint exercises and drills are also carried out with foreign anti-terrorist units. The ITBP trains its men in survival skills and warfare at high altitudes along with courses on border management. Similarly, the SSB has a ring of training institutions providing courses on various subject including border guarding, perception management and survival tactics. The BSF has a network of training institutes across the country imparting specialized training in weapons tactics and counterinsurgency. The CRPF deployed within various states imparts training to its officers through courses on human rights, communal riots, counterinsurgency and law-and-order management. Lastly, the CISF imparts specialized training in firefighting and prevention, VIP protection, vital installations protection, aviation and airport security.

Each CAPF has an officer of Inspector General of Police (IGP) rank, heading the training division. The training methodology has changed over the years. Vertical interaction courses organized by GOI have a fair mix of IPS, CAPF, and state officers in which inter-state coordination, human rights, and case studies of noted successes and failures in operations are taken up. Experts from various areas address the trainees in specialized courses, in which field exercises form an integral part. Before being inducted for counterinsurgency, each unit goes through tactical exercises and familiarization. Thus, CAPFs are self-sufficient in taking care of their training needs. As regular members of contingents serving in UN missions abroad, they also get exposure to conflict situations worldwide.

Comparison with Similar Forces in Other Countries

The CAPFs are perhaps unique in the world with respect to their origin, command, structure, and functions. Paramilitary organizations are mostly helmed by army officers in Asia. In India, except the AR, all CAPFs are headed by Indian Police Service (IPS) officers and do not perform state police duties, but as aid to civil power for managing law-and-order situations and other exigencies. The BSF is armed with police powers only to control inter-state crimes on the border.

Both the Pakistan and Bangladesh paramilitary organizations are helmed by Army officers and structured on army pattern. They patrol the border and sea lines and are also used for internal disturbances. The Chinese People's Armed Police is overseen by the Central Military Commission, with its parent agency being the Armed Forces of the People's Republic of China. The National Guard in the United States comprises the reserve components of the Army and the Air Force and works under dual control of the Center and the states. It is headed by a general from the Army or the Air Force. In Europe, the Italian Carabinieri is also a military police force under the Ministry of Defense with both military and civilian duties. The Spanish La Guardia is, again, structured along military lines and is tasked to cover rural areas for investigating crimes and patrolling the highways.

The German Federal Border Police formed in 2005 is a multifaceted one and comes closest to the CAPF. It is deployed in the railways, the aviation sector, internal security, borders, anti-terrorism and protection of federal buildings. It is also authorized to conduct criminal investigations within its jurisdiction. However, the size of German Federal Border Police (approximately 40,000 personnel) is much smaller than the CAPFs.

Internal Security Review 2000

The Kargil war between India and Pakistan was fought between May and July 1999, when the Pakistani military along with terrorists intruded in the Kargil district of Ladakh, occupying key positions. It was a high-altitude warfare in mountainous terrain resulting in India's decisive victory. A Kargil Review Committee (KRC) was set up to study the incidents leading to the conflict. KRC recommended formation of a Group of Ministers (GoM) in 2000 to review and overhaul the security setup. To guard different international borders more effectively, the GoM laid down the principle of "one border—one force."[1] The GoM lamented that continual demands made by the states for CAPF assistance was diverting the border-guarding forces from their primary role to other duties, adversely affecting their professionalism and efficiency. The Estimates Committee of the Parliament, under the chairmanship of Dr. Murli Manohar Joshi, finalized a report on "Central Armed Police Forces and Internal Security Challenges—Evaluation and Response Mechanism" on March 16, 2018. The report commented, "heavy dependence of states on CAPFs for daily Law and Order duties is diverting the Forces from their more crucial role of anti-insurgency and border guarding." Similarly, another parliamentary committee report, Rajya Sabha in its report on the working conditions of the border-guarding forces, reiterated the views of the earlier committee.[2]

Incessant and varied demands have put the CAPFs under tremendous pressure. This has impacted their efficiency and morale. Even the CISF, mandated to guard important government installations, is called out for duties like the elections and law and order in the states. The CRPF is already stretched, with tasks ranging from counterinsurgency in Jammu & Kashmir and North East to fighting the Maoists in LWE-affected areas and handling law and order situations in various States. Its CoBRA and RAF units, specially trained for deployment in Naxalite-affected and communally sensitive regions, are constantly engaged with little time for rest and recuperation. Deployment in harsh weather conditions and inhospitable terrains also impact their health and morale adversely. Malaria and insect bites are serious health hazards in some areas, debilitating the force.

The CAPFs, in the current scenario, struggle to fulfill their primary duties of border guarding, counterinsurgency, and law-and-order duties. This has led to proposals for raising their numbers, because the states demanding more CAPFs are neither filling up their police vacancies nor sanctioning more posts for policemen in the districts or the State Armed Police (SAP). Another issue is the use of BSF units, sans arms, as aid to law and order, which conflicts with their Standard Operating Procedure (SOP). Under the Act, they are mandated to carry arms, while the law-and-order duties in states require personnel to be equipped with batons only, to handle crowds and processions—keeping a very small armed unit for contingencies.

It is clear, therefore, that neither the GoM directives nor the findings of the Estimates Committee and the parliamentary standing committee for putting an end to the diversion of the CAPFs from their primary roles are being adhered to. This compromises the efficiency and morale of the CAPFs.

CAPF Strength and Implications

It is in this context that the rising strength of CAPF is to be viewed vis-à-vis the Army and the civil police. Since law and order is a state subject, ideally state governments should raise their own force to manage it, but paying for use of CAPF, when needed, works better than keeping a standing force with higher fixed costs. In addition, India's borders extend over 15,000 km with two inimical neighbors, China and Pakistan, and need to be manned with constant vigilance. Applying the "one border—one force" principle, BSF and ITBP are deployed along the Pakistan and China borders, respectively. The ITBP units were manning the posts on the icy heights around Pangong Lake during the India-China skirmishes in the Galwan Valley in June 2020. Similarly, providing security at airports and vital central government installations and buildings all over the country engage the attention of CISF, along with VIP protection.

Each CAPF has been tasked with a specific role but is expected to pitch in for other duties too, such as internal security or disaster management. The border-guarding CAPFs have the firepower and the necessary wherewithal to come to the Army's aid in times of hostilities, while the CRPF is fully equipped to deal with internal security duties and assisting the State Police. Hence the CAPF performs a dual role of aiding the police as well as the military, as the situation demands.

However, any comparison between the Army and CAPF is a redundant exercise since the government is firm about maintaining its distinct role, that is, coming to the aid to state police and to the Army in times of war. CAPF does not have police powers nor is it raised like the Army for combat role. There is no infusion of military officers in CAPF ranks and vice versa.

Each CAPF is governed by an act that deals with all-important issues like its duties and command-and-control structure. Legal protection against prosecution while discharging official duties is also provided by the Act. Under the CRPF Act, the commandant has judicial powers to convict and sentence an offender with any punishment except death. He also has the powers to give summary punishment departmentally without inquiry. This certainly calls for revisiting the Act. Two views are in currency—either create a cadre of judicially trained officers or constitute a special court such as the Security Force Court of the BSF, which comprises three or five senior officers. While disciplinary cases seem to be well handled internally, it is the encounters in J&K and Naxalite areas that rightly attract criticism since in several cases, errant officers are not proceeded against or get off scot-free after inquiries.

Budget Allocation for CAPF

The budget allocations for the CAPF have been increasing over the years but still fall short of burgeoning needs. Roughly 74 percent of the CAPF budget is expended on salaries, as remarked by the Estimates Committee, leaving little for the critical items to ramp up capacities and operational capability.

The Ministry of Home Affairs was allocated Rs. 119,025 crore in the Union Budget 2019–2020, out of which the police share, including the states and the CAPF, was Rs. 98,202 crore. Seventy-three percent of the police budget went to the CAPFs in 2019–2020, amounting to Rs. 7,171,400 crore. While CRPF received 33 percent (Rs. 23,964 crore) of this allocation, BSF with 27 percent (Rs. 19,651 crore) was the second highest recipient. Budgetary allocation increased nearly twelvefold between 2000 and 2020 in nominal terms and 3.3 times in real terms.[3]

Work Environment

Sustained deployment for duties in the hinterland over long periods implies withdrawal from the counterinsurgency grid and border areas, thinning out formations in key theaters of internal security. The SOP dictates that every company, after serving in an operational area for two years, is put under training for the third year. This training exercise is critical not only for debriefing, sharpening of personal skills, and tactical exercises, but is also imperative for rest and recreation. However, constant deployment gives no time to follow these norms strictly.

The Rajya Sabha Parliamentary Committee Report expressed concern over the number of CAPF personnel proceeding on voluntary retirement (around 9,000 per year) and resigning from the CAPF. The housing satisfaction level in the CRPF was just 11.8 percent, the lowest among the CAPF. The poor level of housing could be one of the major reasons for the high attrition rate in the force, the report pointed out. Putting men on duty who are still under training hampers skill development and disrupts the overall training schedule. Almost 98 percent of the training companies are on various temporary law-and-order assignments across the country. As a result, no CRPF company is allowed time for rest and recuperation, which has an adverse impact on the overall operational efficiency of the force.

Discipline and welfare are the key components of man management. CAPF allows a *jawan* in field seventy-five days of total leave in a year. However, due to pressing requirements, leaves are canceled at times, causing huge stress among the personnel. Most personnel rarely enjoy free weekends and work almost twelve to fourteen hours a day. The Union Home Minister's promise in 2019 of 100 days' leave and alleviating the CAPFs' shortage of housing, if adhered to, will be a tremendous morale booster.

Between 2000 and 2018, 700 personnel of CAPFs committed suicide.[4] While a substantial number may be due to personal reasons, some can be attributed to postings for long duration in counterinsurgency areas in inhospitable terrains. Within CRPF, the year 2021 through November has already witnessed forty-eight suicide cases, as opposed to sixty in the previous year. In addition, thirteen fratricide incidents in the last four years led to the loss of lives of eighteen *jawans*. According to MHA data, since 2014, more *jawans* have also died of heart attacks and other ailments than those killed in action.

Worried over such incidents, CRPF senior officers have resorted to "Chaupal" meetings, which are informal village-type get-togethers, allowing the men to speak freely. Several welfare schemes are in place for CAPF personnel and their families. In addition, the prime minister's scholarship scheme is extended to 1,000 boys and girls each, and there is reservation in medical colleges for CAPF officers' wards. A Welfare and Rehabilitation Board was established for the welfare of CAPF and AR personnel and families, including disabled personnel. Additionally, the government has also accepted the recommendations of the 7th Pay Commission for granting various allowances to the CAPFs, like risk and hardship allowance and dress allowance.

The CAPFs themselves have undertaken several stress-alleviating measures. These include, inter alia, transparent leave and transfer policy, regular interaction between enlisted men and officers, improving medical facilities, introducing yoga and other such measures.

To test the efficacy of the welfare schemes in the CAPF, a study was conducted in 2016 by Pramod Phalnikar, IPS, additional director general of police, in conjunction with the Tata Institute of Social Sciences and Jnana Prabodhini Institute of Psychology.[5] The focus of the research was to study "the impact of welfare schemes on subjective well-being of CISF, ITBP and state police personnel." The study advocates compilation and propagation of the best welfare practices and calls for creating better awareness of welfare schemes among the forces. It recognizes the need for stress management and counseling of men. An important recommendation is the empowerment of women in police families and strengthening education-related schemes. Finally, the study suggests closer ties between the rank and file, through interactions on a regular basis.

Morale

Low morale in CAPF personnel can also be attributed to a sense of low self-esteem. They consider themselves at a disadvantage with the civil services and being treated unfairly in comparison with the Army. Despite serving in similar harsh conditions, there is a sizable pay gap between a CAPF constable and an Army *jawan*. While transport and remote hardship allowances are the same for both the forces at the rank of *havildar* (equivalent to a sergeant), the ration money given to CRPF *jawan* is taxable, but it is tax-free for the Army soldier. A CAPF *jawan*'s pension depends on his contributions made to the pension fund, while the Army *jawans* receive one rank, one pension. BSF *jawans* are not entitled to house rent allowance in their hometowns and have much less access to family accommodation as compared to their Army counterparts.

Perhaps the biggest welfare measure yearned for by the CAPF men is clearing up the stagnation in the ranks. This discontent simmers across all ranks. Improvement of service conditions and due promotions are the two basic needs in the CAPF. Promotions are delayed because sudden unplanned recruitment took place at times to tackle Punjab terrorism, Naxalite violence, Jammu and Kashmir insurgency and other similar exigencies. Not matched by creation of increased posts, adverse impact on promotions continues. Creation of posts is a lengthy bureaucratic process, involving a clutch of ministries, including the expenditure ministry.

Leadership

The leadership crisis has been afflicting the CAPFs for some time. The tussle between CAPF officers and the Indian Police Service (IPS) top posts has come out in the open. The CAPF officers argue that they fare better in terms of experience and tactics over the IPS, who serve the CAPFs on short-term deputations only. The tussle had a background in the report of the 6th Pay Commission, which accorded CAPF officers a raise in pay in the next promotional pay scale without attaining the rank—something already applicable to the Group "A" Organized Services, like the Indian Administrative Service (IAS) or IPS, recruited through the Union Public Service Commission (UPSC). The technical term for this is Non-Functional Financial Upgrade (NFFU). The order was held in abeyance by the government until the court ruled in favor of the CAPF officers, awarding NFFU to them. The CAPF officers, however, expected the court to rule on the leadership issue too, but the Court directed that the deputation posts for IPS within the CAPFs would remain the same.

Despite the court decision on the issue, discontent simmers in the ranks of the CAPF officers. According to another view, the CAPF officers seek the perks and privileges of both the armed forces and All-India Services like the IAS and IPS, recruited through the All-India examination conducted by the UPSC. The CAPF officers are also recruited through the UPSC, but their exam does not match the high physical or psychological rigor of the Service Selection Board (SSB) for the armed forces, nor does it compare with the academic standard of the Civil Services Exam. On the other hand, IPS officers, selected through the Civil Services Exam, are well versed in leadership qualities, serving as police chiefs in districts from a very young age and honed in skills through many law-and-order and other trying situations. They also serve as commandants of State Armed Battalions (SAPs) in the states.

The Central Armed Police Forces are no longer called the Para-Military Forces, barring the AR, which is helmed by Army officers at all higher ranks. Behind the change in nomenclature is the intent of maintaining the civilian character of the forces and a conscious design to refrain from using the Army in internal security duties, except in rare circumstances. The deployment of the Army in Jammu and Kashmir is justified on account of Pakistan's unequivocal support of cross-border infiltration causing destabilization in the sensitive border region. The North Eastern states also lie along the sensitive border with China and Myanmar, where the Army is deployed for counterinsurgency duties. The plan is to withdraw the AR from border guarding duties along the Myanmar border and deploy a CAPF.

The IPS leadership, serving across the country in a variety of posts with civil interface, enjoys the trust of the people and represents the civilian face of the administration. The IPS officers led the fight against terrorism in Punjab, under K. P. S. Gill, director general of police, Punjab, with some losing their lives. In the erstwhile state of Andhra Pradesh, IPS officers raised the Greyhounds, a force adept at jungle guerrilla tactics, and took the battle right to the Maoist heartland in the deep jungles. Until today, a clutch of IPS officers, who led the Greyhounds during their time, face an extremely high threat and have been provided with security cover.

Further, the role of a CAPF chief extends beyond tactics and operations to long-term planning, strategy, and, most important, coordination with state governments, police chiefs, and senior-most defense officials at the Center. An IPS officer fits into this role easily with his All-India reach and his long-term experience of managing districts, the armed police, and a variety of other assignments.

Assessment Indicators

How does one assess the role played by the CAPF in internal security? There is no hard assessment made available from either the CAPF or the government. Normally, the statistics of incidents of encounter, terrorists/insurgents killed, or Security Forces (SFs) martyred are used for any presentation or assessment during an internal security review. However, a realistic assessment should include the contributions of CAPF not only in armed confrontations but also in the area of coordination with the SFs, their peacetime activities, level of preparedness, and overall capacity and innate strength to carry out sustained engagement with militants/insurgents.

Internal reviews conducted from time to time by the BSF study figures of border crimes including smuggling of drugs and illegal entry, since it has been given powers under the Customs and Police Acts under its jurisdiction. Punjab faces a drug problem, which is compounded by its vulnerable border with Pakistan, especially the Ferozepur sector, which is quite active. With a fully fenced border, the

35 km long riverine belt is used in ingenious ways to bring in drugs and arms from the Pakistani side. The seizures of heroin by the BSF on the Punjab border have been falling over the years—the haul for 2017, 2018, and 2019 being 277, 231, and 228 kg respectively. This is due to additional deployment of battalions, enhanced technical surveillance, and increased coordination between the BSF, Punjab Police STF, and the Narcotic Control Bureau. The modus operandi for smuggling is also changing, with old networks giving way to new ones. Now drones are the carriers of guns, ammunition, and opium. On June 20, 2020, a Pakistani Hex copter was shot down in Kathua, Jammu Sector, carrying M4 rifles and grenades. On June 27, 2021, two explosive-laden UAVs crashed into the Indian Air Force station in Jammu and Kashmir, injuring two IAF personnel. The BSF is continuously developing counter-drone measures to check cross-border smuggling of drugs and arms.

On the eastern border, the problem of smuggling cattle into Bangladesh persists. The villagers on both sides use innovative ways to evade checks at the border, intertwined as it is in so many places. Certain accomplices in border smuggling from the BSF are apprehended from time to time. Most of them are rogues who act individually or with the help of outsiders and are not part of any crime syndicate. The punishment, however, is quite severe—awarded by the Summary Security Force Court after a trial akin to a court-martial. Figures of court-martials are not released; however, outcomes of some appear in newspapers.

In a recent move MHA has extended the jurisdiction of the BSF to operate in the border states of Assam, Bengal, and Punjab up to a 50 km belt from the international border. The same applies to two other border states, Gujarat and Rajasthan. The reasons for the move as explained by the minister in Parliament was to counter drone attacks and UAV incursions from across the Pakistani border and illegal cattle trade and intrusions along the eastern border. The move is mired in controversy, with opposition states attributing motives on the part of GOI to weaken the federal character of the nation.

New threats require gearing up of security machinery. However, the states are well aware of these threats and that law and order is their problem and they have to take steps to counter these problems. Ideally, both BSF and state police should fight the new age threats jointly, but the politics is clearly blurring the lines of jurisdiction. A statement by the BSF chief about demographic changes being clearly visible in border areas due to illegal entry from Bangladesh on the Bengal border has only added to the distrust between the Center and the states.

The Naxalite Belt

LWE violence was restricted to 251 police stations (PS) in sixty districts of eight states in 2018, in comparison with 330 PSs in seventy-six districts spread over ten states in 2013. The number of violent incidents and deaths also declined by about a quarter (1,136 to 833) and 40 percent (397 to 240). The Maoist movement has suffered a crippling blow, with the killing of some of their top commanders and the surrender of many others. Today, both the geographical spread and the intensity of violence have reduced drastically.[6]

A major share of success can be credited to the CAPFs deployed in the Maoist belt. Initially, with the states unable to provide the manpower, the CAPFs led the fight, taking a fair number of casualties in the process. Over the years, the states have built up their capability, but CRPF is still in the forefront of the anti-Naxal campaign. It has successfully established camps in the deep interior of Chhattisgarh State, like Sukma and Bijapur, hitherto considered as Maoist strongholds. Overall, around 45,000 CRPF men are posted in LWE-affected areas and a new "Bastaria" battalion is being raised, inducting the local tribes of the Bastar region in Chattisgarh.

However, an over-stretched force cannot achieve optimal results. Poor living and sanitation in the makeshift camps in the hot weather conditions have adverse impacts on health and morale. The fact that CAPF deaths from suicides, heart attacks, snakebites and malaria far exceed those from combat duties has been a source of worry, both for the leadership of the CAPFs and the government. MHA has set up a task force headed by DG CRPF to study the reasons of suicide and suggest counter measures.[7]

The biggest threat to the CRPF from the Maoists comes from land mines embedded deep under roads that the mine sweepers fail to detect. Second, time and again, the Naxalites have sprung back with spectacular strikes on the security forces proving their resilience and capability to launch lethal attacks. On March 21, 2020, the Maoists ambushed a CAPF contingent, killing seventeen members of the CRPF, a reminder of the still long road ahead. The see-saw battle continues, with twenty-four Maoists gunned down by state commandos in Gadchiroli district, Maharashtra, on November 13, 2021. Among those killed was a central committee member carrying a reward of Rs. 50 lakhs.

Jammu and Kashmir Sector

Kashmir remains the most sensitive region of deployment of CAPF. Adhering to the policy of "one border—one force," BSF has been withdrawn from counter-militancy and deployed along Jammu and Kashmir (J&K) and Bangladesh borders. The CRPF has been inducted in J&K for duties encompassing a whole range, from anti-militancy, law and order, to VIP security. Questions are often raised over the massive presence and role of the security forces in Kashmir: (a) Is such a heavy deployment justified, reflecting a one-sided security-centric approach to the Kashmir problem? (b) Are the forces using due restraint in anti-militancy operations and adhering to human rights principles? (c) Are there mechanisms in place for speedy disciplinary action against the violators of human rights? (d) Should lethal weapons be allowed to be used against demonstrators?

These issues relate to the Army, CAPFs, and the State Police alike, which are engaged in the battle against militancy in J&K. To make a realistic assessment of the role of CAPFs, it is imperative to give a brief sketch of the internal security situation in this sensitive border area to portray the conditions under which the security forces are working.

The huge cache of weapons seized between 1990 and 2019—including over 32,000 AK47 rifles, 12,000 pistols, 65,000 grenades, and sizable quantities of ammunition, magazines, binoculars and wireless sets—tells the story of Pakistani complicity in sustaining the tempo of violence in Kashmir. Heavy firing along the LOC is often resorted to for facilitating cross-border infiltration by trained terrorists from Pakistan. On September 18, 2016, an Indian Army Brigade HQ in Uri was surprised by four militants in a pre-dawn raid that killed nineteen soldiers. India retaliated by conducting surgical strikes across the border, inflicting an equal number of casualties. A suicide attack against a CRPF bus in Pulwama, Kashmir, in February 2019, killing forty men, again led to the Indian Air Force (IAF) jets flying across the LOC and bombing a known training militant establishment in Balakote, Pakistan. Militant incidents and killing of civilians, terrorists, and SFs from 1990 onward has decreased considerably, with 2019 recording the lowest numbers.

In August 2019, Article 370 of the Constitution, which accorded special status to J&K, was abrogated and the state was bifurcated into the Union Territories of Jammu and Kashmir and Ladakh. As a preventive measure, 300 extra companies of CRPF were rushed in to ramp up the security grid. The terrorists are lying low for the present and violence is at a low ebb, but isolated killings of soldiers and civilians by terrorists continue. Within the valley there is simmering discontent over the move to control channels of communication like mobiles and internet. Even with gradual easing of restrictions and release of political leaders, Kashmir today is still in a state of uneasy calm.

The CRPF works as the third arm against militancy, the other two being the Rashtriya Rifles (RR) of the Indian Army and the J&K Police. The force is often deployed on barricades, temporary *nakas* (checkpoints), and demonstration sites. It is also used for VIP security and protection of key installations. Such a varied range of duties detract from the main task of anti-militancy operations and impact adversely on its capabilities.

Large deployment of security forces in Kashmir has been the focal point of criticism for a long time. However, when militancy erupted in 1989, the state police, limited in strength, had a virtual guerrilla war at hand. By 1996, the insurgency was under control, with the help of increased strength of SFs and sustained counterinsurgency actions. Military strategists found the deployment of forces in J&K justified, considering the requirement to cover 700 km LOC and the area of operations being 122,000 sq. km.[8] Further, the task is not only to contain militancy, but also to contain cross-border infiltrations and their fallout.

A steady decline in the number of militants and incidents has led to change in the separatists' strategy, with huge gatherings on the streets and stone pelting at the SF, as witnessed in 2008. The problem became acute in 2010 and 2016. The CRPF was criticized for using pellet guns, and causing injuries, especially to children. The CRPF claimed that children were instigated to throw stones and funds were provided to engineer protests. Police strategists argue that in delicate law-and-order situations, it is difficult to prescribe the degree of restraint to be exercised while handling such large crowds, especially if they turn violent. Furthermore, in such situations, it is difficult to conceive of harmless, non-lethal standoff weapons since even rubber bullets and pellets cause serious damage to a human body.

Today's militants are small in numbers and more savvy on the internet. Burhan Wani was a poorly trained militant—more active on the internet than in militancy—but attracted huge attention. The CRPF is still trying to contend with the changed scenario, while the state police have to go a long way before taking over the mantle of the anti-militancy campaign.

The North East

Another critical sector of CAPF deployment is North East India, comprising eight states of India, namely, Assam, Tripura, Manipur, Nagaland, Mizoram, Sikkim, Meghalaya, and Arunachal Pradesh.

Sustained counterinsurgency operations by the Army, AR, and the CAPFs, with improved coordination among them and better intelligence, have led to considerable improvement in the North East situation. While Bangladesh, Bhutan, and Nepal have cooperated with India in curbing cross-border infiltration and flushing out militants based along their border, Myanmar has also taken similar action in this regard.

There is a drastic reduction in incidents of violence.[9] Compared to 2013, insurgency-related incidents and civilian deaths were 70 percent and 80 percent lower respectively in 2019. The casualty figures for the security forces during the same period went down by 78 percent. Tripura and Mizoram are free of insurgencies today. Over 600 cadres of National Democratic Front of Bodoland (NDFB) surrendered after signing a peace accord with the government in 2020. The government has been engaging various proscribed insurgent groups in peace talks.

However, allegations of fake encounters and human rights violations have been raised from time to time against the security forces deployed in the North East. Irom Chanu Sharmila, a civil rights activist from Manipur, had been on a hunger strike for nearly sixteen years over the abolition of Armed Forces (Special Powers) Act 1958 that applied to certain areas of North East. Rajnish Rai, inspector general of police,

IG, NE sector, CRPF, indicted a combined team of Assam Police, Army, CRPF, and SSB for staging a fake encounter to kill two militants of NDFB (S) on March 29–30, 2017, in the Simlaguri area of Chirang District, Assam. The Ministry of Home Affairs refused to accept the report, stating that the inquiry could be conducted by the state government only. Allegations have been raised against AR too for high-handedness and human rights violations. A botched operation by the AR that killed fourteen civilians on December 4, 2021, has caused a furor in the state. The Nagaland assembly has since passed a resolution for removal in the Armed Forces Special Powers Act from the state.

Such incidents do cast a shadow on the working of the forces in general in the North East, especially related to encounter killings. Rarely are the officers held guilty and, in most cases, there is no inquiry at all. The general feeling is that since the SFs work in delicate situations, they deserve the benefit of doubt.

The Hinterland

The use of CAPF in the hinterland is mainly dictated by the demands of the states. What draws the maximum attention of the public is the performance of CAPFs during communal disturbances. The RAF battalions are fully equipped to deal with communal clashes, but they work under overall supervision of the state police. In the communal disturbances in February 2020 in Delhi, the police leadership dithered in the beginning and the CRPF had to remain a mute spectator. After only two days of violence, the situation was brought under control with the help of the CRPF. The CRPF will continue to face this disability of playing second fiddle to the state police, despite the capability to act on its own. However, despite the handicap faced by the CRPF, it does not carry any baggage of the state police of being under any influence of the powers in the states where they are deployed.

How does the CRPF leadership view its operational failures? Is there an exercise to hold officers responsible? These cases are studied at the highest level and also discussed in training courses for finding faults and taking preventive measures in future. In J&K, CRPF is deployed on *naka* duties, cordon and search ops, forming the outer ring during encounters, security and patrolling duties and tackling street crowds. Grievous or fatal injuries to the public are caused at times during encounters or while using force to manage crowds. In case of death or serious injury to an innocent, the state police registers a case. Under the CRPF Act, judicial trials can also be conducted by the CRPF commandants. No official figures are available, however, on the trials conducted by the CRPF against its own men.

In Naxalite areas, botched operations have caused the deaths of several CRPF men. Such incidents—like Dantewada where Maoists ambushed and killed seventy-six CRPF men—are probed at the highest level, but there is a general reluctance to act against erring officers. In most of these cases, the laid-down SOP is violated by the commanders on the ground. Cases of unprovoked firing and killing of innocents in encounters have also marred the reputation of the force. While a strong internal mechanism does exist for bringing the culprits to book, the numbers of such cases are indeed few. A judicial commission inquiring into Sarkeguda encounter of 2012 in Chhattisgarh State gave its finding in 2019 that seventeen villagers killed in the alleged encounter were not Maoists. It can be said that the number of officers held accountable are very few in comparison to the number of instances of lapses or failures.

Modernization

Increasing demands on the security forces have led to increasing pressure on the government to sanction more manpower and fill up vacancies. Meanwhile, the CAPFs need upgraded weaponry and equipment. Under the Modernisation Plan III covering the period 2018–2020, around Rs. 1,000 crore have been sanctioned for all the CAPFs, with CRPF getting a major chunk—Rs. 302 crore. According to the MHA Annual Report 2019, these include:

a) Under barrel and multi-grenade launchers, advanced pistols and submachine guns and sniper rifles.
b) Unmanned aerial vehicles, handheld thermal imagers/thermal sights/night vision devices, K9 camera system and bullet resistant boats.
c) Mine-protected vehicles, anti-terrorist vehicles and mine-resistant armored all-terrain vehicles.
d) Communication equipment including jammers and interceptors.

The induction of modern technology in the CAPF needs to be based on the principle of shorter modernization cycles to match the latest threat and tactics of the terrorists. There are some critical areas that merit urgent consideration. Landmines embedded deep beneath the road surface in Maoist areas present the greatest danger while transporting troops. Precious lives continue to be lost due to the limited availability of even the latest-technology mine detectors to detect them. Advanced vehicles equipped with mine detectors for faster mobility are also unavailable. Mine-protected vehicles used as a defensive measure have not matched up to expectations. The CoBRA battalions are in dire need of vehicles and equipment to reach locations as soon as possible after accurate information is received. Perhaps the most critical need for forces in Naxalite areas is a number of UAVs for scanning the immediate terrain before a detachment moves out of its camp for patrol or combing operations.

With the induction of locals in the forces and deeper engagement with the tribes in Maoist areas through a few government schemes implemented by the CRPF itself, SFs are gaining confidence of the villagers and gathering useful intelligence. These need to be supplemented with an upgrade in surveillance and reconnaissance technologies to achieve operational success. There is a sentiment that foreign technology takes time to source and does not often work well in Indian conditions.[10] At present, the National Technical Research Organisation (NTRO) provides valuable information on Maoist movement through its unmanned surface vehicles (UAV). However, upgrades are required in the form of increasing the load capacity of the UAVs and their numbers for better All-India coverage. Detection of Maoist movement in deep jungles with thick foliage remains an outstanding issue, with UAVs still unable to capture the images through the thick cover. The CRPF is also using Defense Research and Development Organization (DRDO) manufactured Netra vertical take-off-and-lift mini-UAV for detecting Maoist movements.

CRPF along with the state police is often exposed to dangerous situations while combating law and order flare-ups. Still, their riot gear leaves much to be desired. While the needs of the CRPF have been expressed various times, they are yet to be supplied with the latest anti-riot gear. Perhaps this is the most pressing need of the CRPF, since safety of the *jawan* on duty is of paramount importance.

Conclusion

The growing strength and extensive deployment of CAPF is a compulsion of India's democratic polity. India's border runs along seven countries and is 15,106.7 km long. Roughly 53 percent of the CAPF is posted on the border, and 15 percent are engaged in security of vital installations and central government complexes. This leaves around 32 percent for deployment in states for law and order and COIN operations.

Under Article 355 of the Constitution, the central government is committed to assisting the states in quelling internal disturbances. This has led to a growing tendency by states to reach out for the CAPFs at the first sign of trouble. Such a trend is expected to continue in future.

Continued deployments have put the CAPF, and CRPF in particular, under severe stress. To ease the burden, the Center aims to fill over 84,000 vacancies and is planning to raise more India Reserve Battalions (IRB)—seventeen IRBs in J&K and four in Maoist-affected states. These are special armed police battalions raised in the states, with the raising costs borne by the Center. A women battalion is also being raised in Kashmir for handling women agitators and stone pelters. Such moves need to be supplemented by the states by augmenting their own police strength and filling up vacancies. Most states continue to have a very poor police-to-population ratio.

The strongest pillar of policing and internal security is the Police Station (PS), which is neglected by the states with most of the police budget allocated only to special forces and schemes. The Center has allocated Rs. 2 crore each for 400 fortified police stations in eighty-three Maoist-affected districts. This has given good results and is also taking pressure off the CRPF and state police to focus on operational matters. The scheme of fortifying police stations should extend to all the 15,000 police stations in the country.

The budget for CAPF will keep increasing every year to keep pace with the demands of modernization and new threats. For instance, there is a critical demand for minesweepers to detect deeply embedded mines beneath the road surface in Maoist-affected areas as well as more UAVs for real-time information on Maoist movements. Purchasing weapons and equipment is a cumbersome procedure, and no headway has been made in this direction to cut down bottlenecks.

However, it appears unlikely that induction of better technology will bring about any reduction in numbers of CAPF personnel. With the proposed withdrawal of AR from the North East border, the CAPF filling in the gap will seek extra manpower for the new job. Each CAPF is also demanding more men to meet the ever-increasing demands.

With a dedicated air wing, NSG's response will be quicker with the already existing four hubs. NSG commandos should also be put on joint exercises with the special forces (these include Para Special Forces units of the Army, Marcos of the Navy, and Garud of the Air Force). Their combined expertise should be a force multiplier for tackling any large-scale terrorist action. Coordination would be smooth since the Special Action Group (SAG) of NSG is headed by a major general of the Army.

The high numbers of suicides and voluntary retirement in the CAPFs are a cause of concern and need to be addressed urgently. The men suffer from a lack of identity and self-esteem. Neither does a CAPF man enjoy the powers of a policeman nor the perks and privileges of an Army man. Harsh conditions of postings, long hours of duty, denial of leave at times, and lack of housing are among the factors that cannot change easily, being the nature of the job. The government has announced a 100 days' leave policy and providing better housing. It is important to give a strong incentive to the men to perform their duties with greater motivation and satisfaction.

The government should consider seriously the often-floated proposal of giving the option to CAPF men for induction in their home state police after completing twenty years of service in the CAPF. With the police being a state subject, the states will have to be included in this. They should agree, considering that vacancies always exist, and the induction would bring them personnel with specialization. This would be a very strong incentive for the men, looking ahead to serve the last ten years or more in their own home state.

Democracies around the world, from the United States to India, are grappling with human rights issues arising out of military and COIN operations. While each military or paramilitary has an institutional mechanism to put such men on trial with civilian oversight in the form of Human Rights Commissions and judicial review in place, a true democracy may still require more transparency and accountability. But instead of creating more disciplinary layers or civilian oversight, it would be better to improve the effectiveness of existing institutional mechanisms.

All democracies are accountable to the people. To this end, a historic legislation, Right to Information (RTI) Act, was passed in 2004. The RTI enjoins all government departments to lay bare all-important details of the organization on their web portals. The department is also bound to give all information sought by an individual within a stipulated time. Information can only be denied if it relates to national sovereignty, the courts and other matters as laid down in Section 8 of the Act.

Twenty-five security organizations have been exempted from the application of this Act—unless the questions relate to human rights violations or corruption. Intelligence organizations and the CAPF are in this exempted list, whereas the police and the defense forces are not. It is time that the CAPF is brought under the ambit of the RTI regime. Questioning its activities and methods will only bring about positive changes and transparency in their working. The Central Information Commission comprising information commissioners is a statutory body. It adjudicates appeals on RTI queries against denial of information by government bodies. Since its enactment, more and more information about government functioning has come into public view. Government authorities are compelled by the Act and the autonomous commission to post information on their websites and become transparent and accountable.

The CAPF should be accountable for their actions since this will align with the tenets of a democratic state and make their role more transparent and meaningful in national security.

Notes

1. Report of the Group of Ministers on National Security, February 19, 2001, Section 4.57.
2. "Parliamentary Standing Committee Report on Home Affairs." *Working Conditions in Border Guarding Forces*, presented to Rajya Sabha on December 12, 2018. Section 4.4.4.
3. Source: Police Modernisation Division, Ministry of Home Affairs.
4. "Central Armed Police Forces and Internal Security Challenges. Evaluation and Response Mechanism by the Estimates Committee of Parliament." *Twentieth Eighth Report* (2017–18), Section 4.17.
5. Pramod Shripad Phalnikar, "Impact of Welfare Schemes on Subjective Well-Being of CISF and ITBP Personnel Submitted to Bureau of Police Research and Development" (MHA, IPS, 2015).
6. "Table of State-wise Extent of LWE Violence during 2010–2018," *Annual Report Ministry of Home Affairs* (2018–2019).
7. Source: Ministry of Home Affairs. .
8. Matthew J. Van Wagenen, "An Analysis of the Indian Government's Counterinsurgency Campaign in Jammu and Kashmir." A thesis presented to the Faculty of the US Army Command and General Staff College. (MAJ, USA, B.S., Marquette University, Milwaukee, Wisconsin, 1991).

9. "Table on Security Situation in Northeast," *Annual Report Ministry of Home Affairs* (2018–2019).

10. Sourav Jha, "India's Para Military Requires an Indigenous Focus," *News18*, June 9, 2015, https://www.news18.com/blogs/india/saurav-jha/indias-paramilitary-modernisation-requi res-an-indigenous-focus-10879-1003697.html, 3/6.

10

The Indian Police

Managing Dilemmas of Internal Security

AKSHAY MANGLA

A capable police force is essential for public order and citizen security. The police are the first line of defense against threats to internal security and the chief instrument by which the state exercises its monopoly on the use of violence. The police have wide-ranging responsibilities that go well beyond routine law enforcement.[1] The security activities undertaken by the police have multiple facets, from ensuring safety of individual citizens, to the maintenance of public order, to the prevention of large-scale episodes of collective violence. In the context of a multi-ethnic democracy such as India, the police also need to balance the use of coercion for collective security with upholding the rights of individual citizens. How the police strike this balance has implications for justice and how citizens experience the state.[2]

This chapter examines how the Indian police manage internal security dilemmas, focusing on the prevention of collective violence between social groups. Drawing on field research conducted in Madhya Pradesh, I find that the state police have developed organizational repertoires for maintaining public order. Using socially embedded tactics, the police draw input from individuals and groups in society for intelligence gathering, to seek out sources of potential conflict, and importantly, to plan and coordinate to prevent sparks from escalating into violence. These organizational repertoires have historical precedents that get reinforced through the police's routine interactions with citizens and societal groups. Similar approaches are used for managing crowd movements, religious festivals, elections, public protests, and other events that can pose security risks.

Yet, the Indian police grapple with sizable institutional constraints that work against socially embedded policing and can contribute to breakdowns in police responses to public order incidents. The militaristic and highly stratified hierarchy of Indian police agencies enables authoritative decision-making and coordination from above, but limits the initiative of frontline officers and information-sharing from below. The lack of frontline personnel, along with institutional biases in the

Akshay Mangla, *The Indian Police* In: *Internal Security in India*. Edited by: Amit Ahuja and Devesh Kapur, Oxford University Press. © Oxford University Press 2023. DOI: 10.1093/oso/9780197660331.003.0010 composition and training of the police, I suggest, makes it more difficult to sustain socially embedded policing. These limitations, in turn, make it more likely for local police agencies to resort to heavy-handed physical tactics during public order situations rather than engaging in conflict prevention strategies.

The rest of this chapter is organized as follows. I first situate the study of policing in India's historical context. The colonial policing structure established a militaristic hierarchy that dis-embedded the police from local society and stressed the use of force to manage public order. Next, I present a case study of socially embedded policing in the state of Madhya Pradesh (MP). Drawing on ethnographic fieldwork conducted in 2017–2019, I show how local police agencies worked to prevent communal violence during the twenty-fifth anniversary of the demolition of the Babri Masjid. I then consider the institutional constraints the police face, as well as the institutional biases favoring the use of force. I conclude the paper with reflections for future research on policing and internal security.

Historical Development of Policing in India

To situate the analysis of police internal security practices, a brief foray into the history of policing in India is required. The British colonial state's primary objectives in India were to collect revenues and maintain a semblance of law and order, in furtherance of the Crown's economic exploits.[3] The institutions and practices of policing evolved within the subcontinent to respond to the political exigencies of colonization and popular resistance to it.[4] The 1857 uprisings set the stage for creating a uniform system of police administration throughout India.[5] The Government of India Act of 1858 transferred authority from the East India Company to the British colonial government. Police reforms that were under discussion became encoded in a series of administrative and legal statutes, including the Code of Civil Procedure (1859), Indian Penal Code (1860), the Code of Criminal Procedure (1861), and the Indian Evidence Act (1872). A police commission appointed in 1860 recommended institutional changes that were reflected in the Police Act of 1861. These laws formed the foundation of India's criminal justice system and continue to influence police practices today. The 1861 Police Act called for the elimination of military police, and in its place established a civil police force overseen by provincial governments. At the local level, the district Superintendent of Police (SP) was made subservient to the District Magistrate (DM), the highest-ranking civil servant in the local bureaucracy.[6]

The 1861 Police Act created a civil police force, but military policing was never eliminated. Instead, a line was drawn between civil police units posted in *thanas* (station houses) and the armed reserve police, posted in barracks. The latter retained a militaristic identity and were periodically summoned to quash communal disturbances and other threats to public order. The creation of a police organization that was partly civil-oriented and partly militaristic was formalized in the Madras Police Act of 1859, which informed the basic structure of policing throughout India. Authority over rural policing was wrested away from landlords (*zamindars*) who traditionally policed the countryside through local headmen (*mukhias*) and watchmen (*chowkidars*) residing in villages. The centralization of authority in the hands of provincial governments enabled colonial authorities to have top-down administrative control of the police.[7] The civil police were designed to maintain distance from local communities, which was evident from the geographic separation of police stations and living quarters from the local public. According to Verma and Subramanian, "the structure stipulated clearly that there was no necessity for involvement of the community in anyway in the policing function."[8] At the top of the hierarchy was the Indian Imperial Police, the colonial predecessor to the Indian Police Service (IPS). To retain British authority over the lower ranks within the police, recruitment into the Indian Imperial Police was closed to Indians until 1920.

The colonial state's apprehension with disturbances to public order became magnified as the anti-colonial movement gained pace and demonstrations became more frequent. In response, the police used force to dissuade rioters, developed town "riot plans" to limit large assemblies, and, together with municipal authorities, created systems to license meetings and processions. In UP, urban centers were redesigned to become "riot-proof" by placing military cantonments and police stations in strategic locations.[9] Despite the creation of a civil police force, the armed reserve forces were frequently called upon to disperse crowds. In practical terms, "public order" within the police meant heavy-handed enforcement of rules and regulations to control crowds and public spaces. Less priority was given to addressing everyday crime and public security.

Following independence, the organizational structure of the police went virtually unchanged. The Constitution gives Indian state (or provincial) governments primary authority over policing. However, internal security is shared with the central government's Ministry of Home Affairs (MHA), which oversees its own set of police forces and specialized branches, including the Central Bureau of Intelligence (CBI) and Intelligence Bureau (IB).[10] Further, the central government has authority over police training, technical assistance for crime investigation, and leads the coordination between states during intelligence operations. Various central bodies exist under the MHA, such as the Bureau of Police Research and Development (BPRD), which supports police training and modernization. Finally, the MHA oversees the recruitment, training, and employment conditions of IPS officers. Officers in the IPS occupy influential posts and wield outsize authority over policing, personnel decisions, and the work conditions of subordinates. The social distance between the IPS and constables posted on the frontlines is sizable and contributes to gaps in communication and information exchange.[11]

Administering Law and Order in Madhya Pradesh: The Anatomy of a Non-Riot

A central feature of policing to uphold internal security has involved the prevention of conflict between social groups. For frontline police officers, there is the ever-present fear of minor disagreements escalating into larger disputes and violence between communities. Additionally, there is the worry that instigators may be encouraged by crowds and large-scale processions to foment violence. These fears are accentuated by the geographic layout of Indian towns and peri-urban centers, with narrow *gullies*, crowded markets, densely populated residential centers, and the prevalence of religious sites and sociocultural symbols. In the backdrop of incredible social diversity and weak administrative capacity, how does the police prevent conflicts from erupting into violence?

This section examines how the police work to prevent communal tensions from escalating into large-scale conflict. I identify two organizational strategies for conflict-prevention: (1) coordinated planning and intelligence gathering; and (2) preemptive conflict management. These strategies have evolved out of the police's routine "law-and-order" practices during elections, religious festivals, and other events. The study of collective violence in India, especially between Hindus and Muslims, has tended to treat the police's role as either incidental or subsidiary to other political and social factors. Attention has been given to the incentives facing politicians, who may choose to deploy the police to protect the minority Muslim community or not depending on the electoral cost and benefits.[12] Alternatively, the security of minorities is thought to have less to do with elections and is instead contingent on the local civic bonds between Hindus and Muslims.[13] In both cases, the police occupy a subservient role to politicians and societal groups. These arguments overlook the possibility that police agencies have both organizational commitment and capabilities to maintain public order, which they can deploy independently of external pressure.

Preventing Communal Escalation in Bhimsen

To illustrate how the police conduct multi-ethnic conflict management for riot prevention, I draw on field research performed in Madhya Pradesh in the period 2017–2019. The study setting is "Bhimsen," a predominantly rural district in central MP.[14] A representative district with respect to sociodemographic indicators, Bhimsen has a population of about 1.5 million, 7 percent of which is Muslim, similar to the statewide average. Bhimsen's literacy rate is also near the MP average of 70.6 percent.

The political context in Bhimsen makes it a crucial case for analyzing police activities around communal violence prevention. My fieldwork oversaw police activities in Madhya Pradesh (MP) surrounding the twenty-fifth anniversary of the demolition of the Babri Masjid. A communally sensitive affair, the tearing down of the mosque in Ayodhya, Uttar Pradesh (UP), on December 6, 1992, and subsequent plans to install a Hindu temple dedicated to Lord Ram on the same site, sparked Hindu-Muslim clashes throughout India. My fieldwork also coincided with the runup to the 2018 state assembly election, a competitive contest between the incumbent BJP and the Congress Party. Over this period, provocative speeches by pro-Hindutva leaders were commonplace and hate-filled messages targeting Muslims made rounds on social media. Organizations involved the Ramjanmabhoomi movement—the movement to construct a temple at Ram's legendary birthplace, on top of the ruins of the Babri Masjid—organized large-scale processions throughout MP, including Bhimsen.

If the propensity for communal clashes in Bhimsen was high, political incentives within the state to protect the minority Muslim population were low. In an important study, Wilkinson finds that the electoral incentives facing state-level politicians account for when and where Hindu-Muslim violence occurs in India.[15] Since the 1990s, Bhimsen has been a political stronghold of the ruling Bharatiya Janata Party (BJP). The district contained the electoral constituencies of senior ministers from the MP state government as well as BJP national leadership, many of whom were outspoken about the intention to build a Ram temple in Ayodhya. In the past, pro-Hindutva organizations operating in Bhimsen's vicinity have stoked communal flames during BJP rule, provoking counter-mobilization by Muslims. In Nusrat Ganj, the peri-urban area within the district, where I conducted ethnographic fieldwork, business owners reported prior incidences of vandalism, stone pelting, and property damage by Hindutva activists and Muslim counter-protesters.[16]

A breakdown in public order and security for Muslims was highly likely in Bhimsen. Surprisingly, the sparks of communal hostility failed to draw oxygen, notwithstanding concerted efforts by Hindutva activists. Below I demonstrate how multi-ethnic policing works to contain communal tensions. My findings are based on in-depth ethnographic field research. I shadowed the district SP, who is ultimately responsible for maintaining public order in the district. While stationed in the SP's office, I observed planning meetings, videoconferences, and informal interactions between local police officers, municipal agencies, and senior police officials based in headquarters in Bhopal. I joined the SP on his local surveillance rounds, observing the in-person and radio communications between the SP and SHOs, who were in charge of public order within their respective station catchment areas. Further, I shadowed the SHO, Sub-Inspectors (SIs), and other frontline officers at the Nusrat Ganj police station (hereafter NG Station), observing their communications with other officers as well as their interactions with citizens while out on their routine patrol "beats." Finally, I conducted participant observation at the police *chowki* (outpost) in central Nusrat Ganj, where a large section of the district's Muslim population lived and worked. The police *chowki* was located between the mosque and a *dargah* (shrine) dedicated to a Muslim saint.

Planning for the Procession

In the weeks and days leading up to December 6, 2017, the anniversary of the Babri Masjid demolition, the police in Bhimsen were on high alert for communal conflict. The projected epicenter of conflict was Ayodhya, Faizabad, and other nearby UP districts, where pro-Hindutva organizations like the Vishwa Hindu Parishad (VHP) and Bajrang Dal had planned religious conclaves, rallies, and other events.[17] Indian Paramilitary forces, including the Central Reserve Police Force (CRPF) and Rapid Action Force (RAF), were posted in large numbers around Ayodhya and major corridors leading to UP from MP. Over the month of November, the district SPs met regularly with the director general of police (DGP) and other senior police officials, and participated in videoconferences to work collectively toward preventing potential sources of Hindu-Muslim conflict.[18]

The administration of policing in MP is separated into six zonal divisions, with an inspector general (IG) assigned to oversee each zone. Bhimsen's SP, "Mr. Saigal," was in frequent contact with the zonal IG for his district, apprising each other of intelligence leads as well as the movements of suspected instigators. The IG shared intelligence from the Special Branch and Police Headquarters, located in Bhopal, the state capital. Similarly, SP Saigal was in regular touch with the SHOs in his district. The SHOs updated him daily on field-level developments as well as leads provided by local informants. Each police station in Bhimsen had a running list of miscreants and local agitators associated with previous conflicts. These lists were critical for police planning around religious festivals, elections, protests, and other large-scale gatherings that posed a threat public order. Frontline officers contacted listed individuals in advance to seek information. As importantly, these communications conveyed the message that the police were vigilant.

Along with information from the streets, social media was a primary mode of intelligence gathering. Police officers in Bhimsen kept a close eye on the Facebook pages of individuals and groups suspected of sharing threats, rumors, and plans to foment conflict. Officers infiltrated WhatsApp groups with support from local informants, who forwarded provocative images and videos in circulation. During one evening at NG Station, I sat with a group of constables as they reviewed WhatsApp messages for suspected leads. They examined messages surrounding cultural events and processions in neighboring districts, which were organized by VHP, Bajrang Dal, and smaller pro-Hindutva organizations. One of the constables showed me a video on his phone of a VHP rally, where a man was inciting the crowd: "*Aisa banda hamare liye bahut khatarnak hai.*" (A man like this is very dangerous.) Upon my asking the officers to elaborate on what "danger" (*khatra*) such a man posed, another constable responded, "*Koi bhi agar yahan zahar phailane aa jaye, khatra to banta hi hai.*" (Anyone who comes to our district to spread poison is dangerous.) Another constable chimed in: "*Fanatical [kattar] elements existed on both* [Hindu and Muslim] *sides."* Both sides of a potential communal dispute had to be monitored closely.

Intelligence-sharing took place between districts as well. During frequent calls between SP Saigal, other district SPs, and the Zonal IG, the police tracked the movements of Hindutva activists and discussed their respective planning activities. After weeks of intelligence work, a lead struck. A WhatsApp video had circulated of a local leader affiliated with the Bajrang Dal giving an inflammatory speech a few weeks prior. Referring to Muslims in derogatory terms, he encouraged the audience to celebrate the Babri Masjid's demolition and to show support for constructing the Ram Mandir by participating in a procession and rally. Officers unearthed plans by the Bajrang Dal to organize a *"Vijay Diwas Yatra"* (Day of Victory Tour) in the zone around Bhimsen. The tour would end at Bhimsen, after passing through the Muslim neighborhood of Nusrat Ganj.

SP Saigal coordinated with the district magistrate (DM) to plan the procession and ensure the smooth flow of traffic. Intelligence revealed multiple inflammatory speeches by the Bajrang Dal affiliate, who was part of the procession and had planned to enter Bhimsen. On the advice of SP Saigal and other senior officers, the DM agreed to institute Section 144 of the Indian Penal Code (IPC), which allows the police to prohibit unlawful public gatherings of five or more persons in cases of impending danger. The police intended to use Section 144 to restrain the Bajrang Dal affiliate from entering the district. While the procession was given clearance to go ahead, the Bajrang Dal leader would not be allowed to enter Bhimsen.

The District Armed Reserve (DAR) police force were summoned by SP Saigal to increase the police presence in Bhimsen and reinforce district borders and checkpoints. Together with civilian police, DAR officers conducted parades through Nusrat Ganj and other town (*kasbah*) and market centers. The parades signaled police control of public space, aimed at building confidence among residents of the area and deterring would-be instigators. Surveillance activities were amplified as the procession approached Bhimsen. Temples, mosques, and other sensitive sites were monitored for suspicious behavior. Constables from NG Station conducted more frequent beats, stopping to interact with business owners as well as mosque and temple authorities. For instance, while patrolling outside of the mosque in Nusrat Ganj, officers met with vegetable stand operators to inquire about their concerns and shared their phone numbers, asking them to report any suspicious activities. Likewise, SP Saigal and the team of senior officers toured the district late into each night, stopping at police *chowkis* and vehicular checkpoints to ensure that passageways were secured.

Managing traffic flows through Nusrat Ganj was central to the police's strategy to prevent conflict. The goal was to move the procession along swiftly and discourage arguments between locals and outsiders. Constables from NG Station were on duty to scan the neighborhood and identify vulnerable pockets that could lead to traffic congestion. Smaller gullies branching into residential blocks were cordoned off with barricades and monitored by officers to create what they called a "*semi-permeable*" membrane, open to local residents but closed to outsiders.[19] Along with traffic, the police closely managed the parking of vehicles and other physical obstructions that could foment conflict. Motorcycles and scooters parked along the main road were repositioned so that they did not jut out, reducing their impact on the traffic flow and limiting the chances of their being knocked over by enthusiastic procession-goers. Pointing to the motorcycles, a sub-inspector described to me how small issues, like the scratching of a vehicle, could lead to a skirmish and then quickly escalate into violence. When such situations erupted, he noted, police had to "*read the crowd*" and find allies to assist in de-escalation. By surveying the area, field officers gained familiarity with local leaders who expressed a willingness to help with procession planning.

In their planning activities, the police paid particular attention to religious sites and symbols that could arouse sentiments. In Nusrat Ganj, many of the Muslim-owned shops carried green flags outside, while Hindu-owned shops were adorned with saffron flags. Shop owners were asked to remove the flags to prevent them from being torn down or damaged during the procession. To improve compliance, the SHO of NG Station sought the help of informal leaders, whose word carried respect among local businesses. Applying painstaking attention to details, frontline officers sought to limit the opportunity for sparks to ignite. On the day before the procession, I joined police officers on foot through Nusrat Ganj as they inspected the market area. Observing that the *durgah* along the main road had a line of green flags stretching across the street, an officer asked residents to help him move the flags to either end, keeping them out of the path of agitators, who may be enticed to tug on the flags when passing by. Another officer spotted a trail of blood on the main road, which led to a back alley with a row of halal butcher shops. The heads of goats were sitting on countertops and hanging from hooks out in the open. The police asked the Muslim shop owners if they would keep the meat out of plain sight during the procession and wash down the animal blood stains along the street. The shop owners readily complied and the ground was swept clean.

The Day of the Procession

On December 6, SP Saigal and his team of senior officers were stationed along the district border. Barricades had been set up at the checkpoint where the procession was due to enter Bhimsen. Upon arrival, leaders of the procession were given the green light to pass through the district, but on the condition that everyone would follow the traffic plans laid out by the police. Importantly, the Bajrang Dal leader who had made the inflammatory speech circulating on WhatsApp was denied entry into Bhimsen, as per the DM's order. Notwithstanding the leader's protests, he was kept outside of the district.[20]

Back in Nusrat Ganj, I stood near the police *chowki*, observing as Civil and DAR officers lined up on both sides of the main road. News arrived that the procession was fast approaching. Shopkeepers began locking up their stores and putting down the shutters. A pair of sub-inspectors on motorcycle informed the NG Station SHO via radio that *"Sab band kar diye hain dukanen"* (All the shops have been closed) and took off to meet him at a checkpoint further down the road. The SHO from another police station arrived with backup. He led a group of DAR officers in riot gear up the main road, creating a formation around the Dargah. The procession's arrival could be heard from a distance. A large truck with "Bajrang Dal" painted on it led the way, carrying loudspeakers that blared songs celebrating Ram's arrival. Behind the truck was a long line of young men riding motorcycles, with orange *tilaks* on their foreheads, waving flags and cheering, *"Jai Shri Ram!"* (Victory to Ram). The procession's movement through Nusrat Ganj continued for more than hour. The truck inched ahead slowly, stopping at various points along the main road as the young men reveled to the music. Some men tried to move through police barricades into the residential alleys, but they were denied entry. *"Udar jaane mat do!"* (Don't let them go there!), an officer shouted to his colleagues.

Residents of Nusrat Ganj looked on from their windows as the crowd passed. Those who lived across from the Dargah maintained a close watch as well. Observing the procession from the police *chowki*, the sheer number of young men and their collective vitality was palpable to me. The police were vastly outnumbered in a narrow street. If the procession-goers ended up in a skirmish with Muslim residents, either willingly or by chance, the police would have had a difficult time maintaining order. The sheer density of the procession, which occupied the entire street from edge-to-edge—several young men grazed me as they road by in pairs on motorcycle—made it practically difficult for officers to reach the site of a potential skirmish. The last few motorcycles sped along and it appeared that the procession had passed through Nusrat Ganj without incident. An officer who stood beside me at the *chowki* turned to me and said, *"Ab thandi sahas lo!"* (Now take a breath of fresh air!).

I joined officers from NG Station to follow the procession. Our destination was the "Ram Lila Point," an open field near the district's edge. The designated endpoint for the procession, the VHP had organized an *aarti* (a ceremony of worship) for Ram, followed by the provision of food and tea for all the participants. While merriment continued among the crowd, I spoke with a VHP leader, who had planned the arrangements in advance with the police. He shared his perspective on the Ram Mandir movement: *"Ham kahte hain ki jab Modi aur Adityanaathji sarkar chala rahe hain, to Ram Mandir nirman aane wala hi hai. . . . Agar ab nahim hoga to kab hoga?"* (We say that since Modi and Adityanaath [the Chief Minister of UP] are running the government, the Ram Mandir will indeed be built. If it doesn't happen now, when will happen?). The VHP leader was clear about the political significance of the procession and the larger moment in India.

Following the completion of the rally at Ram Lila Point, we drove back to SP Saigal's office. During the car ride, a Muslim leader called to thank him for planning the procession. SP Saigal thanked him in return for his assistance: "*Aap ka sahyog hai, tab hi acche se nipat gaya.*" (We have your help, which is why it went off well.) He also asked the Muslim leader to share feedback on the police's work, which they agreed to discuss in person on another occasion.

Back in the SP's office, I looked on as a group of senior officers, SHOs, and sub-inspectors discussed the day's events. SP Saigal congratulated the officers on a job well done. He also asked them to comment on how the procession went and to give their feedback on any operational issues they experienced during the assignment. The ASP of Bhimsen remarked first that the police conducted a flag march the in Nusrat Ganj the day before, covering the full area, which effectively demonstrated their presence to the public. The NG Station SHO chimed in, noting that local-level intelligence was important and that by surveilling the area in advance, the police could prepare themselves and the community for the procession. Others pointed out how planning had begun far in advance and that the sharing of procession dates and traffic management plans was essential.

SP Saigal encouraged the officers to share negative points as well. An SHO commented on the lack of working radio sets, which made it difficult for field officers to follow what was going on as the procession advanced. Organizational gaps within the police were also identified. On this occasion, the ASP remarked, the DAR forces were called in advance and integrated well with the Civil Police. However, the coordination between the DAR and Civil Police force was often very weak. Likewise, a sub-inspector pointed out that, while the police benefited from the cooperation of residents and businesses in Nusrat Ganj, the level of community engagement could have been even greater. Officers, he noted, could not be physically present at every single point of the procession, which made it even more important to coordinate with local residents.

One may raise the question of whether my presence in Bhimsen as a researcher had an influence on police behaviors. For example, field officers were possibly more conscientious in applying conflict moderation techniques knowing that they were being observed. The notion that study participants may act differently if they believe they are being watched dates back to the classic Hawthorne experiments, a topic that has gained renewed interest as police agencies across the world face heightened demands for public accountability.[21] These concerns are valid, but in this case researcher presence likely had a limited effect on the observed behaviors of officers for several reasons. First, the preparations in Bhimsen were underway far in advance of my entry to the field site. I came to learn about police preparations in Bhimsen while researching a different topic (women's security) in another MP district. The field officers that I observed in Bhimsen had already established their presence within the community before my arrival in the district, which was evident from their interactions with shopkeepers and residents. Second, from interviews and informal conversations, I learned that senior and frontline police officers were overwhelmingly concerned about the actual risk of communal violence in the district as well as widespread media scrutiny on the day of the Babri Masjid anniversary. These factors likely swamped the possible influence of my presence in the field. Lastly, field research that I conducted of policing in other MP districts, covering various activities such as beat patrols and the routine intake of cases, suggests that officer behaviors are strongly shaped by hierarchical chain of command, notwithstanding the presence of researchers.[22]

It is notable as well that the police practices identified here, such as event planning and communication with residents and businesses, were not peculiar to this particular district or set of police officers. Across several Madhya Pradesh districts, I observed officers undertaking similar efforts to maintain public order and safety for large-scale events. In police parlance, these *"bandobast"* activities involved elaborate planning and arrangements. For example, during the annual Hindu festival of Rangpanchami, I observed senior police officers from Indore and surrounding districts coordinate to manage traffic movement and the safety of participants. Prior consultations were undertaken with citizens, including members of Village Security Committees (Gram Raksha Samitis), who spread messages encouraging safe behavior and helped monitor checkpoints to prevent public disturbances. Village residents were also recruited to oversee traffic and assist visitors with directions on how to navigate rural roads to reach the festival sites.

In sum, policing activities in Bhimsen complicate our understanding of how the police promote internal security in several ways. The steps taken to prevent communal tensions from escalating into violence—intelligence gathering and surveillance to anticipate threats, micro-level planning with communities, public displays of police force, traffic management, the protection of religious sites, and so on—were administratively complex and required intensive coordination among police subunits, between the police and civilian bureaucracy, as well as between frontline officers and communities.[23] Further, "law and order" was not simply maintained by the police but co-produced by a collaborative network of police officers, state officials, and societal actors.[24] The nature and robustness of co-production in this case depended in large part on the leadership and coordinating efforts of the district SP's office working in concert with mid-level officers, particularly SHOs and sub-inspectors. The efficacy of socially embedded policing practices was also contingent on field officers having clear guidance from above as well as the organizational capacity to plan and coordinate with society, which may not always exist. In the next section, I consider how the institutional constraints facing the police influence the provision of internal security more widely.

Revisiting the Institutional Context of Policing

Having examined how the police in Madhya Pradesh uphold public order through the case study of Bhimsen, this section explores the institutional context of policing and the constraints that agencies experience while managing internal security. Three interconnected themes are discussed: institutional design and capacity, police training and professionalization, and political interference. A lack of administrative resources has been identified as a chief impediment to policing in India.[25] Police agencies face acute shortages of personnel and equipment, such as vehicles, radios, and computers. India's officially reported ratio of 1.58 police officers per thousand population is low by global standards. If one excludes the State Armed Reserve Forces (SAF), a reserve contingent that does not engage in routine policing, India's effective ratio is 1.2 police officers per thousand population. Figure 10.1 shows the variation in this ratio across Indian states. The more populous "BIMARU" states (Bihar, Madhya Pradesh, Rajasthan, and UP) in northern India have significantly lower police to population ratios in comparison to rest of the country.

The lack of adequate human resources puts considerable pressure on district police agencies. As I observed in Madhya Pradesh, when law-and-order events surface, police station staff are expected to be available on demand. A recurring theme in interviews is that frontline officers reported having to drop whatever work they were doing to respond swiftly to law-and-order events. Even when they were immersed in crime investigation or answering citizen complaints, these activities

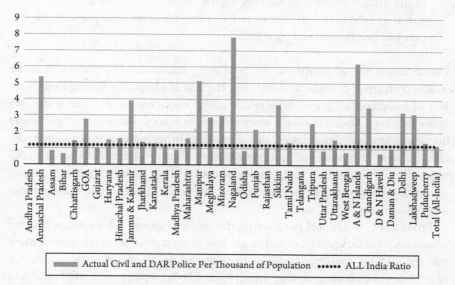

Figure 10.1 Police-to-population ratio across Indian states (per 1,000 persons)
Source: BPRD (2018). Population projections based on Census of India (2011).

were assigned lesser priority and had to be placed on hold. The expectation of being available for law-and-order duty made some officers less inclined to invest effort on citizen-centric tasks. As noted earlier, the Indian police's colonial setup prioritized collective order while downplaying the importance of crime control. The emphasis on law and order continued in democratic India as conflict between societal groups and electoral violence led to crises of governance.[26] Police constraints and pressures undercutting crime investigation are compounded by institutional weaknesses within the larger criminal justice system. India exhibits chronic delays in the dispensation of justice, evident from the backlog of cases, with the high courts reporting 5.8 million pending cases in 2020, a problem that appears to be growing each year. Other weaknesses in the "supply chain" of justice include a lack of coordination between the police and other agencies, as well as uneven prosecutorial effort, which give the police less incentive to allocate scarce resources toward crime-fighting.[27]

Interference from politicians is another impediment for crime investigation and the individual safety of citizens. In a focus group discussion with police constables, "political pressure" (*rajnetik dabav*) was cited as one of the top two reasons why crimes against women were poorly addressed by the police. To illustrate, a constable described how political pressure operated within the policy hierarchy:

> The *neta* [whose son was accused of harassing a woman] is an influential person in the area. He runs the local bus service. The SHO got a call from the *neta* not to pursue *karvai* (action) against his son. Then the SHO [who was away from the *thana* when the girl reported the harassment] called us in the middle of the investigation, saying "*unko chordo*" [let the fugitive go]. If he [the SHO] didn't call to intervene, we could have pursued the case and had the accused punished.[28]

Other officers shared similar narratives of being undermined by politicians in the course of an arrest or crime investigation. The lack of adequate personnel and operational resources (e.g., vehicles) was the second major reason given for ineffective crime fighting. Officers in charge of investigations reported having to stop midway because of law-and-order duties, VIP duties, and other high-priority assignments. Officers were also observed working twelve-to-fourteen-hour shifts on law-and-order duty, with minimal rest, placing stress on their personal health.[29] Several officers reported having to use their own private funds to pay for petrol during routine policing work.

From an organizational perspective, the resource constraints in police stations resembles what Dasgupta and Kapur observe in their study of block development officers (BDOs), local functionaries in charge of development programs. A lack of personnel and resources, they argue, leads BDOs to perform "firefighting" and responding to particularistic issues, which crowds out attention toward managerial tasks and programmatic policy implementation. A similar pattern of managerial overload emerges from ethnographic field research conducted in police stations. The station house officer (SHO), who heads the police station, is responsible for multiple, complex tasks. Moreover, the SHO is accountable to multiple principals, including the district SP, other senior officers, elected officials, unelected leaders, citizens, and the media. External pressures and law-and-order events allow less time for managerial tasks, such as the delegation of staff duties. In twelve police stations across three districts, I observed the SHO lead the morning *ganana*, the daily lineup and briefing of station officers. During this customary interaction, the SHO outlined the main policing tasks and priorities for the day. After a few minutes, the SHO would conclude by asking the subordinate officers if they had any doubts or questions. In all twelve stations, not once did I observe a subordinate officer raise questions or seek clarification from the SHO. Several constables perceived the allocation of field assignments as arbitrary, disconnected from the actual skills or preferences of individual officers.

The paucity of managerial oversight and support stems not simply from the lack of police personnel but also from the skewed hierarchical composition of India's police forces (Figure 10.2). With some differences between states, recruitment into the police happens at four rank-wise entry points: (1) constable; (2) sub-inspector (SI); (3) deputy superintendent of police (DSP); and (4) additional superintendent of police (ASP). The recruitment for ASPs happens through national-level IPS selection, whereas DSP and SI recruitment occurs through statewide selection into the State Police Service (SPS). Both the IPS and SPS have rigorous selection criteria. Recruits have to undertake competitive examinations administered by the Union Public Service Commission and similar professional bodies at the state level. However, the rigor and professional oversight of selection declines as one moves down the hierarchy. The recruitment of constables is comparatively more open to manipulation and bribery, as some police officers noted the "going rates" for positions. At the lower ranks of the organization, constables make up 65 percent of the police force, with another 19.4 percent consisting of head constables.[30] These officers perform critical internal security functions, such as patrolling and surveillance, guarding vital installations, and law-and-order duties, though they do not have authority to conduct crime investigation.[31] The middle ranks, which account for 13 percent of the force, consist of officers with investigative authority. Less than

Senior Ranks (IPS)					Upper-Middle Ranks (SPS)		Middle Ranks (Investigating Officers)			Lower Ranks (Constabulary)		
% DGP	% ADGP	% IGP	%DIG	% AIGP/SSP/SP	% Addl. SP/Dy. Comm	% ASP/Dy. SP	% Inspector	% Sub-Inspector	% Ass. Sub-Inspector	% Head Constable	% Constable	% Others If any
0.01	0.02	0.02	0.02	0.14	0.12	0.54	1.77	6.14	5.63	19.38	65.04	1.18

Figure 10.2 Rank-wise distribution of state police forces
Source: BPRD (2018). Calculated as percentage of actual police personnel strength.

1 percent of the police force consists of officers in the upper-middle tiers of the hierarchy. India has 3,798 IPS officers filling the senior ranks of the police, though more than 10 percent of them are on deputation with the central government. IPS officers hold the post of district SP for a few years before moving to higher-level posts, often away from direct contact with the field. The "middle management" of the Indian police has gained little attention within existing scholarship. These officers belong to the SPS cadres and spend most of their careers in the field, where they supervise subdivisions, or clusters of stations, known as "circles." They are a chief conduit of information and oversight between the senior ranks and police stations.

Taking the rank-wise composition of the police into account gives a fuller picture of capacity constraints within the police and their likely impact on the provision of internal security. Personnel shortages are indicated by the overall vacancy rate of 25 percent, calculated as the percentage of sanctioned posts that are unfilled. The constabulary, which comprises 85 percent of the police force, accounts for the majority of vacant posts. However, the rate of vacancy among higher-ranked officers is even greater, at almost 30 percent. Vacancies in the middle and upper-middle ranks are particularly problematic since officers in these posts are in charge of vital law enforcement duties, such as crime registration. They also perform key managerial functions, such as planning and monitoring events, leading investigations and judicial procedures, overseeing police stations and sub-divisions, and supervising junior officers. Constables also make vital contributions to internal security, as they are close to the ground and in regular touch with communities. However, the police hierarchy grants constables little autonomy over their work, which creates the need for direction and oversight by the SHO.

Why do high vacancy rates persist among the police? One set of explanations suggests that police understaffing is motivated by the criminal tendencies of politicians.[32] Elected leaders with criminal backgrounds may discourage the growth of police professionalism, autonomy, and organizational capacity.[33] For example, politicians may choose to stall the recruitment of police officers to help maintain the flow of illegal rents, or they may prevent rival social groups from gaining employment in the police. If politicians cannot control which ethnic groups get hired, as a second-best option they may block hiring altogether. Some refer to the latter scenario as "state incapacity by design," exemplified in the case of Bihar under the Lalu Yadav government, which actively blocked the filling of vacant police posts over several years.[34]

Amid personnel constraints, it bears mentioning that the recruitment of women into the police has gained heightened attention from state police forces. As illustrated in Figure 10.3, the proportion of women officers in the force has more than doubled to 9 percent in the decade leading to 2018, albeit from a very low baseline. The increase reflects the growing political recognition that crimes against women are a public security concern. Central and state governments in India have undertaken high-profile efforts to improve the police's responsiveness to women,

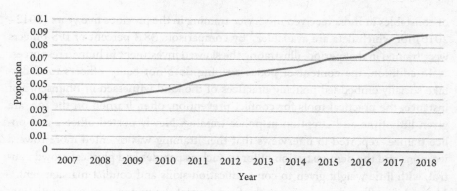

Figure 10.3 Proportion of women in the Indian police force
Source: BPRD Police Statistical Yearbook (various years)

including administrative quotas to hire more female officers, dedicated women's police vehicles to patrol hot spots, Women's Help Lines, and "Mahila Thanas" (all-women police stations). To what extent these interventions are effective in addressing crimes against women is an open question, but they signal important shifts in policy and administration. While hiring women itself is a worthwhile objective, questions remain as to how far women are integrated and supported within the mainstream police force, which overwhelmingly consists of men.

The growing presence of women officers marks an ongoing shift in the composition of India's police agencies. However, the number of personnel overall remains inadequate. To be sure, public administration in India is understaffed across various policy functions, particularly frontline, citizen-oriented services.[35] Within the police, personnel shortages raise particular questions, such as why the armed and reserve police forces have seen such a high proportion of posts filled. The SAF alone accounts for 24 percent of state police forces. These officers remain on guard but do not undertake regular policing duties. One possible explanation is that politicians prefer armed forces since they are more easily controlled by political actors. The armed police are separated from the command structure of Civil Police Forces; the latter are overseen by the police bureaucracy and integrated with local society.

Police capacity constraints are likely amplified by the organizational structure and training of officers. The police abide by a strict, militaristic hierarchy, which provides for a clear chain of command. Although robust hierarchy can be an organizational asset, as observed in the case of Bhimsen, it also carries liabilities. For example, excessive hierarchy can accentuate the social distance between senior police officers (the IPS in particular) and the lower-level constabulary. Constables occupy the frontlines during law-and-order situations and interact regularly with the public. Yet, they have little autonomy to make decisions and receive the least investment in training and professional development. A recent report found that only 6.4 percent of constables in India received in-service training in the previous five years (2012–2016) for which data are available.[36] By comparison, 38.3 percent of IPS officers were trained in that period, illustrating the skewed investment in human resources.

In addition, the content of police training does not equip officers to undertake socially embedded policing practices of the kind witnessed in Bhimsen. For instance, the practical tools for conflict prevention, often learned on the job, are given little time and attention in police training. Newly posted officers and police trainees reported in interviews that their training was oriented more toward weapons and the demonstration of force, such as parades and physical crowd control, with little weight given to communication skills and conflict management.[37] Meanwhile, officer experiences in the field suggest the importance of negotiation, which is an essential skill for community-oriented policing.[38] Police constables receive little, if any, formal training on conflict prevention and de-escalation. These and other deficiencies were identified by the Gore Committee, whose 1971 report suggested the need for officers to receive more training on communication, conflict resolution, and other "soft skills." However, state governments are yet to adopt these recommendations. Adding to gaps in training, the local institutional memory for socially embedded policing by district offices and police stations is made weaker due to frequent transfers of officers.

Finally, the police often do not receive advance warning of internal security threats. These occasions heighten the risk of public disorder and give those who seek to instigate violence the upper hand. When the opportunity for police agencies to plan and coordinate with other departments and societal groups is missing, they become more prone to using physical force and violent control measures.[39] These occasions are precisely when police training on violence prevention, negotiation, de-escalation, and "community policing" practices are useful. As a sub-inspector explained: "*Prevention ki analysis aksar nahim hoti hai. Jab hoti hai, tab ham traffic aur tamam chizon ki dekhbal karte sakte hain. . . . Ham chahte hain ki tatkal jagah pahuchen aur chote star pe muda solve ho jai. Jo primary baat hai, voh secondary baat na ban jaye.*"[40] (Translation: The analysis for prevention [of conflict] often is not conducted. We [the police] endeavor to arrive to the scene immediately and nip small problems in the bud, so that a "primary" [small] issue does not escalate into a "secondary" [larger, communal] issue). As this officer further remarked, the police cannot rely on the "*pistol and latthi*" to disburse crowds, but instead, "need to find support from within the crowd."[41]

Conclusion

This chapter has explored the possibilities and limitations for Indian police forces in managing internal security, based on a combination of field-based evidence, historical sources, and administrative data. The case of Bhimsen suggests that, where given the opportunity, the police can mobilize to prevent violence between communal groups. The elements of an effective response reflected socially embedded policing tactics. These tactics involved intensive coordination between the district SP's office, local police stations, and neighborhood residents. The findings suggest that shared professional commitment to public order guides policing activities. However, gaps in administrative capacity and other constraints make it more challenging to sustain socially embedded policing practices. The paucity of resources and personnel makes it difficult to ensure that trained officers will reach a situation in time to mitigate conflict. As Jauregui's study of the police in Uttar Pradesh demonstrates, police authority is "provisional," left contingent on the local circumstances of policing as well as the nature of societal involvement.[42]

Beyond recognizing the contingencies of policing, this chapter has identified systematic features of police organizations in India that support (and constrain) officers as they work to preserve internal security. Some of these features, such as personnel shortages, have long been apparent from administrative data. Others, such as the quantity and content of police training, require far more research. To what extent police training can encourage the adoption of socially embedded policing practices remains an open question. On the other hand, the police hierarchy provides a strong glue that binds the organization and establishes a chain of command, which in turn makes it possible for the police to address collective violence, even with limited personnel and training. Investigating how organizational capacity, hierarchy, and training interact in the performance of different policing tasks is a fruitful avenue for future research.

This chapter also noted the ways in which the police attempt to work around political constraints. In the case of Bhimsen, senior police officials and frontline officers were aligned on the objective of preventing violence and motivated by a shared aversion to negative media scrutiny. These shared motivations, supported by hierarchical chain of command, acted as a critical bulwark against those instigating collective violence against minorities. The findings from Bhimsen, of police professionalism and aversion to risk, also raise questions about how political interference operates in India and when it leads to breakdowns in public order and collective violence. If police chain of command is strong and centralized, as observed to be the case in Madhya Pradesh, then political interference would seem likely to target the highest levels of the police organization. Moreover, if politicians continually interfere in decision-making by senior police officers, it behooves us to ask what impact these interferences have on frontline officers in the field, and whether the latter can maintain a professional demeanor toward citizens.

The chapter has focused on collective violence, but the security of individual citizens is of equal importance. In that regard, I have noted that the Indian police's institutional tendency toward law-and-order duty supersedes crime prevention and investigation, and thus may come at the expense of individual citizen security. Future research may investigate how different policing functions and tasks get prioritized as well as the possible trade-offs between upholding collective and individual security, especially within resource-constrained police agencies. And finally, while observations and perspectives of police officers provided important data for this chapater, future research should also incorporate citizens' experiences and perspectives to develop a fuller account of internal security.

Notes

1. James Q. Wilson, *Varieties of Police Behavior: The Management of Law and Order in Eight Communities* (Cambridge, MA: Harvard University Press, 1978); Mark Moore, "Problem-Solving and Community Policing," *Crime and Justice* 15 (1992): 99–158.
2. Joe Soss and Vesla Weaver, "Police Are Our Government: Politics, Political Science, and the Policing of Race–Class Subjugated Communities," *Annual Review of Political Science* 20, no. 1 (2017): 565–591, https://doi.org/10.1146/annurev-polisci-060415-093825.
3. Atul Kohli, *Imperialism and the Developing World: How Britain and the United States Shaped the Global Periphery* (New York: Oxford University Press, 2019).
4. David H. Bayley, Police and Political Development in India (Princeton, NJ: Princeton University Press, 1969); David Arnold, "The Police and Colonial Control in South India," *Social Scientist* 4, no. 12 (1976): 3–16.
5. On May 10, 1857, Indian officers in the British East India Company army carried out an uprising in Meerut, a garrison town in western Uttar Pradesh (UP). Peasant rebellions spread over northern and central India. See Thomas R. Metcalf, *Aftermath of Revolt: India 1857–1970* (Princeton, NJ: Princeton University Press, 1964).
6. Variations on this model have existed throughout India. For example, the urban presidency towns of Madras, Bombay, and Calcutta adopted the police commissioner system.
7. The police structure adopted in India followed the Irish policing model, which emphasized accountability to rulers rather than local communities, the separation of the police from the civilian population, and the use of paramilitary arrangements to suppress peasant rebellions. The design of colonial policing in India was at odds with the approach of the Metropolitan Police in London, which aimed to build trust with local communities. See Dilip Das and Arvind Verma, "The Armed Police in the British Colonial Tradition," *Policing: An International Journal of Police Strategies & Management* 21, no. 2 (1998): 354–367.
8. Arvind Verma and K. S. Subramanian, *Understanding the Police in India*, 2nd ed. (Gurgaon: LexisNexis, 2014), 37.
9. Gyanesh Kudaisya, *Region, Nation, "Heartland": Uttar Pradesh in India's Body Politic* (New Delhi: Sage, 2006), 50–58.
10. The Central Armed Police Forces under the MHA have several branches, including the Central Reserve Police Force (CRPF), Central Industrial Security Force (CISF), Border Security Force (BSF), Indo-Tibetan Border Police (ITBP), and the National Security Guard (NSG).
11. Communication gaps between the IPS and constabulary was a recurring theme from my interviews with police officers from across the hierarchy in Madhya Pradesh.
12. Steven Wilkinson, *Votes and Violence: Electoral Competition and Ethnic Riots in India* (New York: Cambridge University Press, 2006), http://books.google.com/books?id=tLpRF bLSxvAC.
13. A. Varshney, *Ethnic Conflict and Civic Life: Hindus and Muslims in India* (New Haven, CT: Yale University Press, 2002).
14. Bhimsen is a pseudonym for the district. The names of locations, police stations, officers, and other individuals have been altered to protect the anonymity of research participants.
15. Wilkinson, *Votes and Violence*.

16. Interviews with local business owners, November 2017.
17. "Tight Security in Ayodhya on Anniversary of Babri Mosque Demolition," *The Times of India*, December 5, 2018, https://timesofindia.indiatimes.com/india/tight-security-in-ayodhya-on-anniversary-of-babri-mosque-demolition/articleshow/66956931.cms.
18. Interviews with senior police officials, Bhopal, November 2017.
19. Interview with frontline officers, November 2017.
20. Interviews with senior officers stationed at the border, November 2017.
21. There is growing interest in policing research on the use of body-worn cameras and whether it produces a Hawthorne effect on officer behavior. See, e.g., David Yokum, Anita Ravishankar, and Alexander Coppock, "A Randomized Control Trial Evaluating the Effects of Police Body-Worn Cameras," *Proceedings of the National Academy of Sciences* 116, no. 21 (2019): 10329–10332.
22. Akshay Mangla and Vineet Kapoor, "The Police in India: Institutional Design, Capacity and Performance," Working Paper. University of Oxford, 2021.
23. State capacity for undertaking complex tasks is theorized in Matt Andrews, Lant Pritchett, and Michael Woolcock, *Building State Capabilities* (Oxford: Oxford University Press, 2017).
24. Elinor Ostrom, "Crossing the Great Divide: Coproduction, Synergy, and Development," *World Development* 24, no. 6 (1996): 1073–1087, https://doi.org/10.1016/0305-750x(96)00023-x.
25. Arvind Verma, *The Indian Police: A Critical Evaluation* (New Delhi: Regency, 2005); Tata Trusts, *India Justice Report* (New Delhi: Tata Trusts, 2019); CSDS, *Status of Policing in India Report 2019: Police Adequacy and Working Conditions*, Common Cause and CSDS Lokniti Program (New Delhi: Common Cause, 2019).
26. A. Kohli, *Democracy and Discontent: India's Growing Crisis of Governability* (New York: Cambridge University Press, 1990).
27. Devesh Kapur and Milan Vaishnav, "Strengthening the Rule of Law," in *Getting India Back on Track: An Action Agenda for Reform*, ed. Bibek Debroy, Ashley J. Tellis, and Reece Trevor (New Delhi: Random House, 2014), 247–263.
28. Respondent 3, Focus group discussion with Constables, Bhopal, April 2017.
29. In the Police Training Academy in Bhopal, a psychologist was hired to assist with the growing stress and mental health issues reported by newly recruited police officers.
30. BPRD, *Data on Police Organizations in India* (New Delhi: Bureau of Police Research and Development, Government of India, 2019).
31. Some states give head constables the authority to investigate minor crimes.
32. Milan Vaishnav, *When Crime Pays: Money and Muscle in Indian Politics* (New Haven, CT: Yale University Press, 2017).
33. As Kapur and Vaishnav suggest, "If there is one principle that unites Indian politicians, it is that a competent, autonomous police force is a threat to their common interests." Kapur and Vaishnav, "Strengthening the Rule of Law," 253.
34. Santhosh Mathew and Mick Moore, "State Incapacity by Design: Understanding the Bihar Story," *IDS Working Papers*, no. 366 (2011).
35. Devesh Kapur, "Why Does the Indian State Both Fail and Succeed?," *Journal of Economic Perspectives* 34, no. 1 (2020): 31–54.
36. CSDS, *Status of Policing in India Report 2019*, 23.
37. Also see Vineet Kapoor, "Human Rights Education and Role Orientation of the Police in Democracy" (PhD thesis, Tata Institute of Social Sciences, 2018).
38. Interviews conducted with police trainees in Madhya Pradesh (May 2017–December 2018).
39. A recent example is police enforcement of the government lockdown imposed for Covid-19.
40. Interview with sub-inspector, November 2017.
41. Ibid.
42. Beatrice Jauregui, *Provisional Authority: Police, Order, and Security in India* (Chicago: University of Chicago Press, 2016).

11

Riots and Rapid Action

The Special Wing of the Central Reserve Police

NIRVIKAR JASSAL AND HANIF QURESHI

A number of nations have established security institutions to quell internal riots or riot-like situations. France's Mobile Gendarmerie, Japan's Kidō-tai, Germany's Bereitschaftspolizei, and Israel's Yasam are such "rapid" units whose goal is to, among others, support the civilian police in quelling civil disorders and unrest. India established its own anti-riot body in 1991: the Rapid Action Force. The assumption underpinning the body's creation was that existing institutions designed to tackle internal violence or insurgency were becoming increasingly overstretched.

In the mid-twentieth century, after India gained independence, the government decided to retain and rename what was called the Crown Representative's Police (1939–1949). This centralized police force, now known as the Central Reserve Police Force (CRPF), would allow the federal government to play a coordinating and counseling role in matters concerning law enforcement, including the ability to establish secondary police organizations that could intervene within states to ensure public order. Sardar Vallabhbhai Patel argued in Parliament that India needed such a centralized force, especially since the nation was retaining a system in which law and order would otherwise be a state subject.[1] Patel argued that, in a period of transition and political upheaval, a centralized force would serve to lower cross-border tension as well as militate against local actors creating "unrest" to "better their own prospects."[2]

By the 1980s, Patel's point was as valid as in 1949; India remained in a "period of transition," and inter-group conflict, insurgency, and secessionism had, if anything, intensified.[3] Local actors, including political elites, used communal violence as a means to advance their own interests.[4] The CRPF, the only Central Armed Police Force (CAPF) with a mandate to assist states (and union territories) in policing operations, was (1) overstretched in tackling the Khalistan movement as well as the violence in Jammu and Kashmir; and (2) had suffered a crisis of legitimacy in its perceived heavy-handedness in those settings.[5] Consequently, the Congress Party

Nirvikar Jassal and Hanif Qureshi, *Riots and Rapid Action* In: *Internal Security in India*. Edited by: Amit Ahuja and Devesh Kapur, Oxford University Press. © Oxford University Press 2023. DOI: 10.1093/oso/9780197660331.003.0011 deliberated over a new, more agile force, that would tackle a very specific variety of conflict, that is, riots and mob violence in the heartland (rather than at the borders). When Narasimha Rao first publicly announced the creation of a new anti-riot body, he did so on the same day that the Congress would offer support for a Ram temple in Ayodhya—a site that would, ironically, later become a major test for his new anti-riot body.[6]

This descriptive chapter attempts to highlight the organization and functioning of the Rapid Action Force or RAF. Broadly, we argue that the RAF faces several challenges—potentially applicable to other Indian security agencies—that may moderate its agility. These challenges include logistical hurdles, a lack of coordination between the Center and states, and political considerations that make governments hesitant about seeking assistance from the RAF. The essay is structured as follows: the section "Organization and Autonomy" describes the organization and hierarchy within which the Force operates, while in "Agility" we use data from the Armed Conflict Location & Event Data Project (ACLED) database to gain a measure of the distance personnel must travel to address a riot. In "Deployments and Constraints," we use the *Times of India* archive to shed light on where the Force has been deployed. In the section on the "Rapid Action Force," we present a brief case study of the Force's deployment during the 2016 Haryana reservation agitation. In the "Discussion" section, we offer concluding remarks while simultaneously highlighting avenues for future research.

Organization and Autonomy

Though law and order is a state subject, the procedure to disperse an unlawful assembly by a civil force is outlined in Section 129 of the Criminal Procedure Code (Cr.P.C.). Under this section, an executive magistrate or officer-in-charge of a police station (e.g., station house officer) may command any unlawful assembly to disperse, and even use force if the command is not obeyed. While the term "civil force" refers to the police, "armed force" falls in the same category.[7] In *Akhilesh Prasad v. Union Territory of Mizoram* (1981), the Supreme Court ruled that the CRPF and other paramilitary forces are indeed "armed forces."

One of these "armed forces," a subsidiary of the CRPF, is the Rapid Action Force or RAF. Data from government reports and answers to parliamentary questions reveal that the Rapid Action Force represents just 1.6 percent of the total paramilitary forces, and 5 percent of the CRPF.[8] While the CRPF is deployed to counteract cross-border terrorism and insurgency in the Red Corridor, North East, and Jammu and Kashmir, the Rapid Action Force is supposed to be deployed largely *outside* those three contexts. Yet, the boundaries between the RAF and the CRPF are highly fluid. The RAF was created after ten CRPF battalions (approximately 1,000 personnel) were simply repurposed and called Rapid Action Force in 1992; this trend continued in 2018 when Battalion Number 114 of the CRPF based at Jalandhar, Punjab, was converted to RAF whereby CRPF personnel simply started wearing blue uniforms.

Organizationally, the RAF is run by one of the CRPF's several inspector generals. Each of the Rapid Action Force's three ranges (Delhi, Mumbai, and Dehradun) houses five battalions (Figure 11.1). One battalion of RAF consists of four companies and has an authorized strength of a little over 1,000 personnel. (A battalion in the CRPF consists of 1,141 personnel, while this number is 1,229 for the RAF.) An RAF battalion is run by a commandant. Each company is commanded by a deputy commandant, has four gazetted officers (GOs),[9] and has an authorized strength of 222 personnel organized into two platoons. Each platoon is commanded by an assistant commandant, has an authorized strength of 97 personnel, and is organized into two teams. Each team is headed by an inspector and consists of an authorized strength of twenty-four. The operational strength of a company, platoon, and team is approximately 120, 60, and 15 respectively. The remaining personnel are required for administrative work, communications, and other duties (Table 11.1). The usual deployment orders from the Ministry of Home Affairs refer to the number of "companies" to be dispatched to a riot-like situation. Once a company reaches a location, the company commander may use his two platoons as per the need of the situation. One platoon consists of four teams, which is the smallest operational unit in the RAF. A team's operational strength comprises three elements: riot control, tear gas, and fire. In other words, in each team, one unit has a *lathi*/cane shield, a second operates with shells/gas, and another with guns.

Every year, 25 percent of the RAF personnel are rotated to the CRPF, drawing an equivalent number of officers from the CRPF to the RAF. The tenure of a CRPF officer in the RAF is usually four years, which, under very special circumstances, can be extended by two years. The ranks in the RAF are like those in the Central Armed Police Forces. The ranks begin from constable and ascend to head constable, assistant sub-inspector, sub-inspector, inspector, assistant commandant, deputy commandant, commandant, deputy inspector general, and inspector general.[10] The junior ranks (up to sub-inspector) are recruited through the Staff Selection Commission (a statutory body created specifically for the purpose).[11] The assistant commandants are recruited by the Union Public Service Commission (and through promotion from junior ranks),[12] whereas the senior ranks of deputy inspector-general and above are promoted from within the CRPF or are drawn from the Indian Police Service.[13]

Some argue that multiple levels of recruitment and the tenure of four years does not allow for institutional loyalty to emerge. Indeed, the Rapid Action Force is *not* an autonomous institution; it is a brief posting for CRPF officials. In other words, by the time culture of the RAF is imbibed by personnel, their tenure in the institution may already be coming to an end. This situation is distinct from other organizations like the Rashtriya Rifles and Assam Rifles, whose troops are drawn from the

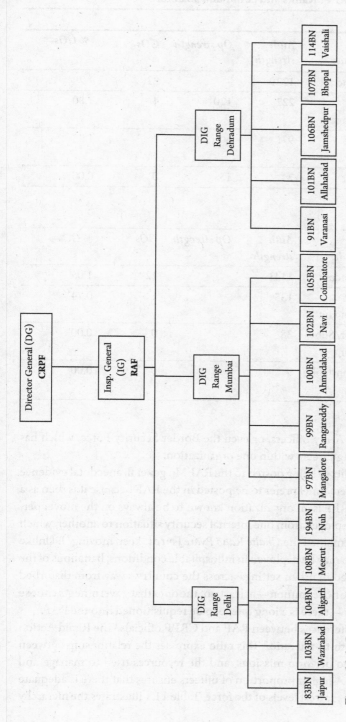

Figure 11.1 Organizational structure of Rapid Action Force (under CRPF)

Table 11.1 **RAF vs. CRPF: Ranks and command structure**

RAF

Unit	Rank of commander	Auth strength	Op strength	GOs	% GOs
Battalion	Commandant	1229	–	22	1.79
Company	Deputy Commandant	222	120	4	1.80
Platoon	Assistant Commandant	97	60	1	1.03
Team	Inspector	24	15	0	0.00

CRPF

Unit	Rank of commander	Auth strength	Op strength	GOs	% GOs
Battalion	Commandant	1141		12	1.05
Company	Assistant Commandant	135		1	0.74
Platoon	Inspector/Sub Inspector	38		0	0.00
Section	Head Constable/ ASI	9		0	0.00

Army and are run by Army officers, or even the Border Security Force, which has personnel with lifelong careers within one organization.

What are the benefits of being posted to the RAF? In general, anecdotal evidence suggests that CRPF personnel prefer to be posted in the RAF because it is seen as a "soft" posting. The CRPF is an organization known to be always on the move; personnel are typically deployed from one internal security situation to another, which is why the body is nicknamed the *Chalte Raho Pyare Force* ("keep moving"). Unlike CRPF personnel, who may be deployed in inhospitable conditions, battalions of the RAF are usually posted in urban settings across the country, away from disturbed areas. Because riots are not common—at least not the ones that governments choose to deploy the RAF for—there is a long queue to be requisitioned into the RAF.

There are other differences between RAF and CRPF officials. The Rapid Action Force has a high "tooth-to-tail ratio." This ratio expresses the relationship between the forces deployed to perform missions, and the resources used to manage and support those forces. A higher proportion of officers ensures that there is adequate supervision even at the lowest levels of the force. Table 11.1 illustrates the hierarchy as well as the number of officers per unit of the RAF versus the CRPF. Considering the battalion as a whole, the RAF has 22 gazetted officers (GOs) (1.79 percent) for 1,229 personnel, whereas the CRPF has 12 GOs (1.05 percent) for 1,141 personnel. Similarly, at the company level, the RAF has 4 GOs (1.8 percent), while the CRPF has only 1 GO (0.74 percent). Finally, a platoon is commanded by an officer (assistant commandant) in the RAF, unlike the CRPF where an inspector or sub-inspector (not a GO) commands a platoon.

Another distinction is that RAF officials, compared to the CRPF, get an extra forty-five days of "conversion" training. In order to avail of an extra 15 percent allowance for being deputed to the RAF, officials have to pass an exam that tests them on operating non-lethal weapons (e.g., rubber bullets, stun grenades, armored vehicle carriers, specialized water cannons) and legal provisions of the Cr.P.C.[14]

When created, an explicit goal of the Rapid Action Force was that it be representative of the broader population, and therefore less likely to be seen as partisan.[15] Yet, data on the representation of minorities in the RAF is scarce. Based on formal answers to questions posed by ministers in Parliament, the representation of minorities (Muslims), Scheduled Castes, and Scheduled Tribes was 17.79 percent, 13.64 percent, and 4.76 percent in 1995–1996.[16] Yet, subsequent answers reveal that the representation of Muslims in the Rapid Action Force declined to 10.93 percent in 1999 to just 5.08 percent in 2004.[17] In 2014, data were provided that outlined the percentage of *incoming* minorities among the cohort of CRPF recruits, but not the total percentage in the organization. Nevertheless, the Rapid Action Force *is* unique in the context of representation for women. The CRPF began a women's battalion in 1986, and six such battalions exist today. Yet, the total representation for women in the CRPF remains less than 2 percent; instead, the presence of women in the Rapid Action Force is—because of a rule mandating that each RAF battalion have at least 96 female officers—close to 10 percent.[18] And so, while the CRPF has separate women battalions, each RAF *company* has at least twenty-four women. However, more research needs to be undertaken as to whether women perform the same roles as men, or whether they face constraints by supervisors and peers when implementing riot control.[19]

Agility

One point made repeatedly in journalistic accounts is the extended period that paramilitary forces—*including* the Rapid Action Force—take to arrive at a hotspot. Some suggest that the Rapid Action Force may not be as agile as was initially intended because battalions are based in only fifteen locations of the country. During the Mumbai terror attacks, for instance, critics questioned whether the Rapid Action Force was truly "rapid" if it took seven hours for personnel to arrive, or forty hours after the demolition of the Babri Masjid.[20] For precisely this reason, Bihar was (in October 2018) permitted a permanent base for RAF troops in Vaishali. Prior to the Vaishali base, the closest RAF battalion that could be deployed to Bihar was based in Jamshedpur, Jharkhand, or Allahabad, Uttar Pradesh.[21]

The organization ACLED has, since 2016, been recording cases of protests and riots across India based on a variety of (English-language) newspapers. ACLED defines riots as "violent events where demonstrators of mobs engage in disruptive acts."[22] Using these data, we attempted to gain a measure for "distance," that is, on average, how far each riot or communal clash takes place from a Rapid Action Force headquarter. We geocode all the instances of rioting in the ACLED database as well as the RAF headquarters. As the left panel in Figure 11.2 reveals, most disturbances took place in Jammu and Kashmir and Punjab in the north, Assam and West Bengal in the east, and Kerala in the south.

Of course, there are challenges with giving equal weightage to every instance of rioting mentioned in the ACLED database. The RAF is *not* the first responder for riots and mob violence, and it would likely be called out in the more dangerous or high-sensitive areas. Therefore, in the right panel of Figure 11.2, we subset the data by looking at only those areas that had one casualty or more from 2016 to 2019. Using the longitude/latitude of the approximately 3,000 unique locations in India where riots took place, as well as the location of the fifteen headquarters, we can calculate the distance a battalion or company must travel. A Rapid Action Force company must travel, on average, roughly 250 km to reach a hotspot from its closest base.

In a country the size of India, it is likely that fifteen battalions cannot cover large distances on road. According to the Rapid Action Force standard operating procedure, the area of responsibility for a battalion stretches to a radius of 400 km. Yet, because the RAF personnel may often have to travel to a hotspot by road, challenges emerge when agitators block highways (as was the case in the 2016 Haryana reservation agitation; see section below). One solution to this problem could be the one used by the National Security Guards—the anti-terror specialized agency of the Government of India—which has access to transport aircraft of the Indian Air Force. Our qualitative interviews suggests that the RAF do not have designated choppers at strategic locations to support personnel deployment.

The ACLED data also reveal other aspects about riots in India. First, as illustrated in Figure 11.3, most *fatalities* related to riots from 2016 to 2019 took place in Jammu and Kashmir, West Bengal, and Haryana. West Bengal and Punjab were also the states that were among the most likely to see riots. Then again, in Figure 11.4—which highlights *where* the Rapid Action Force has been deployed based on information from the *Times of India* rather than ACLED—we find that West Bengal and Punjab are *not* the top five states that the RAF was most frequently deployed to. While Jammu and Kashmir violence is largely the CRPF's domain, the data raise a puzzle as to why West Bengal, for instance, is not the site for more frequent RAF deployments.

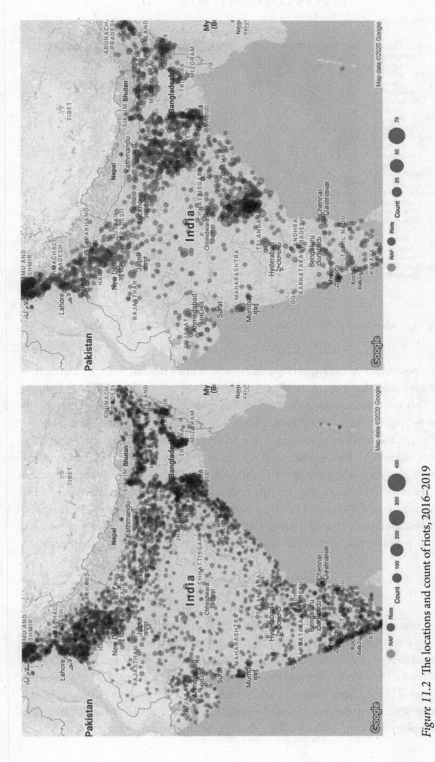

Figure 11.2 The locations and count of riots, 2016–2019

Left: The location and count of riots (and riot-like events) recorded in the ACLED database from 2016–2019. *Right*: The location and count of riots recorded in the ACLED database with 1 casualty or more (N=3,896).

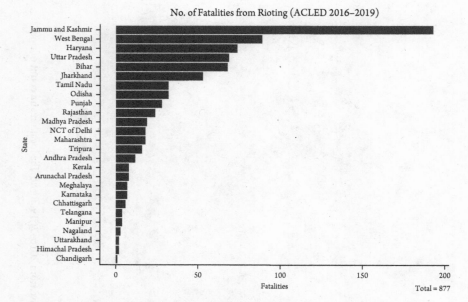

Figure 11.3 Casualties, by state, from riot-like events in the ACLED database

One possibility is that regional parties—which must request RAF deployment—may be reticent about doing so for political reasons, or simply in effort to demonstrate that law and order is a state issue. It is also possible that state governments refuse to request the Rapid Action Force when groups allied with their own political party are involved in clashes.[23] The federal government may also be anxious about sending RAF forces when non-allied regional parties are in power in states. Interestingly, when using the ACLED database to understand which groups/actors most are involved in riots, we find that political parties are particularly likely to be involved; and so, the fact that political parties or their breakaway groups are invariably associated with clashes echoes social science research about how communal conflicts could be perpetuated or supported by political actors for strategic gains.[24]

Deployments and Constraints

While researchers have collected data on riots in India, there is no available source that outlines where, when, and how many Rapid Action Force personnel have been deployed. For this reason, we construct a dataset using ProQuest Historical and LexisNexis to find all mentions of the "Rapid Action Force" from 1992 to present in the *Times of India*. Using this approach, we find that of the roughly 800 mentions of the institution in articles, most describe the RAF engaged in VIP or *bandobast* duties (e.g., deployed annually to Ayodhya during the anniversary of the Babri Masjid

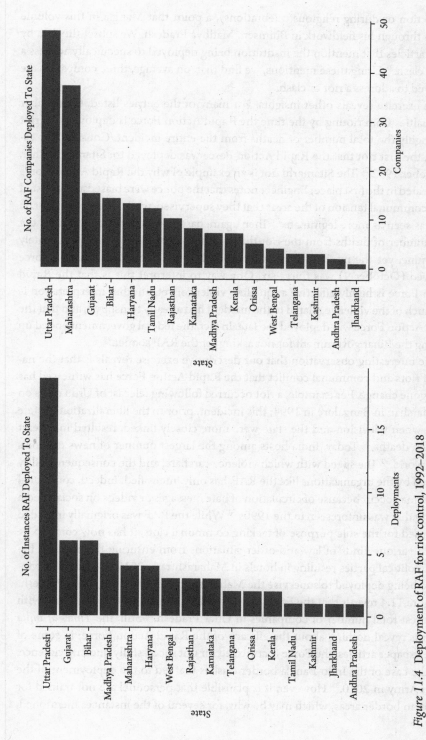

Figure 11.4 Deployment of RAF for riot control, 1992–2018

This figure is an approximation of the number of times (left) as well as the number of Rapid Action Force companies (right) that have been deployed in the state (based on *Times of India* articles from 1992–2018) for riots, mob violence, or ethnic tension destruction or during religious celebrations), a point that Mangla in this volume echoes through his fieldwork in Bhimsen, Madhya Pradesh. We subset the data by all the articles that mention the institution being deployed to specifically address a riot or clash.[25] Using these mentions, we find that, on average, three companies are deployed to address a riot or clash.

The exercise reveals other insights. For many of the entries listed, the number of casualties from rioting by the time the Rapid Action Force is deployed to a riot are roughly the total number of deaths from the entire incident. Consider, for example, the first riot that the Rapid Action Force was deployed to: Sitamarhi Bihar, in October 1992.[26] The Sitamarhi riot is an example of why the Rapid Action Force was created in the first place; Engineer notes that the police were biased and invested in the communal tension of the areas that they supervised, while a new centrally run unit was seen as more legitimate.[27] Then again, based on newspaper accounts, the total number of deaths from the riot that began on October 6 was approximately thirty-nine, yet the number of deaths reported by the time Rapid Action Force deployed (October 9) was thirty-six. One way to interpret this is that the Rapid Action Force is highly effective at quelling violence; yet, another interpretation is that much of the violence related to the incident had already transpired, and that the Rapid Action Force was deployed too late. In fact, the federal government ended up blaming the Bihar government for not asking for the RAF sooner.[28]

One interesting observation that our descriptive exercise reveals is that the nature of riots and communal conflict that the Rapid Action Force has witnessed has undergone change. For example, a riot occurred following telecast of Urdu news on Doordarshan in Bangalore in 1994; this incident, prior to the liberalization of state media when television and the state were more closely linked, resulted in at least eighteen deaths.[29] Today, India hosts among the largest number of news channels in the world.[30] The speed with which violence can flare, and the consequent agility required by the organizations like the RAF, has only intensified. Indeed, communal clashes may occur because of circulation of hate messages or videos on social media in a way that was unforeseen in the 1990s.[31] While the RAF was originally intended to be used for the sole purpose of tacking communal riots, it has now come to be used in various kinds of law-and-order situations from ensuring that a tussle between political parties residing in hotels in Maharashtra in 2019 does not turn violent, to being deployed to supervise the Maha Kumbh in Allahabad, Uttar Pradesh.

Figure 11.4 reveals that the Force is deployed with the most frequency and with the largest total number of companies in Uttar Pradesh.[32] Still, the *Times of India* accounts reveal nothing about the efficacy of the Rapid Action Force; in some of the newspaper articles, the Force is criticized for not successfully quelling violence, as in the case of the Indo-Bangla border clashes that led to the deployment of the Indian Army in 2010.[33] However, it is plausible that personnel are not trained for tension in border areas, which may be why, for several of the instances mentioned, the RAF is deployed *simultaneously* with other paramilitary forces, as was the case with the Jat agitation in Haryana (see below).

One hypothesis for why some accounts highlight the inability of the Rapid Action Force to quell large-scale riots, or those that have already started, is that organizations like the RAF have to be (1) called by the state; and (2) operate under certain constraints when on the ground. Officials from the Rapid Action Force fall under the Central Reserve Police Force (CRPF) Act, 1949 rather than the 1861 Police Act.[34] Because the mandate of the RAF is to assist the state police force, the federal government cannot send the RAF on its own.[35] Ordinarily, the states send a request to the central government, the federal government then assesses the situation, and if satisfied on the grounds of the request, sends in the nearest RAF unit(s) to the affected area. However, to deter moral hazard or local governments' dependency on central forces, the federal government now asks states to assess the requirement of CAPFs by constituting a local committee with representatives of the state police.[36] This is obviously a lengthy bureaucratic process; delays may be caused due to the clearances required throughout this chain of command. Recently, a process to shorten the time required for deployment was put in place whereby district magistrates can directly contact the nearest RAF unit and request deployment. The Inspector-General (RAF) can agree to such a request and send the force for a maximum period of seven days before which the regular permission from the Ministry of Home Affairs arrives.

Aside from the process of being "called-in," RAF officials remain under the supervision of the state government when they are being "hosted." Specifically, operational command always lies with the local district magistrate or superintendent of police. What happens when a *jawan* (who is, let us assume, a member of one of the team elements that carries a gun) perceives the need to use armed force to quell a riot? It is in this context where RAF officials have the most maneuverability. If, for instance, an RAF official has operational instructions by superiors (e.g., the director general of the state police) *not* to open fire, the official may still use force if he or she decides that circumstances on the ground dictate violence. Unlike other paramilitaries, the CRPF/Rapid Action Force have the power to arrest.[37] On July 27, 1976, the Ministry of Home Affairs, Government of India issued Gazette Notification No. J. II-9/74-Adm-(Pers-II/GPA-I), which conferred upon every member of the CRPF of and above the rank of sub-inspector various powers including those under Section 129 Cr.P.C., that is, one of the rights that a police officer holds. Unlike the local police, the RAF are not "socially embedded."[38] Consequently, policymakers assume that if such officials do have to resort to force, and along with the fact that the RAF is theoretically more representative of diverse communities, personnel wearing the blue uniforms will be seen as more legitimate if they must resort to force. Nevertheless, these assumptions have not been systemically tested and thus warrant empirical scrutiny.

Rapid Action Force and the 2016 Reservation
Agitation in Haryana

What set of challenges are most important in determining the Rapid Action Force's efficacy? Structural conditions (e.g., lack of equipment or distance from riot), or lengthy bureaucratic processes of requesting assistance? In the following section, based on interviews with serving RAF officers as well as analyses of government reports, we attempt to tackle this question by using as a case study the Force's deployment during the Haryana reservation agitation in 2016. The Jat agitation represents the kind of incident that the Rapid Action Force was, in theory, explicitly designed to tackle, that is, a multi-day riot based on identity politics within the heartland of the country. Our analyses suggest that not only was the RAF constrained by structural factors, but also that the Force played a largely *supportive* rather than lead role, potentially out of skepticism among state administrators about the RAF's efficacy. Indeed, by most accounts, the reservation agitation was seen as a failure of India's internal security apparatus, especially since ultimately it was the Army that had to be deployed to quell violence.[39]

Between February 7 and 22, 2016, the reservation agitation spilled on to the streets of Haryana, resulting in the blockading of roads and highways, as well as damage to public property. The event that precipitated the state government to call for the Rapid Action Force took place on February 14, 2016, when a Jat Swabhimaan Rally was held in the Sampla village of Rohtak. Between 200 and 250 persons blocked National Highway 10, after which prohibitory orders under Section 144 Code of Criminal Procedure were initiated. The state government, at the request of the police chief of Haryana, requested five companies of the RAF. However, the Ministry of Home Affairs (MHA) allotted only three: one RAF and two BSF (Border Security Force). These units were sent to Sonipat and one company each to Rohtak and Jhajjar, respectively. Between February 17 and 19,[40] a back-and-forth continued between the state government and the MHA about exactly how many companies were to be deployed,[41] as well as where to deploy them. For instance, some CRPF companies allocated to Jind on February 19 were then suddenly relocated to Rohtak the same day. The changing numbers of companies allotted, and the fact that state government had to keep making requests, is emblematic of the bureaucratic process involved in calling in the Central Armed Police Forces, even in the context of fast-moving crises.

According to some of our interviews, the major structural challenge faced by paramilitary personnel were (1) distance to the riot;[42] and (2) blocked highways. One RAF officer informed us that he arrived in Sonipat on February 16, 2016, but was largely immobile simply because agitators had blocked roadways. He also informed us that a major component of RAF activity included setting perimeters and ensuring spaces *not already infiltrated* were protected. For instance, when a collecting mob was moving toward the OP Jindal Global University at Jagdishpur, Sonipat—in which about 3,000 Indian/foreign students reside and study—the RAF unit reached the university before a large crowd could form, and dispersed rioters with tear gas.

Yet, by other accounts, tear gas and anti-riot equipment utilized by the RAF may not have been adequate to quell agitations. For instance, on February 21, 2016, RAF officials were informed about an attempt being planned by rioters to damage Munak Canal. In this instance, tear gas not only proved insufficient, but also RAF officers were overwhelmed by agitators who tried to forcibly acquire their weapons. The RAF ended up opening fire and some individuals were killed.[43] Figure 11.5 illustrates exactly when the Army was called in. Interestingly, the Army faced some of same challenges as the Central Armed Police Forces; it was delayed by almost a day by fallen trees on the roads, and several columns had to be airlifted with helicopters.[44] Eventually, seventy-four columns of the Army were deployed,

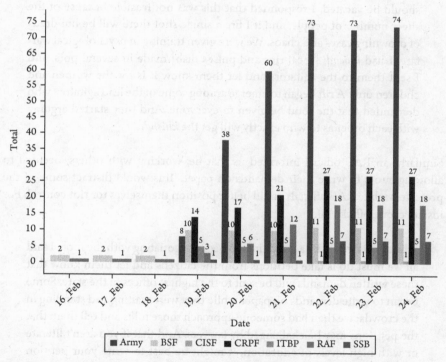

Figure 11.5 Security force deployments to quell the 2016 Jat Uprising in Haryana
The figure represents the breakdown of security agencies deployed to quell the Jat uprising in 2016. The number of non-army deployments are reflected in ``companies.'' The number of army personnel are displayed in "columns" (each column has approximately 75 personnel). The figure shows a dramatic increase in army deployments at the expense of other institutions like RAF, which saw barely any increase. Data based on Prakash Singh Committee Report.

which overwhelmed the manpower of the Central Armed Police Forces, including the RAF.

Some officials that we interviewed did indeed highlight the importance of the Rapid Action Force in quelling violence in Haryana. For instance, an official we interviewed noted that he was posted in Bhopal, Madhya Pradesh, and was informed at 7 P.M. to move to Sonipat on February 23, 2016. (Interestingly, Bhopal is more than 800 km from Sonipat, and so further than the 400 km radius that personnel should theoretically be from a scene.) He reached Delhi airport by plane at 2 A.M., and at 5 A.M. he was on the ground. The official described how he employed some of his training in psychological warfare with the mob. For instance, he highlighted how he used food to sow division between agitators. He said:

> I saw that there were 5,000 persons sitting on the canal and blocking the water passage. The brigadier informed me that by 10 A.M. these people should be vacated. I responded that this was not feasible because of the sheer number of people, and if I fire a single shot there will be hundreds of drowning cases and chaos. We were given training in psychological warfare. I had *khichdi* [local rice and pulses dish] made in several pots, and I sent them to the agitators and let them know it is for the women and children only. A rift began to emerge among some of the lead agitators who demanded that the food be given to everyone. And they started arguing with each other as to who exactly will get the *khichdi*.

Similarly, an RAF official informed us that he, working with others, decided to allow agitators to write their demands on paper. This would distract some of the protesters while RAF officials could better position themselves for riot control. For instance, one official said:

> I thought it would be a good time to begin negotiating with the mob. I said all we must do is take petitions from the citizens and let them know that these written demands will be sent to the highest offices in the state. Some began to write demands on paper while they were waiting and standing in the crowds; we then had someone approach those folks and tell them that the petitions may be challenged by lawyers. And that if you aren't literate or with high levels of education, it might be best to write your petition through a lawyer. In Sonipat, by 5 P.M., a substantial number of citizens had gone elsewhere to try and get some inputs from lawyers.

In this way, some of the RAF officials we interviewed highlighted how their training allowed them to think about ways to disperse mobs *without* resorting to force in Haryana.

Then again, the RAF officials that we interviewed were deployed to the state *after* much of the intense clashes and instances of violence had transpired. Consider Figure 11.5. It depicts the CAPF institutions brought in to quell the rioting in Haryana by day. The figure shows how, as violence and looting continued between February 16 and 18, only *one* company of the RAF was posted in Haryana. By February 19, four other CAPF institutions were brought in, as well as 8 *columns* of the Army. Yet, within the CAPFs, the increase in the number of RAF companies to deal with the rioting was marginal. Instead, aside from the CRPF, it was the Border Security Force—who are *not* trained in riot control—that saw a large increase. From February 20, there was a striking increase in the number of Army columns brought in; yet, once again, the number of RAF companies began to exceed the BSF companies in number only beginning on February 21. Throughout the Jat agitation, the total number of RAF companies never exceeded eighteen. This fact was severely criticized by the Prakash Singh Committee Report, which expressed puzzlement as to why the BSF (and later Indo-Tibetan Border Police or ITBP) were called in before the RAF.[45]

One hypothesis for why Rapid Action Force units were not called in is skepticism on the part of administrators about the ability of the RAF to handle large-scale violence rather than smaller, more concentrated community clashes. One of us (Dr. Hanif Qureshi) was the inspector general of Karnal, Haryana, during the time of the Jat agitation. Based on his experience, much of the violence related to the Jat agitation occurred *prior* to the Rapid Action Force being called in, at a time when a larger number of units were requested but not deployed by the Ministry of Home Affairs. As per the Prakash Singh Committee report, on February 20, there was word that agitators had brought National Highway 1 (Delhi to Chandigarh) to a standstill. On the 21st, agitators had breached Munak Canal, and had stolen a weapon from one of the Sashastra Seema Bal (SSB) *jawans*. SSB officials then opened fire, and a protestor was killed. On the 22nd, agitators had tried to cut off the water supply to Delhi. At 2 A.M., ADC Sonipat, DC Sonipat, IG Railways, and Commando mandated a *lathi*-charge and deployed tear gas to be used on the mob. Eventually, seventy-four rounds of ammunition were fired, and four persons were killed. *Only after* the deaths of four persons did the level of violence begin to subside; and so, by the time that some of the RAF officials that we interviewed had arrived on the scene, and were able to use psychological warfare, there was *already* a diminution in the intensity of violence.

A question that arises is that, if the training of RAF is to deal with clashes like the Jat agitation, why were so few companies sent not only from the very beginning, but also when the violence began to escalate? Why, as the violence intensified on February 19, were the Border Security Force and Sashastra Seema Bal moved into Haryana in larger numbers than the Rapid Action Force? One RAF official informed us:

The government in Haryana likely thought that they could handle the situation without calling in external agencies, including the Rapid Action Force. But by waiting, the violence intensified, by which time it likely became necessary to present a big show of force. RAF officials are deployed across the country, and I for instance was called in from Bhopal. And so, in the heat of the moment, the MHA sent in other agencies, including the Army. There was no big strategy. It really was a game of numbers, and using whatever forces one could get to intimidate the rioters. It is also important to note that the RAF is still called in very rare cases—there remains this association that the organization does not use lethal force. And, for intense clashes that we saw in Haryana, there was an assumption—even shared by the Prakash Singh Committee report—that you do need to use lethal force. Policymakers think, "why should we call troops that have negotiation skills when there is violence and looting in the streets or those troops for whom only 50 percent carry weapons?" We need "real" armed forces is the thought-process.

The official described a mentality among administrators that RAF can likely not deal with escalating riots. In the case of Haryana, the state government had initially asked for more personnel but were allotted far less by the Ministry of Home Affairs; yet, by the time the violence had escalated, the federal government *overcompensated* by deploying personnel from every agency, including the Army. It is also true that there are bureaucratic challenges with deploying just one kind of force; because CAPFs are spread thin in a variety of settings, the RAF is typically deployed *with other* agencies simultaneously. In general, state leaders prefer the disbursal of a variety of forces; deploying sixty-nine companies of CAPFs is seen as better than eighteen companies of the RAF.[46] The reservation agitation was spread across nine districts of Haryana, and eighteen companies of the RAF—which would likely have to be called from several RAF battalion headquarters—would translate to just two companies per district.

The distribution of day-by-day deployments in Figure 11.5 shows the massive deployments of the Army, suggesting that administrators may still depend on the military for large-scale internal challenges. However, the Army is (1) typically ill-equipped for anti-riot activity because they carry heavy weapons; and (2) military deployment—at the expense of CAPFs or the RAF—may undermine the credibility of the country's most trusted institution. Indeed, while the Army carried out flag marches during the Jat agitation, it came with significant cost; several videos emerged showing agitators throwing stones at Army trucks, potentially compromising the status of the Army in the eyes of citizens.

Discussion

In this essay, we attempt to shed light on one of India's Central Armed Police Forces, the Rapid Action Force. The Rapid Action Force was created to address rioting or communal violence in the heartland, which by the 1980s had intensified. The CRPF, which previously had sole responsibility for tackling such forms of violence, became overstretched with large-scale counterinsurgency and cross-border tension. Moreover, state-level police forces, especially after the Emergency, came to be seen as biased. The Rapid Action Force—with their bases across India, specialized training (especially in non-lethal weapons), and emphasis on representation—would theoretically be a boon. The organization has indeed seen a great number of successes since its inception; it was involved in countering the 2001 Indian Parliament attack, rescue operations following the 2004 Tsunami, and saw deployments during the 2008 Mumbai terror attacks.

Yet, in describing the organization of the Rapid Action Force, we also attempt to illustrate some of the challenges that the institution has and will likely continue to face. First, we outline the hierarchy within the Rapid Action Force, and note how the institution is not autonomous. The RAF—a four-year deployment for CRPF officials—is typically seen as a "soft" posting. While CRPF officials sent to the RAF undergo a month-long training course, as a subsidiary of the CRPF and as a likely factor of the short postings, officials do not necessarily generate a loyalty to the institution distinct from the CRPF. Whether the RAF is a more "representative" force is also unclear; still, descriptively, the organization can be said to be more inclusive of women than other paramilitary agencies. Relatedly, hiring more recruits may mitigate against state governments having the need to call-in units from other agencies like the Border Security Force when in crisis.

Second, we point to the fact that, on average, each RAF headquarter is roughly 250 km from a riot-like situation. Combined with the fact that the RAF do not necessarily have equipment like helicopters, there are structural hurdles that constrain personnel from arriving quickly on the ground. Without adequate equipment, RAF personnel can be hindered by simple obstacles such as blocked roadways. Providing adequate equipment to personnel, so that units are not obligated to borrow choppers from the Army or get lifts from other agencies, may improve performance.

Third, we show that on average, three companies of the RAF are typically sent to a riot-like situation. Nevertheless, we also suggest that the bureaucratic processes and red tape involved in requesting CAPFs may not have adapted to the changing environment. As hinted by other chapters in this volume, there has been an evolution of riot-like incidents in India, especially with the advent of social media. And so, instituting more bases for RAF deployment, and potentially ensuring that personnel play a more lead rather than supportive role, may begin addressing the mismatch in terms of states that are most likely to have a riot (or most likely to have fatalities from riots), compared to where RAF personnel are deployed. Indeed, the RAF is typically sent in conjunction with other CAPFs, but if the former is seen as a more neutral, impartial force in their blue uniforms, but remain overpowered by other agencies on the ground, then questions are raised as to whether the RAF are being given the opportunity to deliver in the first place.

We use the reservation agitation in Haryana to illustrate several of the challenges faced by the RAF, and areas for performance improvement. We describe how the body was brought in *along* with other forces during the crisis that may not have had training to deal with riot-like situations (such as the Border Security Force and Army). When on the ground, the RAF did not necessarily retain organizational command. And so, playing largely supportive roles, without robust deployment, the RAF's influence in addressing the agitation may have been overshadowed by its supervising body. In fact, there is some evidence to suggest that state administrators may *prefer* other CAPFs to the RAF; the RAF may be typecast as an agency that is unable to use lethal force to intimidate protesters. This may be one reason why states like Andhra Pradesh, West Bengal, Bihar, and Maharashtra have now created their own state-level Rapid Action Forces. However, further research is warranted as to whether these localized RAF institutions are more agile or simply a way to add layers of bureaucracy without initiating corrective measures to existing institutions.

The chapter makes a case for studying the actors who participate in maintaining law and order in India in a more systematic way, especially because previous scholarly analyses of ethnic or communal violence have focused almost entirely on *why* they occur rather than the *role of actors* responsible for quelling them. Subsequent research, with more comprehensive data, may shed light on why attrition and levels of suicide are high in organizations like the CRPF, whether the deployment of forces like the Rapid Action Force perpetuate moral hazard (i.e., create a dependency upon federal resources and breed inefficiency in the police), or even why state governments ask for paramilitary assistance in some instances, but not others.

We hope that policymakers and scholars will work more collaboratively to share data; at present, accessing even demographic information about the CAPFs is a challenge because such agencies are exempt from the Right to Information Act, as pointed out by Yashovardhan Azad in his chapter in this volume, and the federal government has even stopped providing certain forms of data related to communal conflict, shown by Ahuja and Kapur in their chapter. There may be anxieties among law and order and government officials vis-à-vis researchers potentially exposing structural deficits or painting the security apparatus in a negative light. Nevertheless, greater trust and collaboration between policymakers and researchers may in fact be a win-win situation by not only enabling scholars to carry out research, but also providing government officials a free pool of researchers interested in generating policy recommendations based on data that can increase the agility and efficacy of India's internal security agencies.

Notes

1. Patel's full quote is: "We are passing through a period of transition. In this period we have made so many changes and raised so many forces, upset so many things of the old order—abolition

of *zamindari*, amalgamation of States, removal of old institutions and many other similar things. The present situation is such that we have to be very watchful and careful. Then we have on the borders, due to Partition, several raids being committed by dacoits form the other side or by the forces from the other side. . . . In the industrial centers also there are certain forces which believe in creating trouble, for they think the more unrest they create, the better the prospects for their organization. In all these circumstances, a Central, well-organized and disciplined police force is a boon in these areas. . . . Ours is a vast country, where consolidation has taken place with electric rapidity. . . . Therefore, we have taken care to organize our services, our police force and all the requirements that are considered necessary for keeping law and order in the whole land, so that progress may be as effective and rapid as possible." Lok Sabha, "Constituent Assembly of India (Legislative) Debates" (Legislative Debates: Official Report; New Delhi, 1949).

2. Sabha, "Constituent Assembly of India (Legislative) Debates."

3. For a discussion of this decade marking a deterioration in India's internal security, see the introductory chapter by Ahuja and Kapur in this volume.

4. Steven I. Wilkinson, *Votes and Violence: Electoral Competition and Ethnic Riots in India* (Cambridge: Cambridge University Press, 2006).

5. Stephen P. Cohen and Sunil Dasgupta, *Arming without Aiming: India's Military Modernization* (Washington, DC: Brookings Institution Press, 2013). Each CAPF, established by an act of the Parliament, was created for a specific mandate. The primary goal of the Border Security Force (BSF) is to guard India's border with Pakistan and Bangladesh; the Central Industrial Security Force (CISF) provides security to airports and other public sector infrastructure; the Indo-Tibetan Border Police (ITBP) was raised for guarding duties on the India-China border; while the Sashastra Seema Bal (SSB) secures the borders with Nepal and Bhutan. The National Security Guard is an anti-terrorism unit, and the Assam Rifles guard the Indo-Myanmar border.

6. "Cong. Favours Ram Temple," *The Times of India*, April 17, 1991.

7. Defined under Sections 130, 131, and 132 of the Cr.P.C.

8. For additional information on the other CAPFs, see chapter by Azad in this volume.

9. GOs are senior government officers appointed by the president of India or governor of states; they have power to verify public documents by affixing their seal. In CRPF, assistant commandants and above are GOs.

10. Deputed from the CRPF.

11. 50 percent are promoted from constables, and 50 percent recruited directly from the CRPF.

12. 50 percent promoted from ranks from inspector, and 50 percent recruited directly from the UPSC.

13. The Indian Police Service (IPS) has a cadre strength that includes 40 percent Central Deputation Reserve. This means that 40 percent of IPS officers are meant to serve on deputation in Government of India forces, chiefly in the CAPFs. Currently, as per the recruitment rules of various CAPFs, 20–25 percent of the posts at deputy inspector general level, 50 percent at inspector general level, and 75 percent at additional director general level are manned by IPS officers. The remaining posts are manned by CAPF officers, both directly recruited, or officers promoted from the ranks. All CAPFs in India including the CRPF are headed by IPS officers; J. Frank, E. G. Lambert, H. Qureshi, and A. J. Myer, "Problems Spilling Over: Work–Family Conflict's and Other Stressor Variables' Relationships with Job Involvement and Satisfaction among Police Officers," *Journal of Policing, Intelligence and Counter Terrorism* 17, no. 1 (2021): 48–71. For a few years now, there has been some tension between IPS and CAPF officers over service conditions. The genesis of the legal battle is whether IPS officers should be deputed to CAPFs at the top level (deputy inspector general and above). The Supreme Court in February 2019 ruled that the "grant of status of Group 'A' Central Services to RPF (Railway Police Force) shall not affect (the deputation of) the IPS." The deputation of IPS officers would therefore continue as before. The RPF is not a CAPF. This caused some confusion as to the deputation of IPS officers in CAPFs, as some CAPF officers wanted their own officers to man the top-level posts in CAPFs and not IPS officers.

14. Every year, RAF officials are sent to refresher courses for four weeks.
15. Vinay Pandey, "Novel Approach to Tackle Riots." *The Times of India*, October 28, 1992. The idea that greater representation would ensure a less partisan force was shared by several politicians, some of whom even proposed the creation of segregated *minority-only* paramilitary forces; "Special Anti-Riot Force Plan: Lok Sabha," *The Times of India*, August 2, 1991.
16. Rajya Sabha, "Question No. 217 (Shri Rahman Khan)," Parliament, 1995. In the 1990s, organizations such as the National Commission for Minorities asked that educational and other qualifications be relaxed for minorities entering the CRPF, but this was rejected by the government. Rajya Sabha, "Question No. 412 (Shri Rahman Khan)," Parliament, 2002.
17. Lok Sabha, "Question No. 2056 (Shri Bir Singh Mahato)," Parliament, 1999; Rajya Sabha, "Question No. 122 (Shri Shahid Siddiqui)," Parliament, 2004.
18. Female officers from the Rapid Action Force have also been deployed for international peace-keeping operations, as in Liberia (TOI 2006c).
19. For a discussion of gender in the Border Security Force, see chapter by Ghosh in this volume.
20. Mark Magnier, "India's Response to Attacks Lays Bare Broader Failures," *Los Angeles Times*, December 1, 2008; Manju Parikh, "The Debacle at Ayodhya: Why Militant Hinduism Met with a Weak Response," *Asian Survey* 33, no. 7 (1993): 673–684.
21. Debashish Karmakar, "Permanent Deployment of RAF in State by October," *The Times of India*, August 8, 2018.
22. "ACLED Introduces New Event Types and Sub-Event Types," *ACLED*, https://www.acledd ata.com/2019/03/14/acled-introduces-new-event-types-and-sub-event-types/.
23. Wilkinson, *Votes and Violence*.
24. Sriya Iyer and Anand Shrivastava, "Religious Riots and Electoral Politics in India," *Journal of Development Economics* 131 (2018): 104–122; Wilkinson, *Votes and Violence*.
25. There are, of course, challenges associated with recording mentions of the institution in one English-language newspaper. However, the goal was not to create a comprehensive database, but to gain some descriptive insights about when and how many companies are sent, as well as how many people died (approximately) by the time the Rapid Action Force was called in.
26. "Bihar Riot Toll Rises to 36," *The Times of India*, October 10, 1992.
27. Asghar Ali Engineer, "Sitamarhi on Fire," *Economic and Political Weekly*, November 14, 1992, 2462–2464.
28. "Centre Blames Bihar Govt," *The Times of India*, October 12, 1992.
29. "Bangalore Toll Up to 18: Army Stages Nag Marches; DD Reschedules Urdu News," *The Times of India*, October 9, 1994.
30. Alistair Maclean and Nalin Mehta, *India on Television: How Satellite News Channels Have Changed the Way We Think and Act* (New Delhi: HarperCollins Publishers India, 2008).
31. Debabrata Mohapatra, "Bhadrak Violence Claims Property Worth Rs. 9 Crore," *The Times of India*, April 21, 2017; H. K. Verma and Debashish Karmakar, "Communal Clashes in Bihar District over Video on Deities," *The Times of India*, August 6, 2016.
32. It is also notable that few Rapid Action Force personnel were deployed during the Godhra riots in Gujarat; Kadayam Suryanarayanan Subramanian, *Political Violence and the Police in India* (New Delhi: SAGE Publications India, 2007), 184, argues that the Force was prevented from being able to maneuver during the clashes.
33. "Communal Clash Near Bangla Border, Army Deployed," *The Times of India*, September 8, 2010.
34. CRPF/Rapid Action Force officers, especially under Section 132 of the Code of Criminal Procedure, are immune from most forms of prosecution if a case can be made that officers acted in the interest of the state.
35. The only situation where the federal government may use Central Forces in a state, without the state's consent, is when it concludes that the governance of a state cannot be carried out under the provisions of the Constitution under Article 356 of the Constitution and imposes President's Rule.

36. The Government of India laid out detailed guidelines through a circular issued on October 18, 2017, through which it advised the states that CAPFs cannot substitute state police forces for normal policing duties.

37. However, like other CAPFs, the RAF cannot carry out tasks such as investigations or First Information Report registrations.

38. For a discussion of this term, see Mangla in this volume.

39. Prakash Singh, "Prakash Singh Committee Report: Role of Officers of Civil Administration and Police during the Jat Reservation Agitation (Feb 7–22, 2016)" (2018), 176.

40. From February 17 to 19, there was mob violence in a mall where almost a dozen policemen were taken hostage, confrontations between police and agitators where a BSF official fired and killed a protestor, as well as attacks on the residence of the Haryana finance minister.

41. The federal government first allotted thirty additional companies to the existing three, and later increasing it to sixty.

42. Battalions from the BSF had to travel more than twenty-four hours to reach Narwana from Bikaner.

43. Similarly, on February 22, 2016, the RAF was called upon to disperse a mob of roughly 2,000 personnel who were blocking National Highway 1 at Ladsouli. The RAF then opened fire, in which four people died.

44. A substantial contingent of the Army (five columns) was sent to by the federal government to Munak Canal so that the drinking water to Delhi could be protected.

45. Prakash Singh, "Prakash Singh Committee Report."

46. While facing riots, state governments typically want as many companies as they can get. If they ask for only RAF, they may get only get a dozen or more; whereas if they are open to other CAPFs too, they will most likely get a larger total number of companies. The problem arises in the fact that the RAF were specifically designed to address riots, so if other forces are also brought in, then the point of having a separate RAF—or at least one that cannot be brought in with enough manpower or hold operational command—becomes unclear.

12

Protective Labor and Its Correlates

A Statistical Portrait

PAARITOSH NATH AND ARJUN JAYADEV

> Your Chowkidar is standing firm & serving the nation. But, I am not alone.
> Everyone who is fighting corruption, dirt, social evils is a Chowkidar.
> Everyone working hard for the progress of India is a Chowkidar. Today,
> every Indian is saying-#MainBhiChowkidar.[1]
>
> —Narendra Modi

In the lead-up to the 2019 general elections, the word "Chowkidar" became a politically charged symbol. Prime Minister Narendra Modi deftly reversed criticism of his tenure by claiming to be India's own Chowkidar-in-chief, protecting the country from looting by public officials and ensuring the general security of the country. Members of his cabinet followed his lead in changing their Twitter handles to also suggest a concern with security. In many ways, if 2014 was the year of the Tea-Seller, 2019 was the year of the Security Guard, a potent symbol of an important everyman who is finally getting his due.

That the word had political resonance is due perhaps to the increasing importance of security to the Indian public, both from perceived external threats and from the internal dislocations of social change generated by a rapidly urbanizing, youthful, and liberalizing country. It is perhaps safe to say that security concerns have risen to the top of social and political imagination, especially in urban areas with a young working population, rapid and unprecedented migration, and a changing labor force. What is perhaps interesting about the use of the security guard as a symbol was that the job being referred to is typically a private sector job, a parallel industry that substitutes for publicly provided law and order.

In an era whereby the older forces of trust, commonality, and social arrangements are being disturbed, with official law-and-order institutions increasingly seen to be ineffectual, it is perhaps not surprising that private security is increasingly important in the country.[2] Quick and effective redressal of criminal cases has become rarer

Paaritosh Nath and Arjun Jayadev, *Protective Labor and Its Correlates* In: *Internal Security in India*. Edited by: Amit Ahuja and Devesh Kapur, Oxford University Press. © Oxford University Press 2023. DOI: 10.1093/oso/9780197660331.003.0012 over time. Data from the *Crime in India* reports inform us that the share of IPC cases pending investigation by the police has increased by 11 percentage points between 1984 and 2018.[3] During the same time, the share of IPC trials completed by the courts has fallen by 9 percentage points. In such a scenario, it is not surprising that society is willing to spend substantial resources to provide for crime prevention services.

According to one estimate, India is home to one in three private security guards worldwide and has a private security guard for every 187 citizens.[4] To put this into perspective, the country, going by official estimates, has one doctor for every 1,445 persons.[5] In comparison to other lower-middle-income nations, India's private security fraction at 0.5 percent of the population is quite high, closer to countries such as Guatemala and Honduras, which have the highest share of security workers in their population, as shown in Figure 12.1. Not only is India's private security industry growing, it is also overtaking public institutions entrusted with the task of maintaining law and order. India, it is estimated, has five times the number of private security guards than they have police officers, a ratio second to only Guatemala's 6.2 and just above Honduras's 4.9.[6] The latter two, home to the highest homicide rates in the world along with a widespread network of organized crime cartels, have been well documented for their booming private security industry.[7]

While one can certainly understand why private security is a more important sector of employment than in the past, it is not entirely clear why India appears to have such a high number of private security workers per capita, given the relatively

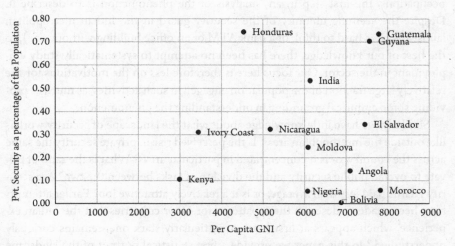

Figure 12.1 Private security as a percentage of the population, lower-middle-income countries, 2015
Source: Guardian study (2017), GNI figures from World Bank
We used the World Bank classification of countries on the basis of GNI per capita in US$ (Atlas methodology), available at https://datahelpdesk.worldbank.org/knowledgebase/articles/906519.

lower levels of violent crime compared to other lower-income countries with similar levels of crime. As such, the role of private security as a parallel law-and-order force is not clear.

Is it really the case that private security guards are indeed primarily providing security services, or is it something more than this? A recent dissertation emphasizes the performative aspect of security guards in molding public space to the favor of dominant classes.[8] In this view, they are not best seen as a substitute for public security as much as a weak, but cheap way of privatizing and filtering public spaces to exclude and control the poor. Another plausible and linked argument is that private security is best seen as a status symbol—a marker of difference in access to public and private space: even if a poor person has a right to access certain public spaces (say, a mall), the presence and arbitrary power of private security may deter him or her.

It may nevertheless be going too far to suggest that private security functions purely symbolically. Employers of such guards do have real expectations that they will guard and protect the space for which they are employed. More formal public security (police, for example) may be more specialized than private security in terms of actual time spent policing and may have a larger jurisdiction of action, but this is a difference of degree and not kind. These are clearly not entirely substitutable jobs, but they do have a clear, common set of core functions. In fact, as we show in the next section, both private and public security occupations have grown together in the last two decades, even if private security has grown faster.

Regardless of the complex socio-political reasons for the rise of security guard occupations, the first step in any analysis of the phenomenon is to describe it. Despite the seeming ubiquity of the security guard in the Indian metropolitan landscape (it is hard to think of a bank ATM or an office building without one), to the best of our knowledge, there has been no attempt to systematically study employment in the sector. Our focus here is therefore less on the motivations for the relatively large fraction of the population engaged in such activities, as much as providing some empirical grounding in understanding the phenomenon.

Similarly, we have little knowledge about what the landscape of security work is like outside the metropolitan areas. Is the perceived rise in private security the same across the country, or is it concentrated in particular areas? What is the ratio of private to overall public security and the division of tasks between the two? Are security guards paid less than average, or is it a relatively attractive job? Earlier attempts have been made to describe these patterns for other countries, but the Indian experience, which appears at first blush a particularly stark one, remains curiously understudied.[9] In this paper we provide a first statistical portrait of the landscape of Indian protective services work. We here attempt to describe the evolution of the security worker landscape and to identify some correlates of the proportion of protective security in general as a pathway to further research. To foreground our findings:

1. Protective services have grown as an important source of employment. Roughly 1–2 percent of the Indian workforce are employed in the sector.
2. Private provision of security has grown more quickly, but the split between private and public protective service work is roughly even. The public sector continues to employ a large fraction of protective service workers, both as a proportion of total workers as well as in terms of the public sector.
3. While the public and private sectors both share in protective service occupations, this hides substantial variation. In urban metropolitan areas, private security provision typically dominates and can be up to six times that of the public sector.
4. On average, security work is slightly better paid than the average, but this differs considerably between subsections. For a public sector protective security employee, wages are higher than average and reflect higher levels of education. The typical private sector protective service worker, by contrast, is a doorkeeper and has much lower than average wages and skills.
5. There were few robust correlates of the extent of protective services in the labor force. Some obvious candidates—the level of inequality, confidence in police institutions, the level of recognized and reported crime, ethnolinguistic fractionalization, and such—did not seem to suggest strong correlation. Only urbanization appears to be a robust correlate, suggesting that the phenomenon may be driven by the rapid changes occurring in urban India.

The rest of this essay is divided into four parts. In the first section we discuss the evolution of protective service work in general, including the geographical and industrial distribution. In section two we describe the individual characteristics of the protective service worker. Section three is a statistical exercise in trying to identify correlates. We conclude by thinking more broadly about protective service occupations, what they tell us about the institutional underpinning of society and the welfare implications of these occupations as a result.

Measuring Protective Service Workers

While there are several private industry reports, in this paper we have focused mainly on official statistics.[10] To estimate the absolute numbers and fraction of the labor force of the pool of protective services, we took the years 1993–1994, 1999–2000, 2004–2005, 2011–2012, and 2017–2018 as the particular snapshots for our analysis. The data for the first four years were obtained from the 50th, 55th, 61st, and 68th NSSO Employment-Unemployment Survey rounds and for the fifth year from the Periodic Labor Force Survey (PLFS), 2017–2018. We used the United Nations' population projection estimates to determine the size of the Indian population (separately for males and females).[11] Worker participation ratios (for those aged fifteen years and above) obtained from the labor surveys were applied to the

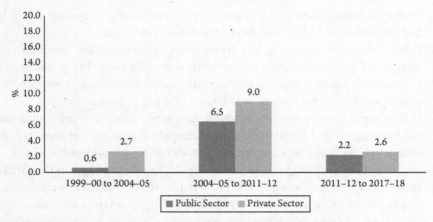

Figure 12.2a CAGR of public and private security workers in India.
Source: Computed using unit-level data from the EUS 55th, 61st, and 68th rounds and the PLFS 2017–2018

population projections to arrive at the overall size of the workforce corresponding to each of these years. We then arrived at the size of the security force in India using the National Classification of Occupation (NCO) information provided in the labor force surveys.

For the first three periods (under NCO 68) we took the occupational codes 571, 573, and 574, corresponding to the occupation groups "Policemen and Detectives," "Protection Force, Home Guard and Security Workers," and "Watchmen, Chowkidars and Gate Keepers" respectively as being representative of protective service workers.[12] Collectively these provide us with an overall estimate of the size of the security workforce in India. For the last two periods, we took the NCO 2004 codes 345, 516, and 915, corresponding to the occupations "Police Inspectors and Detectives," "Protective Services Workers," and "Messengers, Porters, Door Keepers and Related Workers" respectively. Once again, the three occupations collectively give us the approximate size of what may be classified as the security workforce in India.[13]

Figure 12.2a shows that both private and public security have been growing, but private security work has been growing faster. As such, it is difficult to make any statement about any substitution between private and public security.

As Figure 12.2b and Table 12.1 show, between 1993 and 2004 there was a slow but steady rise in the number of people engaged in protective services, with a 26 percent growth rate from 2.3 to 2.9 million. Since then, however, there has been a massive increase. Between 2004 and 2017–2018, the number of individuals nearly doubled from 2.9 to 5.7 million. Similarly, as Table 12.1 shows, around 1.3 percent are involved in protective service activities, nearly doubling from the 0.7 percent in 2004.

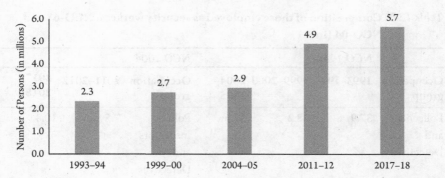

Figure 12.2b Absolute size of those engaged as security workers in India, 1993–1994 to 2017–2018 (in millions)

Source: Computed using unit-level data from the EUS 50th, 55th, 61st, and 68th rounds and the PLFS 2017–2018

Table 12.1 **Absolute number of persons (in thousands) employed as security workers by sex and their share in the overall workforce, various years**

	Absolute Number of Security Workers			Share in the Overall Workforce		
	Male	Female	Total	Male	Female	Total
1993–1994	2,303	33	2,336	0.9	0.0	0.7
1999–2000	2,672	51	2,723	1.0	0.1	0.7
2004–2005	2,864	68	2,932	0.9	0.1	0.7
2011–2012	4,799	113	4,912	1.4	0.1	1.1
2017–2018	5,378	292	5,670	1.5	0.3	1.3

Source: Computed using unit level data from the EUS 50th, 55th, 61st, 68th rounds and the PLFS 2017–2018.

While, as may be expected, women are a minority in the sector, they still constitute a larger fraction than before (0.1 to 0.3 percent of the workforce). We note that around 3 lakh women were employed as security workers in 2017–2018. Fifty-five percent of them were engaged in the public sector, with six in ten working as "protective service workers." Overall, this sub-occupational group contributed to around 50 percent of all female employment in security work. In the private sector, close to two-thirds of female security workers were engaged as "messengers, porters, doorkeepers," etc. Though the share of female security workers has risen marginally over this period, security work in India continues to be a male-dominated occupation, the latter constituting close to 95 percent of the entire security workforce in the country.

Security workers is a large and not wholly commensurate category. The three main sub-categories and their evolution are shown in Table 12.2. Watchmen,

Table 12.2 **Composition of those employed as security workers, NCO-68 and NCO-04 (in %)**

	NCO 1968			*NCO 2004*		
Occupation group	1993–1994	1999–2000	2004–2005	Occupation group	2011–2012	2017–2018
Policemen and Detectives	37.9	38.2	32.6	Police Inspectors and Detectives	7.5	10.4
Protection Force Home Guard & Security Workers	10.6	12.7	17.9	Protective Services Workers	40.4	44.8
Watchmen, Chowkidars, and Gate Keepers	51.6	49.1	49.5	Doorkeepers and others	52.1	44.7

Source: Computed using unit level data from the EUS 50th, 55th, 61st, 68th rounds and the PLFS 2017–2018.

doorkeepers, and gatekeepers (what we may think of as most closely aligning to the "Chowkidar") constitute about 50 percent of the overall category throughout this time. A note of caution on Table 12.2, however: a casual glance would suggest to the reader that there has been a drastic decline in the relative share of "Policemen and Detectives" in 2017–2018 when compared to the earlier rounds (classified under NCO-68). However, as we have already noted above, due to data limitations, we are limited in making any definitive assessments about shifts taking place within the larger security worker classification (sub-occupational groups), as a proper concordance is not possible between the two NCO schemas. The drastic decline in the share of "Policemen and Detectives" between 1993–1994 and 2017–2018 in favor of "Protective Security Workers" is more likely down to the fact that the sub-occupation group "Police Constables" in the old schema (NCO 68 code 571.30) was classified under the broader head "Policemen and Detectives" but as per the NCO 2004 is now part of the "Protective Service Workers" classification (NCO code 5162.10). Given this issue, we can only properly compare long-term trends at the broad aggregate level ("security workers").

In Figure 12.3, we show the share of security workers in each of the main industrial groups (classified on the basis of two-digit National Industrial Classification in 2008) that employed security workers in 2017–2018. Not surprisingly, "Private

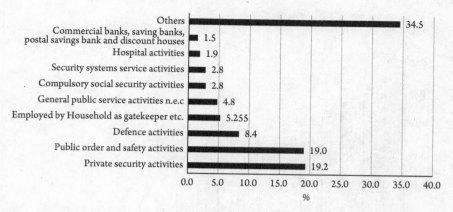

Figure 12.3 Distribution of security workers across major industrial groups (NIC 2008 2-digit), 2017–2018 (in %)
Source: Computed using unit-level data from the PLFS 2017–2018

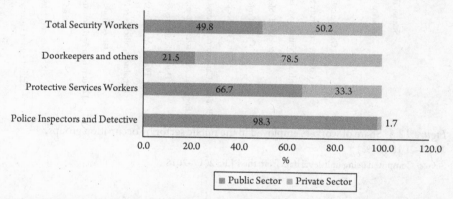

Figure 12.4 Share of security workers employed in the public sector by NCO subgroups, 2017–2018 (in %)
Source: Computed using unit-level data from the PLFS 2017–2018

security activities" and "Public Order and Safety Activities" employed the highest share of security workers (19.2 percent and 19 percent of all security workers respectively), which was followed by "Defense activities" (8.4 percent). The relatively large proportion of security workers employed in these last two groups (primarily state-run institutions) suggests that the public sector accounts for a large share (close to 50 percent) of the employment of security workers in India.

Figure 12.4 further disaggregates this into subgroups. While it may not be surprising that nearly all "Police Inspectors and Detectives" are employed in the public sector, it is also the case that more than two-thirds of "Protective Service Workers" are also employed in it. Private protective services work is dominated by the "Doorkeeper" category.

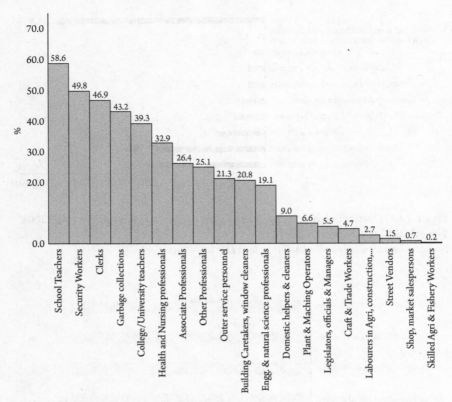

Figure 12.5 Share of workers employed in the public sector by occupation groups, 2017–2018 (in %)
Source: Computed using unit-level data from the PLFS 2017–2018

The importance of the public sector in the provision of protective services is underscored by Figure 12.5. Of all the major occupational groups in the country, only schoolteachers recorded a higher share of their workforce as being employed in the public sector. From the last three rounds, we do note, however, that the share of security workers employed by the public sector has come down by about 5 percent and is still at around 50 percent of the security workforce.

The strong presence of the public sector as an employer is interesting, given that much of the contemporary discussion with respect to security work (as noted above) concerns itself with private security. As the report puts it, the rapid growth of urbanization and changes in the perception of security by the government, business, and the public at large have all led to a massive boom in the private segment of security work, with major potentialities for further growth in the future.[14] The preoccupation with the private segment is possibly due to the fact that, in urban metropolitan areas, private security provision typically dominates and can be up to six times that of the public sector, as seen in Figure 12.6.

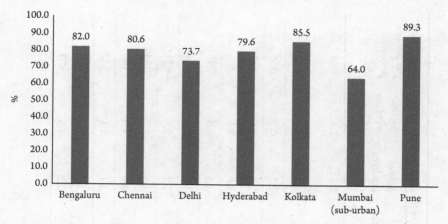

Figure 12.6 Share of security workers employed in the private sector in major metropolitan areas, 2017–2018 (in %)

Source: Computed using unit level data from the PLFS 2017–2018

We used district-level information, as the PLFS does not go beyond that level of disaggregation.

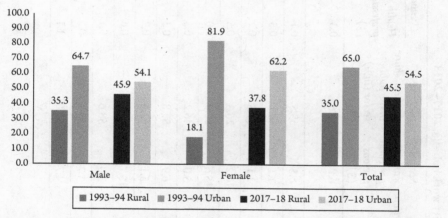

Figure 12.7 Distribution of security workers by sex and sector, 1993–1994 and 2017–2018 (in %)

Source: Computed using unit-level data from the EUS 50th round and the PLFS 2017–2018

We turn now to the geographical dimension of the distribution of protective service occupations. Figure 12.7 suggests an interesting feature. Between 1993 and 2017, the share of security workers who were employed in the rural sector as opposed to the urban sector grew from 35 percent to 45 percent. Both the male and female proportion of security workers in the rural sector grew.

Table 12.3 presents the distribution of security workers across the states of the country. Column 1 provides us with the state-wise distribution of security workers.

Table 12.3 State-wise landscape of security work in India, 2017–2018

State/UT	State wise distribution of security workers (in %) (1)	Index of disproportion (2)	Security workers per 1000 persons (3)	Security workers' share in the public sector (in%) (4)	Occupation group's share in the total workforce (in %)				Population per police personnel (9)
					Health professionals (5)	Nursing professionals (6)	School teachers (7)	Security workers (8)	
Andhra Pradesh	6.2	1.1	6.0	40.6	0.3	0.4	1.8	1.4	916
Assam	3.7	1.6	6.5	68.5	0.1	0.5	3.4	2.0	606
Bihar	2.4	0.4	1.1	50.5	0.3	0.1	2.3	0.5	1,356
Chhattisgarh	1.1	0.4	2.1	71.5	0.1	0.3	2.3	0.5	442
Delhi	3.3	2.5	10.2	26.3	0.5	0.9	1.6	3.1	298
Goa	0.4	3.6	15.6	80.9	0.0	0.5	2.5	4.6	295
Gujarat	5.8	1.2	5.0	46.2	0.3	0.3	1.6	1.4	724
Haryana	3.8	1.8	6.9	57.8	0.3	0.4	2.2	2.3	631
HP	0.8	0.9	5.1	62.4	0.2	0.2	1.9	1.2	434
J & K	3.0	3.7	13.7	92.9	0.6	0.3	4.4	4.6	162
Jharkhand	1.9	0.9	3.0	58.6	0.1	0.2	2.1	1.1	562
Karnataka	4.6	0.8	3.7	38.4	0.3	0.2	1.5	1.0	808
Kerala	3.0	1.2	4.7	51.8	1.1	0.7	2.2	1.5	807

	(1)	(2)	(3)	(4)	(5)	(6)	(7)	(8)	(9)
MP	4.6	0.7	3.2	56.4	0.3	0.1	2.1	0.8	853
Maharashtra	12.0	1.2	5.7	31.1	0.3	0.2	1.6	1.5	572
North East	2.9	2.5	10.6	91.9	0.3	0.7	5.4	3.1	140
Odisha	2.5	0.8	3.1	52.9	0.2	0.2	1.8	0.9	759
Punjab	4.0	1.9	8.0	68.7	0.2	0.5	3.0	2.4	359
Rajasthan	4.6	0.8	3.4	51.7	0.2	0.3	2.5	1.1	844
Tamil Nadu	7.8	1.1	5.7	32.2	0.3	0.5	1.4	1.4	688
Telangana	4.7	1.4	6.9	39.7	0.3	0.3	1.7	1.8	760
UT	0.8	2.6	11.4	74.4	0.7	0.9	2.0	3.2	332
UP	7.2	0.5	1.8	53.8	0.3	0.2	1.8	0.7	783
Uttarkhand	1.5	2.0	7.6	77.6	0.3	0.7	3.0	2.5	527
West Bengal	7.5	0.9	4.1	47.8	0.3	0.2	1.9	1.2	1,031

Source: Columns (1) to (8) computed using unit level data from the PLFS 2017–2018, Column (9) computed from Data on Police Organisations, 2018.

In this exercise, we have combined all the union territories into one group called UT and all the North Eastern states excluding Assam into another group. Maharashtra (12.0 percent) has the highest share of security workers, followed by Tamil Nadu (7.8 percent) and West Bengal (7.5 percent). Column 2 provides us with the ratio of the state's share of total security workers to the state's share of total workers. We calculate this as an index of disproportion. An index score greater than 1 suggests that the state has a disproportionately high fraction of protective service workers while an index value below 1 suggests the opposite. This ratio is highest in Jammu and Kashmir (3.7), followed by Goa (3.6) and the UTs (2.6). At the other end lie Bihar (0.4) and Chhattisgarh (0.4), whose share of the security workforce is relatively much smaller than their overall workforce share.

Goa (15.6), Jammu and Kashmir (13.7), UTs (11.4), and the North Eastern states (10.6) have the highest number of security personnel per 1,000 persons of their population. It is also clear that most of the personnel deployed as security workers in these regions are employed by the state (Column 4).

A similar story presents itself when we look at the data provided by the Bureau of Police Research and Development for the year 2018 (Column 9 in Table 12.3). The North Eastern states Jammu and Kashmir and Goa have the lowest ratio when it comes to total population per policepersons, whereas Bihar and West Bengal have the highest.

One way to examine the relative importance of protective services employment over the years is to compare the presence of security work in our society relative to two other major occupations, viz. (1) health and nursing and (2) schoolteaching, which are also providing quintessential social services. While these may differ in their end goal, their provisioning and purpose may be usefully compared for this reason.

We use the same methodology adopted for security workers to calculate the absolute number of health professionals and schoolteachers for the various time points under study. For calculating health and nursing professionals under the NCO 2004 schema, we have used the codes 222, 223, and 323, whereas for the earlier rounds (coming under the NCO 1968 schema) we used the codes 70–75, 78–79, 84–85, and 89. Similarly, we used codes 232 and 331 under the 04 schema and 151–153 under the 68 NCO schema to calculate "schoolteachers."

In terms of absolute numbers in 2017–2018, there were approximately 8.9 million persons employed as schoolteachers, while the number of persons employed as health and nursing professionals was around 2.6 million. Looking at the growth of these two occupations relative to security work, we note that while in 1993–1994 there were approximately 2.04 schoolteachers to every security worker, this ratio has come down to 1.56 in 2017–2018. Similarly, while there were 0.55 health and nursing professionals to every security worker in 1993–1994, by 2017–2018, this has fallen further to 0.46. Thus, relative to these two professions, security work is growing at a faster rate in recent years, as seen in Figure 12.8.

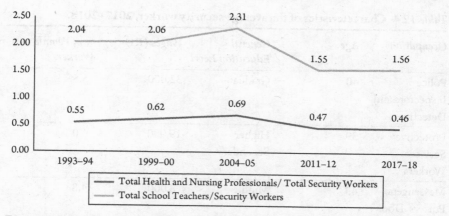

Figure 12.8 Number of health and educational professionals to every security worker, various years

Source: Computed using unit-level data from the EUS 50th, 55th, 61st, and 68th rounds and the PLFS 2017–2018

Interestingly, there are substantial disparities between states in their provisioning of social services (Columns 5–8 in Table 12.3). Kerala is the only state where the share of health and nursing professionals was higher than that of the share of security workers in the workforce. For most states, however, the share of schoolteachers was higher. In only 7 out of the 25 states/UTs was there a higher share of security workers than schoolteachers. The Hindi heartland, which has a disproportionately lower number of security workers and nursing and health professionals by contrast, has a higher than average proportion of schoolteachers. On the other end, Delhi has 1.9 security workers for every schoolteacher, followed by Goa (1.8) and the combined UTs (1.6).

Characteristics of Security Workers

The chowkidar's job is actually unenviable. He works for the haves but belongs to the have-nots and his real task is to maintain a barrier between the haves inside and the have-nots out there.

—Pritish Nandy[15]

We turn now to the characteristics of security workers. As Table 12.4 shows, the median security worker is slightly older than the average worker, disproportionately male, more educated (if in the category of police and detectives), and equally educated in the case of a private doorkeeper. Figures 12A.1 and 12A.2 in this chapter's appendix provide some more disaggregation. From the same, we note that in terms of age distribution there has been a pronounced rightward shift, with security workers being considerably older now on average than in 1993.

Table 12.4 **Characteristics of the average security worker, 2017–2018**

Occupation	Age	General Education Level	Wages (Rs)	% of Female Workers
Police Inspectors and Detectives	40	Graduate	32,000	5.5
Protective Services Workers	39	Higher Secondary	19,000	6.0
Messengers, Porters, Door Keepers	43	Middle	8,000	4.8
Security Workers	41	Secondary	12,000	5.4
Average Workforce	38	Middle	7,715	21.5

Source: Computed using unit level data from the PLFS 2017–2018.

With regard to the average educational attainment of the subgroups, it is observed that "doorkeepers and others" are distinctly to the left tail of the distribution, with the vast majority having at most a secondary education (only about 20 percent have higher degrees). By contrast, "police inspectors and detectives" typically have a diploma or are graduates, as in Figure 12A.2. Those working as doorkeepers, in fact, have roughly the same educational attainment as the overall non-agricultural labor force. On the other hand, the "police inspectors and detectives" and the "protective service workers" categories are disproportionately represented in higher educational categories.[16]

Figure 12.9 provides us with the caste-wise distribution of security workers. Overall, we note that compared to the caste-wise distribution of the entire workforce, scheduled castes (20.6 percent) and others (34.6 percent) are observed to be relatively over-represented when it comes to security workers, while OBCs and STs are found to be under-represented. Given that close to half of the security workforce are employed in the public sector (where caste-based reservations are applicable), we have further broken down the above analysis into caste-wise representation in public and non-public enterprises. We computed a caste-wise representation index, that is, the share of a particular caste group employed as a security worker/share of that caste group in the workforce as a whole. A value greater than 1 indicates an over-representation of that caste category in the occupation group "security

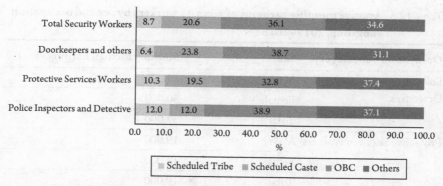

Figure 12.9 Distribution of security workers by social group, 2017–2018 (in %)
Source: Computed using unit-level data from the PLFS 2017–2018

workers," and a value less than 1 represents under-representation. Incidentally, we note that the relative representation of ST security workers employed in the public sector in 2017–2018 has improved (1.13) as compared to the same in 2004–2005 (0.67). The representation index of SC security workers in public segments, however, as gone down from 0.87 to 0.82 during the same time period. OBCs both in 2004–2005 and 2017–2018 find themselves relatively under-represented in both the public and non-public sectors.

With respect to religious groups, we find that in 2017–2018, 83 percent of all security workers are Hindus, while Muslims account for 7 percent and Christians 5 percent. We note that the representation of Muslims in security work is lower than their representation in the overall workforce both in the public (index value: 0.79) and private sector (index value: 0.64) while for Christians it is much higher (index value of 1.26 and 2.13 in the public and private segment respectively).

Given these facts, it is perhaps not unsurprising to see that labor incomes of security workers also vary substantially. Table 12.5 shows the average monthly earnings of security workers. Among the various sub-occupational categories within security workers, "police inspectors and detectives" in 2017–2018 had the highest average monthly wage, followed by "protective service workers." Across the categories, the wages of male security workers are higher than that of female security workers.

Comparing the average (median) earnings in different occupation groups relative to security workers, we note that eleven out of the eighteen other occupation groups, reported to be earning less than what security workers earned in 2017–2018.

We now turn to look at the conditions of work of those who are employed as security workers. From Table 12.6 we note that between 2004–2005 and 2017–2018, the share of strongly formal security jobs has fallen by more than 11 percentage

Table 12.5 **Average monthly earnings of security workers by sex and occupation subgroup, 2017–2018**

Occupation Subcategory	Sex	Monthly Median Earning (Rs.)
Police Inspectors and Detectives	Male	33,000
	Female	30,000
	Total	32,000
Protective Services Workers	Male	19,000
	Female	14,000
	Total	19,000
Messengers, Porters, Door Keepers and Related Workers	Male	8,000
	Female	7,000
	Total	8,000
All Security Workers	Male	12,000
	Female	9,000
	Total	12,000

Source: Computed using unit level data from the PLFS 2017–2018.

Table 12.6 **Shift in share between 2004–2005 and 2017–2018**

Sector	% Shift	Type of Employment	% Shift
Unorganized	4.0	Strongly Formal	−1.9
		Weak Formal	0.5
		Informal	1.4
Organized	−4.0	Strongly Formal	−12.3
		Weak Formal	7.0
		Informal	5.4
Total	0	Strongly Formal	−11.8
		Weak Formal	4.9
		Informal	6.9

Source: Computed using unit level data from the NSSO EUS 61st round and the PLFS 2017–2018.

points in favor of both informal and weakly formal jobs.[17] There is thus a rising informality among security workers in India. Moreover, there has been a 4 percentage point rise in the share of security workers that are employed in the unorganized sector.[18]

The Correlates of Protective Security Work

The body of work dedicated to understanding the rapid rise of security work in the past few decades has identified a number of plausible reasons for the same high levels of inequality in modern society, rising ethnic tensions, rapid pace of urbanization, and concerns brought forth by increasing migration, just to name a few.[19] In the following section, we have made an attempt to correlate the share of security workforce in a given region with some of these aforementioned explanations in order to understand whether there exists a relationship between the same in the Indian landscape.

The first measure that we used was the state-wise per capita NSDP (2017–2018) to note whether richer states tend to be associated with a higher share of security workers. State-wise Gini Coefficients based on the NSSO's 2011–2012 Consumer Expenditure survey were then used to see whether inequality in a region tends to have any relation with the number of security workers in the state as a share of the workforce. The assumption is that the more unequal states would employ a larger security force given the social unrest arising out of that inequality.[20] We captured urbanization rates based on the PLFS 2017–2018 to note if there exists any evidence to link urbanization with varying security shares across states. The rate of total cognizable crime was collected from the NCRB (National Crime Research Bureau) data for the year 2017 to explore whether states with a higher crime rate tend to deploy a larger security workforce. We also used information from the IHDS-II survey to relate security work with the confidence and trust that people of a region have in their institutional policing structures.

Alongside the state-wise analysis, we also tried to look at some possible correlates of security work at the district level.[21] The district level analysis was taken up to account for the heterogeneity of an area's population and the impact that it might have on the overall share of the security force deployed— information that one cannot meaningfully hope to capture at the aggregated state level. Migration, for example, is known to be an intra-state phenomenon in India rather than an inter-state phenomenon. With district-wise migration (which we captured from the Census 2011 migration tables)[22] we have also tried to examine whether a relationship exists between a district's security share and its share of non-Hindu population,[23] and the level of its ethno-linguistic fractionalization.[24] We also tried to see the correlation between a district's share of security workers and the IPC crimes per one lakh population for major metropolitan areas located in those districts.[25]

What we noted from this exercise was that surprisingly some of the obvious candidates—the level of inequality, confidence in police institutions, the level of recognized and reported crime, ethnolinguistic fractionalization, and migration— did not seem to suggest a strong correlation with a region's share of the security

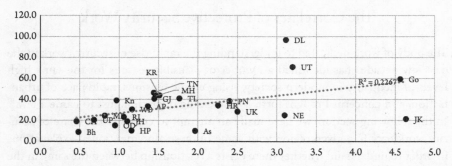

Figure 12.10 Correlating share of security workers in a state's workforce with the state-wise urbanization rate (in %)

Source: Computed using unit-level data from the PLFS 2017–2018, statistically significant (95%)

workforce. Of all the variables taken up for study, only urbanization, in Figure 12.10, appears to be a robust correlate, suggesting that the phenomenon may be driven by the rapid changes occurring in urban India.

Conclusion: Guards and Welfare

We conclude our chapter here with a discussion of the welfare implications of the industry. In national accounts statistics and the job figures, the rise of the security services industry must perforce be a "good thing": providing some services and value added in an otherwise bleak labor market landscape. But from a broader viewpoint this is questionable. To us, the sharp growth in the security guard industry is likely symptomatic of twin failures in the Indian growth process, especially in urban India. On the one hand, an inability to generate high-quality jobs for the relatively unskilled and on the other hand a skewed pattern of growth whereby an enclave urban economy is increasingly distanced from the vast majority around it. The security guard may be a way of controlling the fraught intersection between these spaces. It is also possible that unequal growth has heightened security needs and a sense of threat, especially in urban areas, from the gale forces of migration and aspirations that have been released. Private security services can be seen, in some sense as a defensive expenditure, albeit for the relatively wealthy.

We are certainly not the first to make the point about security being a defensive expenditure. As early as 1939, John Hicks wrote that "the services of police, justice and defense do contribute to production, and may be thought of as used in production in the same way as power and fuel."[26] The question was also important to Simon Kuznets, and the fundamental concern as to how to include these in the national accounts—either as intermediate goods or final goods—was a point of major deliberation.[27] The decision has deep implications for the assessment of economic well-being. As John Joseph Wallis and Douglass C. North showed, many goods and services that they call transactional (which includes but is not limited to defensive expenditures) account for a much larger fraction of GDP over time.[28] Kenneth Boulding, for example, proposed somewhat wryly that every country maintains two sorts of accounts: a national income and a national cost account, with guard labor being put into the latter.[29] The most explicit recognition of the difficulties of evaluating defensive expenditures was made by Nordhaus and Tobin, in their seminal 1973 paper. They termed any activities as being "defensive" if they "are evidently not directly sources of utility themselves but are regrettably necessary inputs to activities that may yield utility."[30] Clearly the expenditure on security guards falls under examples of defensive expenditure,[31] focused specifically on security services, and suggested the need to consider these as actual intermediate inputs. As he puts it: "The final output is always the goods and services being produced, and the police necessary to protect them are simply a cost of that final output. Treating police services on this basis would enable us to avoid the anomaly of showing increases in real GNP as both crime and the police efforts to hold it in check rise apace."[32]

Of course, even before this, classical economists found the difference between what they termed "unproductive" and "productive" activities to be central to their analysis of the economy. Marx stressed that the capitalist system needed a whole range of unproductive workers whose purpose was to maintain the status quo distribution of rights as well as to help in the realization of value.

An additional question that arises is whether these "regrettable" expenditures are best borne privately or publicly. Except for the most extreme libertarian viewpoint, security is seen across the board as something that is best provided publicly since law and order is essentially a public good.

In India's case, then, the question is how to treat the rise of the security industry. India is, by far, the largest employer of private security guards. We wonder if the breathless excitement of the security guard industry as a source of employment is misplaced, and instead that the correct way to view this is as a symptom of a sharpened social schism. Societies that enjoy high-quality social relationships—say, high levels of interpersonal trust—possess an important input that allows for production and that is not priced by the market. Thus, for example, shopping malls in Scandinavia or Europe typically do not require you to be subjected to a security check before entering (by contrast, this is ubiquitous in urban India). Conversely, societies that have low levels of trust are forced to "invest" resources to enhance transactional security and elicit production. If our thrust is correct, we ought to see this industry as a glaring example of what may be termed "Marxian Waste." This is

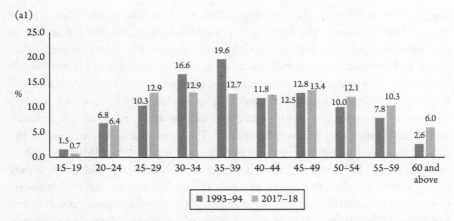

Figure 12.A1 Age-wise distribution of workers employed as security workers, 1993–1994 and 2017–2018 (in %)

Source: Computed using unit-level data from the NSSO EUS 50th round and the PLFS 2017–2018

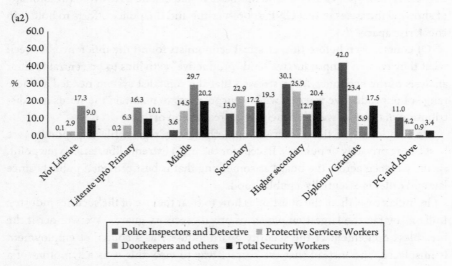

Figure 12.A2 Distribution of security workers by NCO subgroups and general education status, 2017–2018 (in %)

Source: Computed using unit-level data from the PLFS 2017–2018

the waste associated with the need for maintaining the institutional features of society that allow for enduring capital accumulation but that are not directly productive (in the classical sense themselves).

Understanding the drivers of this societal arrangement is certainly an important task for future research, especially in India.

Notes

1. Narendra Modi (@narendramodi), "Your Chowkidar is standing firm & serving the nation. But, I am not alone. Everyone who is fighting corruption, dirt, social evils is a Chowkidar." Twitter, 16 March, 2019, 9:00 AM https://twitter.com/narendramodi/status/11067595 55315314689

2. As per a survey conducted by Lokniti (2018), only three in every ten people had significant levels of trust in senior police officers and two in every ten in the local police. Similarly, only three in ten respondents had significant trust in the courts.

3. https://ncrb.gov.in/en/crime-in-india.

4. Claire Provost, "The Industry of Inequality: Why the World Is Obsessed with Private Security," *The Guardian*, May 12, 2017, https://www.theguardian.com/inequality/2017/may/12/industry-of-inequality-why-world-is-obsessed-with-private-security.

5. https://medicaldialogues.in/one-doctor-for-every-1445-patients-in-india-still-behind-who-prescribed-11000-govt/.

6. https://docs.google.com/spreadsheets/d/1D1DtDTupI-ildBLWIQGswypRCsRzjB--39rQ QBGgqSU/edit#gid=75703183.

7. https://www.insightcrime.org/news/analysis/private-security-necessity-central-america/.

8. Damien Carrière, "Filtering Class through Space: Security Guards and Urban Territories in Delhi, India. Geography," Université Sorbonne Paris Cité; University of Minnesota (Minneapolis, MN, 2018).

9. Samuel Bowles and Arjun Jayadev, "Guard Labour," *Journal of Development Economics* 79, no. 2 (2006): 328–348; Samuel Bowles and Arjun Jayadev, "Garrison America," *The Economists' Voice* 4, no. 2 (2007): 1–7.

10. See, e.g., https://www.grantthornton.in/globalassets/1.-member-firms/india/assets/pdfs/private_security_services_industry_in_india.pdf;
    http://ficci.in/spdocument/20966/FICCI-PwC-Report-on-Private-Security-Indus try.pdf.

11. See https://population.un.org/wpp/.

12. Of course, what constitutes a private security person is also dependent on regulatory categories. Guards deployed by private security agencies are mandatorily governed under the Private Security Agencies Regulation Act, 2005 (PSARA) and are monitored by the respective controlling authorities of the states that grant them licenses for operating in the state based on the parameters laid down in the law. Recently, the Ministry of Home Affairs issued a draft Private Security Agencies Central (Amendment) Model Rules, 2019, which seeks to amend certain provisions that were laid out in the 2006 model rules.

13. It is to be noted that a clean concordance (for comparability between the two NCO schema, 68 and 2004) requires the data to be available at the six-digit level. Lack of availability of data at this disaggregation, however, prevents us from making a proper concordance. At best we were able to arrive at only a close approximation.

14. FICCI-Grant Thornton, "Private Security Services in India" (New Delhi, 2015).

15. Pritish Nandy, "You Want to Be a Chowkidar?" *Mumbai Mirror*, March 27, 2019, https://mumbaimirror.indiatimes.com/opinion/columnists/pritish-nandy/you-want-to-be-a-chowkidar/articleshow/68587186.cms.

16. We use information from the PLFS 2017–2018 to compare the educational qualifications of security workers with that of the overall non-agricultural workforce. This gives us some indication as to the educational qualifications that are needed to be part of the security workforce when compared to the workforce average. We calculated the following ratio: share of security workers (disaggregated by occupational groups) found in a particular educational category/share of non-agricultural workforce found in that category. Again, it is an index of disproportionality, with a value greater than 1 indicating that the occupation represented higher than average in that category and a value less than 1 indicating the opposite.

17. The labor bureau surveys brought out by the NSSO provide us with two different indicators that are generally used to measure the degree of formality/informality of work, that is, (1) nature of job contract and (2) access to social security. Combining the two, attempt to define one's employment type as "strongly formal," "weak formal," and "informal." If an individual has access to any form of social security and also has a written contract, their employment type would be strongly formal. Access to any one of these benefits would see them as working in jobs that are weakly formal and none of these benefits would imply their employment is informal in nature.

18. We use the NCEUS definition to calculate the unorganized-organized dichotomy.

19. Tim Hope, "Inequality and the Clubbing of Private Security," in *Crime, Risk and Insecurity: Law and Order in Everyday Life and Political Discourse,* ed. Tim Hope and Richard Sparks (Oxford and New York: Routledge, 2000), 84–106; S. A. Bollens, "Managing Urban Ethnic Conflict," in *Globalism and Local Democracy: Challenge and Change in Europe and North America,* ed. R. Hambleton, H. V. Savitch, and Murray Stewart (London: Palgrave Macmillan, 2003), 108–124; Michael Pacione, *Urban Geography: A Global Perspective* (Oxford: Routledge, 2001); UN-Habitat, *Enhancing Urban Safety and Security: Global Report on Human Settlements* (London: Earthscan, 2007).

20. Samuel Bowles and Arjun Jayadev, "Guard Labour," *Journal of Development Economics* 79, no. 2 (2006): 328–348.

21. State-wise per capita NSDP obtained from the *Handbook of Statistics on Indian Economy,* RBI website; R^2: 0.1378 (Statistically significant −95%); Gini Coefficients taken from Chauhan et al. (2016), R^2: 0.0034 (Not significant). Degree of Confidence in police institutions taken from IHDS-II unit level data. R^2: 0.0082 (Not significant). Rate of cognizable crime taken from *Crime in India, 2017,* Volume I published by the NCRB; R^2: 0.0117 (Not significant).

22. Using migration tables (D-2) from the 2011 Census, we ranked districts according to the share of migrant workers in the total district population (in descending order) and took the top 25% for this analysis; R^2: 0.0339 (Statistically significant-95%).

23. Using data from the PLFS 2017–2018, we ranked districts according to the share of non-Hindus (in descending order) and took the top 25% for this analysis; R^2: 0.0459 (Statistically significant-95%).

24. Using data from the PLFs 2017–2018, we ranked districts according to their ELF value (in descending order) and took the top 25% for this analysis; R^2: 0.0091 (Not significant).

25. Computed using unit level data from the PLFS 2017–2018; IPC crime data for major metropolitan area taken from the NCRB webpage for the year 2016. https://ncrb.gov.in/sites/defa ult/files/crime_in_india_table_additional_table_chapter_reports/Table%201B.1_0.pdf. We used district data since PLFS does not provide information at the metropolitan level. R^2: 0.0265 (Not significant).

26. John R. Hicks, "Public Finance in the National Income," *Review of Economic Studies* 6, no. 2 (1939): 147–155.

27. Simon Kuznets, "Government Product and National Income," *Review of Income and Wealth* 1, no. 1 (1951): 178–244.

28. John Joseph Wallis and C. Douglass North, "Should Transaction Costs Be Subtracted from Gross National Product?" *Journal of Economic History* 48, no. 3 (1988): 651–654.

29. Kenneth E. Boulding, *Collected Papers, Vol III: Political Economy* (Boulder: Colorado Associated University Press, 1973).

30. William D. Nordhaus and James Tobin, "Is Growth Obsolete?" *Cowles Foundation Discussion Papers 319* (Cowles Foundation for Research in Economics, 1971).

31. Robert Eisner, "Extended Accounts for National Income and Product," *Journal of Economic Literature* 26, no. 4 (1988): 1611–1684.

32. Eisner, "Extended Accounts for National Income and Product."

13

India's Intelligence in Internal Security

SAIKAT DATTA

Spanning a history of nearly 135 years, the Intelligence Bureau (IB) has served as the bulwark of India's internal security apparatus. Created as an agency to monitor Indians by a colonial power, post-independence saw the organization evolve into a leviathan that is omnipresent in every state and Union Territory. Its primary role is to generate intelligence for the federal government on a variety of subjects, of which internal security is a significant aspect.

Due to a combination of several factors, the IB has not only emerged as the most significant internal security organization, it also wields enormous influence on political and economic affairs. This reflects a key philosophy that has existed since the days of the master-strategist Kautilya (also known as Chanakya), who advocated for intelligence as a key aspect of statecraft aimed at ensuring the stability of the state.[1]

The IB's overarching role in India's internal security is a result of several reasons, not the least being its historical legacy as a key instrument of colonial power. Its role evolved with independent India's first major crisis when it went to war with Pakistan soon after independence over the state of Jammu and Kashmir. The Kashmir crisis also blurred the distinction between internal and external security with those of political stability, propelling the IB into a position of eminence for every federal government in power since independence.

However, as this chapter argues, the historical legacy, structure, and dominant position of the IB in India's internal security matrix has led not only to successes, but also to many failures and resulted in unintended consequences.

This has created a paradigm in which the IB has emerged as the preeminent agency for internal security and enormous influence even in non-security-related policies with minimal accountability and oversight. Such power and influence has undermined the IB's core charter to protect India against all domestic threats.

The role of intelligence in decision-making at India's apex political and strategic levels has grown significantly over decades. This is due not only to the fact that there

Saikat Datta, *India's Intelligence in Internal Security* In: *Internal Security in India*. Edited by: Amit Ahuja and Devesh Kapur, Oxford University Press. © Oxford University Press 2023. DOI: 10.1093/oso/9780197660331.003.0013 is a formal recognition that information is power and there is now more information and big data that the government is able to collect than ever before, but also to the complexity of threats the state faces.

Since the mid-1980s, India has aspired for regional and global power status. However, such a status is incumbent on a nation's ability to stay ahead of its rivals in terms of information, innovation, and economy. This is especially true in a world that is dominated by internet-based technologies that have blurred traditional geographical boundaries and provided access for inimical actors to tap into pools of discontent and dissent contained within national boundaries earlier. But this is where India's century-old intelligence apparatus is out of sync with its great power ambitions as well as modern security precepts.

Both in terms of influence and budget, the IB holds a premier status. With a budget slightly above Rs. 2,575 crore ($340 million), the IB works under the federal government with offices in every state and Union territory.[2] In the states the IB works as Subsidiary Intelligence Bureau (SIB), usually headed by an officer of the rank of Joint Director, with some key states like the erstwhile state of Jammu and Kashmir having an Additional Director (see Figure 13.1).

This gives the IB a national footprint and an institutional relationship with the state police forces. The senior leadership of the IB comes almost entirely from the Indian Police Service (IPS), making it a police-dominated body that draws on its relationship with the state police forces. Most of the IPS officers come to the bureau on deputation from the federal government and stay for five years or more, after which, with mutual consent, they are declared as "hardcore" and allowed to serve for longer periods, beyond the seven-year cap that remains for other federal deputations. The

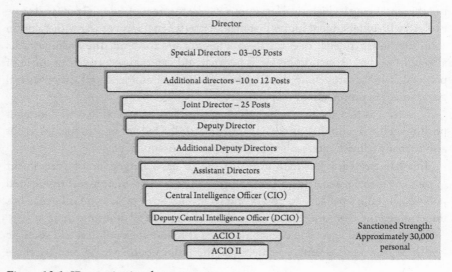

Figure 13.1 IB organizational structure

predominance of the IPS leaves an enormous impact on the functioning and ethos of the IB and is discussed later in the chapter. Those in the ranks of Deputy Director and below are drawn from a nationwide examination where successful candidates are recruited as Assistant Central Intelligence Officers—Grade 2 (ACIO-2). These cadre officers serve up to a middle rank before retiring since the senior leadership is always reserved for the IPS.

As a federal body, not only does the IB play an enormous role in informing the federal and state governments on all forms of security challenges; it also plays a leading role in shaping all internal security postures and policies. This is even more significant when the footprint of the IB's role is examined. It plays a key role in collecting political intelligence on the rivals of the government in power, and also gives inputs in the appointment of senior bureaucrats and senior judiciary.

The IB has been at the heart of the Indian state's response to insurgencies. From the insurgencies in the North East, to those in Kashmir, Punjab, and in the LWE-impacted states, the IB has worked in conjunction with the security forces. The difference between the IB and other security agencies would be its omnipotent and omnipresent role throughout the life of the conflict. While other agencies like the Indian Army or federal police agencies would come in to control or quell the armed insurgency (see chapters by Shakti Sinha, Sushant Singh, and Yashovardhan Azad in this volume), the IB would not only play the lead role in gathering intelligence, but also influence other agencies, and calibrate the role of the federal government in pursuing a "kill strategy" or initiating negotiations as part of its conflict mitigation strategy. This has been largely true for all armed insurgencies and internal security challenges since then.

While the role of the IB in ending insurgencies in the state of Mizoram or Punjab are seen as definitive successes, its inability to anticipate and mitigate many other security challenges also indicates systemic failures. Many of these insurgencies, the Indian government has claimed consistently, are aided by foreign powers like Pakistan and China.[3]

This is due to many historical and structural factors. For instance, the lack of powers to carry out arrests, a legacy from its colonial-era foundations, has allowed the IB to work outside the ambit of the law. It is not bound by the need to prosecute its cases in trial courts. Hence, the need for gathering evidence is left to other organizations. This, instead of restricting the IB's role, instead expands it, giving it much more leeway than its sister agencies that are bound by limitations imposed by specific laws that govern them.

The IB is an organization that has not been created by an act of Parliament and therefore remains beyond any form of public scrutiny. This is coupled with the lack of a specific charter, allowing the federal government to use it in many ways. This in turn affects its role and enhances its influence in managing India's internal security.

The role and efficacy of the IB within the framework of India's democratic structure can be examined using the benchmarks set by the Geneva Centre for the Democratic Control of Armed Forces (DCAF).[4] It lays down the following:

- Domestic intelligence and collection are subject to national laws.
- Separation of foreign versus domestic intelligence require an effective coordination of intelligence collection.
- Coordination is performed by an executive branch entity.
- Joint assessments are ideally taken by an independent body.
- Executive, legislative, and judicial branches exercise oversight.[5]

Clearly, the IB fares very poorly on these benchmarks, as will be discussed later in this chapter.

India has tried to delineate its intelligence apparatus between its external and internal security scenarios for over five decades, without looking at reforming it. As a result, what has passed off as reform has actually been cosmetic change at best, leading to repeated failures at key junctures. This plays out differently when dealing with external and internal security challenges.

For internal security, the repeated failure of intelligence has led to perpetuating conflicts rather than resolving them. Many failures stem from the political structure of the intelligence community in India. This is a legacy of the past.

The origins of India's intelligence apparatus lie in colonial times when surveillance and subjugation of the native population was paramount. Post-independence, while incremental reforms have taken place to improve efficiency, the gains have been limited.

While independence brought about a change in objectives of India's internal security apparatus, its traditional approach and institutional frameworks largely remained the same. This not only has led to a resistance to any reform, it also creates an inherent conflict between the institutions and the stated aims of a modern constitutional republic. Naturally, this has a major impact on India's internal security that continues to remain reactive and crisis-prone.

The same malaise dogs India's internal security institutions created after independence. The National Investigation Agency (NIA) was created in the aftermath of the terror attack on Mumbai on November 26, 2008 (popularly referred to as 26/11). The creation of the NIA is mired in controversy when it was revealed that "constitutional boundaries" had been stretched to set up the agency.[6]

Like the creation of the Intelligence Bureau (IB), most intelligence or security-related organizations like the Research and Analysis Wing (R&AW), India's external intelligence agency, the NIA, or even the Central Bureau of Investigation (CBI) have weak legal foundations. This has led to legal challenges being mounted in India's various courts questioning the constitutional validity of an agency like the CBI.[7] This undermines any attempt to reform these organizations and creates a cycle of repeated failures and incremental changes to pacify public sentiment.

Historical Accident: From Colonial to Unconstitutional

The IB, like many other institutions tasked with India's national security, was inherited from the departing colonial British. A writ petition filed in India's Supreme Court in 2012 by the Centre for Public Interest Litigation (CPIL), a New Delhi–based non-profit, seeking directions for the passage of laws for governing India's intelligence agencies as directed by the Constitution details the historical antecedents of the organization:

> The Intelligence Bureau has its origins in the Thuggee Office set up in Jabalpur by Colonel (JL) Sleeman in 1835 to gather intelligence about the movements and modus operandi of the "thugs" and dacoits who rampaged the plains of northern India in the 18th and 19th centuries. After the Great Indian Mutiny of 1857, when the reins of government of the Indian Empire were taken over from the East India Company by the British Crown, the Thuggee Office was renamed the Intelligence Bureau and began to collect political and other non-criminal intelligence. In December 1887 the Secretary of State for India set up the Central Special Branch. At the beginning of 20th Century, it was renamed the Central Criminal Intelligence Department. By 1918 the word "criminal" was dropped and the agency started looking after internal security rather than crime. Two years later, it was designated as Intelligence Bureau or IB. It was recast as the Central Intelligence Bureau in 1947 under the Ministry of Home Affairs. Soon after Independence, the agency was given back its old name and became the IB.

Officially, the IB came into existence through a telegram sent by Her Majesty's Secretary for India to the then Viceroy, Lord Dufferin, on December 31, 1887.[8]

Post-independence, the IB was the sole federal intelligence organization undertaking domestic as well as international intelligence collection and analysis. The military had its separate intelligence branches that were largely tactical and focused on operations.

T. G. Sanjeevi Pillai, who served as the first director of the IB after independence between 1947 and 1950, was sent to the United States in 1949 to study how the American intelligence community functioned,[9] so that he could come back and help usher the IB into a post-independence role and also create a Foreign Intelligence Division to gather external intelligence.[10]

India's first federal home minister, Sardar Vallabhbhai Patel, recognized the difficulties of setting up an intelligence capability that could cater to the needs of a modern republic. "I realise how difficult it is to organise our system of intelligence and how the legacy of past prejudices against one community or another against certain types of individuals or others and the monopoly of Europeans in the branch of police service has retarded our progress," he said while addressing the All-India Conference of Police Chiefs on January 12, 1950.[11]

The early years of the IB witnessed a major role in the accession of the erstwhile princely state of Jammu and Kashmir (J&K). This would become a permanent feature of India's dealings with and in the state and also shape the IB's role in internal security. Colonel I. S. Hasanwalia was independent India's first intelligence official in the state of Jammu and Kashmir and would spend ten years (until 1959) coordinating intelligence from the state. His role would become the cornerstone of the IB's relationship with Kashmir affairs, and by extension, its dominant role in internal security as well as in policymaking.

Colonel Hasanwalia was commissioned into the Army Service Corps of the British Indian Army before he sidestepped into signals intelligence.[12] He was one of only two assistant directors in the newly restructured IB who was picked up to head the state unit known as the Subsidiary Intelligence Bureau (SIB) soon after its accession to India.[13] Posted to Jammu and Kashmir in 1949 as the head of the IB station, Hasanwalia would keep a close watch over Kashmir's then prime minister, Sheikh Mohammed Abdullah. IB reports from the state indicated how Abdullah was sidelining the Hindu-leaning opposition Praja Parishad Party, thus edging out the interests of the Jammu and Ladakh regions of the state.[14] These fault lines would remain, leading to the end of Jammu and Kashmir's constitutionally mandated "special status" by the abrogation of Article 370 in August 2019. Hasanwalia's reports to the Indian government would also document how Abdullah was now raising a tirade against India, and his apparent plans to seek independence for the state.

Seen as an officer close to both Prime Minister Nehru and the federal Home Minister Patel, Hasanwalia was initially looked upon with great suspicion by Sheikh Abdullah. He bitterly complained against Hasanwalia and finally came around to accepting him and even developing a "warm professional equation."[15] However, scholars such as veteran journalist Ved Bhasin have been critical of Hasanwalia's role in the early days of Kashmir. Bhasin believed that Hasanwalia and the activities of the IB in the state provoked Abdullah, leading to events that finally led to his dismissal and the appointment of his right-hand man, Ghulam Bakshi, as the second prime minister of the state.[16]

Hasanwalia reported directly to the Director, IB, Bhola Nath (B. N.) Mullik and would operate from Gupkar Road in Srinagar. This has remained as the IB's official residence and office in the state since then.[17] Hasanwalia would also regularly brief both Nehru and Patel and also stay in touch with Bakshi, and he is believed to have been instrumental in the events that led to Abdullah's dismissal.[18] The role that the IB played in conflating a political decision with internal security would prove to be a defining moment in the bureau's relationship with its political masters. This would also shape the IB's role in other insurgencies in independent India.

Mullik, the IB's second chief after Sanjeevi Pillai, would also forge a personal equation with Nehru, virtually mirroring his tenure as India's first prime minister. Mullik would lead the organization for fourteen years from July 1960 to October 1964.[19] His role in the early years of the Kashmir crisis would cement the IB's pre-eminent position among security agencies as well as a tradition of proximity to the prime minister. While the IB was placed under the Ministry of Home Affairs (MHA) as a charter of its role in internal security duties, it continued to have special access to the Prime Minister's Office.

Another key element that would shape the IB in the coming years would be its symbiotic relationship with the Indian Police Service (IPS). The IPS was another colonial handover that became one of three functions labeled as the All-India Services Act, enacted by India's Parliament in 1951.[20] The All-India Services Act had its origins in the administrative setup created by the East India Company and later promulgated as the "Imperial Services" under the Government of India Act, 1919. In 1946, the then Central Cabinet decided to create the Indian Administrative Service to replace the Imperial Civil Service and the IPS.[21] (The Indian Forest Service [IFS] was added to the All-India Services Act in 1967).

The debates led by Patel in the Constituent Assembly from October 1949 offer an insight into how Patel looked at the All-India Services.[22] Patel was insistent that the services, and therefore the police, need to have an independent role. He also saw the services as a bureaucratic institution that would help resolve India's many contradictions and competitive aspirations of the various states. "The Union will go—you will not have a united India, if you have not a good all-India service which has the independence to speak out its mind, which has a sense of security that you will stand by your word and, that after all there is the Parliament, of which we can be proud, where their rights and privileges are secure."

Patel also defended the police and envisaged them as apolitical and professional to ensure that the proposed law would resist any attempt to politicize their role. "The Police which was broken has been brought to its proper level and is functioning fairly efficiently. The Heads of the Departments of the Police in every province are covered under this guarantee. Are you going to change that? Are you going to put your Congress (Party) volunteers as captains? What is it that you propose to do?"[23]

Despite the passing of the All-India Services Act, the legacy of inheriting the intelligence apparatus of a departing colonial power had its share of challenges. While Patel saw the newly created IPS as apolitical and professional, this did not necessarily impact the IB to adapt to the needs of a modern democratic republic. The fact that it remained close to the center of power did not help it shed some of its colonial legacies.

For example, it inherited its suspicion of communist movements in India from the departing British. New inductees into the IB would receive lectures on communism to maintain a dedicated wing to monitor the Communist Party and its affiliates.[24] Trainee officers would be sent to states that had strong communist movements (Kerala, Bengal, and Andhra Pradesh), traditionally seen as a rival of the ruling Congress Party.[25] This ensured that the IB would be tasked to also monitor domestic political movements as a part of its charter to maintain internal security. Keeping the government in power, briefed on domestic politics, was seen as a part of ensuring the stability of the ruling dispensation, and therefore integral to internal security. This shaped the IB's approach to traditional internal security challenges such as armed insurgencies in the North East and groups that were predecessors of the CPI (Maoist), a banned armed insurgent group.

The Intelligence vs. Policing Tussle

As a result, India's post-independence intelligence apparatus was dominated by the officers from the police service, whose role as intelligence officers was also shaped by their proximity to their political masters. This has major implications for domestic intelligence functions while tackling internal security. The domination of IPS officers also needs to be seen in the context of the IB's preeminent role in managing internal security.

The IB's role in independent India began with a close relationship with Prime Minister Nehru and his Home Minister Sardar Patel. Naturally, the first Director of the IB was drawn from the police services, setting a precedent that ensured IPS officers would get to head the organization. Intelligence, thus, came to be seen as an *adjunct* of policing, rather than a separate function of internal security. For many IPS officers, who would on occasion be hand-picked by the director himself, a stint in the IB meant an opportunity to serve in an elite organization that had the years of the highest political office in the country.

The IPS gained from its dominant association with the IB, thus making it impossible for an intelligence culture to evolve independently from a culture of traditional policing. It also ensured that the relationship between the IB and its counterparts in the state police forces remained ambiguous. While law and order is a state subject by constitutional mandate, the IB is federal. As a result, while the bulk of policing is left to the state police, its role in gathering intelligence is left to specialized departments called either the Special Branch/Cell or the Criminal Investigation Department (CID). Like their counterparts in the IB, the state police intelligence departments have to deal with political and security intelligence with far less resources. This results in the state intelligence departments keeping tabs on political intelligence for the state's chief minister, while intelligence relevant to traditional internal security challenges such as terrorism is largely left to the IB.

Most IPS officers spend the early years of their careers managing districts, which are administrative units in the state and primarily involve a variety of law-and-order functions such as registration and investigations of crimes, managing traffic, and security of prominent officials. As a result, intelligence is often viewed as the last priority in policing and therefore a poor career choice. After a few years of service in the state, those who choose to take up intelligence as a career apply for a deputation with the federal government either in the IB or in the R&AW. Paradoxically, a career in intelligence at the federal level is now seen as an elite career choice.

Both federal intelligence organizations also directly recruit personnel who are referred to as "cadre appointments." In the case of the IB, cadre officers start at the bottom of the hierarchy and if age permits, retire at lower-level management positions. This ensures that IPS officers remain at the middle and upper echelons of the IB, thus preserving their dominance. Ironically, those who were recruited directly to be "central intelligence officers" are left at the bottom of the rung, while those on deputation from the police remain in control.

The recruiting of traditional policemen into intelligence roles, especially at the higher echelons, leads to a number of challenges for India's intelligence community.

According to IPS cadre rules, officers are eligible for recruitment into the IB after a minimum of five years of service.[26] This leads to a piquant situation where IPS officers come to intelligence roles after considerable experience in policing. This is further compounded by the fact that the upper age limit for recruits into the civil services is thirty-two years. Efforts to reduce the upper age limit over the years have been consistently set aside by successive governments due to political reasons.

Recruitment at older ages coupled with the minimum five-year tenure in the police leads to institutional challenges for the IB's professional ethos. Not only does it delay the retraining of police officers in intelligence tasks, it also leads to lack of specialization in specific areas.

The SIBs, which are the IB's subsidiary units in the states, are tasked with maintaining liaison with their police intelligence counterparts. However, this has been found to be "inadequate," with the states looking at the IB as political agents of the federal government.[27]

The lack of major reforms within the IB is largely due to resistance from within and the lack of political vision of elected governments. The political gains of keeping a powerful internal intelligence agency moored in its colonial avatar offered many advantages that came at the cost of a constitutional republic's need for an efficient, accountable, and lawful internal intelligence and security service.

Intelligence Reform: Between Denial and Reluctance

The need or reforms in intelligence are manifold. A key aim is to prevent the misuse of intelligence by government. The other is to improve the intelligence cycle, a process that involves five stages—planning and detection, collection, all-source analysis and production, and finally, dissemination of intelligence.[28]

There are several examples of interventions by legislative bodies to address systemic deficiencies in the intelligence cycle, while building oversight mechanisms and accountability. A classic example of legislative interventions are the several attempts by the US Congress to address the misuse of intelligence by President Nixon's administration following the Watergate scandal.[29] The US Congress established two committees to examine issues of alleged misuse of intelligence by the Nixon administration. The report and recommendations of one of them, the Pike Committee, were never published officially and were only available publicly when leaked to the media.[30] The Church Committee report was published, leading to a major push for greater oversight and democratic control of the US intelligence community. However, India has not seen any successful parliamentary initiative for reform of the country's intelligence community.

Instead, attempts at reforms in intelligence have been reactionary and piecemeal as a response in the aftermath of a crisis. There has never been seen an attempt to proactively reform the IB and its practices through legislative and administrative interventions.

The IB's performance received close scrutiny when it failed to predict the 1962 Chinese invasion. The proximity between the IB's second Director, B. N. Mullik, to Prime Minister Nehru, leading to inaccurate assessments being accepted without challenge, was partly to blame. Mullik continued to present an inaccurate assessment to Nehru, claiming that the Chinese would not react to his "Forward Policy" of using the Indian Army to occupy posts hitherto held by China.[31] As scholars have pointed out, while Mullik and the IB's assessment should have first gone to the Joint Intelligence Committee as a part of the intelligence process, it went directly to Nehru.[32]

The first attempt at reforming India's intelligence community and structure came in 1968, when its foreign intelligence division was excised to create the Research and Analysis Wing (R&AW). Unlike the IB, which was an overt agency, the R&AW was to be a clandestine agency that would work on gathering external intelligence. In 1965, the Indian Army blamed the IB for lack of adequate intelligence and put this on record giving fresh impetus for a new agency.[33]

The next significant review of the intelligence establishment happened in the aftermath of the limited war with Pakistan in the Kargil sector between May and August 1999. A committee headed by the retired bureaucrat K. Subrahmanyam proposed major security reforms. This was followed by setting up task forces to address specific areas including intelligence that finally went to a group of ministers to consider recommendations and implement them. These efforts post-1999 were arguably the most comprehensive review of India's intelligence capacities and an attempt to improve them, especially in terms of operational capabilities and adding structures for better coordination between the producers and consumers of intelligence.

These reforms were also an attempt to situate and structure intelligence agencies within the higher echelons of India's security architecture starting from the Prime Minister's Office and its subordinate offices. This became an ambitious attempt at identifying a charter for each agency and attributing specific responsibilities.

The impact of this assessment by the Kargil Review Committee sought major changes in internal security. While such changes led to a structural reorganization, it failed to address the systemic issues that plagued the IB.

The recommendations from the Committee helped establish the Multi Agency Centre (MAC) with similar structures known as subsidiary MACs (S-MACs) in the states. The bulk of the intelligence-related recommendations remained focused on external threats and intelligence.

The relationship between intelligence agencies and political representatives has always been fraught with contradictions. On occasion, intelligence agencies may function beyond the pale of democratically elected policymakers. The secrecy and clandestine activities, integral to the intelligence process, also leads to politicization of intelligence, but without adequate checks and balances, erodes its professional ethos. This is largely the case for India's internal intelligence apparatus.[34]

An early failure in reforming intelligence occurred soon after the Constitution was promulgated. Entry 8 of List 1 of Schedule VII of the Indian Constitution lists a "Central Bureau of Intelligence and Investigation" that gave the Union government the power to create an intelligence agency through an act of Parliament.[35] However, no government in post-independent India has ever used this constitutional provision to enact laws that will create and govern an intelligence agency.

There have been individual legislative attempts, such as the one made by then Congress Member of Parliament Manish Tewari to pass a Private Member's Bill in 2011.[36] Tewari introduced a draft bill that would give intelligence agencies a legal statute, a charter, besides internal, parliamentary, and judicial oversight.[37]

However, the bill did not pass muster since no private member's bill has been passed by Parliament since the 1970s, and Tewari being a member of the Indian National Congress, which was a leading constituent of the ruling coalition government at that time.

Interestingly, while India inherited its intelligence mechanism from colonial Britain, a similar debate in the United Kingdom led to a slew of reforms within the British intelligence community. In 1989, the UK Parliament passed the Security Service Act, giving its internal intelligence agency, the Security Service (earlier known as MI-5), a legal basis to exist.[38] Similarly, its other agencies such as the Secret Intelligence Service (earlier known as MI-6) and GCHQ, were brought under the Intelligence Services Act, 1994.[39]

Another impediment to meaningful reforms is the lack of holistic inquiries into intelligence failures. For instance, the massacre of seventy-five federal policemen drawn from the Central Police Reserve Force (CRPF) by armed cadres of the CPI (Maoist) in the district of Dantewada, Chhattisgarh, should have led to an inquiry that examined the process of intelligence collection, analysis, and dissemination between the federal government and its agencies and the state.[40]

Historically, most of the collection of intelligence has been left to the cadre recruits in the IB, while the IPS officers would dominate the analysis. However, no such inquiry specific to the functioning of intelligence was carried out. While two internal inquiries were carried out by the CRPF followed by a comprehensive assessment by a retired police official, E. N. Rammohan, the role of intelligence in assessing the impending attack remained secret.

When Kao was tasked with creating R&AW, he hoped to change this IB model and instead recruit from what he envisaged as "the open market." His vision led to the creation of the Research and Analysis Service (RAS), a dedicated intelligence cadre of officers who could be picked up outside the proscribed government rules of selection. Kao hoped that this would also give him the freedom to spot not only talent, but also expertise in various disciplines that IPS officers may lack.

"The political, bureaucratic, military and intelligence establishments appear to have developed a vested interest in the status quo. National security management recedes into the background at the time of peace and is considered too delicate to be tampered with at the time of war and proxy war," the KRC noted.[41]

Caught between the IPS, officers on deputation, and cadre officers, India's intelligence community never managed to evolve, unlike in the United States or United Kingdom, the two countries that provided templates for Indian policymakers. This has now produced systems that are inward-looking and not amenable to cooperation. It struggles to build relationships with organizations like the CIA and the SIS that are staffed by career intelligence professionals who not only give permanence but also build a professional "intelligence culture."

The KRC noted that unlike the United States, which reformed its intelligence structures after 9/11, in India, the process of intelligence dissemination and evaluation at the highest levels is broken. While India transitioned from the Joint Intelligence Committee (JIC), a British legacy, to the National Security Council (NSC), borrowed from the United States, the change has not produced the desired results. "The Committee has drawn attention to deficiencies in the present system of collection, reporting, collation and assessment of intelligence. There is no institutionalized mechanism for coordination or objective-oriented interaction between agencies and consumers at different levels. Similarly, there is no mechanism for tasking the agencies, monitoring their performance and reviewing their records to evaluate their quality. . . . All major countries have a mechanism at the national and often at the lower levels to assess the intelligence inputs received from different agencies and sources," the Kargil Review Committee recorded in its findings.[42]

The need for reforms in intelligence is a continuous process. But the lack of re-form within India's intelligence apparatus, when compared to similar exercises elsewhere, offer a sharp contrast. The 9/11 attacks triggered a Director of National Intelligence–led overhaul of the intelligence community in the United States. A 500-day plan was developed and executed to improve interagency collaboration as well as intelligence generation and sharing. Intelligence failure–triggered crises have not produced similar reforms in India.

Unless these gaps are resolved, the reformation the IB will continue to function sub-optimally. The need to create a new professional culture within the IB has been proposed several times but never followed through.[43]

A String of Intelligence Failures

The history of India's intelligence in internal security is replete with failures. Intelligence has repeatedly failed to stop serious internal security challenges—from communal riots to terror attacks, and often ended in spectacular lapse. Indian intelligence failed to anticipate serial blasts in Mumbai in 1993 and 2006. It failed to stop the audacious attack on the city by ten members of the Lashkar-e-Toiba in 2008.

At the height of the armed militancy in the state of Punjab led by Sikh separatists, inadequate intelligence from the IB contributed to a messy military action called "Operation Bluestar" to eject armed Sikh militants from the Golden Temple.[44] Operation Bluestar would lead to the assassination of Prime Minister Indira Gandhi, which the IB failed to stop. The IB also failed to prevent the assassination of her son, Prime Minister Rajiv Gandhi, while he was campaigning for the general elections on May 21, 1991.[45] The IB, which has a special division for VIP security, is tasked with gathering intelligence on serving and former prime ministers and their families. While Gandhi was out of power and seeking a re-election when he was assassinated, it was the IB's charter to gather intelligence on any threat to him. However, none of these failures brought about any attempts to reform the intelligence community in a bid to improve its track record on internal security.

India's intelligence capabilities in internal security have been further undermined as terrorists embraced internet-based technologies to communicate and plan attacks. In 1999, the KRC had pointed out this gap: "The United States has grouped all its communication and electronic intelligence efforts within a single organization, the National Security Agency (NSA). The desirability of set-ting up a similar organization in India with adequate resources for this extremely important and non-intrusive method of gathering technological intelligence calls for examination."[46]

Twenty years later, India's technical intelligence capabilities are still inadequate. India's internal intelligence apparatus still lacks a proper information management system or even the ability to carry out big-data analysis.[47] Its analytical procedures are still largely left to officers who read through reports maintained on paper while carrying out intelligence analysis.[48]

An opportunity to reform India's intelligence services rose in the aftermath of the attack on Mumbai by the Pakistan-based Lashkar-e-Toiba (LeT) on November 26, 2008 (also known as 26/11). There was considerable unhappiness within the Indian intelligence and diplomatic community in that the United States held back intelligence from India that could have prevented the attack.[49] However, there was no introspection that the IB's technical wings had failed to access any intelligence that indicated the impending attack. Despite credible intelligence inputs from the CIA in September and November 2008, there was no analysis done by the IB that could have predicted this attack.

It is believed that a key source for much of the intelligence on 26/11 came from David Coleman Headley, an American of Pakistani origin. Former Indian diplomats and intelligence officials who dealt with the case believe that the United States held back intelligence on the assumption that Headley was a US "double agent." His detailed interrogation by India's National Investigation Agency (NIA) in 2010 reveals the extent to which he was a part of the initial reconnaissance and planning that culminated in the final attack.[50]

However, the failure to either track Headley or apprehend him is the beginning of a series of blunders that further exposed the systemic failures within Indian intelligence. The Bureau of Immigration (BOI) is manned by the IB, affording it access to data on the travel histories of all foreign nationals visiting India.[51] The absence of big-data analytical tools contributed to the IB's failure to detect any pattern of Headley's visits to India and his earlier travels to Pakistan. The fact that Headley traveled to Pakistan frequently, while also traveling to India to map targets for the Lashkar-e-Taiba attackers, using the same passport, did not set off any alarm bells.[52]

When intelligence inputs from the CIA were passed on to the IB by R&AW, a senior official of the rank of additional director was dispatched to Mumbai to meet senior police officials from the state.[53] Inadequate cooperation between the IB and the state police ensured that the intelligence inputs received from the CIA could not be used to prevent the attack. Neither the IB nor the Mumbai Police set up a joint task force using other agencies such as the R&AW and the National Security Guards (NSG) to further develop these intelligence leads, war game scenarios, and prepare for a possible attack.

The other key source of information about the 26/11 plot came from Zarar Shah, who was a key plotter and the technology chief of the Lashkar-e-Taiba. The British intelligence group Government Communication Headquarters (GCHQ) was monitoring Shah's online activities. According to documents leaked by the National Security Agency contractor Edward Snowden, GCHQ was able to track down details of the impending attack, as well as Shah's efforts to set up VOIP calls that would enable the Pakistani handles to maintain communication with the attackers.[54] However, the IB remained clueless about the plans to attack Mumbai that were in Shah's laptop.

The government made another attempt to reform the IB in the aftermath of the attack on Mumbai.[55] A slew of reforms was planned after the attack by the then United Progressive Alliance (UPA) government headed by Prime Minister Dr. Manmohan Singh, which included granting the IB legal status through an act of Parliament, and ensuring a defined charter and oversight mechanism.[56] The then Union Home Minister P. Chidambaram would also try to bring about changes in processes, the first of its kind since the KRC recommendations after the Kargil war.

Chidambaram viewed intelligence as a part of a cycle and he made an attempt to what he called a "bold, thorough and radical restructuring of the security architecture at the national level."[57] He reformed and expanded the role of the Multi Agency Centre (MAC), an organization first mooted within the IB after the Kargil war to improve cooperation between different intelligence agencies. The MAC was part of a slew of reforms that were initiated to improve coordination and build accountability to the intelligence generation, analysis, and sharing mechanisms.[58] Besides the MAC, the then Vajpayee government created the Strategic Policy Group (SPG), the Intelligence Coordination Group (ICG), Technical Coordination Group (TCG), and the National Intelligence Board (NIB) to try to ensure that the producers and consumers of intelligence could work together.[59]

The role of the MAC was to help the various agencies coordinate their intelligence to build comprehensive assessments and threat perceptions. The SPG would be the senior-most members of the cabinet who would look at the available intelligence for taking policy decisions. It was also hoped that the senior-most cabinet members would also become de facto arbitrators between the various competing agencies seeking credit for their work. The ICG was a platform that would place the consumers and producers of intelligence together to discuss issues of need and quality of the information sought and produced. The TCG was to serve as a body that would coordinate all issues relate to TECHINT, including purchases and deployments.[60]

Chidambaram's attempt was to take this further and build on the earlier process by reforming the architecture significantly. He wanted central agencies like the IB to be connected to state police forces through the Subsidiary MAC (S-MAC), a mirror of the central MAC at the state level. He laid the foundations of the National Intelligence Grid (NATGRID) and the National Counter Terrorism Centre (NCTC). The NCTC, as envisaged by Chidambaram, was to be the crux of his vision, expanding the existing MAC and adding investigations (by making the NIA an adjunct to it) and giving it an operations wing (by adding the NSG).[61] However, resistance from within the government and the existing agencies ensured that the bulk of these reforms never took off.[62] Chidambaram returned to the Ministry of Finance, and a change of government in 2014 ended these proposals permanently.

Had these proposals and the ones made after the Kargil war gone through as they were originally envisaged, India's intelligence capabilities would have been very different. For the IB, the reforms would have led to a major reorganization, which would force it to change its ethos, but also enabled it to notch up more successes in a far more complex world.

But are these systemic intelligence failures a result of the "ideological element to the management of internal security," as Paul Staniland argues in Chapter 6? As far as the role of intelligence in internal security is concerned, this is highly unlikely. Intelligence as a function and an organization in the Indian context has always been close to those in power. As a result, it has remained ideologically ambivalent, switching quickly to adapt to whichever government is in power. This has ensured systemic failures in intelligence, but none of that can be attributed to ideological biases. Instead, as Ahuja and Kapur argue in their Introduction to this volume, "information processing, interagency coordination and assessment generation are the key challenges," despite the fact that its surveillance capabilities continue to expand.

Intelligence Successes in Internal Security

In the early hours of February 26, 2019, a number of Mirage 2000s took off from their base in India and headed toward Balakot, a small town in the Khyber Pakhtunkhwa province in Pakistan.[63] Their target was a seminary just on the outskirts of the city of Balakot, considered to be a training camp of the designated terror group Jaish-e-Mohammed (JeM). This would be the first time since the war in 1971 when Indian combat jets would cross into Pakistani airspace to bomb a target.

The combat aircraft were on a mission to retaliate against an attack by the group on February 14, 2019, in Indian-Administered Kashmir that killed forty federal policemen from the Central Reserve Police Force. The failure of the IB to generate specific information that could have stopped this attack led to the usual rounds of "intelligence failure." But the subsequent plan to hit Balakot would come from a success of the IB, which began work on these targets through the MAC soon after the attack on Mumbai in 2008.

For decades, Indian diplomats had blamed Pakistan for sponsoring terror groups to carry out attacks against India. But the careful mapping of the facilities where men like Ajmal Kasab, one of the ten attackers of Mumbai in 2008, had been trained, was yet to be carried out as a joint exercise between various intelligence agencies. The MAC, housed within the IB, began this work, drawing in experts from the R&AW, the Indian Air Force, NTRO, and other relevant agencies to piece together a map of every facility that purportedly trained armed insurgents to carry out attacks in India. The JeM training camp in Balakot was one such facility.[64] Drawing on decades of intelligence that the IB had built from interrogations and source reports helped them piece together a detailed mapping of these facilities. In parallel, the R&AW began to work on finding ways to infiltrate these training areas and generate real-time intelligence from these areas. Once again, Balakot emerged as a key success, where both organizations scored. Not only did they manage to identify the camp, they also found sources willing to provide coordinates and valuable intelligence.

For an agency that has lived in virtual anonymity for decades, the IB has always been hard-pressed to showcase its successes. As the lead agency of the federal government on all major internal security threats, the IB notched up several successes. These began as classic intelligence operations to elicit tactical and strategic intelligence to weaken targeted organizations and force them into negotiations.

Insurgencies in the North East of India saw the IB claim several successes. In the 1960s, the Mizos rose against the Indian state under the leadership of a charismatic leader, Laldenga, who formed the Mizo National Front and the Mizo National Army.[65] The armed insurgency turned into a protracted guerrilla war. By 1986, the IB had managed to infiltrate Laldenga's camp and start a series of negotiations that led several Mizo military commanders to defect.[66] The pressure created by the defections forced Laldenga to start formal talks that led to the Mizoram Accord in 1986. The Mizo success would be replicated in Punjab when it was in the middle of one of the most violent insurgencies in India.

After the IB's failure to counter the growing threat from Sikh separatism in the aftermath of Operation Bluestar, the then DIB, M. K. Narayanan created a special directorate to specifically gather intelligence on the Khalistan movement.[67] Three officers, Kalyan Rudra, Maloy Krishna Dhar, and Ajit Doval, were handpicked by Narayanan to set up a new directorate to ensure that the state and federal police agencies would use actionable intelligence on Khalistani separatists to launch counter attacks. The Punjab experiment proved to be a success with Operation Black Thunder II and earned the IB's Doval a Kriti Chakra (India's second-highest peacetime gallantry award), the first for a serving IPS officer in independent India.[68]

The IB not only identified and neutralized top Sikh separatist leaders, but also forced them into secret negotiations.[69]

By the mid-1990s, the specter of Islamic terrorism, partly fueled by events in Afghanistan and Pakistan, began to rise. For the IB, home-grown outfits like the Indian Mujahideen would prove to be a major challenge. However, the IB's vast network across the country and its ability to tap into local communities contributed to major successes. The capture of the terrorist Mohammed Ahmed Sidibapa, popularly known as Yasin Bhatkal, in August 2013 demonstrated its ability to carry out complex operations in India's neighborhood. The IB's subsidiary unit in the state of Bihar was tipped off by a source that Bhatkal was stationed in Nepal. Months of painstaking intelligence gathering led to confirmation about his presence and a few of his colleagues. Working with their counterparts in the R&AW and Nepal Police, the IB brought back Bhatkal to India. Bhatkal's capture is considered a major intelligence coup, and his interrogation reports show how influential he had become across several terror networks targeting India.

But while the IB notched up a steady string of successes, it was still struggling to become a modern intelligence organization that was also in tune with India's democratic underpinnings. The decades of opposition to any major systemic reform have undermined its performance.

The Rocky Road Ahead

The IB's insignia has an octagonal shape in its outermost layer that "symbolises multiplicity of directions and stands for multi-dimensional responsibilities."[70] The "multiplicity of directions" and "multi-dimensional responsibilities" of the IB can be cited as one of the key reasons for undermining its focus on internal security.

Can the IB continue to discharge its primary responsibility to generate intelligence for India's internal security, while also generating political intelligence for the political party in power? Can it still remain as an effective instrument of statecraft for a democratic and constitutional republic without being bound by legislative statute, judicial accountability, and parliamentary oversight?

There have been attempts to reform the process for intelligence gathering and dissemination. For instance, during his tenure as the director of the IB, M. K. Narayanan created an intelligence doctrine built on three pillars:[71]

- Intelligence Generation
- Directive
- Response

This was documented to create a process that would recognize collection, analysis, and dissemination in a more structured manner than what was prevalent before him. Many within the IB agree that the process started by Narayanan helped bring about changes in the processing of intelligence within the organization.

However, these measures did not address issues of interagency cooperation, or build a professional institutional culture that can address India's complex internal security challenges. As a case in point, there is criticism that India's current intelligence culture and practice has led to Open Source Intelligence (OSINT) being passed off as Human Intelligence (HUMINT) and "operational tasks" attracting better human resources than field intelligence or counterintelligence.[72] The lack of knowledge and expertise in "target areas" has led to an erosion in the quality of intelligence that is generated.[73]

There is divided opinion on how far the IB has been able to adapt to essential analytical tools and processes to enable a culture of big-data analysis.[74] A case in point is the adaptation of some rudimentary big-data analytical tools that were introduced to the IB in 2004. According to a former DIB, their adaptation has been slow across the agency and more often discarded by officials who prefer to pore through files manually rather than look for patterns within big data using modern software tools.

Unlike most private ventures that now routinely use threat models to input data and derive analysis, the IB continues to function without one. As a result, key intelligence functions like predicting threats or attacks remain laborious manual processes and are at times, as was evident in the months preceding the attack on Mumbai in 2007, incapable of arriving at accurate predictive analysis.

The IB has not modernized its database management systems. NATGRID, which is supposed to digitally facilitate access to twenty-one databases, was supposed to go operational by October 2021 but is still on hold, at the time of writing this chapter.[75]

The advent of internet-based technologies has impacted and reimagined intelligence processes globally. This has been particularly difficult in India and is intricately linked to its archaic structures. Technologies have also brought new legal structures including the role of privacy in modern societies, now recognized as a fundamental right following the unanimous decision of a nine-judge constitutional bench of the Supreme Court.[76] This has led to clamors for reimagining India's intelligence structures and processes and given a push for an Indian personal data-protection bill on the lines of the General Data Protection Regulation (GDPR) framed by the European Union (EU).[77]

Envisaged as a catch-all information database, NATGRID was supposed to be the mother repository of information that would not only facilitate quick access to information, but also provide predictive analysis after parsing through petabytes of information. However, the IB was keen that the organization remain as an adjunct of its operational requirements and mostly serve as a database, rather than emerge as a parallel organization that would have ambitions to generate intelligence.[78] This rivalry put the project into a deep freeze for years until the founding Chief Executive Officer was eased out in 2014 and a senior IB official was appointed as its new head. The organization returned to its original charter of accessing and interlinking twenty-two databases, to be made available as and when required.

However, organizations such as NATGRID also serve as a key example of how India's democratic frameworks work at cross-purposes with its internal security apparatus. By August 2017, a nine-judge constitutional bench of the Supreme Court had ruled that privacy was a fundamental right. This called for new laws that would zealously safeguard the data of Indian citizens and deny access to state agencies unless under national security exceptions. An organization like NATGRID, which was envisaged and created years before the 2017 Supreme Court judgment, had already managed an exemption from the Right to Information Act, a major transparency law. It is now seeking exemption from proposed privacy regimes that seek to enforce privacy as a fundamental right.

Interagency coordination between the IB and other security agencies both at the federal and state levels remains fraught. State police agencies often complain that intelligence provided by the IB is "vague" and "lacks specifics."[79]

A key reason why interagency cooperation has not improved between the IB and its state counterparts is the institutional culture to restrict information sharing. The balance between secrecy and openness that can promote efficacy is a delicate one.[80] This can be managed by creating structures that will enforce sharing of information as an institutional culture, as was attempted post-1999 and 2007 by the Atal Behari Vajpayee and Manmohan Singh governments. Both failed to take off due to a number of reasons already discussed in this chapter.

While India inherited the Joint Intelligence Committee from the United Kingdom, it continues to function far below its intended outcomes. The role of the Joint Intelligence Committee is clearly defined in the United Kingdom, whereas in India it doesn't have a publicly available charter.[81] It was dismantled in 1998 when India adapted the National Security Council (NSC) and the National Security Council Secretariat (NSCS) as the apex body for intelligence analysis.[82] The JIC was subsequently brought back as a part of the NSCS and its Chairman has been re-designated as one equal to a deputy national security advisor and given a tenfold rise in budget. However, there is no institutional mechanism available to study its efficacy with its expanded budget and personnel.[83]

India's internal security architecture is also plagued by the lack of specialization for intelligence roles. Until the 1970s, the IB had also followed the "earmarking" system for recruiting IPS officers into the organization.[84] Entry would be limited to the top positions of any graduating class from the Sardar Vallabhbhai Patel National Police Academy (SVNPA). Out of these, those who were keen on a career in intelligence would undergo background checks and interviews before being inducted. At best, they would get only six to eight months with their allotted state police cadre, before being inducted into the IB.[85] This was abandoned in the early 1980s, leading to the current dominance of a police culture at the expense of building an intelligence ethos and culture within the organization. The IB and its state police counterparts will continue to work despite their systemic inadequacies. However, their contribution to managing India's internal security will remain marginal until systemic reforms are introduced to prepare them for challenges of the future.

Notes

1. For a fuller discussion on Kautilya and his views on the use of intelligence see Dany Shoham and Michael Liebig, "The Intelligence Dimension of Kautiliyan Statecraft and Its Implications for the Present," *Journal of Intelligence History* 15, no. 2 (2016): 119–138.
2. Demands on Grants 2020–2021, Ministry of Home Affairs Demand No. 48—Police: 157.
3. Report of the Group of Ministers on National Security, Chapter 2, paragraphs 2.24 to 2.30 2002.

4. James Burch, "A Domestic Intelligence Agency for the United States? A Comparative Analysis of Domestic Agencies and Their Implications for Homeland Security," *Homeland Security Affairs* 3, no. 2 (June 2007).

5. Ibid.

6. Nirupama Subramaniam, "NIA Pushes Constitutional Limits, Chidambaram Told FBI," *The Hindu*, March 19, 2010. Also available at https://www.thehindu.com/news/the-india-cab les/NIA-pushing-constitutional-limits-Chidambaram-told-FBI/article14953597.ece.

7. Judgment of the Guwahati High Court WA No 119 of 2008, in WP © No 6877 of 2005 dated November 6, 2013, http://ghconline.gov.in/Judgment/WA1192008.pdf. Also see https://indianexpress.com/article/india/india-others/sc-stays-gauhati-high-court-order-declaring-cbi-unconstitutional/.

8. Vijay Shukul, IPS, "Sleeman Sahib Ki Jai," *Indian Police Journal* 53 (December 2012): 4; Saikat Datta, "Created by a Telegram, IB Finds Itself Standing on Thin Legal Ground," *Hindustan Times*, November 14, 2013, https://www.hindustantimes.com/india/created-by-telegram-ib-finds-itself-standing-on-thin-legal-ground/story-UFrue3ywW4P96DhvQFtadM.html.

9. Bashyam Kasturi, "Intelligence Services: Analysis, Organisation and Function," Lancer Paper 6, Lancer Publishers and Distributors, 1995: 28–29.

10. Ibid., 28.

11. Ibid.

12. Interview with Colonel I. S. Hasanwalia's son-in-law and founding chairman of NTRO, R. S. Bedi, November 11, 2021.

13. Interview with Colonel I. S. Hasanwalia's son H. S. Hasanwalia in Delhi on January 21, 2022.

14. Praveen Swami, "Secret Life of Article 370: Nehru's Use of Ruthless Force to Integrate Kashmir behind Veil of 'Special Status' Offers Lessons for Today," Firstpost.com, August 19, 2019, https://www.firstpost.com/india/secret-life-of-article-370-nehrus-use-of-ruthless-force-to-integrate-kashmir-behind-veil-of-special-status-offers-lessons-for-today-7187891.html.

15. Interview with Colonel I. S. Hasanwalia's son H. S. Hasanwalia in Delhi on January 21, 2022.

16. See "Riots Changed J&K Politics," an interview with Ved Bhasin available at https://ikashmir.net/storm/chapter11.html.

17. Praveen Swami, *India, Pakistan and the Secret Jihad: The Covert War in Kashmir, 1947–2004* (London and New York: Routledge, 2007), 5, 30.

18. Interview with the family of Hasanwalia conducted in 2007 by the author.

19. Elizabeth Roche, "Report on India's Defeat in 1962 War Revealed," March 19, 2014, https://www.livemint.com/Politics/VnlRYckt2cIqfnzA2jiviP/Forward-Policy-of-Jawaharlal-Nehru-govt-blamed-for-1962-deba.html.

20. See http://legislative.gov.in/sites/default/files/A1951-61_0.pdf (accessed February 26, 2020).

21. Prof. R. K. Barik, "Baswan Report," https://dopt.gov.in/sites/default/files/BaswanReport.pdf (accessed February 26, 2020).

22. Constituent Assembly Debate, October 10, 1949. Available at http://164.100.47.194/Loksa bha/Debates/cadebatefiles/C10101949.html.

23. Ibid.

24. T. V. Rajeshwar, *India, the Crucial Years* (Gurugram: Harper Collins India, 2015), 10–11.

25. Ibid.

26. MHA, GOI Office Memorandum dated March 30, 2010, https://ips.gov.in/pdfs/TenurePol icy-300310.pdf.

27. Maloy Krishna Dhar, *Open Secrets: India's Intelligence Unveiled* (New Delhi: Manas Publications, 2005), 86.

28. Ibid.

29. Faith Karimi, "Watergate Scandal: A Look Back at a Crisis That Changed US Politics," https://edition.cnn.com/2017/05/17/politics/watergate-scandal-look-back/index.html.

30. John Prados and Arturo Jimenez-Bacari, "The White House, the CIA and the Pike Committee, 1975," https://nsarchive.gwu.edu/briefing-book/intelligence/2017-06-02/white-house-cia-pike-committee-1975; and "The CIA Report the President Doesn't Want You to See," The Village Voice Archives, https://www.villagevoice.com/1976/02/16/the-cia-report-the-president-doesnt-want-you-to-read/.

31. Elizabeth Roche, "Report on India's Defeat in 1962 War Revealed," *Livemint.com*, March 19, 2014, https://www.livemint.com/Politics/VnlRYckt2cIqfnzA2jiviP/Forward-Policy-of-Jaw aharlal-Nehru-govt-blamed-for-1962-deba.html.

32. Srinath Raghavan, "After 50 Years of RAW, There Are Still No Declassified Documents or an Official History," *ThePrint.In*, September 18, 2018, https://theprint.in/opinion/why-was-raw-formed-and-what-has-india-learnt-after-50-years-of-its-existence/119811/.

33. Ibid.

34. Ibid.

35. See https://www.mea.gov.in/Images/pdf1/S7.pdf

36. Manish Tewari, MP, The Intelligence Services Private Member Bill of 2011, https://timesofin dia.indiatimes.com/india/manish-tewaris-bill-sought-to-regulate-ib-raw-ntros-operations/articleshow/21134566.cms.

37. Manish Tewari, MP, Bill on Intelligence Reforms, March 29, 2011, Observer Research Foundation, New Delhi, https://www.orfonline.org/research/bill-on-intelligence-agencies-reforms/. Disclosure: The author of this chapter was a member of the group of experts set up under the aegis of ORF, New Delhi, to frame the Bill for Mr. Tewari.

38. See http://www.legislation.gov.uk/ukpga/1989/5/pdfs/ukpga_19890005_en.pdf.

39. See https://www.sis.gov.uk/; http://www.legislation.gov.uk/ukpga/1994/13/contents.

40. Saikat Datta, "Death of Illusion," *Outlook*. April 19, 2010, https://www.outlookindia.com/magazine/story/death-of-illusion/265013.

41. *From Surprise to Reckoning: The Kargil Review Committee Report* (New Delhi: Sage Publications, 1999), paragraph 614.1, p. 252.

42. Ibid., paragraph 6.6, p. 109.

43. Interview with a former director, Intelligence Bureau, and with former national security adviser Shiv Shankar Menon.

44. For background, see "Operation Bluestar: What Happened 37 Years Ago," https://www.hin dustantimes.com/india-news/operation-bluestar-what-happened-37-years-ago-10162293 7941625.html, *Hindustan Times*, June 6, 2021; and "What Happened during 1984 Operation Bluestar?," *India Today*, June 6, 2018, https://www.indiatoday.in/fyi/story/1984-operation-blue-star-amritsar-1251681-2018-06-06.

45. See http://news.bbc.co.uk/onthisday/hi/dates/stories/may/21/newsid_2504000/2504 739.stm.

46. *From Surprise to Reckoning*, paragraph 14.8, p. 254.

47. Saikat Datta, "India's Intel Agencies Make No Use of Big Data Analytics," *Deccan Chronicle*, June 26, 2020, https://www.deccanchronicle.com/opinion/columnists/260620/saikat-datta-indias-intel-agencies-make-no-use-of-big-data-analytic.html.

48. Interview with a senior Indian intelligence official.

49. Interviews with two former R&AW officials and two former Indian ambassadors to the United States.

50. Saikat Datta, "The Union Republic of Terror," *Outlook*, October 11, 2010, https://www.outlo okindia.com/magazine/story/the-union-republic-of-terror/267300.

51. https://boi.gov.in/.

52. Megha Sood, "David Headley, the Man Who Mapped Mumbai for LeT Attack," *Hindustan Times*, November 5, 2018, https://www.hindustantimes.com/mumbai-news/david-headley-the-man-who-mapped-mumbai-for-let-attack/story-QeZvYSivMiCnHqk53iC SfK.html.

53. Interview with a senior Indian intelligence official.

54. Sebastian Rotella, "The Hidden Intelligence behind the Mumbai Attacks," *ProPublica*, April 21, 2015, https://www.propublica.org/article/the-hidden-intelligence-breakdowns-behind-the-mumbai-attacks.

55. Interview with Shiv Shankar Menon, former national security advisor, India.

56. Ibid.

57. P. Chidambaram, IB Endowment Lecture, delivered on December 23, 2009, Union Home Minister, India, https://casi.sas.upenn.edu/sites/default/files/iit/Intell%20Bur%20-%20Chidambaram%20-%20Related%20Resources.pdf.

58. Saikat Datta, "Low on the IQ," *Outlook*, July 4, 2005, https://www.outlookindia.com/magazine/story/low-on-the-iq/227823.

59. Ibid.

60. Ibid. This section has also benefited from a conversation with the former deputy national security advisor in the Vajpayee government, Amb. Satish Chandra.

61. Chidambaram, IB Endowment Lecture.

62. Interview with a former DIB and a serving senior intelligence official.

63. Saikat Datta and Kunwar Khuldune Shahid, "Indian Fighter Jets Hit Targets inside Pakistan," *Asia Times*, February 26, 2019, https://asiatimes.com/2019/02/indian-fighter-jets-hits-targets-inside-pakistan/.

64. Interview with several Indian security officials.

65. John Zothansanga, "28 Years On, Laldenga Is Still Mizoram's Tallest Leader," *Indian Express*, July 14, 2018, https://indianexpress.com/article/north-east-india/mizoram/28-years-on-laldenga-is-still-mizorams-tallest-leader-5258952/.

66. Subir Bhaumik, "I Told Atalji Negotiating with a Rebel Group Is Like Wooing a Lady: Zoramthanga," *The Telegraph*, September 17, 2020, https://www.telegraphindia.com/north-east/i-told-atalji-negotiating-with-a-rebel-group-is-like-wooing-a-lady-zoramthanga/cid/1743523. Also see Zothansanga, "28 Years On, Laldenga Is Still Mizoram's Tallest Leader."

67. Interview with a former director, Intelligence Bureau.

68. See https://www.indiatimes.com/trending/social-relevance/ajit-doval-facts-james-bond-of-india-559860.html and https://www.youtube.com/watch?v=M1UN3UYzuaw

69. See "Old Men and Their Official Secret Acts," *Times of India*, September 3, 2006, https://timesofindia.indiatimes.com/Old-men-and-their-Official-secrets/articleshow/1951335.cms.

70. Bureau of Police Research and Development (BPR&D), *Indian Police Journal* 59, no. 4 (October–December 2012): viii.

71. Interview with a former DIB.

72. Rana Banerji, "A Case for Intelligence Reforms in India—IDSA Task Force Report" (2012), 55.

73. Ibid.

74. Interview with a former DIB.

75. PTI, "National Intelligence Grid to Finally See Light of Day," *The Hindu*, September 12, 2021, https://www.thehindu.com/news/national/national-intelligence-grid-to-finally-see-light-of-day/article36414741.ece.

76. Krishnadas Rajagopal, "Right to Privacy Is Intrinsic to Right to Life and Liberty, Rules SC," *The Hindu*, August 24, 2017, https://www.thehindu.com/news/national/privacy-is-a-fundamental-right-under-article-21-rules-supreme-court/article19551224.ece.

77. See https://www.prsindia.org/theprsblog/personal-data-protection-bill-2019-all-you-need-know; https://gdpr.eu/.

78. Interview with a former IB official and two former NATGRID officials.

79. Media reports often cite state police officials who blame the lack of specific and actionable intelligence from the IB. See https://www.indiatoday.in/magazine/the-big-story/story/20130311-hyderabad-blasts-bomb-im-indian-mujahideen-762281-2013-03-01; https://frontline.thehindu.com/cover-story/pulwama-attack-intelligence-inputs-ignored-national-security-leak-compromise-balakot-bjp-win-2019/article33889516.ece; https://m.dailyhunt.in/

news/india/english/telanganatoday-epaper-dhb85c4349317f4e1ea92a85cfd14b6a8f/intel
ligence+bureau+intel+before+delhi+riots+was+unsubstantial+in+nature-newsid-n168635
126;   https://economictimes.indiatimes.com/news/politics-and-nation/ib-should-mobil
ise-correct-information-about-terror-strikes/articleshow/3510214.cms?from=mdr; https://
www.wionews.com/india-news/received-alert-by-ib-of-possible-attack-in-ayodhya-uttar-
pradesh-adg-179313.

80. For a fuller discussion between the balance between secrecy and efficacy, see Rob
    Johnston, "Analytical Culture in the U.S. Intelligence Community: An Ethnographic Study"
    (Washington, DC: Center for Study of Intelligence, CIA), 11, https://irp.fas.org/cia/prod
    uct/analytic.pdf

81. See https://www.gov.uk/government/groups/joint-intelligence-committee.

82. Tara Kartha, "The Rejig of India's National Security Architecture Has Been a Long Time in
    Coming," *The Wire*, October 17, 2018, https://thewire.in/security/ajit-doval-national-secur
    ity-council-secretariat.

83. Ibid.

84. Interview with a former director, Intelligence Bureau.

85. Ibid.

PART IV

INTERNAL SECURITY

Intra-Organizational Changes within the Security Providers

14

Included but Not Equal?

Debating Gender and Labor Reforms within the Border Security Force

SAHANA GHOSH

In February 2020, the Supreme Court of India ruled to allow permanent commission to women in the Indian Army on par with male officers.[1] This landmark case brings to the fore enduring tensions with regard to women and security forces in India and beyond: questions of inclusion and equality. In the case of the Army, arguments made for equal opportunities beyond limited inclusion and fewer pathways for professional success ranged against objections raised that the rural and male rank and file would not accept women in command positions and that biological differences made women unfit for certain roles. The Court's dismissal of these objections as contravening gender equality under the law and reinforcing regressive gender stereotypes is a milestone on the path for a more equal future for female officers in the Army, arguably the most prestigious armed force in India.[2] The contestations in this case resonate beyond the Army, across all the security forces that now include women, and merit sustained attention. From the United Kingdom, United States, and Canada in the Global North to postcolonial countries like South Africa and Turkey, negotiations over gender and sexuality—its meanings, mutability, and the management of difference—have been acute at every stage of women's inclusion in security forces.[3] This chapter examines the ongoing institutional transformations in the Indian Border Security Force (BSF) with the inclusion of women in all ranks of the Force. The broad question at its heart is about the relationship between such reforms and the norms and culture of gendered labor *within* the institution. Drawing on ethnographic research with members of the BSF between 2014 to 2019, it focuses on discourses about institutional change, including gender norms, policies, and infrastructures, with women's inclusion in the BSF. While there are normative policy debates about what institutional change should be like and studies of the effects of gendered security institutions on conflict, counterinsurgency, and local communities amid whom forces work, empirical research and analysis on the

Sahana Ghosh, *Included but Not Equal?* In: *Internal Security in India*. Edited by: Amit Ahuja and Devesh Kapur, Oxford University Press. © Oxford University Press 2023. DOI: 10.1093/oso/9780197660331.003.0014 experiences of serving members of labor reforms—in this case relating to gender—within security institutions is rare. This chapter provides a grounded perspective on the BSF during an ongoing period of radical transformation. An anthropological approach enables us to see how individual and collective experiences are shaped by, and in turn shape, discourses on gender and labor, by foregrounding how men and women at different ranks grapple with the aspirations and contradictions engendered by institutional reform.

Comparative studies of gender reform in armed forces across the world show tremendous variation, and it is unmistakably clear that the socio-political and historical context of the institution within each nation-state greatly shapes the outcomes of very similar reforms.[4] For instance, the trajectory of gender reforms in the South African military cannot be understood apart from the specific history of race, colonialism, and the political economy of the apartheid regime.[5] In the Indian policy context, the role of the state in addressing gender norms to foster and achieve equality within public institutions has been studied extensively, especially in terms of affirmative action.[6] While theoretical discussions about legislation and evaluating the effect of such policies are invaluable, in this chapter I suggest that we think of the life of policy anthropologically, in two ways. First, rather than evaluate policy implementation as success or failure, I follow anthropological understandings of policy *as processes* that themselves produce new debates, shifts in power, and meanings attached to the issues of concern; in this case, gender equality and the labor of soldiering.[7] Taking an ethnographic approach that centers gender as a core relationship of power demands that we view the issue of women in the BSF not as an additive one—that is, what does this mean for the women employed and deployed?—but rather a substantive one that affects all members of the institution, its structure and culture—as in, how does this reshape masculinities and femininities of all members and the gender norms and value of soldiering labor.

Second, scholarship on the management of difference (gender, race, ethnicity, caste) within the armed forces makes clear that policies of inclusion of women (i.e., numerical participation) do not necessarily have gender equality either as its goal or its effect. I consider discourses on institutional reform *within* the BSF to be a dynamic site generative of normative debate. In doing so, I draw on anthropological work on the state that has revealed the importance of both disaggregating different scales and agents of the state as well as attending to the contingencies and forms of power (of gender, caste, and class, for instance) that constitute the state and its relationships to society.[8] Taken together, the chapter shows that the life of these policies is shaped not only by national and transnational policymakers but the people who are its targets of reform—the BSF officers designing and managing these policies in the everyday, the male troops whose daily life, labor, and meanings of work come to be shaken up due to this radical change, and the new female recruits. The conception of gender as a dynamic social construction and relation of power may have become commonplace in critical social sciences,[9] but its conflation with sex as immutable, essential difference underlies significant policy frameworks and institutional discourses on gender reform. As I will show, with ethnographic examples, the categorical distinction between "inclusion" and "integration" of women is key to understanding the relationship between policy frameworks and discourses about gender norms and culture within the BSF. In the sections that follow, the stakes of this distinction for gender equality will become clear. I will also reflect on what this means for the efficacy of the BSF as an internal security institution.

I outline the key fractures along which the inclusion of women and the ongoing transformations that such inclusion entails are experienced and debated by members of the Force. In what follows, I describe the organizational structure of the BSF and the historical context of its duties within which women come to be recruited, trained, and deployed. I draw out the significance of this model of inclusion of women in the previously all-male Force in juxtaposition to the model used by its close institutional kin, the Central Reserve of Police Force (see chapter by Azad in this volume for a comparative overview of the CAPFs). Three sections will consider the key fractures that emerge with the inclusion of women, followed by a reflection on the potential of social transformations that surface from the experiences of female constables themselves. I conclude with some conceptual and empirical questions pertaining to gender, labor, and equality in the contemporary BSF as an internal security institution.

A Brief History of the BSF

The BSF was raised in 1965, to be an armed force prepared for war, guarding India's borders at all times. It took over the border-guarding mandate as well the bulk of its starting troops from the police of India's border states. Established under the leadership of a decorated police officer, K. Rustamji, the inaugural cadre of officers were trained by a combination of Army and police officers with a balance of soldierly and policing skills.[10] The recurrent experiences of fighting wars and militancy—the Liberation War of Bangladesh, and militancies in Punjab, Kashmir, and most recently the Maoist insurgency—have entrenched a soldierly ethos of war-preparedness into the Force. This ethos combines with the BSF's mobility—any given battalion spends five years at one location after which they move to the next posting—to impart a character of perpetual emergency to it. So, for instance, a battalion posted in northern West Bengal spends five years in these densely populated villages along the India-Bangladesh border after a stint in Bhuj, Gujarat, where they rarely had any "civilian interaction." As they shift rapidly from duty at the hostile India-Pakistan border where soldiers reported "shoot-at-sight" orders, to the officially friendly India-Bangladesh border with an avowed zero-shooting goal, failures to adjust result in frictions with borderland communities along the eastern border.[11]

Since a Supreme Court ruling in 2011, the BSF use a combination of non-lethal and assault weapons along this border.[12] In other words, the BSF's own theaters of duty present sharp contrasts, contradictions even, in what is expected of them in terms of border security practice, attitude, and responsibility in civilian interaction. As the Introduction to this volume and the chapter by Azad note, the CAPFs, notably the BSF and the CRPF are stretched to perform additional duties such as disaster management, election protection, and humanitarian relief, none of which was originally within their mandate, placing their already-diverse internal security tasks under pressure. In the BSF, officers and troops alike struggle to make the adjustments necessary to balance their national security tasks and goals with varied local cultural norms and the demands of democratic principles across these distinctive theaters of duty.

Reports of border security from both the western and eastern borders highlight the limitations of the male soldiers of the BSF in detaining and searching women in border villages, whether during routine patrolling or planned raids and operations. Moreover, trained as soldiers and prepared to defend national security against external aggression and infiltration in any form or manner, male troops found themselves ill-equipped to deal with frequent interactions with members of the public, especially women and children in regions they are culturally unfamiliar with. It is in this context of the changing demands of border security, especially in the last two decades, that the inclusion of women has emerged as a grounded need in the BSF. In borderlands such as those along the geographically, ecologically, and demographically variegated border with Bangladesh or in border villages in Punjab, where the BSF cohabit with and encounter everyday local communities, male troops are limited in their ability to search women suspected of smuggling or raid homes and private properties where women and children are present. The CAPFs like the BSF and CRPF in addition to the Indian Army also have a record of sexual and human rights violations from counterinsurgency operations to borderlands, as the editors of the volume observe in their Introduction.[13] The inclusion of women in its troops has been considered to be a step toward improving its relations with local communities amid whom they live and work as well as improve their public image as a caring and "people-friendly" Force.

The BSF, under the jurisdiction of the Ministry of Home Affairs, took a decision to incorporate women in the Force in its constabulary in 2008. This decision was further strengthened by the recommendation of a Parliamentary Committee on the Empowerment of Women to undertake gender-based reforms in the paramilitary forces with the grounded needs of the BSF to address the growing involvement of women in cross-border smuggling.[14] The existing gendered nature of the Force was foregrounded as inadequate to the changing national security needs, and a decision that would serve both functional and normative goals was made conceivable. Institutional discussions about the terms of inclusion, both theoretical and practical, make clear that distinctions between "inclusion" and "integration" were at play from the very beginning: where would the female constables stay? What new infrastructures would need to be added to existing border security architectures to make living and working conditions adequate? What kinds of deployments and assignment of duties to female constables would fulfill the need for female policing, but keep existing practices of personnel management in the Force largely unchanged?

While women were recruited nationally in 2008 and the first batches were trained in 2009, *mahila* constables, as they are referred to in official parlance, were not deployed to all parts of India's borders with Pakistan and Bangladesh where the BSF are deployed. In 2014, I was living in the border villages of northern West Bengal in the district of Cooch Behar, when female constables of the BSF were first deployed to that part of the 4,096 km-long India-Bangladesh border. Since 2014 I have been conducting ethnographic research with female constables, their male colleagues, and male officers in the BSF as they live and work in barracks and outposts along the Bangladesh border, in areas under the North Bengal and Guwahati frontiers.[15] This has included accompanying female constables on duty at gates and other checkpoints along the border fence, spending time together during off-duty hours, in activities of leisure and pleasure. I also draw on focused group discussions and interviews with officers and subordinate officers at different levels in three battalions that have female constables attached to them and deployed at the India-Bangladesh border in northern West Bengal. In this chapter, I draw on this range of structured and unstructured interviews as well as participant observation to describe the experiences of the BSF personnel, both constables and officers.

In 2009 the first batches of 735 female constables were trained at the BSF training center in Punjab, through a forty-six-week-long basic training course that is standard for all constables recruited to the Force.[16] Upon completion, they were assigned to join different battalions along the border with Pakistan. As reported jubilantly in the media in the months that followed, their specific duties were to frisk women in border villages and "build rapport" with communities in the Punjab borderlands.[17] As more women are recruited and trained, they are being deployed gradually to more locations along India's borders under the jurisdiction of the BSF, under the "one border—one force" doctrine inaugurated after the Kargil War, as discussed by Azad in this volume.

The BSF's model of incorporating women is distinctive from the CRPF, which has had women in its constabulary since 1982. In the CRPF women are structured into the Force through female-only battalions; at present there are a total of six. The BSF by contrast assigns female constables into existing battalions, within the total sanctioned strength of the organizational structure. In a press release in 2016, the BSF announced that "the tasks entrusted and performed by them are at par with men '*praharis*' and as such they are performing all operational, security and intelligence-related tasks."[18] At present there are 4,147 women in the BSF, a mere 1.66 percent of the total constabulary.[19] There are fifteen female inspectors and one female officer who directly entered the Force at these ranks.[20] While the female constables are trained in female-only batches, recruits at other higher ranks are trained in gender-mixed batches. In the gender-mixed batches it becomes clear that male and female recruits are held to different standards of physical fitness, like the IPS outdoor training, though trainers and trainees asserted that other aspects such as weapons training and technical skills were expected to be the same. While the broad structural parameters of this model of inclusion were decided upon prior to the implementation of the policy, each of these aspects and their minutiae are intensely debated by BSF personnel, thus making the terms of inclusion highly fluid and contingent. Practical details need to be worked out and a series of decisions need to be taken across multiple ranks to concretize the stated policy objectives of inclusion: the next three sections show how discourses about institutional change and gender norms shape this process of ongoing reform and its implications for a security institution.

Who Will Guard the Guards?

Consider the discourse of functionality. The argument from within the BSF seeking the inclusion of women emphasizes the organization's improved effectiveness for border security purposes. To that end, as I learned from my fieldwork along the India-Bangladesh border in West Bengal, newly trained and deployed female constables are assigned to duty at gates along the border fence. Gates along the fence India has built along its serpentine border with Bangladesh are opened thrice a day for an hour each. During this opening, Indian residents of border villages are allowed to go through the gates to work on the land or go to the homes that fall in the area between the fence and the actual border.[21] Men, women, and children pass through these gates between the hours of 6–7 A.M., 12–1 P.M., and 4–5 P.M. Since the male BSF soldiers are not allowed to search and frisk women, they have allegedly come to be the most effective carriers of goods for smuggling. This phenomenon, evident in these borderlands, densely inhabited by the agrarian poor, had made itself known as an urgent demand for "gender-sensitive policing" in policy-making circles.[22]

Imagine, then, that into this beleaguered scene of border security enter Mala and Aditi, two female constables.[23] They are the newly trained, young soldiers whose presence promised to revolutionize border security in favor of the BSF and the Indian state. In their first month of duty and at briefings in the border outpost to which they had been assigned, they learned that they were not to go on duty in "buddy pairs," as is typically the case with male constables, but that each buddy pair would be further accompanied by a senior male constable. On one afternoon shift we were a group of four sitting in a makeshift bamboo shelter, built for patrolling soldiers by the border fence. To my question about such an arrangement—of a "buddy pair" being accompanied by a senior constable—being usual for all new soldiers when they were first deployed, the senior male constable accompanying the female pair replied: *"Jawan ko to hum phek dete hain. Larkiyo ko aise kaise kare. Unko akela chhor nahi sakte."* (We throw the jawans in. How can we do that to the girls. We cannot let them go alone.) While the inclusion of women as soldiers is "de-gendered" by recruitment, training, and professionalization processes that are emphatically the same for men and women, such experiences of inclusion reveal the cultural logics through which the BSF is "re-gendered" to "reify hierarchical gender differences" that mark out female recruits structurally.[24]

Mala's and Aditi's opinions on the matter bring another aspect of this functionalist discourse to light. On one occasion they had finished duty at a border fence gate and were walking their cycles back to the barracks about a kilometer away, savoring the time alone as the male constable had cycled away. I invited them to accompany me to the nearby border town and wondered if they might plan a day off. Aditi, the more outspoken of the two, responded, "We are guards, but they always send a guard to guard us. No *chance* of going out with you." She went on to relate her experience from the previous week when she was feeling unwell and wanted to see a gynecologist in that border town. The officer in charge of the border outpost had arranged for her to be driven to and from in his jeep with another male constable "on duty." These two men waited outside the doctor's chamber while she visited and Aditi recalled the embarrassment she felt at using up all these resources. "Then we will have to hear that we get *special treatment*, I am sure of that."[25] With no power to resist such "special treatment," Aditi was not only infantilized but also held responsible for it by her male colleagues. Women and men in the BSF are hardly alone in grappling with the wide gap between gender reform ideals and existing social realities, such as those considered by commanding officers in keeping female constables accompanied and protected. Inter-governmental agencies such as the UN Women and the UN Peacebuilding Commission have committed to military and peacekeeping reforms to achieve gender equality, especially since the 1990s.[26] Even though studies of such efforts of "gender balancing," that is, the degree to which women and men are represented in and participate across the full range of activities within military forces and operations, are overwhelmingly limited to international peacekeeping or forces of the developed world, the emergent patterns of gender reform in the BSF echo many of their findings. If critiques of women's role in peacekeeping are that they hinge on an essentialized understanding of women as natural caregivers, mothers, and naturally inclined to peace, here we see that Indian women's deployment alongside Indian men and amid local communities presumed to be patriarchal rest on the assumption that female soldiers need protection as women despite being a professional soldier. These kinds of experiences accumulated: while some men and women narrated them as remarkable and undesirable, most referred to the underlying patriarchal logic as a given. Such a reification emphasizes perpetuates an essentialized distinction between men and women, where women are not capable of the same responsibilities as men and therefore must be treated differently.

These experiences are crucial to understand the patriarchal principles underlying micro-decisions governing the deployment and incorporation of female constables and the form that such structural arrangements cumulatively take. In many ways it is analogous to the paternalistic disciplinary mechanisms, colonial and racialized in origin, that structure the interactions between police officers and rank and file that Jauregui draws attention to in her contribution to this volume. In the BSF, it is specifically through the cultural logic of patriarchy that female soldiers are *simultaneously* heralded as an institutional asset as a special kind of soldier—to be lauded and utilized for limited purposes—and as an institutional liability in need of "special treatment," as a woman.[27]

For many women, including those at the rank of inspectors,[28] the perceived power and valor of the uniformed soldier had drawn them to this profession in the first place. Aditi, who had been a competitive athlete in high school and college and was used to traveling long distances on public transport alone to attend sports meets, chafed at the male protectionist discourse that framed women's limitations within the Force. She made it clear that she was disappointed—and quite surprised—by the ways in which female constables were being cloistered. This is a common theme for female recruits in security forces as Anthony King shows, based on a study of the British army. Valor in uniform is the kind of power that women aspire to in being soldiers, indeed even willing to fit the bill to be what in the British context has been described as "an honorary man."[29] However, the ability to embody this power and valor was severely circumscribed through these daily distinctions by which they were marked as inferior and in need of someone else's protection. Aditi experienced and narrated this not only as patronizing but also as discriminatory. "We wear the same uniform, but we are not given the same opportunities," she reflected bitterly on the value of soldiering labor within the institution. Feminist scholars of gender reform in militaries have demonstrated that increasing numbers of women in such deeply masculinist institutions does not necessarily translate into better outcomes for such women. Even in the Israeli military, where the conscription of men and women is mandatory, women consistently suffer discrimination as less able and weaker.[30] South Africa has the highest number of women in the military on the African continent, yet as Lindy Heinecken argues, this goal of increasing numerical representation in a quest for "gender mainstreaming"[31] has cemented the masculinist critique of women's selections and progress "simply because they are women."[32]

For the BSF's masculinist decision-making ethos, however, this is precisely what they see as "high risk":[33] women's performance of valor and potential injury is a liability and public cost they are not willing to take.[34] Taking seriously dominant patriarchal notions of the need to protect women in women's interest as well as for the sake of the institution's honor and dignity, masculinist to be sure, illuminates how the presence of women is made consonant with existing gender hierarchies and culture within the BSF. Writing about gendered counterinsurgency operations of the US military, Synne Dyvik (2017) notes that female soldiers were deployed in special teams in Afghanistan to advance military effectiveness even as the US ban on women in combat was still in place. She argues that evidence from this and other cases of such functional inclusion of female soldiers suggests that while there is "a certain amount of recognition for their efforts," it changes little in institutional norms and culture around the gendered labor of soldiering.[35] Such a functionalist argument holds in this case too: the inclusion of female constables in the Force was to fulfill a specific and limited purpose. They could frisk the women and children and search their bags and thereby put an end to a pervasive range of smuggling that included petty consumer goods, perishables, and drugs and narcotics. In all my interviews with BSF officers and constables across all ranks, not a single person mentioned the recommendations of the parliamentary committee on the empowerment of women as an impetus for the recruitment of women in the BSF. Rather, the sole rationale—and objective—for the inclusion of women was for specific policing tasks that required women. In this dominant institutional discourse about the rationale for including women in the BSF, gender equality, integration, and equality of opportunity were framed as low priorities, even at odds with institutional needs.

To Integrate or Not: Discourses of Standards and Professionalization

BSF battalions are universes unto themselves. While officers often move from one battalion to another as they are promoted, frequently occupying roles that are not attached to any single battalion, the young men and women who join as constables typically spend their entire career in a single battalion. A constable's service record often reflects the biography of the "unit," as battalions are referred to as the smallest sphere of autonomous decision-making in the BSF. Within this unit, everyday decisions such as about assigning duty, further training, and leaves affect the battalion's performance as an effective operational team. But its operational effectiveness is also significantly shaped by its sense of community and camaraderie that is built and maintained over a long time. Here the distinction between inclusion and integration with regard to female constables becomes particularly acute, with implications for Force cohesion and effectiveness. Female constables, though included into the existing structures of the Force, are done so with a departure from the practice of constables belonging to a single battalion over the course of their entire career. Women are posted to locations in their home states or the nearest options. Numerous men and women referred to this as "police *jaisa* posting" to signal the restriction to one's home state and the limited prospects of postings within that smaller ambit.[36] In this section I consider the significance of this manner of inclusion through the discourses of equal standards and professionalization.

In a focused group discussion with six company commanders of a battalion stationed under the North Bengal frontier, my question about the challenges of managing personnel with the inclusion of female constables sparked a heated debate. The group's mix of young direct-entry officers and older officers who had been promoted through the ranks from the inspector level is fairly representative of the overall composition of BSF officers, especially at the level of the company commander. On one side were those who advocated for women's-only battalions, a segregation model of inclusion, whose members could be posted to specific sites to fulfill limited duties. Arguments for this ranged from its cost-effectiveness to that it least disturbed the existing institutional status quo. Female constables in this view were an instrumental necessity for a Force, whose masculinist labor, community, and ethos was deemed to need no gender reform overall. Some vocal advocates of this position went so far as to suggest that the integration of female constables imposed from above created "manpower shortages" and actively damaged the sense of bottom-up *fraternal* community of soldiers. Women constituted the total strength of an outpost but given their limited duties, it meant allocating their male colleagues with more work (for the same pay). Countering this view were officers who believed that gradually enhanced integration was not only possible with women's improved and expanded training, duties, and performances, but in fact necessary to maintain the overall standards, community cohesion, and professional effectiveness of the Force as a modern organization. Expressing this view, one of the company commanders referred to a neighboring battalion that had deployed a female inspector to lead a platoon post (a subsidiary post under a border outpost, with fewer troops) with no problems. He credited the progressive leadership of the battalion's male commander for creating this opportunity and recommended other steps such as assigning women to night patrols that would allow women to demonstrate their abilities in these expanded duties and combat roles.

At stake in the institutional discourses around gender—whether taken to be an essential difference or dynamic and socially constructed—is the idea of inclusion through integration, a framework that does not foreclose the equality of opportunities, unlike the segregationist model. Studying male soldiers' resistance to women's integration in the US military, Carol Cohn argues that existing gender stereotypes about immutable differences in physical capacity (e.g., "they can't do as many push-ups as us") may entrench feelings of resentment but find expression through the ostensibly neutral ideology of the "standards discourse."[37] As we see in this case too, a conception of immutable gender difference is marshaled to voice a critique of gender equality as unfair. On the other hand, stories of exceptional female soldiers growing into expanded combat roles, including ones of leadership and frontline soldiering, are double-edged. While they are premised on a conception of gender difference as shifting and open to change, in stressing the exceptionality of individual cases, they risk occluding the structural inadequacies and norms that remain unchanged. As Aditi confronts the prohibitions of the "special treatment" with which female constables are managed, naturalizing their limited abilities and prospects in the Force as soldiers, the systemic work of patriarchal discrimination that both individualizes and naturalizes hierarchical gender difference becomes visible. From the limited roles that soldiers like Aditi are *structurally* encouraged to perform—and that they critique and resent—officers can generalize that female constables do not and cannot perform all functions of a soldier and that instances where they do, are exceptional at best. As feminist scholars of reforms in law have argued, changes in law alone cannot ensure the substantive changes in institutional culture, beliefs, and dynamics upon which rest the experience and realization of equal opportunities.[38] Instances of female soldiers advancing from conservatively assigned roles toward a greater degree of equality show the importance of progressive leadership at all ranks in addition to the capacity and training of female recruits themselves to overcome male-normed soldiering standards. Together these represent new openings and opportunities to improve the prospects of female soldiers and their value as soldiers.

The importance of community and its interrelatedness to professional development and knowledge within the Force comes into sharp relief with the peculiar nature of women's incorporation. Take, for example, the case of Sujata Roy, posted in the North Bengal Frontier. In 2018, she was very familiar with her battalion's entire area of duty, having worked at several different border outposts, as well as the needs and functioning of the frontier headquarters having been posted there since 2011 when she finished training. She had developed a deep and broad understanding of the BSF's organizational structure and different aspects of work, arguably much more than a male constable with six or seven years of experience typically only in border outposts. She had just been reassigned to a new battalion that had arrived a month prior to take the place of what had been her "parent" battalion and she wondered whether or not—and how—her knowledge and skills would be valued in this new and unknown unit. Over five years, Sujata and eleven of her female batchmates, who had joined the battalion fresh out of training, had come to be socialized into the larger institutional culture and structure of the BSF through this primary home and finite community.[39] They imbibed the dominant philosophy of and identification with what is called a parent unit, for constables signifying the individuals they will get to know and work with closely every day for the rest of their careers. Far from their own families, who they visit typically once a year, this finite community of the battalion becomes kin and a vital support system. These social and emotional ties also become the conduits for the exchange and consolidation of knowledge, experience, and expertise. Sujata's professional growth from a fresh recruit to a relatively senior female constable had been witnessed by the head constables and inspectors and other colleagues of her parent unit. Beyond the skills and experiences recorded in her official file, this familiarity constituted the basis on which Sujata's work and abilities were appreciated, the opportunities and responsibilities she was allocated, and her own aspirations for future development were forged. Accomplished and ambitious, Sujata reflected that she had no doubt that over time the officers and senior constables in the new battalion would also come to recognize and value her abilities and experience. Nevertheless, the time and labor to forge these new relations of trust and acquaintance was an additional cost, hard to measure or quantify, to be borne by female constables. Research on the management of diversity—gender and race—in the British Army finds that the framework of professionalization has been vital in changing gender norms around ability within the institution, leading to a greater acceptance of women.[40] In this case, to the contrary, we learn from Sujata Roy's anxiety how questions of professional progress are intimately connected to the value of institutional community as the basis of social ties, support, and knowledge, especially for female constables. Thus, it is within and despite the patriarchal culture of the BSF that it is possible for female soldiers to foster professional development and aspirations through ties and recognition within their immediate soldiering units.

Infrastructures of Privileged Inclusion

Whatever their disagreements, officers and troops alike are bitterly critical of policy directives that are informed not by the ground realities of security work in multiple settings but by abstract policy and political objectives. Evidence of such a mismatch could be seen in the GOI's announcement in 2016 of reserving 33 percent of the constabulary for women in the CISF and the CRPF and 14–15 percent in the border-guarding forces of the BSF, ITBP, and SSB. Even those in favor of a radical transformation of the Force with gender reform were critical of this policy given the lack of institutional preparation, capacity, and social outreach. No one I spoke to, whether female constable or male officer, was surprised that even by 2019, filling up this quota of recruits has been slow and difficult despite secure pay and the stability of scarce central government jobs.[41] Female soldiers remain a socially exceptional figure. And in the absence of the radical infrastructural and normative changes necessary within the institution to allow female soldiers to thrive, once they join, numerous female constables in their early twenties are already considering leaving. In addition to the unresolved question of "manpower shortage," which would become critical if the current structure of women's limited inclusion is scaled up without addressing the negative impacts on collegiality, mutual respect, Force cohesion, and effectiveness, the domain in which the subject of institutional preparedness is most contentious is infrastructure.

Female recruits cannot be sent to border outposts without adequate housing facilities. Such a consideration rules out 71 out of 177 battalion locations across the country, which are classified as "hard" or "very hard."[42] Further, among the remaining 106 locations classified as "soft," the primary determinant of which outpost comes to receive and house a deployment of women is the feasibility of providing gender-segregated and adequately private housing. New border outposts being built along the India-Bangladesh border are designed to have a female barrack in addition to the standard components and layout of outposts: male and female barracks share the same facilities and features. Existing outposts that have been modified to prepare for the *mahila* constables, however, present a sharp contrast in the infrastructural provisions for women compared to men. For instance, in one of the BOPs that I've seen transformed, six women share the barrack that previously ten men used to share. A bathroom has been built on to this barrack while all the male troops continue to share a makeshift structure with toilets and taps. In two other BOPs, two rooms for officers have been converted into a barrack for women while the commanding officer now occupies what was a guest room for visiting senior officials. In short, in an already constrained system of material resources, newly recruited female constables receive greater infrastructural investment than their male counterpart. Ensuring physical privacy through enclosures and attached bathrooms for female barracks is clearly given the utmost importance, an infrastructural measure appreciated by women. However, in BOPs where hierarchy and value in the Force are given spatial form, the stark differences between the living conditions of male and female soldiers is on display for all to see. There are beds of flowers outside the officers' rooms, not of the *jawans*' barracks, and the buildings where the arms and ammunitions are stored are central and prominent in the BOPs layout. The symbolism of the female constables coming to occupy structures that were previously inhabited by officers and are thus in much better condition than other structures in the older outposts, then, is up for debate. To be sure, these are differences that may be eliminated over time—especially if a concerted institutional effort is made to do so—but during this protracted period of transition, in whispers and in jokes a discourse and perception of un-deservingness attaches to the position of female soldiers and the material benefits available to them.

If the implementation of gender reform has come with certain measures of infrastructural preparedness, such as facilities in border outposts, there is a whole host of examples that reveal the masculinist blinders behind the conception and planning of this policy. A constable's day is broken up into six hourly shifts alternating between being on duty and off duty. When the new recruits first arrived to the border outposts in Coochbehar district and began to patrol gates and other checkpoints along the border fence in six hourly shifts, they were shocked to find that there were no bathrooms they could use other than the ones in the BOP. Using bathrooms in the homes of border villagers was deemed to reduce the dignity of the Force and lead to potential compromises, thus ruled out as an option.[43] Officers in charge resorted to reducing the hours of female constables, a practice that became common, adding to the litany of complaints that male constables have about the reduced work and demands of their new colleagues. From an organizational perspective, these are clearly issues of state capacity and resource constraints, like those that the police forces at the district level (Mangla, this volume) also struggle with. However, in such matters of institutional failures in infrastructural provision,[44] female recruits come to be blamed for the short-term solutions used to address these problems within the dominant male chauvinism of the institution. These instances are important to push policy conversations beyond a simple listing of the lack or provision of infrastructure. Instead, such experiences of infrastructural investments demonstrate the complex ways in which the terms of inclusion can themselves deepen existing patriarchal convictions about the capacities of women. What's more, they provide ammunition for the resentment and disrespect toward colleagues on the grounds of unfairness and partiality, greatly undermining a progressive discourse and agenda for gender equality.

Wrapped around the tangible, built structures that enable women to join the BSF's work amid India's varied borderlands, are the equally critical but less visible infrastructures governing life and well-being. As the editors of the volume note in the Introduction, and Jauregui describes regarding the police rank and file, rising deaths from suicides, mental and chronic health issues are a serious concern that receives little public attention.[45] In security institutions such as the BSF, such dire matters of well-being have been connected directly to the inadequacy and unpredictability of leaves and holidays, especially for the constabulary. For female soldiers, leaves and special absences from duty due to pregnancies or other medical needs are heavily stigmatized in a Force that has not only never had to deal with them, but considers them to be inconsequential to the workforce as they know it. Such stigma and expressions of this inconsequence came across emphatically in almost all my interviews and group discussions. Male officers and constables referred to their own sacrifices regarding family life, with the skepticism that women could ever do that. Given that the dominant model of BSF community is a disavowal of family ties in favor of complete immersion in service and the life of the Force, older officers especially are reluctant to reimagine responsibility to one's children and family coexisting with one's responsibility to the Force.

Seventy percent of the women being recruited in the BSF are under twenty-five.[46] For instance, in one of the three battalions under study in this chapter, there are forty-six women currently in its rolls. Nearly half of this number were married or widowed at the time I conducted interviews in 2018 and 2019. Several others had plans to marry and were waiting to understand the system better as well as gain some experience and seniority in it before making personal decisions that would affect their professional advancement. This reflects an understanding of a system that worked through individual discretion and ability to maneuver rather than an accountable and transparent system of rules and policies that could be relied upon. There is an official policy in place for maternity and parental leave that two women in this battalion had already utilized. Both women lived in the family quarters of the battalion headquarters with their small children; one constable's husband lived and worked from home and shared childcare responsibilities while the other constable's mother lived with her to help with childcare as her husband had a job elsewhere.

Both, however, were anxious that this arrangement could be disrupted any time if they were deployed to the border. To recall the challenges of personnel administration discussed in the previous section, officers and senior constables in this battalion repeatedly cited the requests of such female constables to remain in the headquarters as evidence of being "unwilling" to do even the limited work they were explicitly hired for: patrolling at gates and checkpoints along the border. Unless adjacent infrastructures and policies for childcare and family housing at or close to border outposts are conceived and invested in by the Force, individual women will have to bear the burden of making feasible arrangements and being stigmatized while doing so. Most important, the BSF's institutional inability to register complaints and concerns in a systematic and fair manner from the constabulary on any matter becomes particularly acute with the issue of leaves, decisions over which are entirely in the discretionary power of their immediate superiors. Noting the colonial institutional resonances in this unreformed structure within police institutions, Jauregui writes in her contribution that the rank and file suffer from having nowhere to address their complaints. In the BSF, the case of female constables brings into sharp relief the inadequacies of current institutional structures and the urgent need for reform of such structures in order to support the kinds of personnel changes entailed with the recruitment of women. The slow uptake in recruitment of women despite reservations has the further pernicious effect of being explained in terms of women's *inherent* unsuitability and unwillingness to the BSF and soldiering rather than a scrutiny of the infrastructures of equal opportunities that make this a viable career choice for young women.[47]

Radical Transformations or Status Quo Re-established?

Does the inclusion of women in the BSF result in a radical transformation of the institution or is the status quo re-established despite this important reform? The short answer to this question is neither, while the longer and more complicated kind of answer that this chapter has suggested is that it is indeed a bit of both. The question also is what the yardstick for change is and should be for measuring the BSF's accomplishments: whether it should be understood in relation to social change in Indian society at large, with regard to the BSF's own goals and institutional history, or some normative standard that a Force like the BSF should aspire to emulate.

Through the debates I have presented internal to the BSF, I would suggest that the presence of women compels members of the Force to confront questions of gender equality in theory and in practice, debating intensely and carefully a model of inclusion by segregation in comparison to one of integration. Even when there are seemingly irreconcilable positions on what to do about these issues, the ideal of fostering an environment free from discrimination and harassment so that overall discipline and cohesion can be maintained is acknowledged as vital to the interest of the Force. Although not a predictable starting point for conversations about equal opportunities for women, this acknowledgment makes space for an institutional commitment to gender reform that could align with progressive goals from the standpoint of gender and labor equality and institutional efficiency. As I have shown with ethnographic examples, these internal debates expose the masculinist and frequently chauvinist principles, ethos, and practices of the institution that continue to set the measure of honor, valor, and expertise in the labor of soldiering to members of the Force in ways that would never have arisen otherwise. This includes renewed demands for the betterment of the predominantly male labor force. While solutions may not be easy or speedy, given the finite budgets upon which the Force is dependent, the inclusion of women has forced the related issues of family and leave policies—facilities in BOPs, family housing, leave policies, medical facilities including mental healthcare—for *all* members of the Force to the center stage. For instance, the care taken to provide adequate infrastructure and conditions of work and living for women has foregrounded the dismal conditions under which many *jawans* live and work; improvement of these conditions for all has become a priority. So, the inclusion of women shifts the needle for the welfare of *all* soldiers in the Force.

Radically different, even contradictory, issues are at stake for the different actors in the BSF, all affected by the incorporation of women. This ongoing period of transition is a particularly important one because while it is open to being pushed in multiple directions and institutional precedence being established or reified, these issues are now are likely to become foundational. As the company commanders and male and female troops alike drew on their own experiences or those of their friends in other battalions to support or challenge normative positions, it becomes clear that their opinions and decisions at these micro-scales do shape the terms of gender reform in the present and have the potential to dramatically direct its contours in the future. This can have tremendous significance for women in combat and leadership roles in armed/security forces and police broadly. The impact of the inclusion of women in the BSF requires critical reflection on the two primary stated aims: improved organizational efficacy and gender equality.

Does the inclusion of women in the BSF lead to greater organizational effectiveness for the BSF? At first glance, it appears that the stated aims of intercepting and reducing the involvement of women and children in unauthorized cross-border activities along India's borders with Pakistan and Bangladesh has been successful. However, as I have suggested in this chapter, this narrow view of functionality poses a dangerous problem for overall organizational cohesion and a balanced distribution of tasks. Inadequacies on these two aspects prevents the BSF from realizing its full capacities to perform. With the Supreme Court pushing for greater integration of women in the armed forces, it is imperative to have an institutional roadmap for what that might look like based on the needs and mandates of each CAPF, like the

BSF. As the editors note in the Introduction, India appears to be without an over-arching internal security doctrine. Studying the BSF as an institution, it becomes evident that such radical labor reforms with tremendous potential are occurring without a larger functional and ideological vision. Instituting mechanisms— training and combat role goals, infrastructure expansions, leave policies, internal mechanisms of complaint, to take a few examples—by which women can be more fully integrated would allow for their functional roles to be supported and enhanced and the overall effectiveness of the institution to be realized.

Does the inclusion of women in the BSF herald a shift in organizational cul-ture, especially toward gender equality? This is a difficult question, one that scholars of gender in the armed forces have been debating across a variety of distinct contexts. I have categorically avoided judgments about success or failure and tried to paint with a finer brushstroke the emergent contradictions and tensions as experienced by different members of the Force. I have focused my discussion to broadly three aspects: the discourse of protection and risk in the inclusion of women as soldiers; the question of standards, profession-alization, and community; and the infrastructures of inclusion. My goal with this focus has been to examine the extent to which systemic reform challenges and shifts hegemonic social norms *within* the institution—in this case patriar-chal understandings of the hierarchical difference between men and women— and disaggregate the kinds of shifts and contestations that do become possible. I have drawn attention to these openings and internal contestations in the BSF while suggesting that security forces such as these must address the patriarchal norms of soldiering labor at its heart so that its members, whether male or fe-male, can thrive.

A rigorous understanding of the emergent nature of inclusion in the BSF—part integration, part segregation—suggests that perhaps the functional argument of in-clusion could be a bridge to the integration model based on principles of gender equality, by slowly shifting norms and infrastructures from within the institution. Lawmakers across a number of contexts, such as in the EU, have observed that even when women join they remain in the minority in military roles, especially in higher ranks.[48] They are faced with an environment and institution designed for success by and for men; proactive policies are required to change this to recruit and re-tain women at *all* ranks. Making an active commitment to improving the working conditions of all soldiers of the BSF will require emphasizing a respectful balance of professional and family lives beyond patriarchal expectations that are harmful for all. Given that the BSF is one of India's numerically largest and most signifi-cant security institutions and also one of the world's largest border security forces, these questions broadly resonate with the Indian state and society. Policymakers would do well to think in terms of short-term and longer-term changes they wish to enact: at this juncture, the BSF has the opportunity to lead the way in institutional and social change.

Notes

1. Sushant Singh, "Explained: What Supreme Court Said on women in the Army," *Indian Express*, February 17, 2020.
2. The Supreme Court judgment in the case of *Babita Punya and Others v. Ministry of Defence, Government of India*, in February 2020. It is interesting that the judgment specifically listed honors and recognitions bestowed by various UN peacekeeping operations to female officers as evidence of their distinguished service to the nation.
3. For a collection of studies on gender reform and issues of gender and sexuality more broadly in militaries, see Rachel Woodward and Claire Duncanson, *The Palgrave International Handbook of Gender and the Military* (London: Palgrave Macmillan, 2017).
4. Broadly speaking, gender reforms in militaries have come at distinct political-historical junctures, such as after World War II, during the UN decade of focus on women and gender, and so on. For a broad overview and discussion of the findings of a comparative study, see Mayesha Alam and Robert Egnell, eds., *Women and Gender Perspectives in the Military: An International Comparison* (Washington, DC: Georgetown University Press, 2019).
5. Alon Peled, *A Question of Loyalty: Military Manpower Policy in Multiethnic States* (Ithaca, NY: Cornell University Press, 1998).
6. Rikhil R. Bhavnani, "Do Electoral Quotas Work after They Are Withdrawn? Evidence from a Natural Experiment in India," *American Political Science Review* 23, no. 35 (2009): 23–35; Raghabendra Chattopadhyay and Esther Duflo, "Women as Policy Makers: Evidence from a Randomized Policy Experiment in India," *Econometrica* 72, no. 5 (2004): 1409–1443; Lakshmi Iyer et al., "The Power of Political Voice: Women's Political Representation and Crime in India," *American Economic Journal: Applied Economics* 4, no. 4 (2012): 165–193.
7. See Wedel et al., "Toward an Anthropology of Public Policy," *Annals of the American Academy of Political and Social Science* 600, no. 1 (2005): 35–51.
8. Begona Aretxaga, "Maddening States," *Annual Review of Anthropology* 32 (2003): 393–410; Nayanika Mathur, *Paper Tiger: Law, Bureaucracy, and the Developmental State in Himalayan India* (Cambridge: Cambridge University Press, 2016); Ajantha Subramanian, *The Caste of Merit: Engineering Education in India* (Cambridge, MA: Harvard University Press, 2019).
9. Following from Judith Butler, *Gender Trouble: Feminism and the Subversion of Identity* (New York: Routledge, 1999).
10. Interviews with a member of the first batch of BSF officers. For an overview of the Indian Home Ministry's policies on internal security, see Sinha, this volume.
11. In theory, battalions going from "hard" postings are supposed to have a period of rest and all changes to be preceded with regional and cultural orientation. In practice, neither of these two is adequately observed.
12. TNN, "Soft Diplomacy: Non-Lethal Weapons at Bangla Border," *The Times of India*, March 13, 2011, https://timesofindia.indiatimes.com/india/Soft-diplomacy-Non-lethal-weapons-at-Bangla-border/articleshow/7689296.cms.
13. Human Rights Watch, *"Trigger Happy": Excessive Use of Force by Indian Troops at the Bangladesh-India Border* (New York: Human Rights Watch, 2010); United Nations High Commissioner for Human Rights, *Report on the Situation of Human Rights in Kashmir, 2016–2018* (Geneva: United Nations, 2018); Samreen Mushtaq et al., *Do You Remember Kunan Poshpora: The Story of a Mass Rape* (New Delhi: Zubaan Books, 2016); see also Ahuja and Raghavan, this volume.
14. Parliamentary Committee on Empowerment of Women, evaluations submitted in *Women in Paramilitary Forces*, Sixth Report of the Committee on Empowerment of Women (2010–2011).
15. These frontiers are headquartered in Siliguri and Guwahati respectively. While I have conducted research in battalion and frontier headquarters, the bulk of the ethnographic research has been carried out in border villages under the jurisdiction of these frontiers.

16. K. Ganesh, "Induction of Women Combatants in BSF: Issues and Effect on the organization," *Indian Police Journal* 66, no. 2 (2019): 36–47.

17. "Starry-Eyed Young Women Set to Guard Borders," *News 18*, July 26, 2009, https://www.news18.com/news/india/women-bsf-guards-2-321342.html.

18. PTI, "Border Security Force to Induct More Women in Force," *Economic Times*, November 27, 2015, https://economictimes.indiatimes.com/news/defence/border-security-force-to-induct-more-women-in-force/articleshow/49950542.cms.

19. Ganesh, "Induction of Women Combatants in BSF."

20. My own ethnographic data as of 2019.

21. There are reportedly 146 villages that fall in the areas between the fence and the border fence that have not relocated despite efforts by the BSF.

22. Sabrina Karim and Kyle Beardsley, "Female Peacekeepers and Gender Balancing: Token Gestures or Informed Policymaking?," *International Interactions* 39, (2013): 461–488; and Donna Bridges and Debbie Horsfall, "Increasing Operational Effectiveness in UN Peacekeeping: Toward a Gender-Balanced Force," *Armed Forces & Society* 36 (2009): 1, for discussions of functionalism arguments on the relation between gender reform and operational effectiveness in UN Peacekeeping. See Santana Khanikar, "Women Police in the City of Delhi: Gender Hierarchies, 'Pariah Femininities' and the Politics of Presence," *Studies in Indian Politics* 4, no. 2 (2016): 155–177, for discussions of this theme with regard to the Delhi police.

23. I use pseudonyms and am deliberately unspecific about the names and locations of border outposts to protect the identity of individuals and their battalions.

24. Orna Sasson-Levy and Sarit Amran-Katz, "Gender Integration in Israeli Officer Training: Degendering and Regendering the Military," *Signs* 33, no. 1 (2007).

25. English words in italics indicate their usage as such in Hindi speech.

26. The UN Security Council Resolution 1325 passed in 2000 centered the important role women play in peacekeeping, security, and conflict resolution. Since then, the numbers of women in peacekeeping forces have increased.

27. Santana Khanikar (2016) argues that women in the Delhi police maneuver being a *police*woman and a police*woman* for different situations and power relations.

28. Studying the contradictions that female inspectors face with regard to a profoundly hierarchical institution where respect and authority accrues to rank but daily indignities subtly subvert their authority is especially insightful and an arena for further research.

29. Anthony King, *Gender and Close Combat Roles*, in *The Palgrave International Handbook of Gender and the Military*, ed. Rachel Woodward and C. Duncanson (London: Palgrave Macmillan, 2017), 305–317. There is a longer discussion to be had about the question of gendered aspirations and role models more widely prevalent in society, which greatly affects the extent to which men and women in the Force are complicit in upholding masculinist notions of valor and heroic labor.

30. Sasson-Levy and Amran-Katz, "Gender Integration in Israeli Officer Training."

31. The language of "gender mainstreaming" comes from and the UN 1325 resolutions and has become standard part of bureaucratic discourse on gender reforms within governmental institutions.

32. Lindy Heinecken, "Transitions and Transformation in Gender Relations in the South African Military: From Support in Warfare to Valued Peacekeepers," in *The Palgrave International Handbook of Gender and the Military*, ed. Rachel Woodward and C. Duncanson (London: Palgrave Macmillan, 2017), 355–369.

33. Ganesh, "Induction of Women Combatants in BSF."

34. A study of the distribution of female military personnel in UN missions has similar findings; see Karim and Beardsley, "Female Peacekeepers and Gender Balancing."

35. Synne Dyvik, "Gender and Counterinsurgency," in *The Palgrave International Handbook of Gender and the Military*, ed. Rachel Woodward and C. Duncanson (London: Palgrave Macmillan, 2017), 319–333.

36. Frequent comparisons to the police and the Army in different conversations emphasized the in-between status of the BSF as an institution. Depending on the context, the comparisons to posting like the police were both positive and negative.

37. Carol Cohn, "'How Can She Claim Equal Rights When She Doesn't Have to Do as Many Push-ups as I Do?': The Framing of Men's Opposition to Women's Equality in the Military," *Men and Masculinities* 3, no. 2 (2000): 131–151.

38. Srimati Basu, *The Trouble with Marriage: Feminists Confront Law and Violence in India* (Berkeley: University of California Press, 2015); Neema Kudva and Kajri Misra, "Gender Quotas, the Politics of Presence, and the Feminist Project: What Does the Indian Experience Tell Us?," *Signs: Journal of Women in Culture and Society* 34, no. 1 (2008): 49–73.

39. The total number of female constables in this battalion was thirty-eight. As with male constables, they were distinguished among themselves in seniority based on years of experience.

40. Rachel Woodward and Patricia Winter, "Gender and the Limits to Diversity in the Contemporary British Army," *Gender, Work and Organization* 13, no. 1 (2006): 45–67.

41. Ananya Bhardwaj, "No Takers for Women's Quota in CRPF, CISF or BSF as Forces Strive to Fulfil Modi Govt Plan," *The Print*, March 19, 2019, https://theprint.in/india/governance/no-takers-for-womens-quota-in-crpf-cisf-or-bsf-as-forces-strive-to-fulfil-modi-govt-plan/207485/.

42. Ganesh, "Induction of Women Combatants in BSF."

43. The eastern borderlands in Bengal, Assam, etc. is reportedly different in this regard from the border villages in Gujarat, Punjab, Rajasthan, along the western border where the troops enjoy sympathetic relations with local communities.

44. To be fair, these are being addressed and remedied—in 2018 and 2019 I saw bathrooms and provisions for running water being built into the new watchtowers being built along the fence. No doubt this will exacerbate fault lines between the BSF and local communities who will surely be debarred from using these facilities, but that is a different story.

45. See Introduction and Azad, this volume. Heart attacks and suicides were the cause of more deaths than operations in the BSF in the past decade. https://economictimes.indiatimes.com/news/defence/bsf-adopts-ways-to-curb-suicides-depression-among-jawans/articleshow/60141797.cms?from=mdr.

46. Ganesh, "Induction of Women Combatants in BSF."

47. Bhardwaj, "No Takers for Women's Quota in CRPF, CISF or BSF as Forces Strive to Fulfil Modi Govt Plan."

48. Committee on Equality and Non-Discrimination, Council of Europe, "Women in the Armed Forces: Promoting Equality" (Doc 14073, 2016).

15

Security Labor and State Suppression of Police Worker Politics

BEATRICE JAUREGUI

In 2018, two in-service Uttar Pradesh Police (UPP) constables, Prashant Chaudhary and Sandeep Kumar, were involved in an extrajudicial killing colloquially known as an "encounter." Chaudhary and Kumar claimed that they were conducting a routine stop of a speeding car overnight on September 29 in the UP state capital of Lucknow, and that they had to shoot in self-defense when the driver suddenly tried to mow them down. The constables were soon charged with murdering a man in the car named Vivek Tiwari, who happened to be a sales manager with the Apple corporation.[1] Many rank-and-file police across UP considered the criminal charges against their colleagues unjust, in a context where police perform these kinds of killings routinely and with impunity.[2] Some of these police engaged in protest actions that consisted mostly of posting on social media sites images of themselves or their fellow constables holding protest signs or wearing black bands on their arms, traditionally a symbol of mourning. Some protesting police also shared with one another things like screen shots of their bank account statements verifying contributions of a few hundred rupees to a crowd sourced fund to support Chaudhary's and Kumar's criminal defense.

Several in-service constables and sub-inspectors were reportedly suspended from service (with a 50 percent pay cut) for participating in or ostensibly allowing these protests.[3] The most extreme punitive measures were taken against two former UPP constables who, like many others, were sharing news of the protests on social media. One was a civil police pensioner named Brijendra Singh Yadav. The other was a family man in his late thirties named Avinash Pathak.[4] Yadav, who since the 1980s has been litigating against what he argued was personal mistreatment and unjust dismissal by the UPP, founded a police union called the Rakshak Kalyan Trust/Araajpatrit Police Workers Association (RKT/APWA), or Security Workers Welfare Trust/Non-gazetted Police Workers Association. Pathak, who has collaborated with Yadav and other police unionists while litigating to overturn

Beatrice Jauregui, *Security Labor and State Suppression of Police Worker Politics* In: *Internal Security in India*. Edited by: Amit Ahuja and Devesh Kapur, Oxford University Press. © Oxford University Press 2023.
DOI: 10.1093/oso/9780197660331.003.0015

his own dismissal in 2004 from the UP Provincial Armed Constabulary (PAC), founded an organization called the Police Parivar Kalyan Samiti (PPKS), or Police Family Welfare Association. On October 17, 2018, as the police protests around UPP constables Chaudhary's and Kumar's arrests heated up, Pathak and Yadav were detained in synch on opposite sides of the state, allegedly for engaging in activities that "were prejudicial to the maintenance of public order and have disturbed the normalcy of the society."[5] Both men were denied bail and released on the same day exactly twelve months after they were taken into custody, and without ever being produced in a public court to face criminal charges. Though they never had public hearings according to due process, the one-year detentions were deemed lawful on the grounds that Yadav and Pathak had violated: (1) the 1922 Police Incitement to Disaffection Act; (2) several sections of the Indian Penal Code (IPC);[6] and (3) the National Security Act of 1980 (NSA).

Encounter killings or "encounters" as a category of police practice, or even as specific cases of police violence, are challenging to analyze for lack of definitive data and the localized politics of (under or mis-) reporting their occurrence.[7] Human rights advocates and other analysts who write about this extreme form of police brutality generally suggest that it reinscribes endemic public insecurity in the name of eradicating "terrorism" or "anti-national" activity or more-or-less organized forms of "criminality."[8] Some scholars have analyzed how encounter killings may be considered legitimate not just by police but many other public citizens, often in the name of a feckless legal system or cultural concepts of cosmic justice.[9] My contributions to this volume, and my reasons for beginning with this particular case, do not center the truism that threats to the "internal security" of the people in democratic India manifest in encounters and other common forms of extreme police violence. Rather, I view the constable protests and state responses around this case through a lens that frames police as "security labor" in order to critically reflect on how the extremely poor living and working conditions of many rank-and-file police reflect and reproduce public insecurity at large.[10] Put another way, this chapter highlights the insecurity of "cutting-edge" police officials themselves, and constables in particular, as a crucial piece of the puzzle of their simultaneously excessive and inadequate provision of security to the public. The discussion sounds a clarion call for new modes of engagement around police reform that apply democratic principles of equity, welfare, and social justice for all, including police personnel.

This analysis demonstrates how state government actions like the yearlong detention of Yadav and Pathak represent an ideology that constructs rank-and-file police who engage in "police worker politics" as always already potential insurgents, even "enemies of the state."[11] This ideology has a long history that is rooted in colonial governance, but has intensified and crystallized following independence. The questionably legal and legitimate confinement of these two former constables for allegedly being threats to "public order" falls in line with a plethora of other instances of state suppression of police attempts to critique the government that employs them, and by association to critique the social order they work to uphold. Based on almost two decades of fieldwork, interviews with current and former police in several states, and content analysis of various kinds of documents—including but not limited to government commission reports, internal police memos, court writs and judgments, and interactions on social media—this essay makes two primary claims. First, there is robust evidence that for well over a century, the imbrication of official police organizational hierarchies with unofficial forms of social inequality—especially those related to socioeconomic status or "class"—have led most government leaders, including senior police officials, to perceive cutting-edge police workers unions and advocacy as a significant internal security threat. Second, this hegemonic suspicion of potential police insurgency, and the effects of the suppression of police worker politics, comprise significant factors in endemic police discontent that reproduces both a conflictual structure of relations within the police institution, and a generalized lack of capacity to maintain public order and security.

In what follows, I will support these claims through an ethnographic and historical account of how the founding and ongoing functioning of police organizations in India reinforce broad-based social inequalities and perpetuate conflict and insecurity. First, I will demonstrate how the inability of police to legally and legitimately express work-related grievances today is rooted in colonial forms of knowledge and administration related to "discipline" that figure police as an overextended, underresourced labor force. Next, I will detail how this figuration of police personnel negatively impacts their physical, social, and political welfare in line with broader forms of structural violence in contemporary India. I will then analyze how the Indian state has repeatedly suppressed attempts by police to unionize or find other avenues for voicing labor concerns, and how this reinforces public insecurity. Finally, I will suggest some means through which changes in relational structures—rather than the more common recommendations of increasing manpower or resource allocation—may realize substantive improvements in police practice and effectiveness that could enhance "internal security," both within the police institution and also among Indian society more broadly. The insights of this critical examination of long-entrenched class warfare within and around policing as *itself* a threat to internal security must be foregrounded in ongoing debates about how best to reform policing in the world's most populous democracy.

Police "Discipline" as Subjugation

In 2007, while conducting long-term fieldwork with police in Uttar Pradesh, I was invited to observe routine activities on the Lucknow Civil Police Lines. One day, I arrived just before 6 A.M., watched the flag raising, parade, drill, and inspection of the armory; then proceeded with the host, an assistant superintendent (ASP) whom I will call Praveen Kumar, to the *aadesh kaksh*, orderly room.[12] The room appeared to be a blending of administrative office, court bench, and commemorative lounge, furnished with a desk and chairs, and decorated with flags, trophies, official portraits, and plaques listing names of various leading officers dating back to the 1950s. As "inspirational" adornment hanging behind the presiding officer's desk, there was a painting of a famous photograph of Mahatma Gandhi and Prime Minister Jawaharlal Nehru, sitting together smiling, with a caption reading, "Confession of errors works like a broom. Broom sweeps away the filth and confession does no less. —Mahatma Gandhi."

After Kumar seated himself at the desk, constables began to enter marching in formal goosestep, saluting, stomping, and then standing stiffly while the ASP read whatever reports or requests they had brought for his review and signature. After several minutes of this, a single constable soberly marched in empty-handed, donning more formal attire than the others, including ceremonial headdress. Appearing old enough to be Kumar's father, the constable stood stone-still while his case file was presented to the ASP by another younger (but according to sleeve stripes higher-ranking) constable, who explained that this man was found to be missing from his post for nine hours and was being disciplined for dereliction of duty. ASP Kumar looked at the paper laying out the details of the reported offense and asked the constable to explain himself. The constable responded that his son had come to him needing food, so he had gone home with him and fed him, and by the time he returned to his post, the report against him had already been issued. Following this testimony, the ASP turned to me and said in English that he believed the constable was being honest, and that, "since he has not made up lies about being 'biimar' [sick] or something . . . I have decided not to punish him, but instead will just give him one day's involuntary leave." This meant the constable would lose a full day's pay. Kumar scribbled some writing on the paper, gave it to the younger file-carrying constable, and pronounced his decision to the older constable being sanctioned, who then saluted and marched away silently behind his file.

When one raises with senior police officers the orderly room's paternalistic disciplining procedures for alleged minor infractions by constables, the officers tend to respond with a mixture of surprise (that a civilian even has knowledge of it), embarrassment, and defensiveness. Many will make some reference to it being a problematic colonial military "hangover" or "relic." Yet, most will not acknowledge how this social artifact reproduces a dialectic of senior officer authority/superiority and subordinate personnel silencing/inferiority that is a key element in constructing constable views of what they call "afsar [thana]shahi," or "dictatorship of [senior] officers."[13] Some officers will go so far as to claim that orderly room offers rank-and-file police a space to submit complaints related to work. This claim does not hold water. Constables being disciplined are given a singular moment to explain their case in front of an arbitrating senior officer who has absolute discretion. Being compelled to defend oneself against an accusation of misconduct by one's boss does not equate to provision of adequate and supportive space for airing job-related grievances, especially systemic problems. Moreover, the rigid structure of orderly room does not allow constables to initiate complaints themselves. To do this, police personnel must either submit an individual application in writing or raise the issue at a *masik samelan* or *durbar* (monthly meeting, public congregation, or hearing). The second option might seem more promising, especially if a complainant can garner support from colleagues. But in practice, *samelan* either do not happen at all due to some apparent "exigency" like understaffing, or, as attested by many constables, these meetings tend to become spaces for senior officer didactics and reprimand (group "discipline") rather than a space for subordinate personnel to express their own concerns.[14]

Orderly room procedures represent one of the more functionally regularized and ritualized police institutional procedures that shows how the long shadow of colonial governance continues to reinscribe both class warfare between seniors and subordinates, and generalized insecurity among the rank and file, which gets passed on to the general public (see also chapter by Mangla in this volume regarding the "social distance" between IPS offices and constables that "contributes to gaps in communication and information exchange"). Another procedural form is the system (or lack thereof) for ensuring that rank-and-file police personnel receive the full amount of leave from work to which they are entitled, an amount that many argue is itself inadequate in comparison with their senior officers.[15] There are two types of leave that may be taken by police in Uttar Pradesh and in many other Indian states. "Earned leave" is accumulated over time and dependent upon years of service. One year of service earns thirty days of leave, and a person may choose to take extra salary in lieu of taking the leave. This "thirteenth month" of salary benefit seems to be the preferred option for the vast majority of rank-and-file police, since they are also officially entitled to a second type of leave called "casual leave," which may be used any time with immediate effect by anyone providing a "good reason." Senior officers are given fifteen days of casual leave per year, while sub-inspectors and constables are given thirty days of casual leave annually. Some senior officers have noted that they receive fewer official casual leave days annually because "as a rule" they have Sundays off, while their subordinates do not.[16]

Besides the fewer days of leave officially provided to subordinate ranking personnel—an inequity that unionists place front and center in their campaigns for police *karmchariyon kalyan*—the bigger problem for most constables is that they are very often unable to take the casual leave to which they are entitled. Casual leave must be requested in writing and is granted solely at the discretion of one's immediate superior officer. Constables' requests for leave are routinely refused, often on the grounds that they are needed because of staff shortages (again, a chronic problem), sometimes for no better reason than the boss simply assumes they are lying about their reasons for the request.[17] Notably, casual leave does not roll over to the next fiscal year—so you either use it or lose it. And if you happen to have a boss that consistently refuses to authorize you to use it, then that is just your bad luck, and you have little recourse. Many constables have told me that they make efforts to discover which senior officers will be the most lenient or understanding, and therefore likely to allow leave. And a few have readily admitted that if they cannot find such a person, then they will make up an outrageous story to procure needed time off, if that is what it takes.

This relational structure of inequity in the guise of bureaucratized discipline stems from the very formation of police institutions themselves under colonial rule. As multiple police scholars, practitioners, and many members of the general public in India know, policing across the sub-continent is still mostly organized under principles established in the 1861 Police Act.[18] What is less commonly considered is how the commission that drafted this Act—a commission composed entirely of British military and civil service leaders—did so with two primary goals in mind: (1) "civil-izing" security administration in the colonies and (2) minimizing expenditure on said administration in order to maximize revenue (again, see Mangla, this volume, who notes that the "British colonial state's primary objectives in India were to collect revenues and maintain a semblance of law and order, in furtherance of the Crown's economic exploits."). Crucially, the report the commission issued in 1860 made explicit declarations that civil police work purportedly demands *less* "strict discipline [than that considered] essential in a military body," and therefore police workers would require "fewer reliefs" from duty than soldiers.[19] This was then written into the 1861 Police Act as police being "always on duty." As the British Crown consolidated administrative control over its South Asian colonies in the following decades, the expressed assumption that civil police could, and should, do variegated tasks for longer hours without significant provisions for relief confronted (and arguably engendered) struggles to recruit and keep adequate numbers of personnel deemed fit for the job.[20] What became a perennial challenge of maintaining enough "manpower" to keep the "peace" produced an organizational culture demanding that rank-and-file police essentially be "on call" all day every day, without clear distinctions between times they were on or off duty, and without sufficient time for recuperative leave from work.

In sum, British colonial administrators created a new class of supposedly "disciplined" security laborers fundamentally defined by simultaneous overextension of their labor power and minimal expenditure on their pay and welfare, a working class that now comprises the vast majority of police in India.[21] Over time this social structure has generated an increasingly disenchanted and seemingly "insubordinate" collective of rank-and-file police personnel. State government responses to any expression of discontent among these security laborers have reflected anxieties about the possibility that "grievously overworked . . . disheartened and dispirited" constables might, like soldiers had in 1857, rebel against their overlords.[22] Giving these allegedly "less-disciplined" laborers fewer reliefs from often ill-defined and exhausting work, with no clear or functioning avenues for redressal of grievances or negotiations over working conditions, has rendered a smoldering spirit of alienation among the rank and file, which feeds fears by senior officers and other governing elites of insurgencies from below. These fears have hardened into harsh legal restrictions on and state reactions to police unionization across India. These restrictions and reactions work to instigate and reproduce the very things the state wishes to prevent: mass protests by police, as well as a host of police malpractices that worsen public insecurity and disorder, from encounter killings and fabrication of evidence to routinized bribe-taking and discriminatory treatment of common citizens.[23] In the next section I will delve further into how this systemic lack of "relief" and other elements comprising the poor living and working conditions of police personnel impact both their vitality and their ability to participate as full citizens in independent India.

Expendable Police Life and Disenfranchisement

One of the most striking and disturbing social facts about police life in India is the extraordinarily high number of police deaths on duty, the vast majority of which, over 90 percent, are constables or head constables. Recent reports have indicated that "between 1947 and 2019, more than 35,000 police personnel have lost their lives in the line of duty."[24] At its most conservative estimate, that is an average of more than 486 police deaths per year since India became an independent nation-state. In 2020 the total recorded number of police deaths in the line of duty was 526, 70 percent of which were categorized as "accidents"; and the total recorded number of police injuries was 1,506 for that year only.[25] The figures vary widely state to state, fluctuate year to year, and are usually proportional with general population figures. So more populous states like Uttar Pradesh, Maharashtra, and Tamil Nadu often incur the highest numbers of annual police casualties, though there are occasional exceptions—for example in 2020, 78 of the 526 police killed on duty that year were in Chhattisgarh, most of which were attributed to Maoist insurgents. Even accounting for India's superlative population figures, however, these casualty numbers are astonishing, leaving far behind analogous statistics of police deaths per population in other world regions, and even soldier deaths in many war zones.[26] And yet, in aggregate they rarely garner much critical attention on the local or national level except briefly and ceremonially during national Police Commemoration (or Remembrance) Day, which is observed annually on October 21. This is arguably because most of the violence experienced by police personnel is structural, just like most of the violence experienced by the Indian public at large. This section aims to shed light on how structural violence that manifests in poor living and working conditions of police harms them not only physically and psychologically, but also socially and politically in ways that both reflect and reproduce insecurity across the country.

Regarding structural violence that harms the body specifically, the available official data show that the vast majority of police deaths in the line of duty, usually between 75 percent and 95 percent annually, are attributed to mundane accidents, illness, suicide, or undefined "natural causes."[27] Of the 526 police personnel listed as "killed in police operations" in 2020, 72 percent of those deaths were reported as occurring either "in accidents" (70 percent) or "accidentally with Self weapon" (2 percent).[28] Even if they do not suffer death or serious injury, cutting-edge police personnel generally experience high levels of work-related stress and fatigue that have been documented for decades by official and non-governmental organizations, or NGOs.[29] But it was only in the past few years that, for the first time, an independent survey of both police personnel and their family members in twenty-one states was conducted, which focused primarily on police vulnerabilities and turned a critical eye on their poor living and working conditions across the country.[30] Titled the *Status of Police in India Report* (SPIR), and combining published official statistics with new data from more than 22,000 interviews in over 100 locations, this research study reaffirmed in a consolidated "All-India" fashion what millions of police and their associates have known and have been trying to voice for years: that rank-and-file police across the nation are overstretched, under-resourced, and generally miserable. As the SPIR authors rhetorically inquire, "Why should anyone be surprised if police personnel come across as bitter, exasperated or fatigued?"[31]

The SPIR findings included, among many other things, that police personnel across India work for fourteen hours a day on average, with about 80 percent working far more than eight hours a day, the global standard for a full-time shift.[32] It also found that 50 percent of police personnel report having no weekly days off; and that approximately 80 percent of police who work what officially counts as "overtime" do not receive pay for this labor.[33] As with compiled statistics on police deaths and injuries, reported working hours varied state-to-state, with police in Nagaland reporting an average workday of eight hours,[34] while police in Odisha and Punjab reported an average workday of seventeen to eighteen hours.[35] These more quantitative "labor time" measures were further nuanced by findings that 75 percent of police believe that their workload has a negative impact on their physical and mental health;[36] that 84 percent of police personnel and 88 percent of their relatives feel that time spent together is "insufficient"; and that over 75 percent of police personnel feel their work load makes it difficult to do their job well.[37] This is all congruous with earlier ethnographic findings among rank-and-file police in Uttar Pradesh (UP), who widely lament that they often do not receive full pay for work completed; are on call "24/7"; and have fewer days off than senior officers, especially the top brass Indian Police Service, or IPS officers.[38] And there remains so much that we do not know, even as rigorous research findings related in the SPIR begin to fill in some of the gaps of official government reports on things like poor living and working conditions. The government of India would do well to start systematically collecting data on the amount of leave that police request versus the amount they are actually permitted to take; the quality of police housing and equipment; the numbers and types of complaints that police register regarding job-related grievances; rates of resignation or dismissal from the job; and rates of suicide among police across the country.

The previous section of this chapter outlined the challenge that many rank-and-file police face obtaining permission for work leave in line with official entitlements. This challenge is further complicated by the fact that some state governments place geographic restrictions on personnel postings as part of what in UP has long been referred to as the "border scheme." In order to prevent presumed "vested interests" in one's home locale supposedly translating into "corrupt" activity of some sort, police constables may not be posted in their home district; nor may they even be posted in a district that borders their official residence (hence, the name border scheme). Whatever nebulous and nefarious designs this policy may in fact prevent, it also has the destructive social effect of separating massive numbers of police personnel from their families and communities. This is not always the case, certainly. Some constables are able to secure family housing provided by the government, which is in short supply (and often poorly maintained—see CC & CSDS: 50–52), or may find an affordable rental home in their current district of work. But the majority are compelled to live separately from their loved ones, often in barracks that are overcrowded, unhygienic, and insecure from things like theft, extreme weather conditions, or other potential harms to person or property. It is crucial to understand how these isolating and depressing living conditions intersect with or directly contribute to other problems within the police institution that fall under seemingly unrelated categories of policy, such as employment benefits and internal disciplining procedures like those discussed in the previous section. For example, if a constable requests a few days of leave from work to travel a long distance home in order to attend to a family emergency—or even to join a happier occasion, like a wedding—and the leave is not granted for some reason, then in desperation, they may go anyway, and then be disciplined for "dereliction of duty." As noted above, constables are commonly refused leave even when claiming dire need, and often for no better reason than the caprice, cynicism, or indifference of the senior officer making the decision.[39]

An equally or perhaps even more significant negative effect of these geographically restrictive posting policies relates to their de facto disenfranchisement of masses of police personnel. Journalistic accounts coming out of multiple states and union territories suggest that hundreds of thousands of cutting-edge police are unable to vote in regional and national elections, either because they are not provided with leave in order to return to their home district, or because they are not provided in a timely manner with the other resources allowing them to vote from a distance.[40] I have spoken about this with numerous current and former police personnel, most of whom seem resigned to being excluded from the right to suffrage. One UP police constable, whom I will call Ashish Kumar, told me, "I have never cast my vote in an election . . . and I am 42 years old." When asked why, he responded that senior officers do not give permission for leave, nor provide the necessary forms to vote by mail, which he says can only be given by the department. When I press him on why he thinks his senior officers do not provide him with the necessary forms, he claims they prefer that subordinates "just take orders rather than express political opinions." Considered from another angle, that of politicians themselves, one retired officer noted in his critique of state responses to police protests that "there does not seem to be many votes in the redressal of grievances of policemen."[41]

Constable Kumar and erstwhile constable Avinash Pathak both have been mentored by a longtime police worker activist named Ram Ashish Rai. Rai was the cofounder and general secretary of an organization called the Rajya Police Karmchari Parishad (RPKP), or State Police Workers Council, and was imprisoned for more than four years in the 1970s for alleged security threats as a police unionist leader.[42] Rai, who at the time of writing is still alive and survives mostly on alms and a meager pension won through years of litigation, continues to work to gain support for a legally registered and officially recognized police union, conducting *yatra* (pilgrimages), holding meetings, and recruiting in-service personnel to the cause, which he sees as the exercise and survival of democracy itself. Rai has told me, "We have a democratic system, but I feel a constable has no freedom." He goes on to say (in translated Hindi for readability):

> I want that the police should run on a democratic system, to be there for serving and not beating the people. Seeing the Indian police today, you will have fear in your heart, you will not feel secured. . . . [People talk of] democracy here [but] in fact, the rich are powerful and worshipped everywhere . . . whereas the poor will just sit quietly and get nothing . . . [perhaps] plain bread . . . polluted water. . . . I feel police are the backbone of our democratic system that can help develop and nourish all. . . . Police are supposed to give protection to all. But our police is broken.

Rai's declarations about police being "the backbone" of democracy, potentially working to "develop and nourish" the demos, the people, echoes not only statements made by late Prime Minister Indira Gandhi but also claims made by other police worker activists in contexts as far-flung as Chicago in the United States.[43] His wish that police "run on a democratic system" could be interpreted as a call for more "democratic policing" that adheres to international human rights law, is accountable to independent oversight bodies, and responsive to public needs.[44] But it also could, and arguably should, be read as a call for what some scholars have termed police "workplace democracy," where rank-and-file police personnel have a voice in institutional decision-making and policy reforms that help them realize workers' rights.[45]

Ram Ashish Rai has conducted his police unionist activities for a half century in what he considers a spirit of "true democracy" that demands equity and enfranchisement for all. And he has been branded a security threat and suffered greatly for it, not unlike the anti-colonial revolutionaries with whom police unionists frequently compare themselves. These unionists claim they are fighting not merely for civil rights like equitable access to their voting franchise, but moreover for their dignity and human rights (*"manvadhikar"*), particularly the rights to health, to a living wage, and generally to benefit from fair labor practices, among others listed in the International Covenant on Economic, Social, and Cultural Rights, which India ratified in April 1979. In the next section, I will consider how official restrictions placed on the rights of police workers to organize *as security laborers* has transformed and intensified over the past half century in ways that reinforce the insecurity of rank-and-file personnel and reinscribe social inequities suffered by the Indian public at large.

Police Aspirations to Democratic Rights and Security

The punitive and preemptive ideology framing police unionists as enemies of the state crystallized in the 1970s, a particularly turbulent time in Indian political history marked by the 1971 war with Pakistan, and the Emergency period between 1975 and 1977. Interspersed among these seismic regional events were the country's two most lethal and widespread police uprisings. The first occurred in Uttar Pradesh in May 1973. In March of that year, the RPKP cofounded by Ram Ashish Rai, who was then a young civil police constable, managed to register officially under the 1860 Societies Registration Act. This alarmed senior officers, some of whom lobbied the UP Vidhan Sabha to ratify the national Police (Restriction of Rights) Act of 1966, which banned police from forming or joining unions.[46] While the causal chain of ensuing events remains in dispute, what is known is that within a couple of months, police across the state began to gather in protest at more than one dozen sites, including at Lucknow University and at various battalion grounds of the armed auxiliary wing of the Provincial Armed Constabulary (PAC). On May 20, the UP government declared a state of emergency, and over several days tense stand-offs and at least three lethal shootouts occurred between national Army soldiers and rank-and-file police in Kanpur, Lucknow, and Varanasi.[47]

A similarly dispersed, if slower moving, and even more "All-India" scaled uprising of police personnel began in May 1979, after a MLA reportedly assaulted a constable in Patiala for not saluting as he passed, and alleged that the constable was "dead drunk."[48] A medical examination revealed the constable had reported to duty while extremely ill. It is unclear whether he requested leave and was refused, or feared even making such a request. In any case, news of the assault apparently set off protests among police across the state. Over the next few days, agitations spread like wildfire outside of Punjab, leading to police strikes and confrontations with senior officers in fourteen other states. There were also mass protests, some of which turned lethal, among personnel with several central police forces, including the Central Industrial Security Force, Central Reserve Police Force, and Intelligence Bureau. Most of the 1979 police protests were peaceful demonstrations expressing grievances related to "inadequate emoluments, lack of housing, long hours of duty . . . inadequate promotional opportunities and absence of institutional machinery for redressal of grievances."[49] Notably, however, there were also complaints about "use of policemen for personal work of officers" and "senior officer 'tanashahi' [dictatorship]."

Whatever their legal or political classification—as insurgencies or even "terrorism"—what I wish to highlight here are the conditions of possibility that gave rise to these protests.[50] These conditions remain essentially unchanged today even in the face of periodic pay commissions, policy changes, and budget allocations oriented toward "modernizing" police across India. It is tempting to think that police living and working conditions have substantively improved over the past half century, since there seem to have been relatively few violent protests of police around welfare and workers issues since the 1980s, and smaller localized incidents receive little media attention.[51] But a historically and ethnographically informed analysis demonstrates that the apparent lack of spectacular events associated with collective organizing by discontented personnel likely has more to do with powerful campaigns of state "lawfare" successfully suppressing police unionist activities.[52] Moreover, a plethora of personal pressures to keep a hard-won if miserable job, among other endemic social and political factors, work against the cohesion and consensus-building required for a police workers association to gain strength (to say nothing of public legitimacy) and to make any headway on specific demands. Caste loyalties, communal conflicts, and other cultural cleavages fragment police unionist efforts just as they do so many other social movements and their potential progress across India.[53] Regional linguistic divides and lack of knowledge of how fellow police personnel may organize as security labor in other parts of the country limit the imaginations and organizing capabilities of many local unionists. And crucially, many people in India in myriad social positions still hold fast to a potent imaginary (which is, to a limited extent, a reality) that a government job—any government job, even one that seems to extract far more than it provides—offers a person, their family, and their close associates the best chances of stability, success, and a semblance of security.[54]

This imaginary of state employment supremacy itself is rooted in practices and ideologies of colonial governance, which over many decades forged structures of feeling and interaction that configured all aspects of livelihood, from language and art to the ways in which various forms of labor, especially security labor, would be configured and valued.[55]

Government work generally, and police work specifically, reproduce broader relations of social inequity, discrimination, and devaluation among state workers themselves and among the public at large. While these relational structures play out in complex and sometimes counterintuitive ways among all levels of the official police hierarchy, they are revealed most starkly in the alienation between the senior-most officer class of the IPS and the rank-and-file masses of constables. It would be a gross oversimplification to claim the existence of an overarching IPS "culture" of ignorance, indifference, or exploitation in relation to subordinate police personnel; and certainly there are countless instances in which police of all ranks work together sometimes to good effect in ensuring security (see Mangla, this volume, for some examples). That said, it is also undeniable that prevalent and patterned social practices, including but not limited to orderly room, constitute these senior-most gazetted officers as enemy number one—or at least gatekeeper or obstacle number one—for many rank and file police personnel. This is the very meaning of officer "tanashahi" or dictatorship.

The acrimonious alienation between many senior officers and subordinate personnel is widely known, and has been analyzed at length in ethnographic study of everyday police life, with particular attention to constables claiming they must sometimes pay bribes for duty assignments or do non-mandated and often physically taxing *"begaar"* or forced labor, like building construction, pond digging, quarry mining, and animal husbandry.[56] But these matters are completely ignored in most research and official reports on police institutions in India, which is not particularly surprising when we consider that the collection and tabulation of such data are usually overseen by senior officers themselves, or by analogous officials in the civil services. To date, the most critical quantitative analysis of these forces and relations of senior-subordinate strife at an All-India level comes from the previously cited SPIR, though again they have been revealed in a rather limited capacity. The SPIR found that 25 percent of rank-and-file police personnel reported that senior officers ask their juniors to do their household/personal jobs even though they are not meant to do it.[57] It also found two in five police personnel report the use of "bad language" by senior officers; three in five report a lack of "equal treatment" of junior and senior level personnel, and a full 75 percent express that they are permitted to do "only those tasks that are asked by their seniors."[58] While the language framing these problems in the survey is at best vague and tepid, in aggregate, the responses of those surveyed hint at the prevalence of not merely a lack of working "autonomy" among the majority of cutting-edge police, but more important, a systemic rot of top-down abuse of police personnel by their own bosses.

While SPIR provides invaluable information on a host of infrastructural shortcomings and problems in policing, its authors suggest that the poor service conditions, including and especially the "inhuman duty hours" that most police suffer, "can be directly attributed to the inability of the States to fill the sanctioned strength of the police force . . . [which negatively] impacts on the efficiency and overall functioning of the police."[59] Undoubtedly, a lack of resources, including shortcomings of "manpower" and "force multipliers," is one piece of the puzzle of police inadequacy and insecurity. But I would argue that a much larger and more fundamental piece involves the history, structure, and meaning of these conflictual and exploitative relations between senior officers and subordinate personnel, which at least one retired official has claimed "should be more like that of employer and employee than of [military] major and private."[60] Indeed, it is the oppressively disciplining, disregarding, and disenfranchising structure of relations among police themselves—and the concomitant conceptualizations of what police work is, and what police workers are for—that must change before there will be any hope of inducing police reforms that could substantively help improve public security.

One issue that demands further attention as we consider how to reconfigure demands for transforming police institutions is the gendered nature of policing as security labor, a matter that is highlighted in the previous chapter by Sahana Ghosh. Ghosh notes explicitly how "the care taken to provide adequate infrastructure and conditions of work and living for women [in the BSF] has foregrounded the dismal conditions under which many *jawans* live and work; improvement of these conditions for all has become a priority. So, the inclusion of women shifts the needle for the welfare of all soldiers in the Force." The police unionists in UP that I have engaged to date have been exclusively men. These leaders would do well to place women's issues in a more central position in their political platforms, and to invite more women activists to collaborate on and even lead their campaigns. At the time of writing, RKT/APWA leader Brijendra Singh Yadav has recently founded his own political party, the Rakshak Jan Morcha Party (RJMP), and one of their key strategies has been reaching out to women's rights groups. It remains to be seen how other police worker organizations will incorporate and address concerns around gender in their calls to action.

In any case, police reform programs in India generally must place front and center the long history of neglect of the welfare and the voices of rank-and-file police personnel. As demonstrated here, most police workers in India have virtually no functioning avenues for collective bargaining in the name of their *own* security, nor any effective means of self-representation as security laborers with basic civic and human rights. There must be a radical transformation in how police reform gets discussed and done, specifically by inviting the active and sustained inclusion—indeed, following Sahana Ghosh's analysis, the genuine "integration"—of subordinate-ranking police in high-level conversations, and not only that but by providing space for them even to *initiate and lead* some discussions. Otherwise, the vicious cycle of fearful oppression, eruptive anger, and generalized insecurity will continue indefinitely. At times this cycle, which some may liken to the mythical *chakravyuha*, may be writ large and lethal, as it was throughout the 1970s.[61] More often, though, it likely will continue to be writ small and recurrent, for example in the occasional eruptions of sometimes violent protests by police against lawyers—or by lawyers against police—which have occurred in UP in 2004 and 2007, Tamil Nadu in 2009, and in Delhi in 2019, among other times and places across the country. If we wish to inspire just and sustainable policies and practices that will put India on the path to providing genuine security for the public and police alike, then we must break the extant *chakravyuha* of fear and ferocity by creating new and inclusive spaces for democratic debate regarding reforms. To quote reformer and retired senior officer S. K. Ghosh one more time, to date it appears that "[t]hough the police have their place in a democracy, there is [still] no place for democracy in the police!"[62]

Creating New Spaces for Democratic Policing and Social Justice

Police in South Asia began trying to form workers unions as early as 1920, in what is now Tamil Nadu, Bihar, and West Bengal.[63] Some of their activities led directly to the Police (Incitement to Disaffection) Act of 1922, which as mentioned above, was invoked in the detention of police unionists Yadav and Pathak in 2018. Notably, this colonial Act partially exonerates police acting in *"good faith . . . for the purpose of promoting the welfare or interest* of any member of a police force by inducing him to withhold his services *in any manner authorized by law."*[64] This provides a small opening for accommodating some existing police organizations. Unfortunately, to date this provision has only intensified the class warfare within the police institution since it has served primarily to support "professional associations" for already well-resourced and strongly networked senior officers. Rank-and-file police are left to fend for themselves, and subject to the aforementioned disciplining measures, or worse.

For one of the more disturbing examples of how this plays out, consider how in November 2018, in the Bihar state capital of Patna, a police protest following the death of a constable who was allegedly denied medical leave resulted in the suspension of 27 constables and full dismissal of 175 personnel.[65] Media outlets commented that this was "the first time that an action on such a scale has been taken against the constables."[66] Perhaps the scale of dismissals and suspensions is somewhat less shocking when we consider that the constable (in fact, a new recruit) who died of dengue was a woman, as were most of those who were ultimately let go.[67] Again, we would do well to keep in mind the analysis of Sahana Ghosh in this volume, regarding the ongoing struggle for gender equity in security institutions, in India and globally. And just as disturbing, of course, is the case with which I began, that of Avinash Pathak and Brijendra Singh Yadav, who were *detained for an entire year* under the 1980 National Security Act for allegedly "anti-national" activities.

In June 2016, in the southern state of Karnataka, there was a strike threat by constables, thousands of whom applied simultaneously for leave. The organized event made national headlines. Like similar events occurring a century before, the strike did not actually come to pass, and many attributed this to the "strong arm of the law" manifesting in the arrest of Shashidar Venugopal, the leader of a police union called the Akhila Karnataka Police Mahasangha (AKPM), or All Karnataka Police Federation. Similar to Pathak and Yadav in UP, Venugopal, who related in an interview that he had registered the AKPM as an NGO back in 1986, was charged with "sedition" and other crimes for allegedly instigating the strike via social media. But importantly, the Karnataka state government responded to the strike threat rather differently from how the UP government responded to the mostly social media–based protests by constables. Karnataka government leaders immediately formed a committee headed by Assistant Director General of Police Raghavendra Auradkar to review issues of pay, promotion, housing, and other living and working conditions of rank-and-file police across the state. The committee worked unusually quickly and within days recommended a 30 percent pay hike and increased allowances for things like uniform replacement and fitness maintenance. However, by February 2019, the recommendations still had not been implemented, which spurred Venugopal to lead further mass protests. He was again arrested and charged with sedition, criminal conspiracy, and other violations of the IPC for allegedly instigating police personnel, their families, and other organizations to rise up and demand implementation of the recommendations of the Auradkar Committee. The Karnataka state government eventually reported that a revised pay scale for all police in the state *except* for the senior-most IPS officers, with salary increases of approximately 50 percent across the board, would take effect in August of that same year.[68]

The case of Karnataka may give some encouragement to people like Pathak, Rai, Yadav, and other current and former police personnel in UP and across India who hope that organizing a union to collectively negotiate for improved living and working conditions will realize substantive transformation. But even in this particular context—a southern state in what many people consider a relatively more "progressive" region of the country—the government response still entailed the public defamation and detention of a unionist leader before there was any change in rules and regulations. Therefore, this incident may also be read as a less-than-optimistic example of what is currently possible, or probable, since it still falls well within the ambit of the long-standing state ideology of conceiving as a security threat police who express any kind of critique or protest regarding their own feelings of insecurity. There is still much work to do to understand the complex tensions between demands for security and social justice revealed by police unionism. And it remains an empirical question what the role and structure of police unions in India can and ought to be, as well as how or whether concessions like increased wages and benefits may actually translate into improved police performance and relations with the public.

With the well-known routinization of encounter killings, custodial deaths, torturous interrogations, and countless other types of violent and neglectful interactions between the police and the public in India, it is more than reasonable to be concerned and critical about police unionism, and about other more or less organized forms of what we may call police worker politics. We need look no further than the problematically powerful police unions in world regions like North America, which are widely considered to be bastions of white supremacy and one of the most significant obstructionist forces in ongoing debates around police reform and social justice.[69] But we must also remember that in India, as elsewhere, police violence is arguably a symptom rather than the root cause of public insecurity. And in this regional context, the specific history of police institutional foundations in structural violence dressed as hierarchical discipline and masking an exceptional poverty of working conditions among rank-and-file police demands that at least some of the unionist leaders' calls for change be heeded to some extent.

History clearly shows that techniques like "strike threats" by large groups of serving police have resulted in limited negotiations and infrequent actions, and in recent cases like that of Venugopal in Karnataka, it has resulted in criminal charges and detention of some individuals. Unless there is a concerted effort to acknowledge and transform the structural conditions of alienation between senior officers and subordinate personnel, and diffuse the concomitant low-intensity class warfare within and adjacent to civil police institutions as part of the larger state security apparatus, then state leaders will continue, consciously or not, to perceive rank-and-file police, unionized or not, as themselves an ongoing internal security threat. Simply allowing the formation or strengthening of police unions will not resolve these and other structural tensions. But neither will prejudicial suppression of every effort by police personnel to express work-related dissatisfaction or to form associations that may allow them some kind of platform for collegial support, voicing of concerns, and "good faith" negotiations with their governmental supervisors and employers. State leaders and policymakers need to consider how they can forge sustained and productive working relationships with cutting-edge police rather than relying on the repeatedly reinvented *chakravyuha* of feckless top-down commissions and committees that receive little to no bottom-up input from the workers most directly affected by their recommendations.

Countless months have been expended on research conducted and reports issued by "police reform" committees and commissions over the long twentieth century, and in the early decades of the twenty-first century. Pay commissions recommend new salary scales every five years or so. Training courses on leadership and management for mid-career senior officers abound. Non-governmental organizations and think tanks continue programs dedicated to critical study of police reform and safety trends and reporting of crime. Countless crores of rupees are expended in all these efforts. But even with the best of intentions, sometimes significant resources, and some of the most knowledgeable and hard-working actors on the case, many of the suggested policy changes put forward by these and other social institutions in the past, present, and future have and will come to naught without a focus on creating spaces of deep and sustained dialogue that include rank-and-file police personnel themselves at the proverbial table—whether they have a well-organized and officially recognized union or not. We must all work together to conceive new interactive spaces in which senior officials, policy advisors, scholar experts, and police personnel of all ranks can collectively address long-standing neglect of rank-and-file police welfare and subjugated status. Only then will the apparent "threat" to internal security of disgruntled police begin to abate, and institutional and individual performance perhaps begin to improve.

Notes

1. Fatal "encounters" with police often involve persons associated with social minority groups (especially Muslim people), and are rarely investigated thoroughly, with strong credence given by the government to police claims of "self-defense." In this particular case, beyond the very suspicious circumstances of the killing itself, it seems that the public outcry associated with the victim's elite social status as an upper-class Hindu Brahmin was key to the BJP-led UP government taking the unusual step of swiftly arresting and charging the two constables directly involved in the killing.
2. Julia Eckert, "The *Trimurti* of the State: State Violence and the Promises of Order and Destruction," *Sociologus* 55, no. 2 (2005): 181–217; Jyoti Belur, *Permission to Shoot? Police Use of Deadly Force in Democracies*. (London: Springer, 2010); Neha Dixit, "A Chronicle of the Crime Fiction That Is Adityanath's Encounter Raj," *The Wire*, February 24 2018, https://thewire.in/rights/chronicle-crime-fiction-adityanaths-encounter-raj (accessed December 8, 2020).
3. Pathikrit Chakraborty, "Vivek Tiwari Murder: Police Personnel Removed for Leading Protest in Support of Accused Cop," *Times of India, Lucknow Edition*, October 5, 2018, https://timesofindia.indiatimes.com/city/lucknow/vivek-tiwari-murder-six-cops-suspended-for-leading-black-day-protest-in-support-of-accused-constable/articleshow/66088266.cms (accessed December 8, 2020); Nilanshu Shukla, "Indiscipline Not Tolerated, Says DGP on Cops Supporting Accused in Vivek Tiwari Murder," *India Today*, October 9, 2018, https://www.indiatoday.in/india/story/indiscipline-not-tolerated-says-up-dgp-on-cops-supporting-accused-in-vivek-tiwari-murder-1358948-2018-10-09 (accessed 7 July 2019).
4. Since many of my interlocutors and their affiliated organizations are named in publicly available legal documents or news and social media sources, I use their real names on occasions when discussing general matters that are already part of the public record. However, when relating any information or direct quotations by police personnel that are not already published, or that I feel may pose some legal or social risk to interlocutors over and above what is already present in their daily lives, then I use generic titles like "constable" or "senior officer" or "unionist leader" in the interest of protecting confidentiality. I occasionally use pseudonyms and will explicitly signal this.
5. Some details from Yadav's case may be found in the text of this writ petition for habeas corpus filed in March 2019, which was ultimately dismissed by the judges: https://indiankanoon.org/doc/12121110/. Pathak has shared his own case files with me, but at the time of writing none has been posted publicly online.

6. These include charges under IPC codes 419, 353, and 500, which respectively involve "cheating by personation, fraud"; "assault or criminal force to deter public servant from discharge of his duty"; and "punishment for defamation."

7. Beatrice Jauregui, "Law and Order: Police Encounter Killings and Routinized Political Violence," in *A Companion to the Anthropology of India*, ed. Isabelle Clark-Deces (Malden, MA: Wiley-Blackwell, 2011), 371–388.

8. Grace Pelly and Jai Singh, *State Terrorism: Torture, Extra-judicial Killings, and Forced Disappearances in India.* Report of the Independent People's Tribunal 9–10 February 2008; Sanjoy Hazarika and Sarthak Roy, " 'Encounter' Killings: India Must Honour Its Pledges to the UN Human Rights Council." Commonwealth Human Rights Initiative, December 18, 2019.

9. Eckert, "The *Trimurti* of the State"; Beatrice Jauregui, "Just War: The Metaphysics of Police Vigilantism in Northern India," *Conflict and Society* 1 (2015): 41–59.

10. Beatrice Jauregui, "Lawfare and Security Labor: Subjectification and Subjection of Police Workers in India," *Law and Social Inquiry* 47, no. 2 (2022): 420–448.

11. Beatrice Jauregui, "Police Worker Politics in India, Brasil, and Beyond," *Comparative Policing Review* 32, no. 3 (2022): 271–290.

12. I was told that while the senior superintendent or SSP generally only presided over OR on Fridays, on other days a subordinate IPS officer, usually the ASP, does it; and that if the SSP must attend to some other urgent duty, the ASP will do it on Fridays as well.

13. Beatrice Jauregui, "Police Unions and the Politics of Democratic Security in Postcolonial India," *Qualitative Sociology* 41, no. 2 (2018): 145–172.

14. A chronic problem, see Common Cause and the Centre for the Study of Developing Societies (CC & CSDS), *Status of Policing in India Report 2019: Police Adequacy and Working Conditions* (2019), https://www.commoncause.in/uploadimage/page/Status_of_Policing_in_India_Report_2019_by_Common_Cause_and_CSDS.pdf (accessed January 12, 2021).

15. Cf. Ghosh, this volume, who describes gender discrepancies in the Border Security Force, and how rank-and-file male *jawans* with the BSF often blame their female colleagues for the "special treatment" the latter seem to receive regarding more days of leave from work or more posh living quarters, benefits that resemble those of senior officers.

16. There is no concept of "shift-work" for subordinate police in Uttar Pradesh. While there may be unofficial attempts to rotate workers on duty every eight to sixteen hours, depending on the types and necessities of duty, there is no legal protection dictating a limit of hours. Most of the police in and around the UP state capital of Lucknow with whom I worked were essentially "on call" twenty-four hours a day (see also NPC 1: 2.19).

17. Beatrice Jauregui, "Intimacy: Personal Policing, Ethnographic Kinship, and Critical Empathy," in *Writing the World of Policing: The Difference Ethnography Makes*, ed. Didier Fassin (Chicago: University of Chicago Press, 2017), 62–90; and Beatrice Jauregui, "Police Labor and Exploitation: Case Study of North India," in *Oxford Handbook of Ethnographies of Crime and Criminal Justice*, ed. Sandra Bucerius, Kevin Haggerty, and Luca Berardi (New York: Oxford University Press, 2021).

18. Anandswarup Gupta, *Crime and Police in India up to 1861* (Agra: Sahitya Bhawan, 1974); Anandswarup Gupta, *The Police in British India: 1861–1947* (New Delhi: Concept Publishing, 1979); Arvind Verma, *The India Police: A Critical Evaluation* (New Delhi: Regency Publications, 2005); K. S. Dhillon, *Police and Politics in India: Colonial Concepts, Democratic Compulsions: Indian Police 1947–2002* (New Delhi: Manohar, 2005); Common Cause and the Centre for the Study of Developing Societies (CC & CSDS), *Status of Policing in India Report 2019*.

19. Police Commission Report (PCR), Appendix IV: Extract from Report No.5 of the Military. (1860), section 161; cf. Ghosh, this volume, and Partha Pratim Shil, *Police Labor and State Formation in Bengal, c. 1860 to c. 1950* (unpublished PhD diss., University of Cambridge, 2016), 84.

20. Cf. Dirk H. A. Kolff, *Naukar, Rajput and Sepoy: The Ethnohistory of the Military and Labour Market in Hindustan: 1450–1850* (Cambridge: Cambridge University Press, 1990).

21. Bureau of Police Research and Development (BPRD), Data on Police Organizations, Annual Report, Ministry of Home Affairs (New Delhi, 2019), https://bprd.nic.in/WriteReadD ata/userfiles/file/202001301028101694907BPRDData2019-19forweb-2.pdf (accessed December 8, 2020).

22. Police Commission Report (PCR), Appendix IV: Extract from Report No. 5 of the Military (1860), section 157.

23. Beatrice Jauregui, *Provisional Authority: Police, Order, and Security in India* (Chicago: University of Chicago Press, 2016); Verma, *The India Police*; Dhillon, *Police and Politics in India*; Human Rights Watch (HRW), *Broken System: Dysfunction, Abuse and Impunity in the Indian Police* (New York: Human Rights Watch, August 2009), http://www.hrw.org/sites/default/files/reports/india0809web.pdf (accessed December 8, 2020).

24. Dheera Sharma, "Phenomenon of High Casualties among Police Personnel Must Be Probed and Addressed," *Indian Express*, July 15, 2020, https://indianexpress.com/article/opinion/columns/police-killed-in-line-of-duty-casualty-rate-6505954/ (accessed December 8, 2020); see also Ahuja and Kapur, Introduction to this volume.

25. National Crime Records Bureau (NCRB), "Crime in India" (2020), https://ncrb.gov.in/en/Crime-in-India-2020.

26. Jauregui, *Provisional Authority*, 88.

27. Ibid., 107–108; National Crime Records Bureau (NCRB), "Crime in India" (2019), https://ncrb.gov.in/en/crime-india-2019-0.

28. The year before, 2019, the proportions were even larger: of the 424 police personnel listed as "killed in police operations" that year, 87 percent of those deaths were reported as occurring either "in accidents" (84 percent) or "accidentally with Self weapon" (3 percent). It is important to note the lack of clarity regarding what counts as an "accident" as well as what constitutes a discrete "police operation," in contrast to one simply being "on duty" while incurring an injury. It is also important to note that these figures do not include deaths of police with central armed police forces (CAPF), 104 of which were attributed to accidents and 36 of which were attributed to suicide in 2019; https://ncrb.gov.in/sites/default/files/Accidental-Dea ths-Suicides-in-India-2019cpfb.pdf. See also Ahuja and Kapur, Introduction to this volume.

29. National Police Commission of India (NPC), "First Report" (New Delhi, 1979); S. K. Ghosh, *Police in Ferment* (New Delhi: Light and Life Publishers, 1981); M. B. Chande, *The Police in India* (New Delhi: Atlantic Publishers and Distributors, 1997); Human Rights Watch, *Broken System*.

30. Common Cause and the Centre for the Study of Developing Societies (CC & CSDS), *Status of Policing in India Report 2019*.

31. Ibid., 14.

32. Ibid., 44.

33. Ibid.

34. This was unique: police in every other state surveyed reported a minimum daily average of 11–18 hour work shifts.

35. Common Cause and the Centre for the Study of Developing Societies (CC & CSDS), 48.

36. Ibid., 44.

37. Ibid., 51–54.

38. Jauregui, *Provisional Authority*; Jauregui, "Police Unions and the Politics of Democratic Security in Postcolonial India."

39. Jauregui, "Lawfare and Security Labor."

40. Hemani Bhandari, "For Police Officers on Poll Duty, Voting Is Another Challenge," *The Hindu*, March 22, 2019, https://www.thehindu.com/news/cities/Delhi/for-officers-on-poll-duty-voting-is-another-challenge/article26562995.ece (accessed December 8, 2020); "Without Postal Ballots, Policemen Unable to Vote," *Times of India*, November 19, 2018, https://times

ofindia.indiatimes.com/city/dehradun/without-postal-ballots-policemen-unable-to-vote/articleshow/66684516.cms (accessed December 8, 2020); "Why 24,000 Cops in Mumbai Can't Vote Today," *NDTV*, February 16, 2012, https://www.ndtv.com/mumbai-news/why-24-000-cops-in-mumbai-cant-vote-today-572767 (accessed December 8, 2020).

41. Ghosh, *Police in Ferment*, 13.
42. He should not be confused with the BJP-affiliated MLA for Deoria in UP, who is also named Ramashish Rai.
43. Jauregui, "Police Unions and the Politics of Democratic Security in Postcolonial India."
44. David Bayley, *Changing the Guard: Developing Democratic Police Abroad* (Oxford: Oxford University Press, 2006); N. Pino and M. D. Waitrowski, eds., *Democratic Policing in Transitional and Developing Countries* (Hampshire: Ashgate, 2006); Andrew Goldsmith and James Sheptycki, *Crafting Transnational Policing: Police Capacity Building and Global Police Reform* (Oxford: Hart Publishing, 2007).
45. David Sklansky, *Democracy and the Police* (Palo Alto, CA: Stanford University Press, 2008); Monique Marks and David Sklansky, *Police Reform from the Bottom Up: Officers and Their Unions as Agents of Change* (New York: Routledge, 2012); cf. Ghosh, *Police in Ferment*.
46. It remains unclear why the UP Vidhan Sabha did not ratify the 1966 Act before March 1973.
47. "Centre to Help UP in Reorganizing PAC," *Hindustan Times*, May 26, 1973, 12; "Tripathi Offers to Quit Even with Majority Support," *Hindustan Times*, May 28, 1973, 1; S. R. Arun, *U.P. Police ka udbhav evam vikaas tathaa: P.A.C. ka itihaas (The Origin and Development of the U.P. Police: A History of the PAC)* (Uttar Pradesh: UP PAC Director General, 1995).
48. Ghosh, *Police in Ferment*, 6.
49. Ghosh, *Police in Ferment*, 9.
50. Joseph McQuade, *A Genealogy of Terrorism: Colonial Law and the Origins of an Idea* (Cambridge: Cambridge University Press, 2020).
51. Chande, *The Police in India*.
52. Jauregui, "Lawfare and Security Labor."
53. Jauregui, "Police Worker Politics in India, Brasil, and Beyond."
54. Jauregui, *Provisional Authority*.
55. Bernard S. Cohn, *Colonialism and Its Forms of Knowledge: The British in India* (Princeton, NJ: Princeton University Press, 1996).
56. Jauregui, *Provisional Authority*; Jauregui, "Police Unions and the Politics of Democratic Security in Postcolonial India."
57. Common Cause and the Centre for the Study of Developing Societies (CC & CSDS), 44. Not surprisingly, the study also found SC, ST, and OBC personnel are more likely to report this than other caste groups.
58. Ibid., 44, 55–57.
59. Ibid., 45.
60. Ghosh, *Police in Ferment*, 15.
61. Jauregui, "Just War."
62. Ghosh, *Police in Ferment*, 15.
63. David Arnold, *Police Power and Colonial Rule: Madras 1859–1947* (Delhi: Oxford University Press, 1986); Lata Singh, "Locating the Bihar Constabulary, 1920–22: An Exploration into the Margins of Resistance," *Social Scientist* 30, no. 9/10 (2002): 47–71; Shil, *Police Labor and State Formation in Bengal, c. 1860 to c. 1950*; Partha Pratim Shil, "The 'Threatened' Constabulary Strikes of Early Twentieth-Century Bengal," *South Asian Studies* 33, no. 2 (2017): 165–179; Michael Silvestri, "'A Fanatical Reverence for Gandhi': Nationalism and Police Militancy in Bengal during the Non-cooperation Movement," *Journal of Imperial and Commonwealth History* 45, no. 6 (2017): 969–997.
64. Ali Kabir, *Commentaries on UP Police Regulations with Allied Laws*, revised by Ram Nath Mishra (Allahabad: Hind Publishing House, 2005), emphasis added.

65. Avinash Kumar, "175 Cops Dismissed for Violence in Patna Police Lines over Woman Constable's Death." *Hindustan Times*, November 5, 2018, https://www.hindustantimes.com/patna/175-cops-dismissed-for-violence-in-patna-police-lines-over-woman-constable-s-death/story-NI4YBAfhAiaxPOx1gUJI4H.html (accessed January 12, 2021), cited in Common Cause and the Centre for the Study of Developing Societies (CC & CSDS), *Status of Policing in India Report 2019*, 45.

66. Kumar, "175 Cops Dismissed for Violence in Patna Police Lines over Woman Constable's Death."

67. Avinash Kumar, "Police vs. Police in Patna over Dengue Death of Woman Constable, Several Injured," *Hindustan Times*, November 3, 2018, https://www.hindustantimes.com/patna/police-vs-police-in-patna-over-dengue-death-of-woman-constable-several-injured/story-62I0CD9qZWJcE1pL8XIcVK.html (accessed January 12, 2021).

68. Madur, "All You Need to Know about the Auradkar Committee," August 2, 2019, https://www.karnataka.com/govt/auradkar-committee-recommendations/.

69. Luke Broadwater and Catie Edmonson, "Police Groups Wield Strong Influence in Congress, Resisting the Strictest Reforms," *New York Times*, June 25, 2020, https://www.nytimes.com/2020/06/25/us/politics/police-reforms-congress.html (accessed December 8, 2020).

INDEX